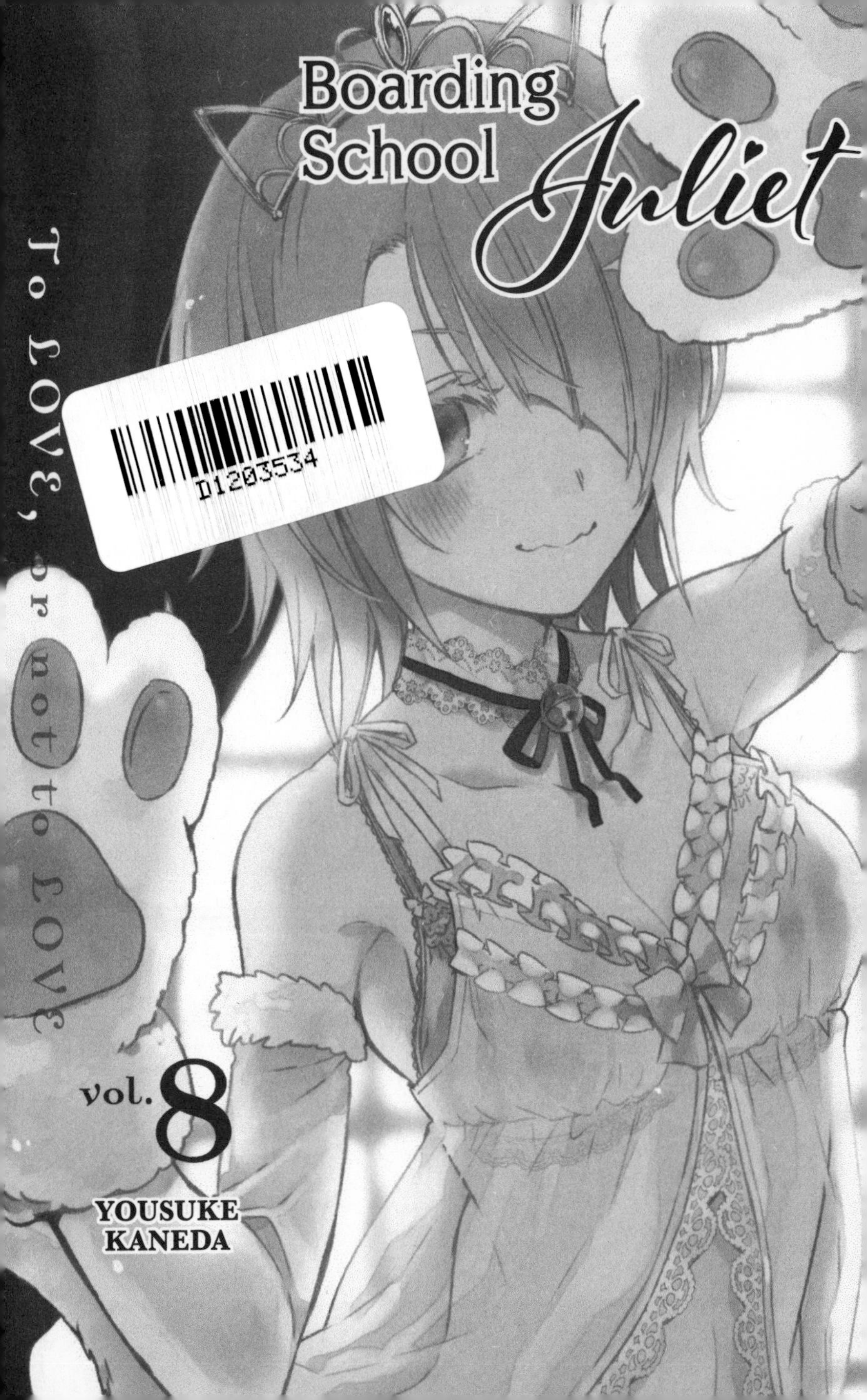
Boarding School Juliet
To LOVE, or not to LOVE
vol. 8
YOUSUKE KANEDA

THE PLAYERS

character

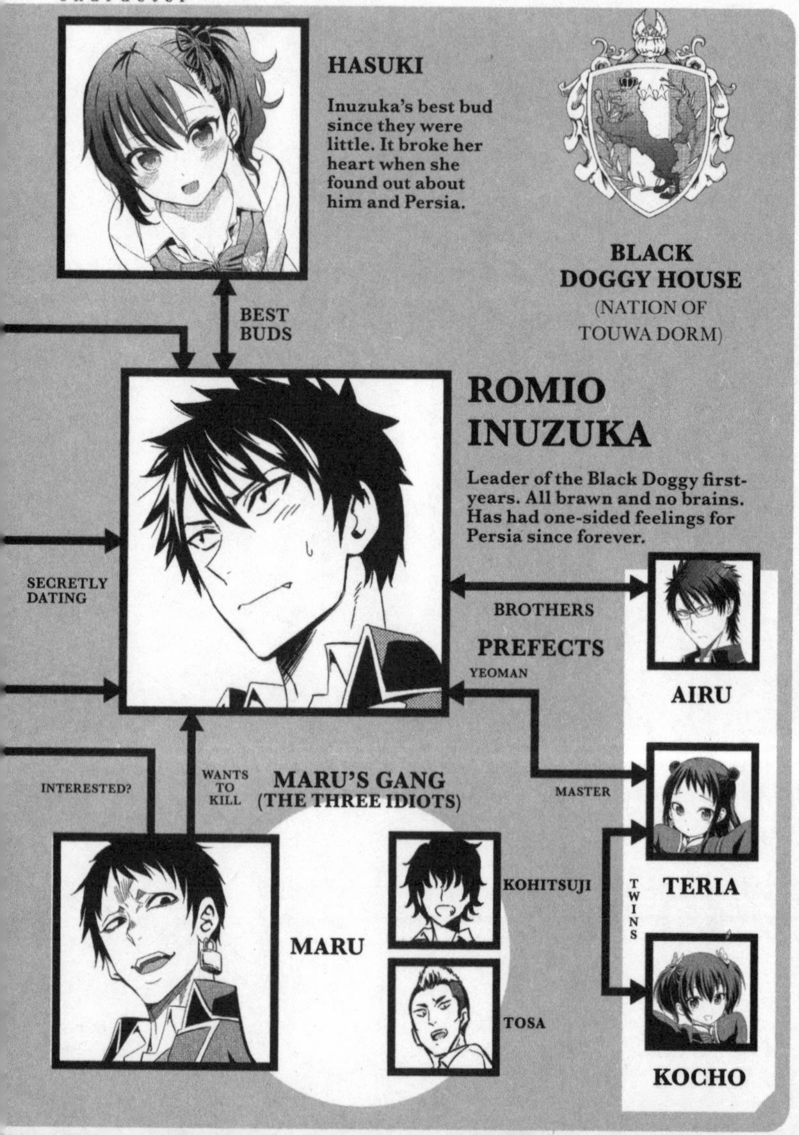
HASUKI
Inuzuka's best bud since they were little. It broke her heart when she found out about him and Persia.
BLACK DOGGY HOUSE (NATION OF TOUWA DORM)
BEST BUDS
ROMIO INUZUKA
Leader of the Black Doggy first-years. All brawn and no brains. Has had one-sided feelings for Persia since forever.
SECRETLY DATING
BROTHERS
PREFECTS
YEOMAN
AIRU
MASTER
INTERESTED?
WANTS TO KILL
MARU'S GANG (THE THREE IDIOTS)
TERIA
TWINS
KOHITSUJI
MARU
TOSA
KOCHO

BOARDING SCHOOL JULIET

To LOVE, or not to LOVE

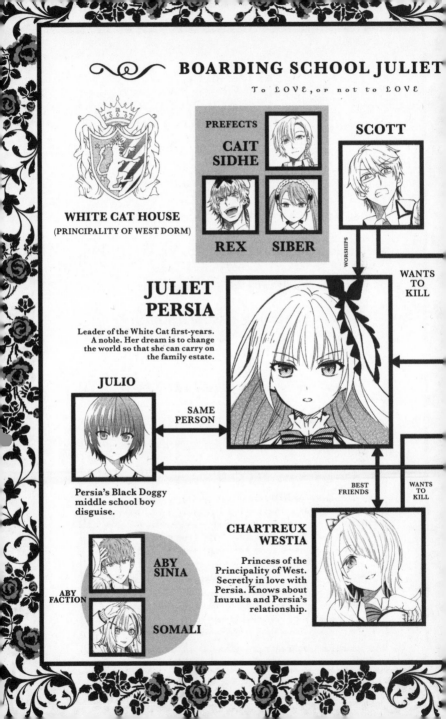

PREFECTS

CAIT SIDHE

REX

SIBER

SCOTT

WHITE CAT HOUSE
(PRINCIPALITY OF WEST DORM)

WORSHIPS

WANTS TO KILL

JULIET PERSIA

Leader of the White Cat first-years. A noble. Her dream is to change the world so that she can carry on the family estate.

JULIO

SAME PERSON

Persia's Black Doggy middle school boy disguise.

BEST FRIENDS

WANTS TO KILL

ABY SINIA

ABY FACTION

SOMALI

CHARTREUX WESTIA

Princess of the Principality of West. Secretly in love with Persia. Knows about Inuzuka and Persia's relationship.

contents

story

At boarding school Dahlia Academy, attended by students from two
feuding countries, one first-year longs for a forbidden love. His name:
Romio Inuzuka, leader of the Black Doggy House first-years. The apple
of his eye: Juliet Persia, leader of the White Cat House first-years. It all
begins when Inuzuka confesses his feelings to her. This is Inuzuka and
Persia's star-crossed, secret love story...

Romio becomes a School Festival Committee Member as part of a plan
to go on a festival-patrolling date with Persia without having to sneak
around. But on the big day, who should he catch sight of but Maru, chasing
Julio! Thanks to some crazy misunderstandings, Inuzuka and Maru are
about to throw down, with Julio caught in the middle!

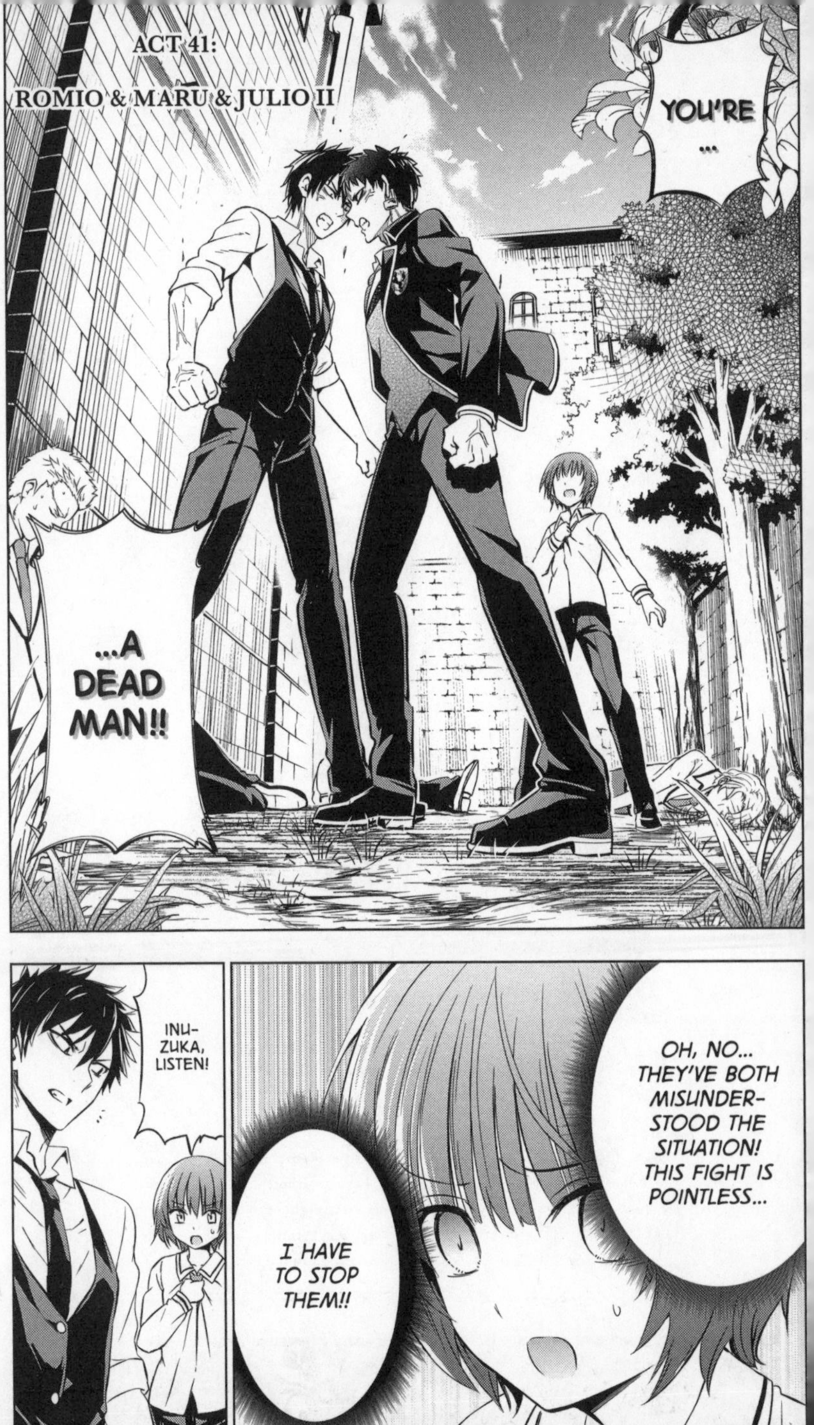
ACT 41:
ROMIO & MARU & JULIO II
YOU'RE ...
...A DEAD MAN!!
OH, NO... THEY'VE BOTH MISUNDER-STOOD THE SITUATION! THIS FIGHT IS POINTLESS...
I HAVE TO STOP THEM!!
INU-ZUKA, LISTEN!

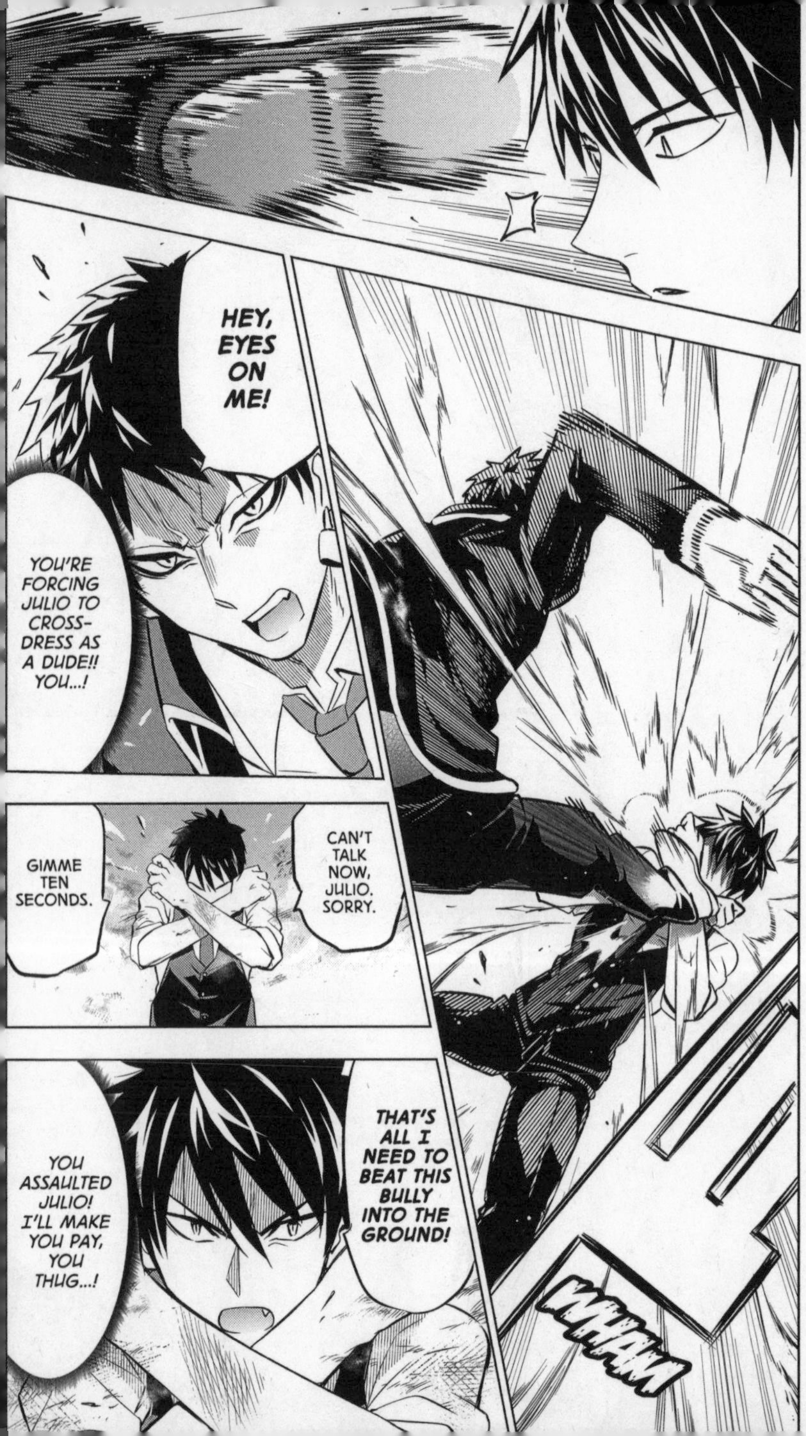
WHAM
HEY, EYES ON ME!
YOU'RE FORCING JULIO TO CROSS-DRESS AS A DUDE!! YOU...!
CAN'T TALK NOW, JULIO. SORRY.
GIMME TEN SECONDS.
THAT'S ALL I NEED TO BEAT THIS BULLY INTO THE GROUND!
YOU ASSAULTED JULIO! I'LL MAKE YOU PAY, YOU THUG...!

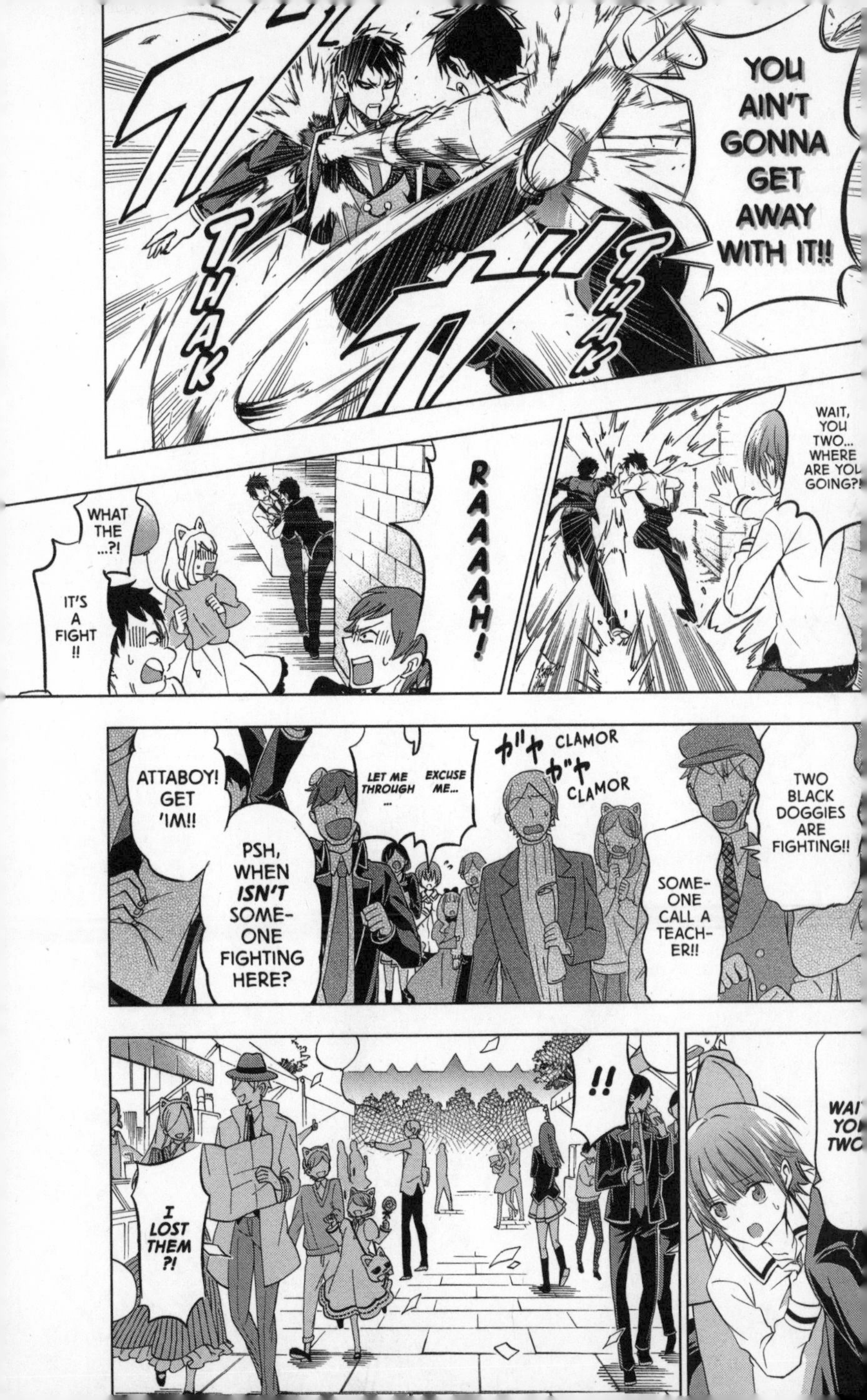
YOU AIN'T GONNA GET AWAY WITH IT!!
THAK
THAK
WAIT, YOU TWO... WHERE ARE YOU GOING?!
RAAAAAH!
WHAT THE ...?!
IT'S A FIGHT !!
TWO BLACK DOGGIES ARE FIGHTING!!
ガヤ CLAMOR
ガヤ CLAMOR
SOME-ONE CALL A TEACH-ER!!
EXCUSE ME...
LET ME THROUGH ...
ATTABOY! GET 'IM!!
PSH, WHEN *ISN'T* SOME-ONE FIGHTING HERE?
WAI YO TW
!!
I LOST THEM ?!

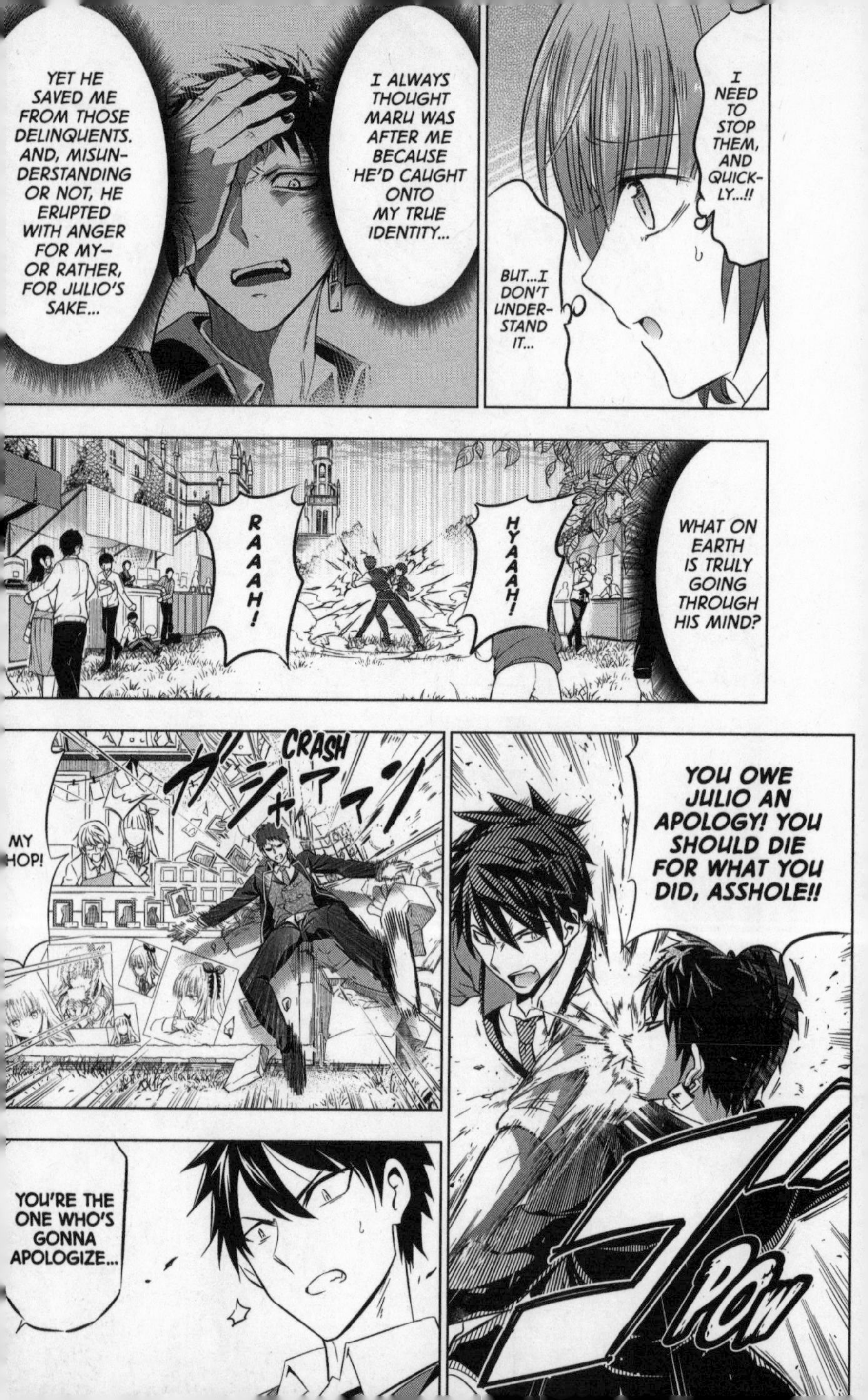
I NEED TO STOP THEM, AND QUICKLY...!!
BUT...I DON'T UNDERSTAND IT...
I ALWAYS THOUGHT MARU WAS AFTER ME BECAUSE HE'D CAUGHT ONTO MY TRUE IDENTITY...
YET HE SAVED ME FROM THOSE DELINQUENTS. AND, MISUNDERSTANDING OR NOT, HE ERUPTED WITH ANGER FOR MY— OR RATHER, FOR JULIO'S SAKE...
WHAT ON EARTH IS TRULY GOING THROUGH HIS MIND?
HYAAAAH!
RAAAAH!
YOU OWE JULIO AN APOLOGY! YOU SHOULD DIE FOR WHAT YOU DID, ASSHOLE!!
POW
CRASH
MY HOP!
YOU'RE THE ONE WHO'S GONNA APOLOGIZE...

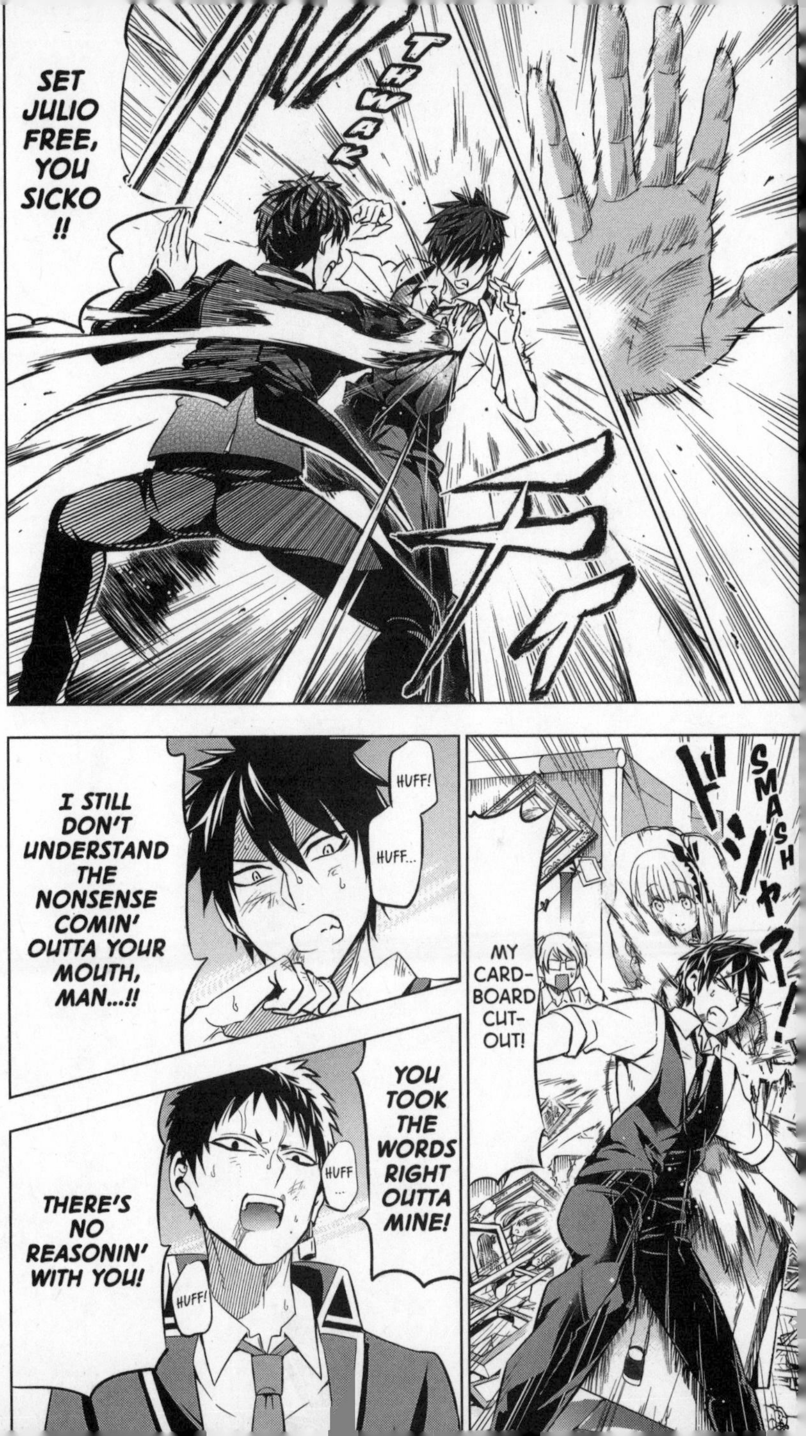
THWAK
SET JULIO FREE, YOU SICKO!!
SMASH
MY CARDBOARD CUT-OUT!
HUFF!
HUFF...
I STILL DON'T UNDERSTAND THE NONSENSE COMIN' OUTTA YOUR MOUTH, MAN...!!
YOU TOOK THE WORDS RIGHT OUTTA MINE!
HUFF...
THERE'S NO REASONIN' WITH YOU!
HUFF!

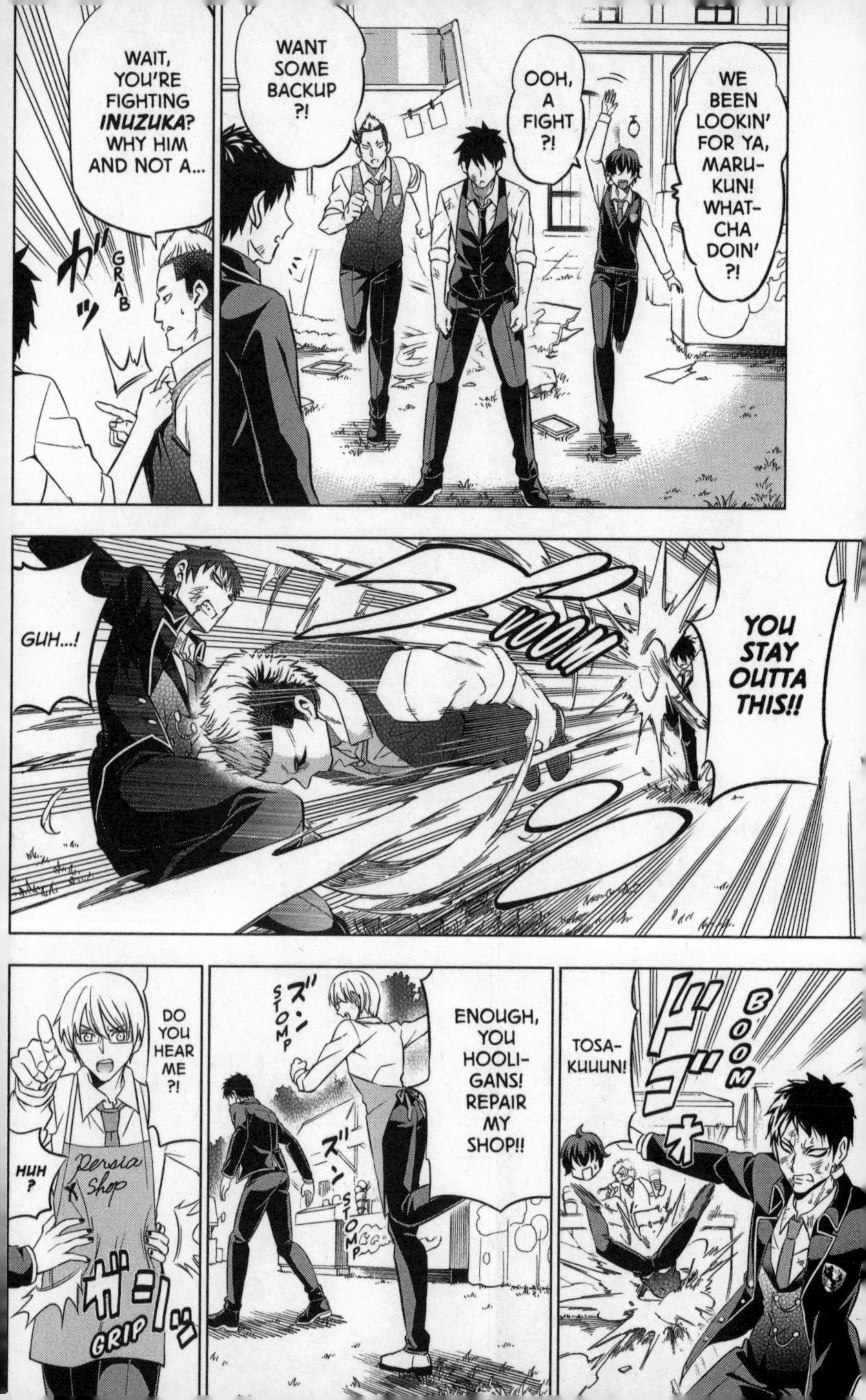
WE BEEN LOOKIN' FOR YA, MARU-KUN! WHAT-CHA DOIN' ?!
OOH, A FIGHT ?!
WANT SOME BACKUP ?!
WAIT, YOU'RE FIGHTING INUZUKA? WHY HIM AND NOT A...
GRAB
YOU STAY OUTTA THIS!!
VOOM
GUH...!
BOOM
TOSA-KUUUN!
ENOUGH, YOU HOOLI-GANS! REPAIR MY SHOP!!
STOMP
STOMP
DO YOU HEAR ME ?!
HUH ?
Persia Shop
GRIP

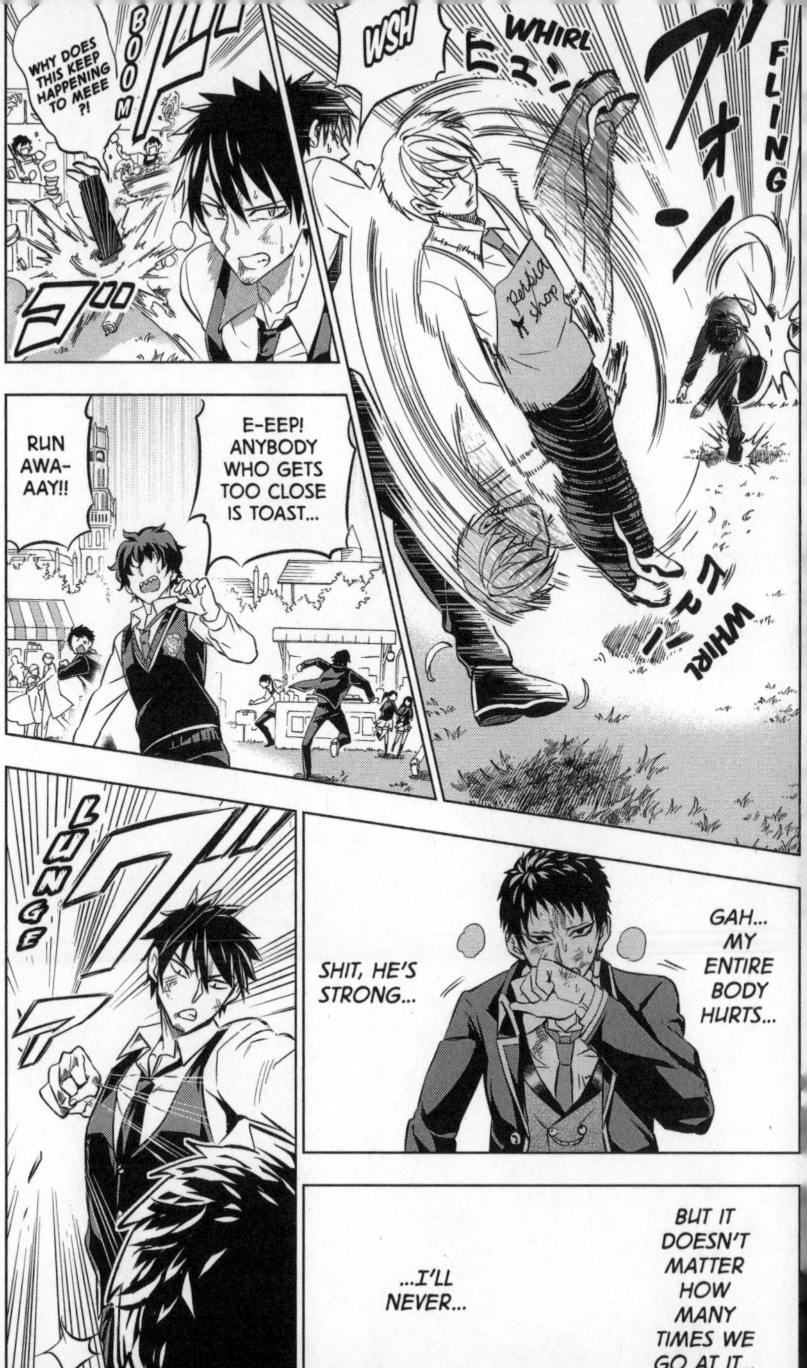
FLING
WHIRL
ヒュン
WSH
WHIRL
BOOM
WHY DOES THIS KEEP HAPPENING TO MEEE ?!
E-EEP! ANYBODY WHO GETS TOO CLOSE IS TOAST...
RUN AWA-AAY!!
GAH... MY ENTIRE BODY HURTS...
SHIT, HE'S STRONG...
BUT IT DOESN'T MATTER HOW MANY TIMES WE GO AT IT...
...I'LL NEVER...
LUNGE

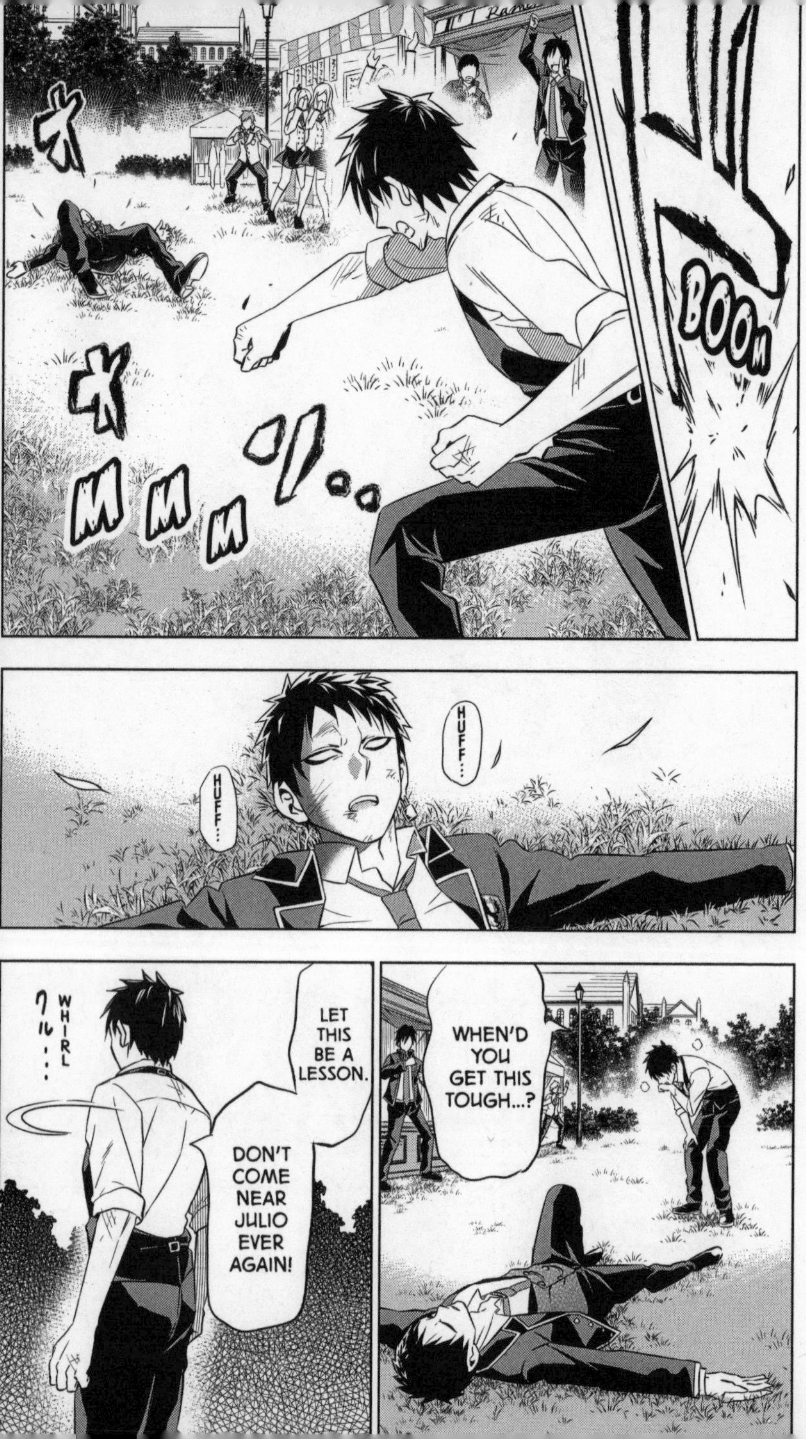
BOOM
オ
オ
HUFF...
HUFF...
WHEN'D YOU GET THIS TOUGH...?
LET THIS BE A LESSON.
DON'T COME NEAR JULIO EVER AGAIN!
WHIRL
クル...

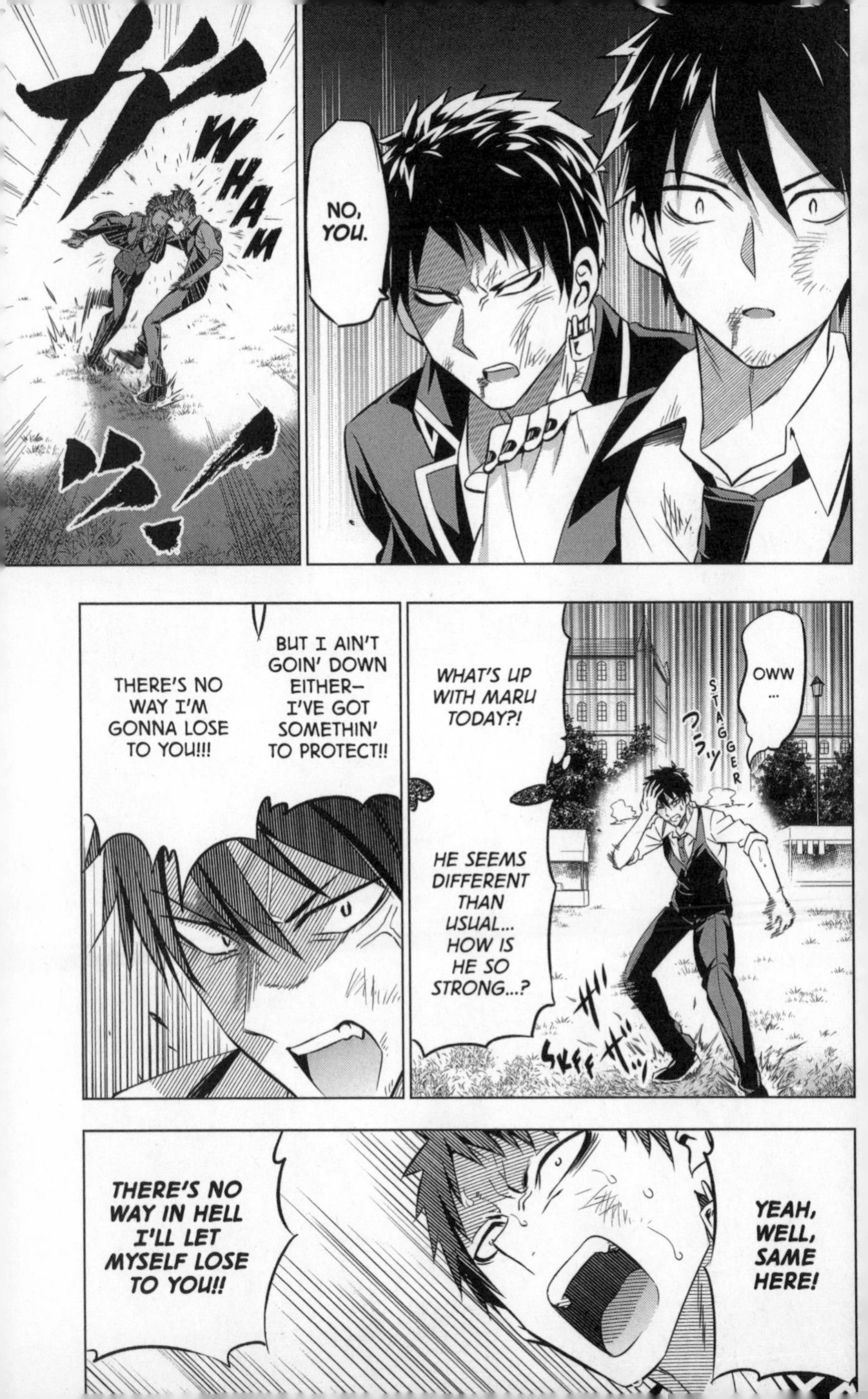
NO, YOU.
WHAM
OWW ...
STAGGER
WHAT'S UP WITH MARU TODAY?!
HE SEEMS DIFFERENT THAN USUAL... HOW IS HE SO STRONG...?
SKFF
BUT I AIN'T GOIN' DOWN EITHER— I'VE GOT SOMETHIN' TO PROTECT!!
THERE'S NO WAY I'M GONNA LOSE TO YOU!!!
YEAH, WELL, SAME HERE!
THERE'S NO WAY IN HELL I'LL LET MYSELF LOSE TO YOU!!

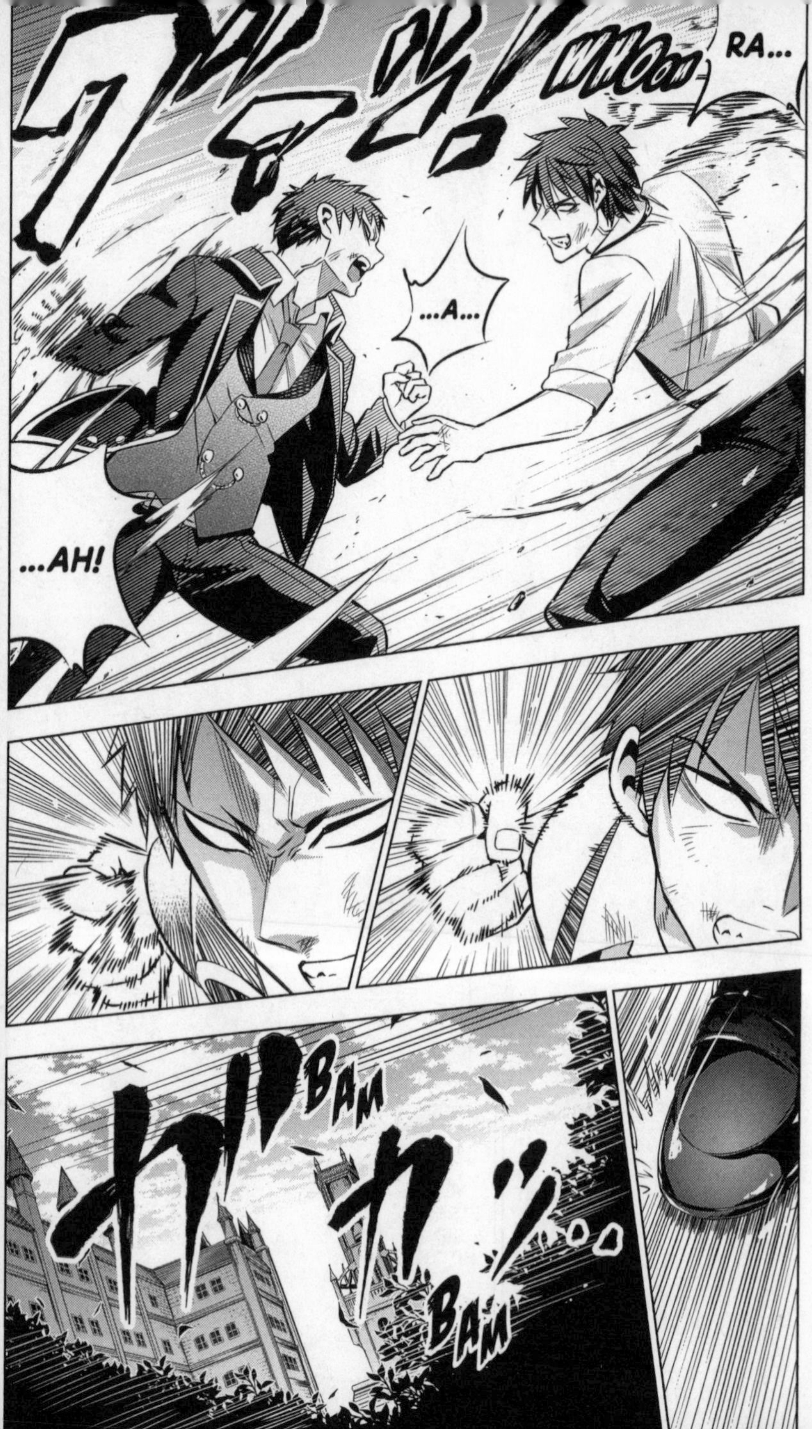
RA...
...A...
...AH!
BAM
BAM

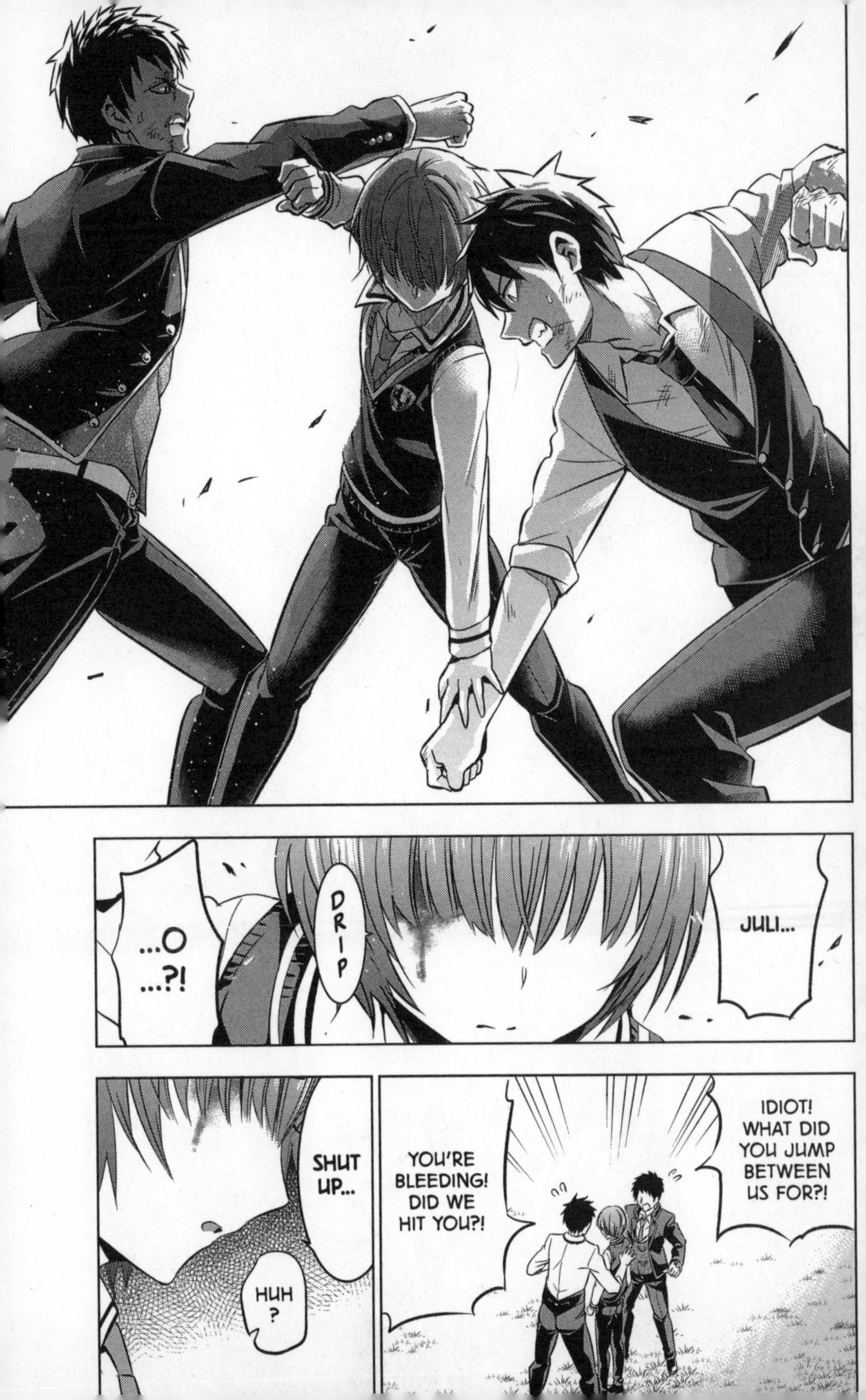
JULI...
DRIP
...O ...?!
IDIOT! WHAT DID YOU JUMP BETWEEN US FOR?!
YOU'RE BLEEDING! DID WE HIT YOU?!
SHUT UP...
HUH ?

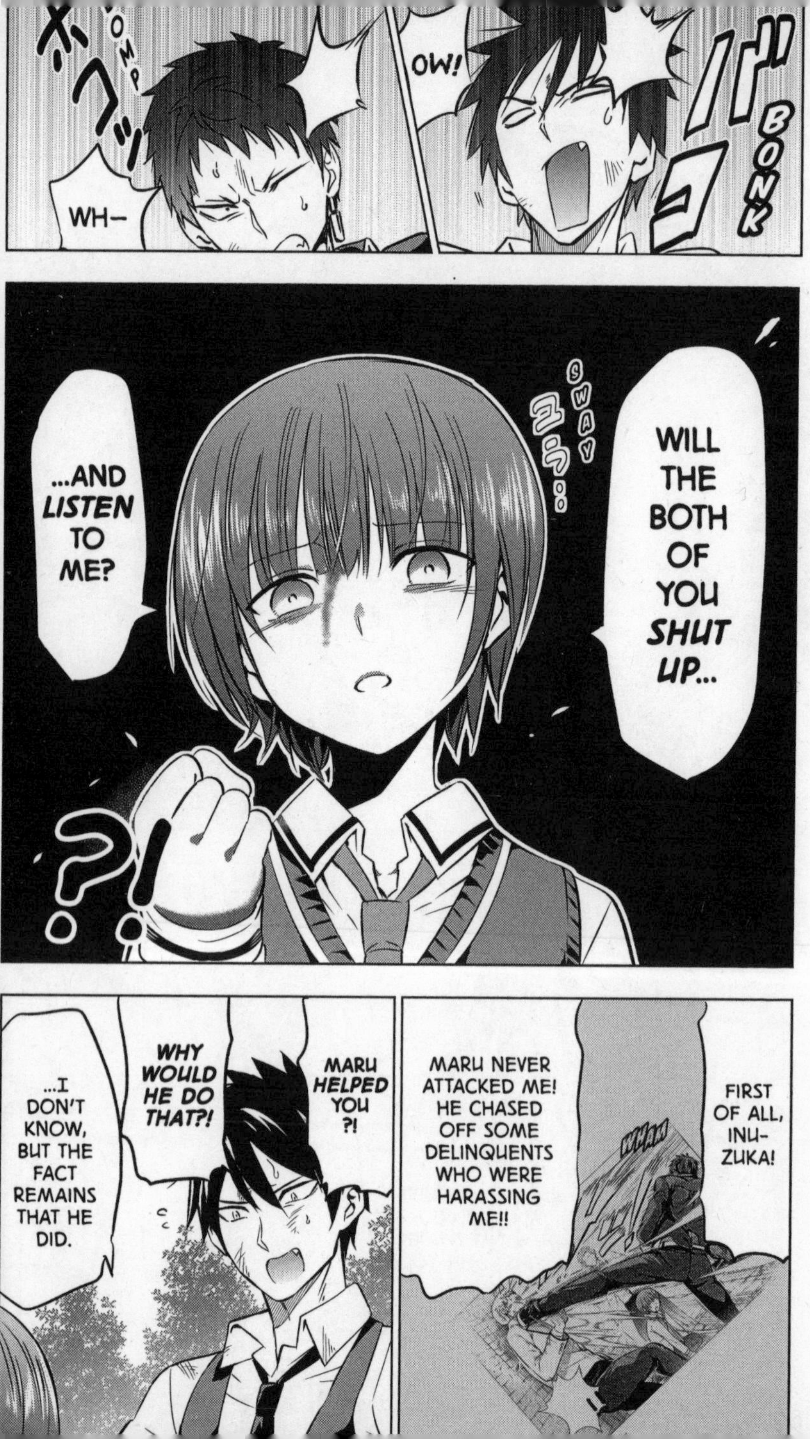
BONK
OW!
OMP
WH–
WILL THE BOTH OF YOU *SHUT UP*...
SWAY
...AND *LISTEN* TO ME?
?!
FIRST OF ALL, INU-ZUKA!
MARU NEVER ATTACKED ME! HE CHASED OFF SOME DELINQUENTS WHO WERE HARASSING ME!!
MARU *HELPED* YOU ?!
WHY WOULD HE DO THAT?!
...I DON'T KNOW, BUT THE FACT REMAINS THAT HE DID.

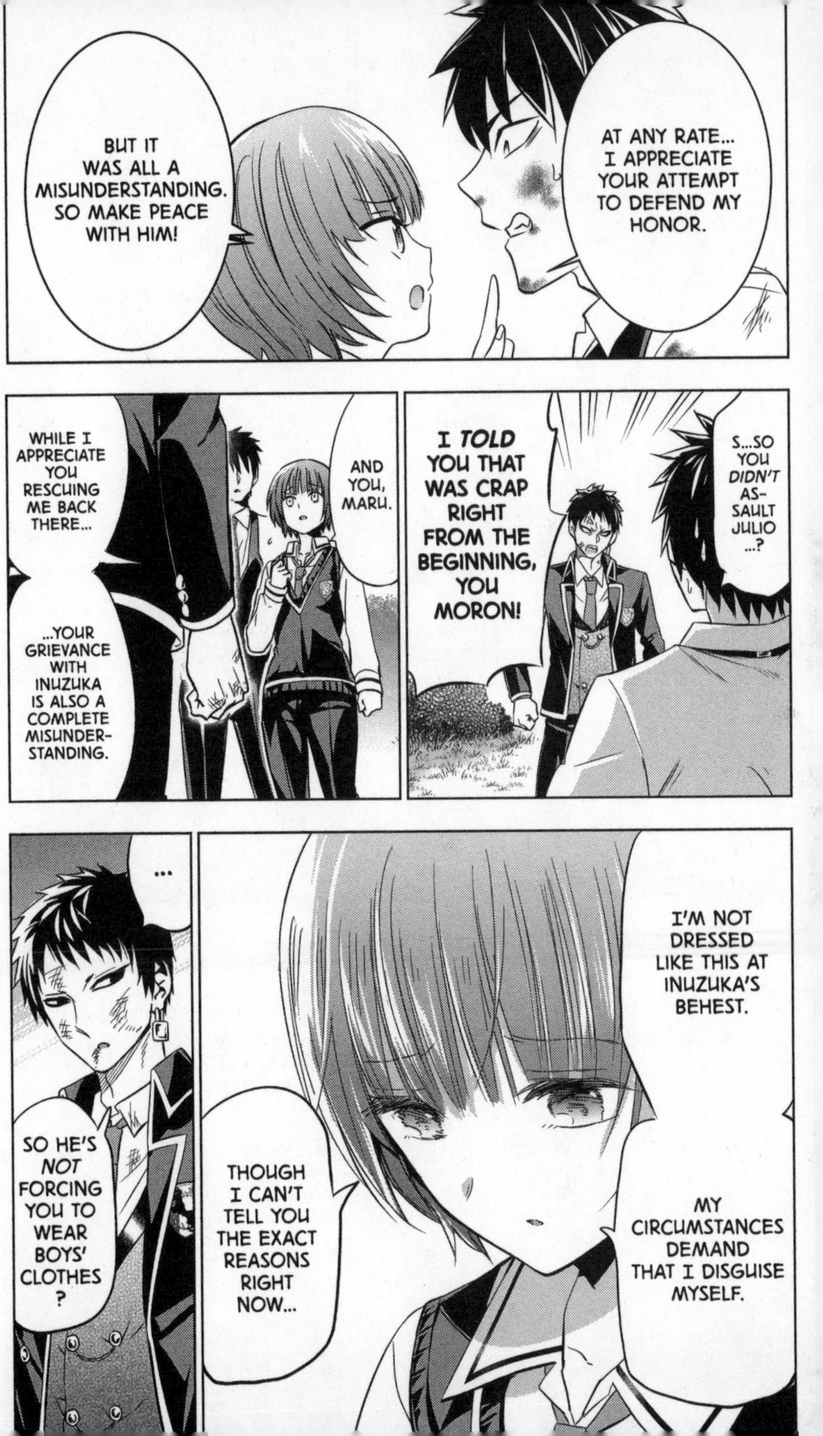
AT ANY RATE... I APPRECIATE YOUR ATTEMPT TO DEFEND MY HONOR.
BUT IT WAS ALL A MISUNDERSTANDING. SO MAKE PEACE WITH HIM!
S...SO YOU *DIDN'T* AS-SAULT JULIO ...?
I *TOLD* YOU THAT WAS CRAP RIGHT FROM THE BEGINNING, YOU MORON!
AND YOU, MARU.
WHILE I APPRECIATE YOU RESCUING ME BACK THERE...
...YOUR GRIEVANCE WITH INUZUKA IS ALSO A COMPLETE MISUNDER-STANDING.
I'M NOT DRESSED LIKE THIS AT INUZUKA'S BEHEST.
MY CIRCUMSTANCES DEMAND THAT I DISGUISE MYSELF.
THOUGH I CAN'T TELL YOU THE EXACT REASONS RIGHT NOW...
...
SO HE'S *NOT* FORCING YOU TO WEAR BOYS' CLOTHES ?

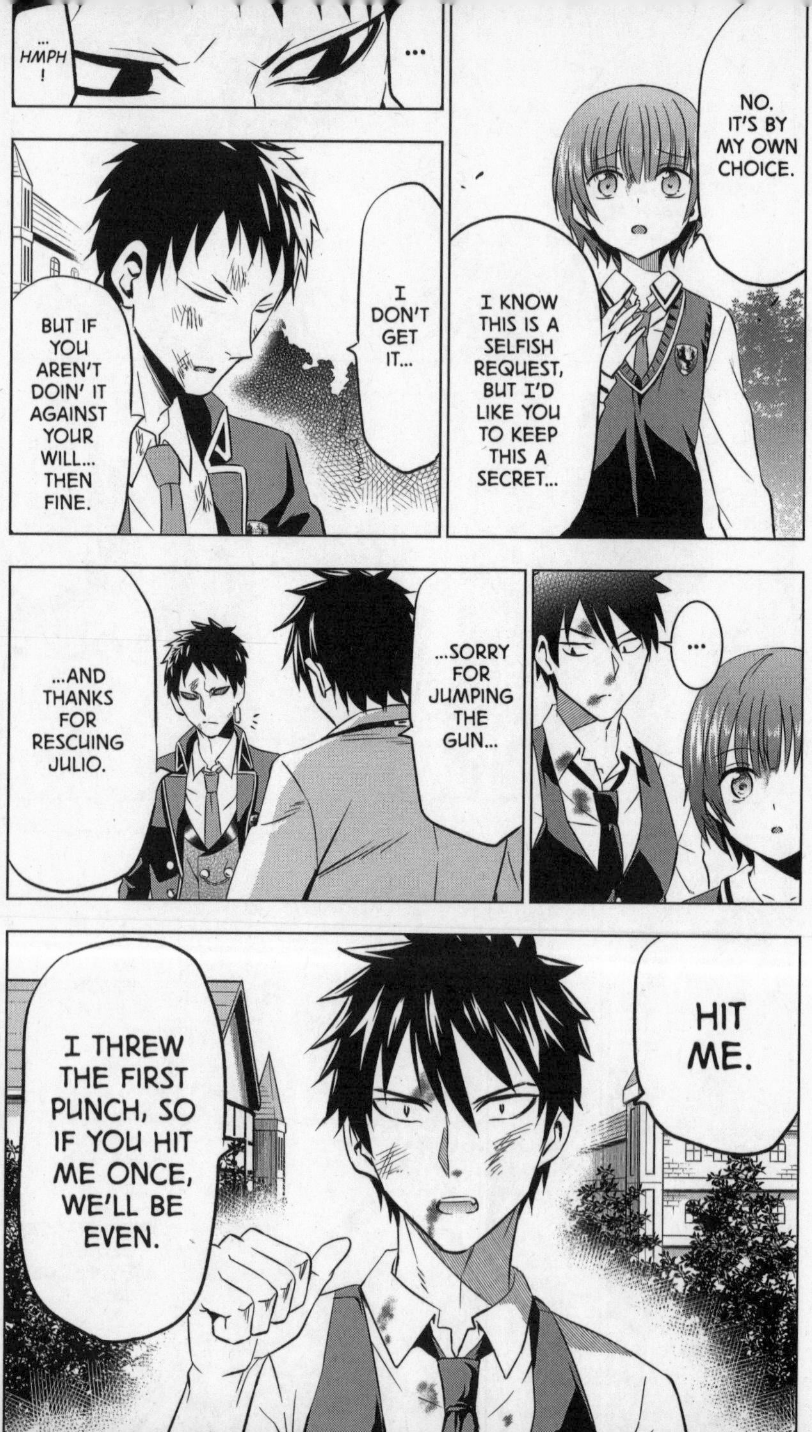
NO. IT'S BY MY OWN CHOICE.
I KNOW THIS IS A SELFISH REQUEST, BUT I'D LIKE YOU TO KEEP THIS A SECRET...
...
... HMPH!
I DON'T GET IT...
BUT IF YOU AREN'T DOIN' IT AGAINST YOUR WILL... THEN FINE.
...
...SORRY FOR JUMPING THE GUN...
...AND THANKS FOR RESCUING JULIO.
HIT ME.
I THREW THE FIRST PUNCH, SO IF YOU HIT ME ONCE, WE'LL BE EVEN.

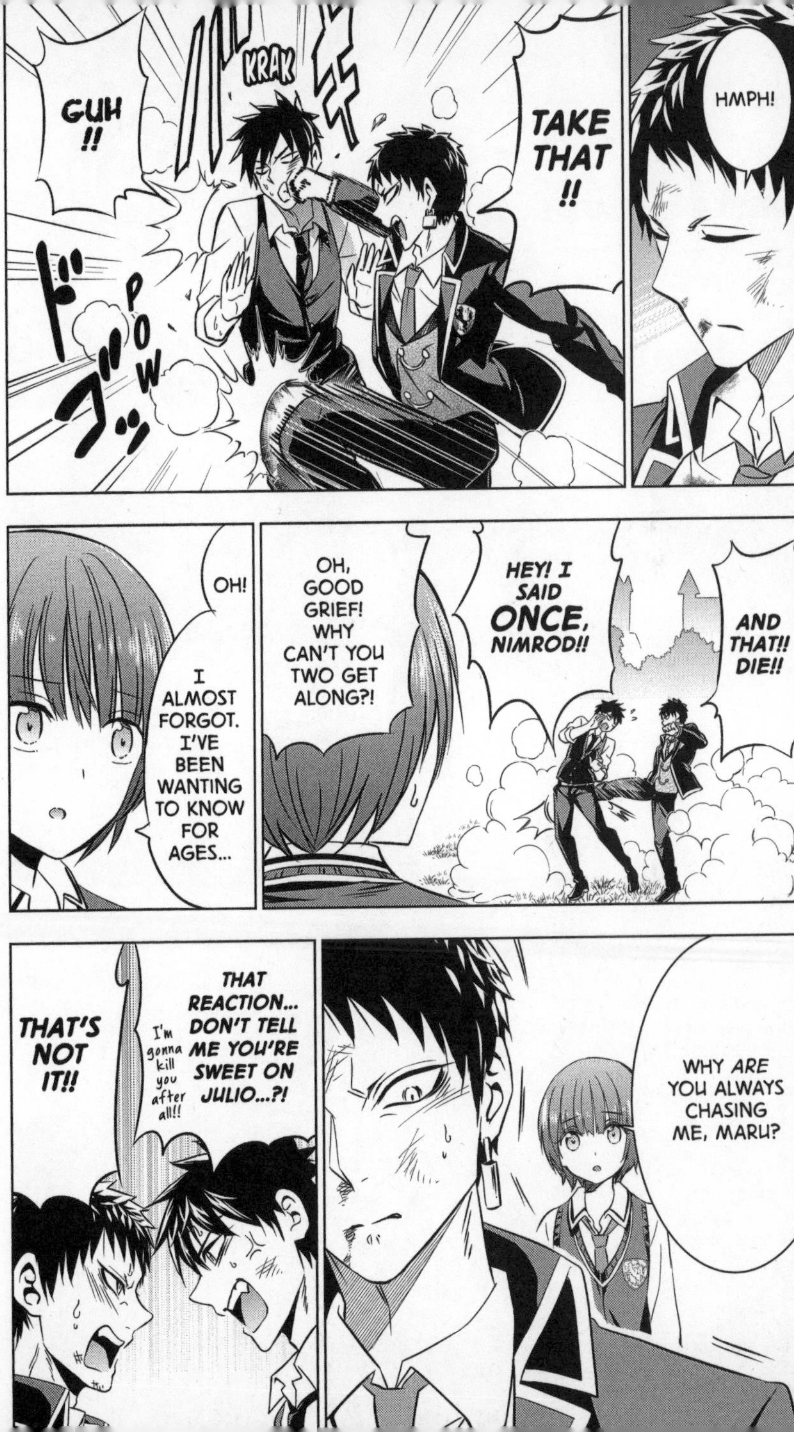
HMPH!
TAKE THAT!!
KRAK
GUH!!
POW
AND THAT!! DIE!!
HEY! I SAID ONCE, NIMROD!!
OH, GOOD GRIEF! WHY CAN'T YOU TWO GET ALONG?!
OH!
I ALMOST FORGOT. I'VE BEEN WANTING TO KNOW FOR AGES...
WHY ARE YOU ALWAYS CHASING ME, MARU?
THAT REACTION... DON'T TELL ME YOU'RE SWEET ON JULIO...?!
I'm gonna kill you after all!!
THAT'S NOT IT!!

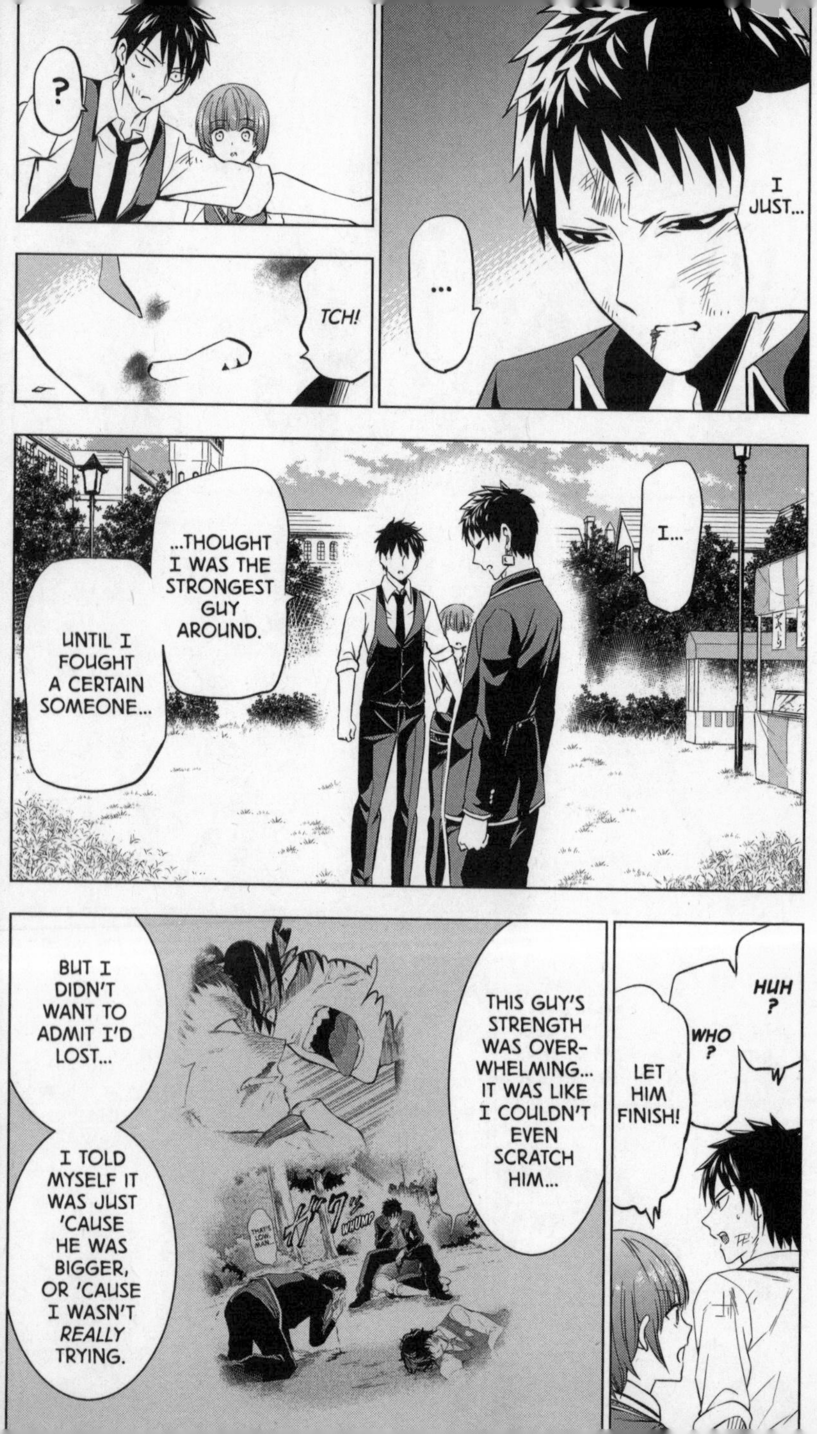
I JUST...
...
?
TCH!
I...
...THOUGHT I WAS THE STRONGEST GUY AROUND.
UNTIL I FOUGHT A CERTAIN SOMEONE...
HUH?
WHO?
LET HIM FINISH!
THIS GUY'S STRENGTH WAS OVER-WHELMING... IT WAS LIKE I COULDN'T EVEN SCRATCH HIM...
WHUMP
THAT'S LOW, MAN.
BUT I DIDN'T WANT TO ADMIT I'D LOST...
I TOLD MYSELF IT WAS JUST 'CAUSE HE WAS BIGGER, OR 'CAUSE I WASN'T *REALLY* TRYING.

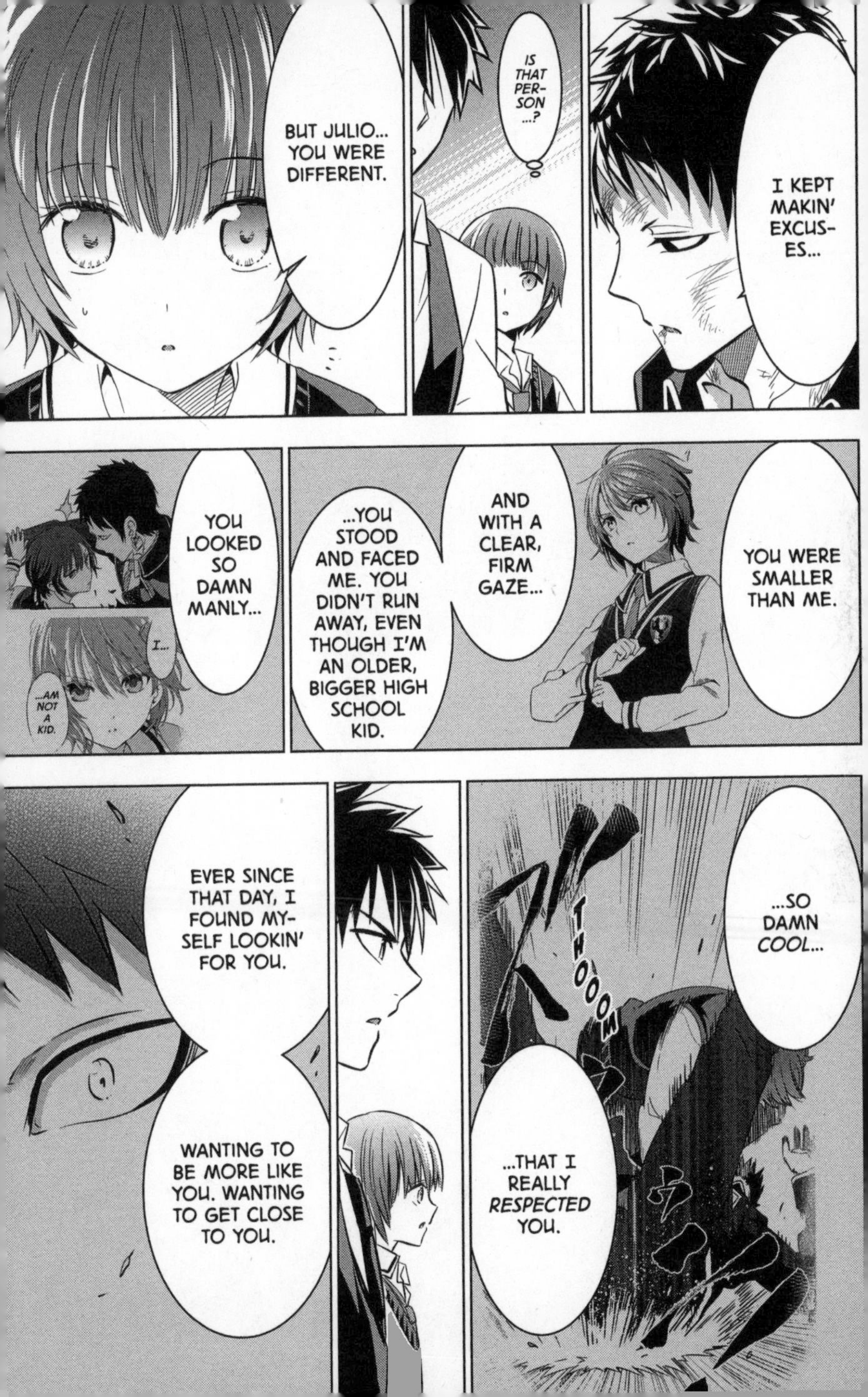
I KEPT MAKIN' EXCUS-ES...
IS THAT PER-SON ...?
BUT JULIO... YOU WERE DIFFERENT.
YOU WERE SMALLER THAN ME.
AND WITH A CLEAR, FIRM GAZE...
...YOU STOOD AND FACED ME. YOU DIDN'T RUN AWAY, EVEN THOUGH I'M AN OLDER, BIGGER HIGH SCHOOL KID.
YOU LOOKED SO DAMN MANLY...
I...
...AM NOT A KID.
...SO DAMN *COOL*...
THOOOM
...THAT I REALLY *RESPECTED* YOU.
EVER SINCE THAT DAY, I FOUND MY-SELF LOOKIN' FOR YOU.
WANTING TO BE MORE LIKE YOU. WANTING TO GET CLOSE TO YOU.

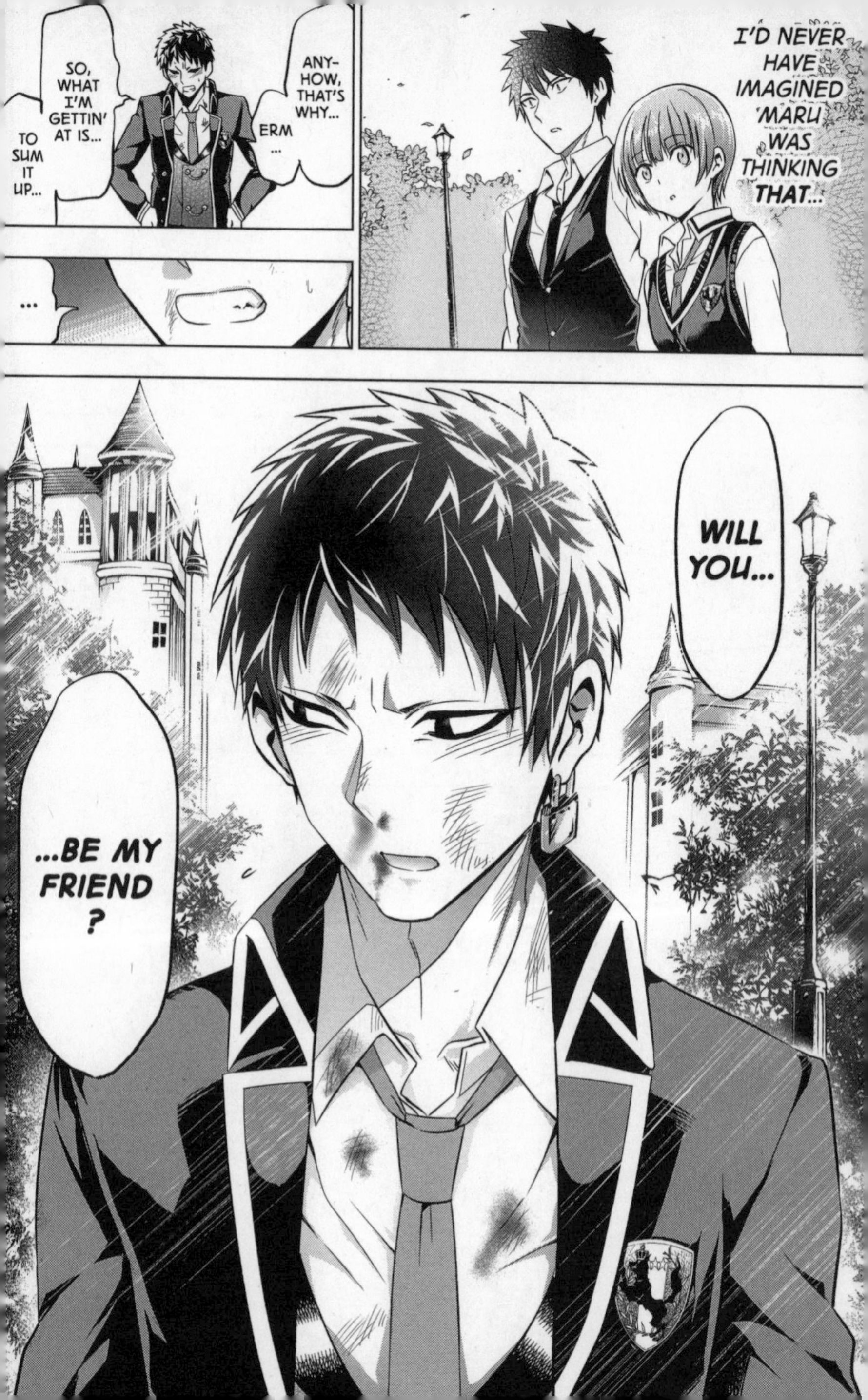

I'D NEVER HAVE IMAGINED MARU WAS THINKING THAT...
ANY-HOW, THAT'S WHY...
ERM ...
SO, WHAT I'M GETTIN' AT IS...
TO SUM IT UP...
...
WILL YOU...
...BE MY FRIEND ?

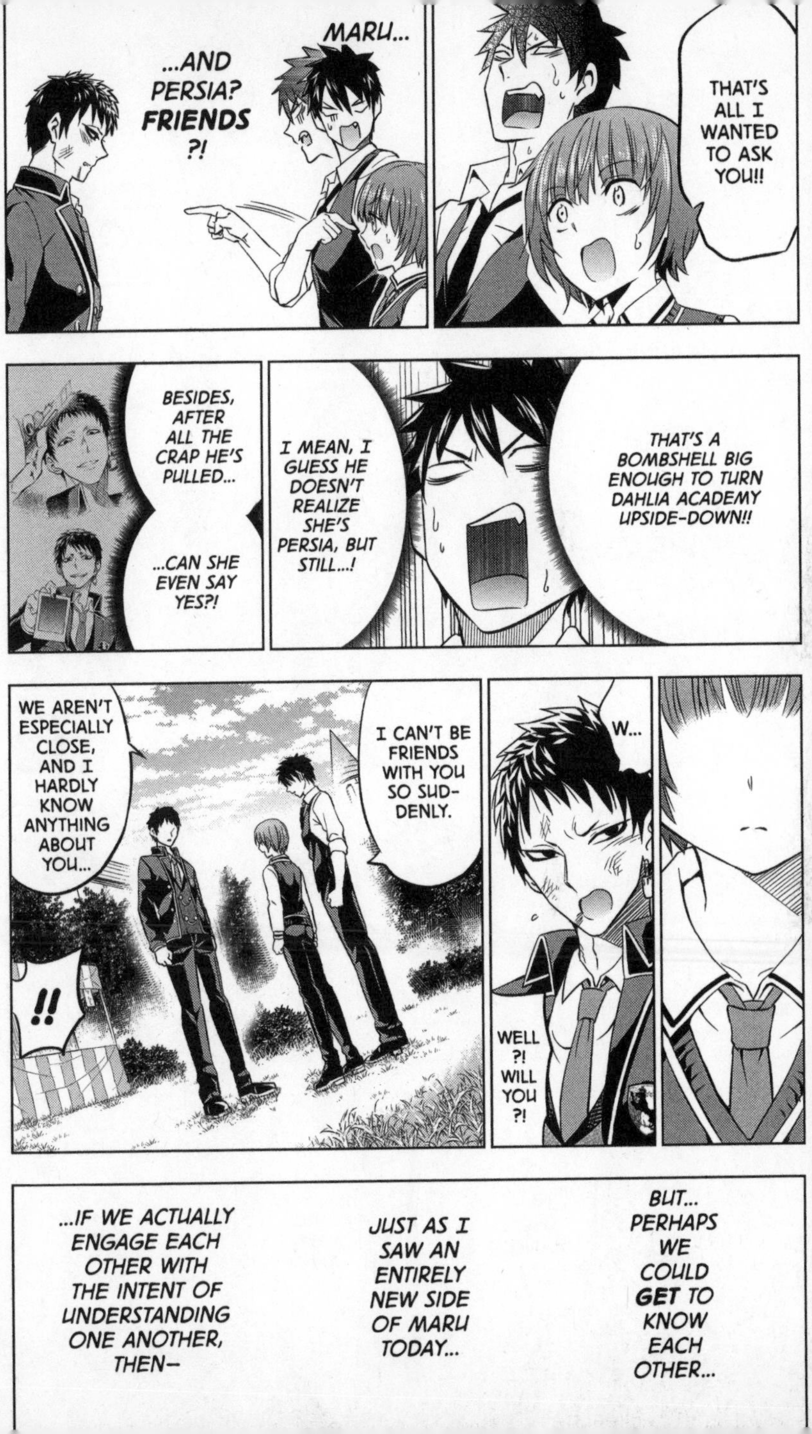
THAT'S ALL I WANTED TO ASK YOU!!
MARU...
...AND PERSIA? **FRIENDS**?!
THAT'S A BOMBSHELL BIG ENOUGH TO TURN DAHLIA ACADEMY UPSIDE-DOWN!!
I MEAN, I GUESS HE DOESN'T REALIZE SHE'S PERSIA, BUT STILL...!
BESIDES, AFTER ALL THE CRAP HE'S PULLED...
...CAN SHE EVEN SAY YES?!
W...
WELL?! WILL YOU?!
I CAN'T BE FRIENDS WITH YOU SO SUD-DENLY.
WE AREN'T ESPECIALLY CLOSE, AND I HARDLY KNOW ANYTHING ABOUT YOU...
!!
BUT... PERHAPS WE COULD **GET** TO KNOW EACH OTHER...
JUST AS I SAW AN ENTIRELY NEW SIDE OF MARU TODAY...
...IF WE ACTUALLY ENGAGE EACH OTHER WITH THE INTENT OF UNDERSTANDING ONE ANOTHER, THEN–

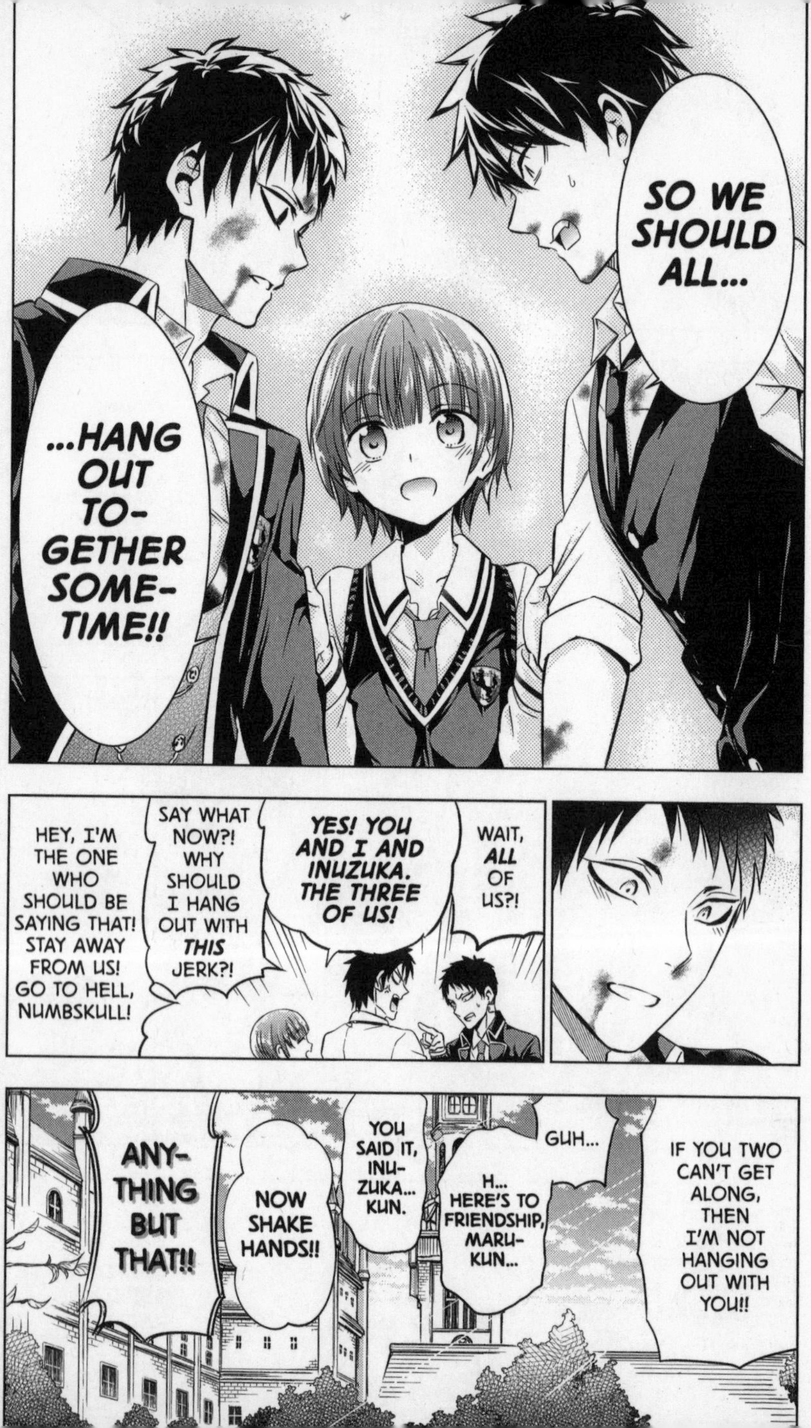
SO WE SHOULD ALL...
...HANG OUT TO-GETHER SOME-TIME!!
WAIT, ALL OF US?!
YES! YOU AND I AND INUZUKA. THE THREE OF US!
SAY WHAT NOW?! WHY SHOULD I HANG OUT WITH THIS JERK?!
HEY, I'M THE ONE WHO SHOULD BE SAYING THAT! STAY AWAY FROM US! GO TO HELL, NUMBSKULL!
IF YOU TWO CAN'T GET ALONG, THEN I'M NOT HANGING OUT WITH YOU!!
GUH...
H... HERE'S TO FRIENDSHIP, MARU-KUN...
YOU SAID IT, INU-ZUKA... KUN.
NOW SHAKE HANDS!!
ANY-THING BUT THAT!!

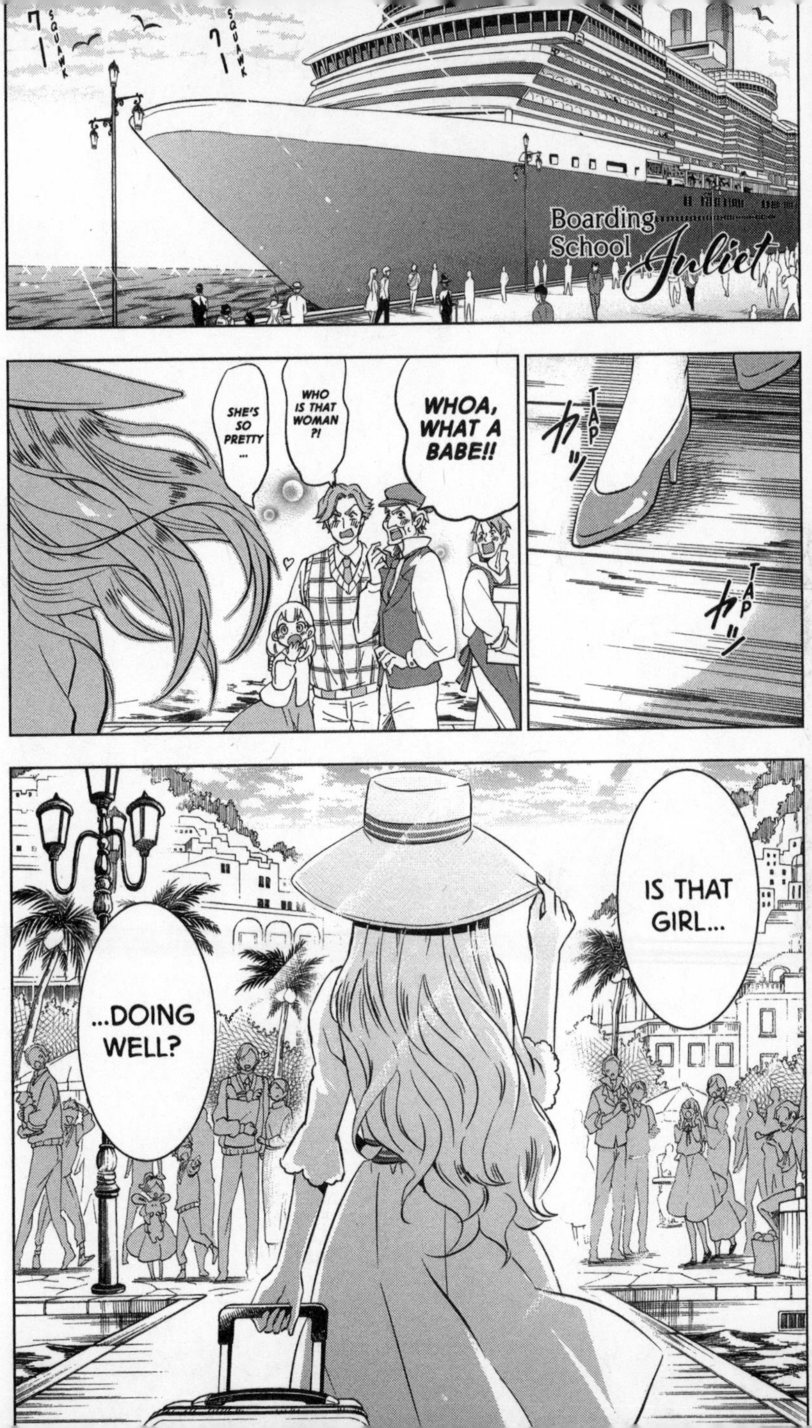
SQUAWK
SQUAWK
Boarding School Juliet
TAP
TAP
WHOA, WHAT A BABE!!
WHO IS THAT WOMAN?!
SHE'S SO PRETTY...
IS THAT GIRL...
...DOING WELL?

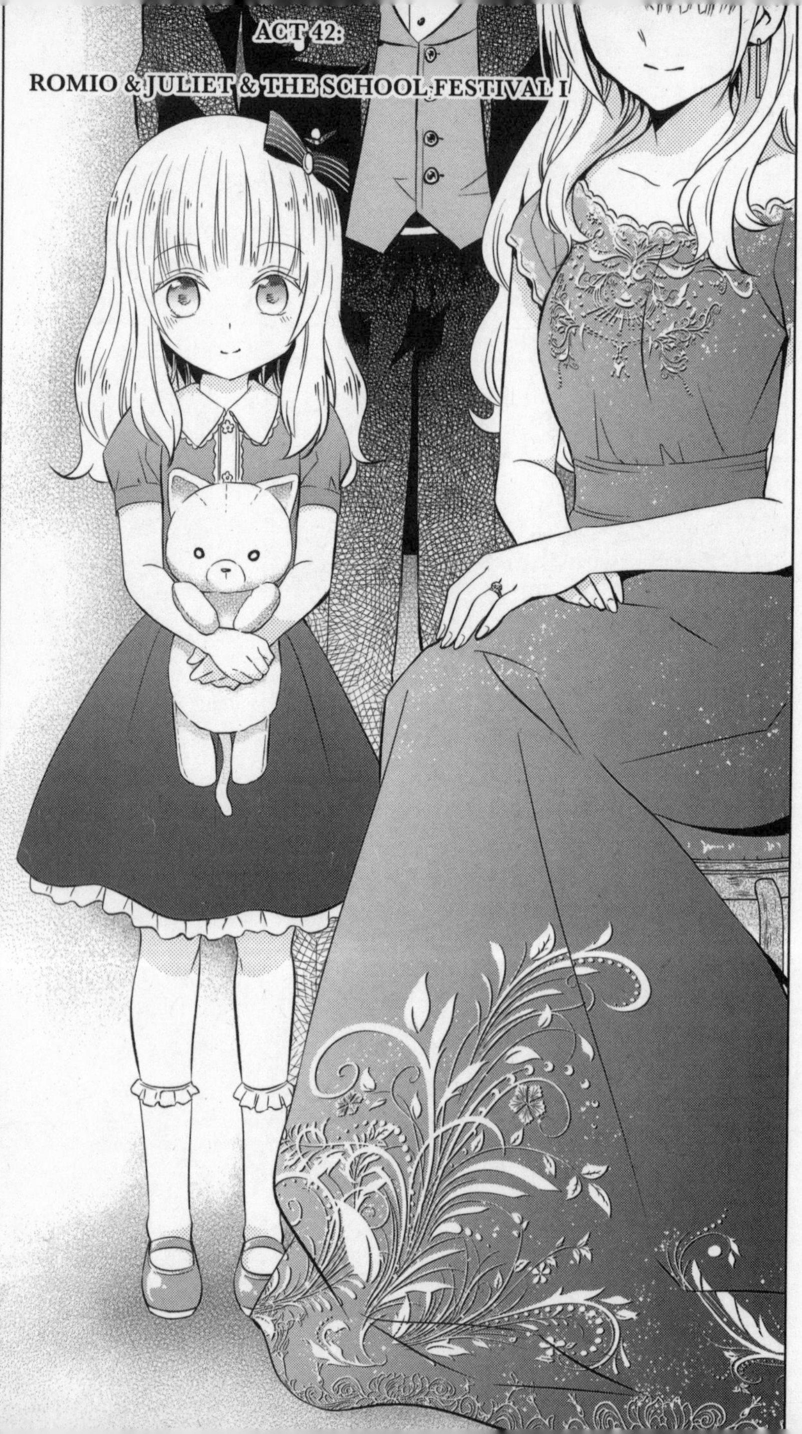
ACT 42:
ROMIO & JULIET & THE SCHOOL FESTIVAL I

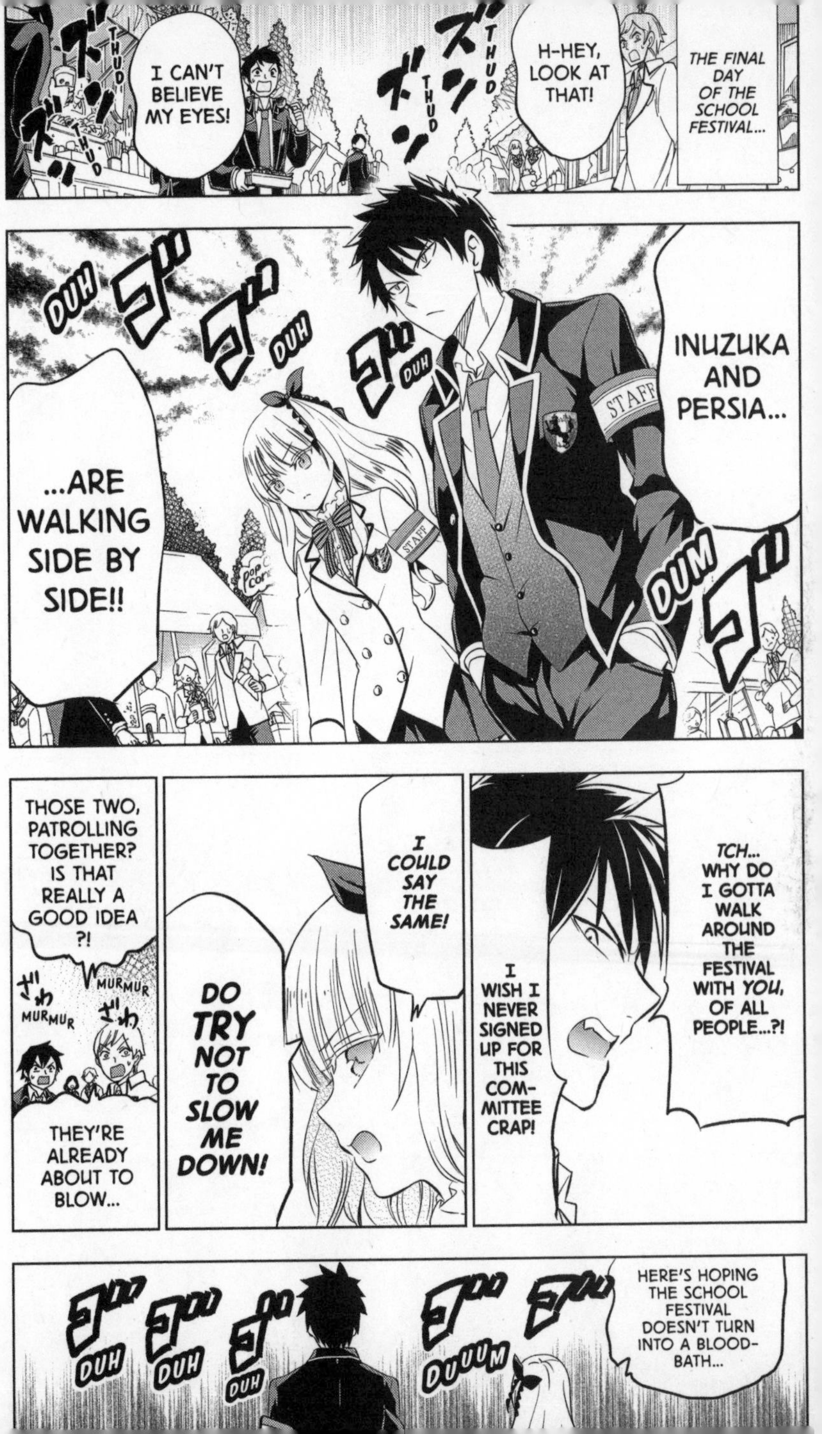
THE FINAL DAY OF THE SCHOOL FESTIVAL...
H-HEY, LOOK AT THAT!
THUD
THUD
I CAN'T BELIEVE MY EYES!
THUD
THUD
INUZUKA AND PERSIA...
DUM
DUH
DUH
DUH
...ARE WALKING SIDE BY SIDE!!
TCH... WHY DO I GOTTA WALK AROUND THE FESTIVAL WITH *YOU*, OF ALL PEOPLE...?!
I WISH I NEVER SIGNED UP FOR THIS COM-MITTEE CRAP!
I COULD SAY THE SAME!
DO TRY NOT TO SLOW ME DOWN!
THOSE TWO, PATROLLING TOGETHER? IS THAT REALLY A GOOD IDEA?!
MURMUR
MURMUR
THEY'RE ALREADY ABOUT TO BLOW...
HERE'S HOPING THE SCHOOL FESTIVAL DOESN'T TURN INTO A BLOOD-BATH...
DUUUM
DUH
DUH
DUH

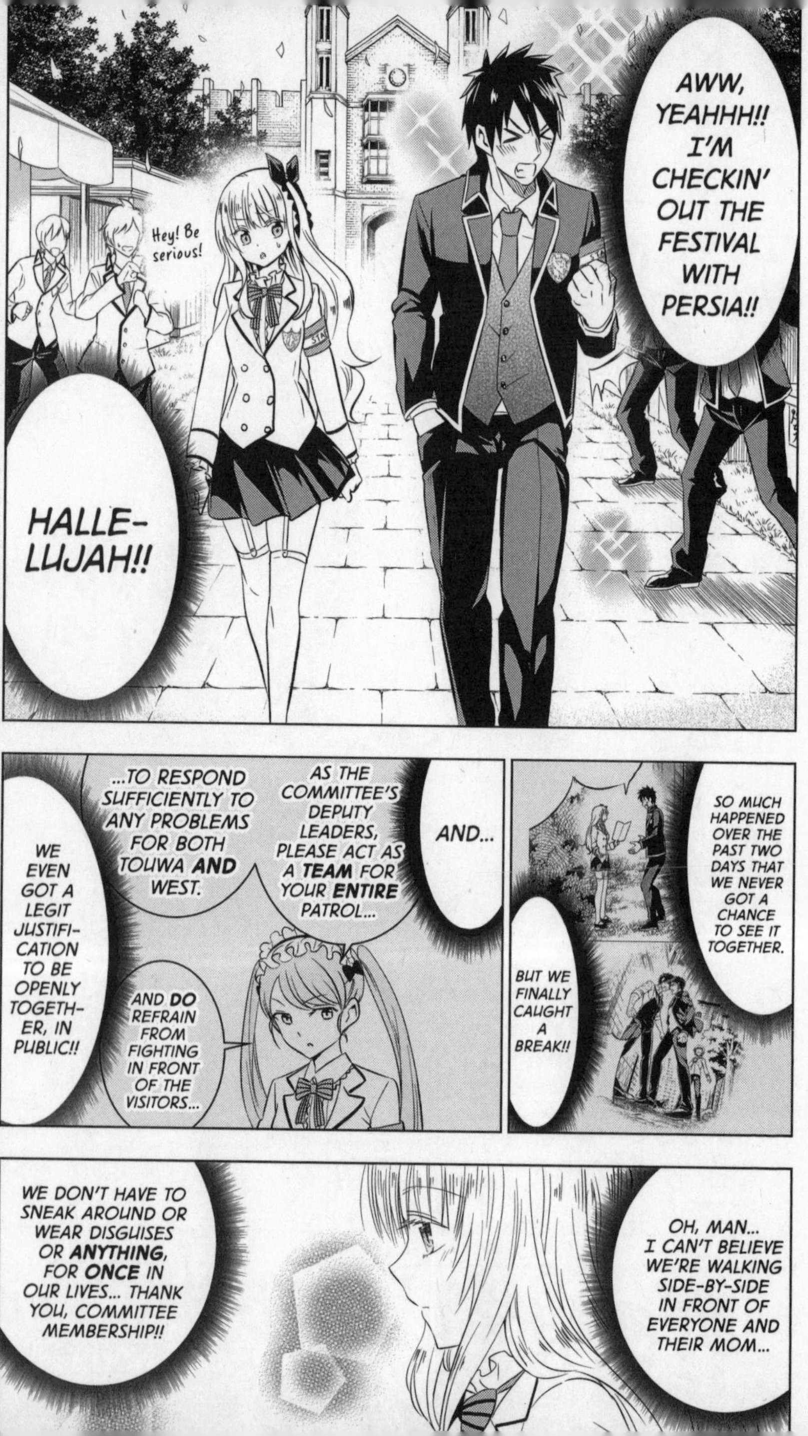
AWW, YEAHHH!! I'M CHECKIN' OUT THE FESTIVAL WITH PERSIA!!
Hey! Be serious!
HALLE-LUJAH!!
SO MUCH HAPPENED OVER THE PAST TWO DAYS THAT WE NEVER GOT A CHANCE TO SEE IT TOGETHER.
BUT WE FINALLY CAUGHT A BREAK!!
AND...
AS THE COMMITTEE'S DEPUTY LEADERS, PLEASE ACT AS A TEAM FOR YOUR ENTIRE PATROL...
...TO RESPOND SUFFICIENTLY TO ANY PROBLEMS FOR BOTH TOUWA AND WEST.
AND DO REFRAIN FROM FIGHTING IN FRONT OF THE VISITORS...
WE EVEN GOT A LEGIT JUSTIFI-CATION TO BE OPENLY TOGETH-ER, IN PUBLIC!!
OH, MAN... I CAN'T BELIEVE WE'RE WALKING SIDE-BY-SIDE IN FRONT OF EVERYONE AND THEIR MOM...
WE DON'T HAVE TO SNEAK AROUND OR WEAR DISGUISES OR ANYTHING, FOR ONCE IN OUR LIVES... THANK YOU, COMMITTEE MEMBERSHIP!!

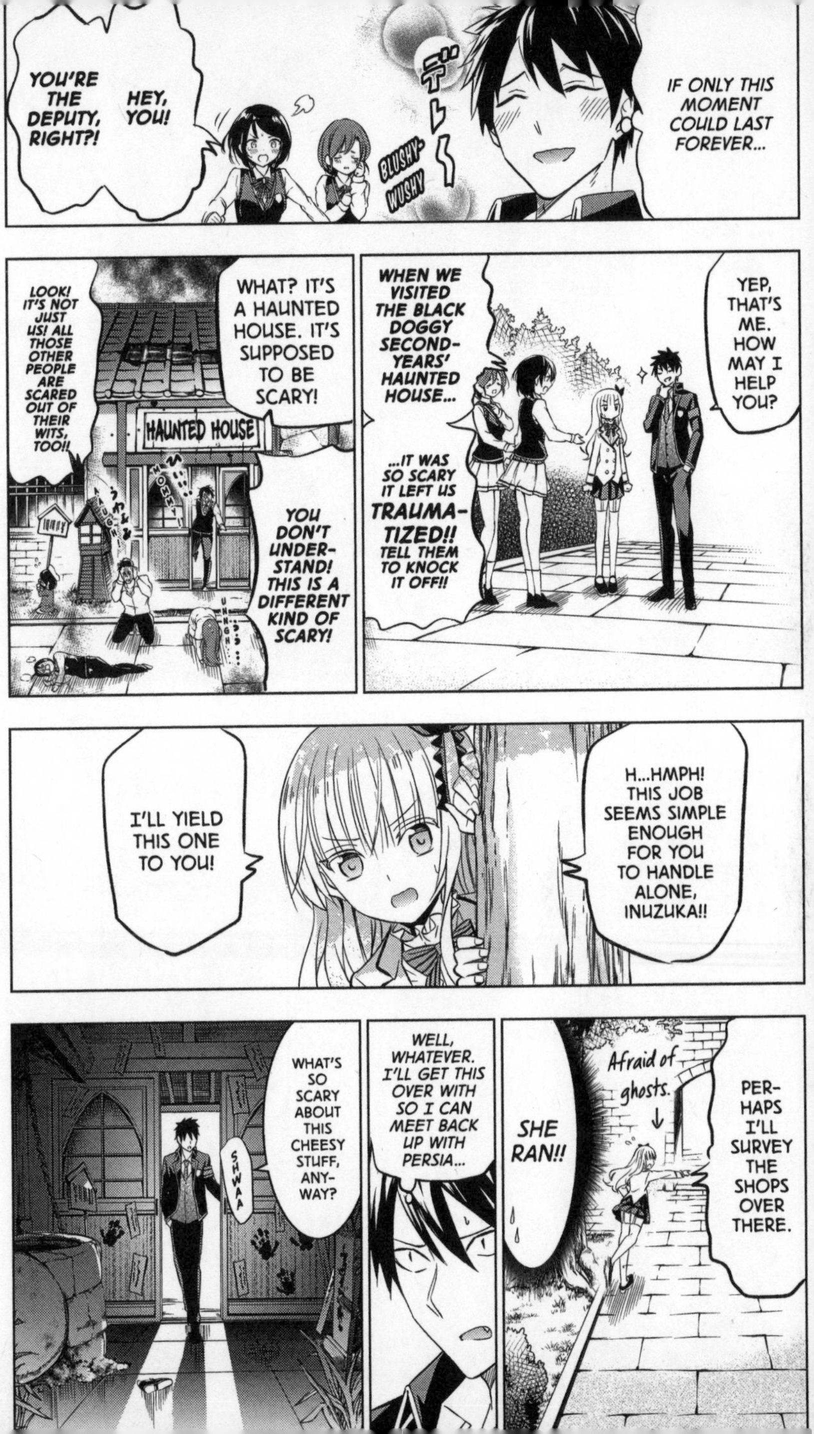
IF ONLY THIS MOMENT COULD LAST FOREVER...
BLUSHY-WUSHY
HEY, YOU!
YOU'RE THE DEPUTY, RIGHT?!
YEP, THAT'S ME. HOW MAY I HELP YOU?
WHEN WE VISITED THE BLACK DOGGY SECOND-YEARS' HAUNTED HOUSE...
...IT WAS SO SCARY IT LEFT US TRAUMATIZED!! TELL THEM TO KNOCK IT OFF!!
WHAT? IT'S A HAUNTED HOUSE. IT'S SUPPOSED TO BE SCARY!
LOOK! IT'S NOT JUST US! ALL THOSE OTHER PEOPLE ARE SCARED OUT OF THEIR WITS, TOO!!
HAUNTED HOUSE
MOMMY!
YOU DON'T UNDERSTAND! THIS IS A DIFFERENT KIND OF SCARY!
H...HMPH! THIS JOB SEEMS SIMPLE ENOUGH FOR YOU TO HANDLE ALONE, INUZUKA!!
I'LL YIELD THIS ONE TO YOU!
PERHAPS I'LL SURVEY THE SHOPS OVER THERE.
Afraid of ghosts.
SHE RAN!!
WELL, WHATEVER. I'LL GET THIS OVER WITH SO I CAN MEET BACK UP WITH PERSIA...
WHAT'S SO SCARY ABOUT THIS CHEESY STUFF, ANYWAY?
SHWAA

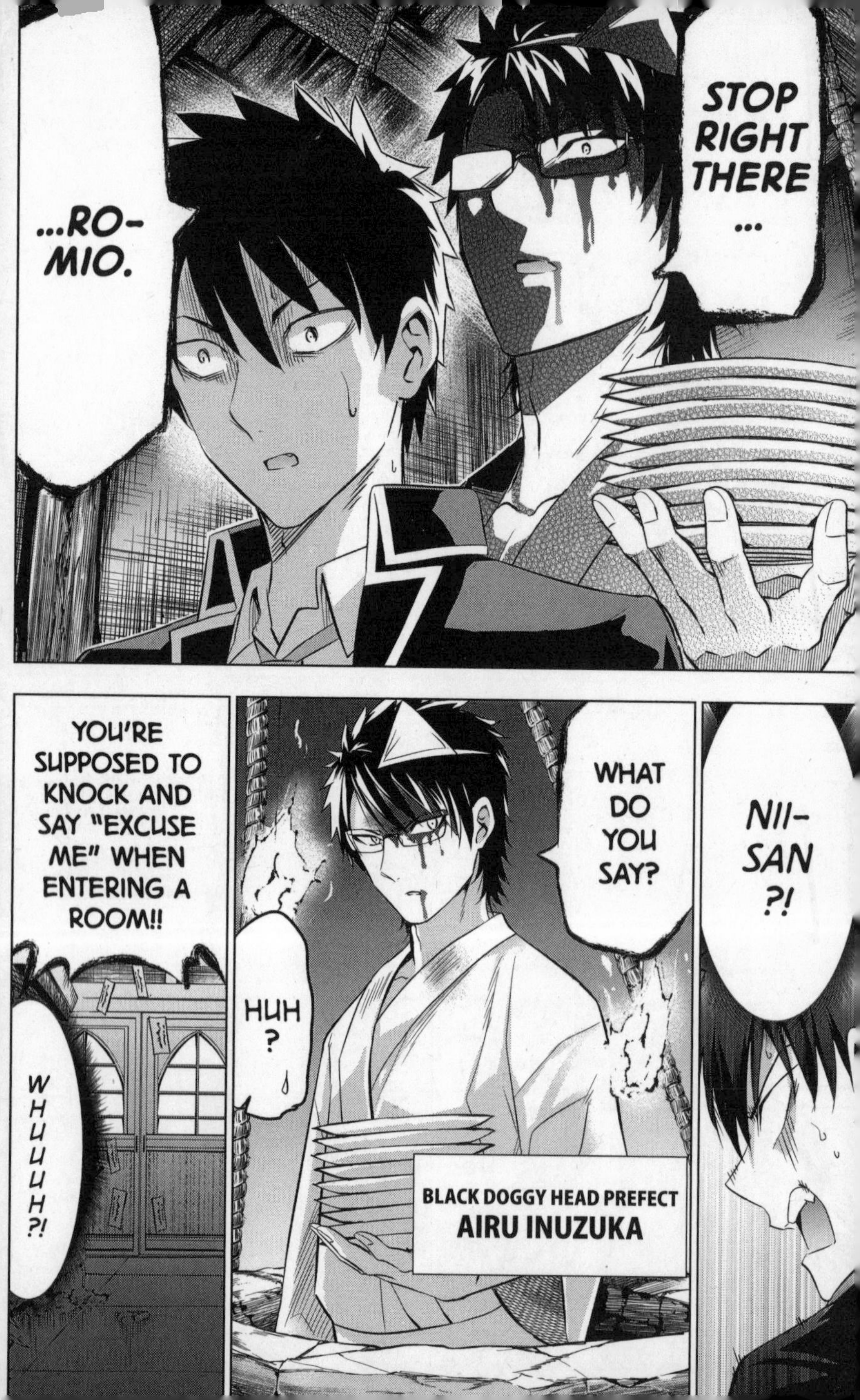
STOP RIGHT THERE ...
...RO-MIO.
NII-SAN ?!
WHAT DO YOU SAY?
HUH ?
BLACK DOGGY HEAD PREFECT
AIRU INUZUKA
YOU'RE SUPPOSED TO KNOCK AND SAY "EXCUSE ME" WHEN ENTERING A ROOM!!
WHUUUUH?!

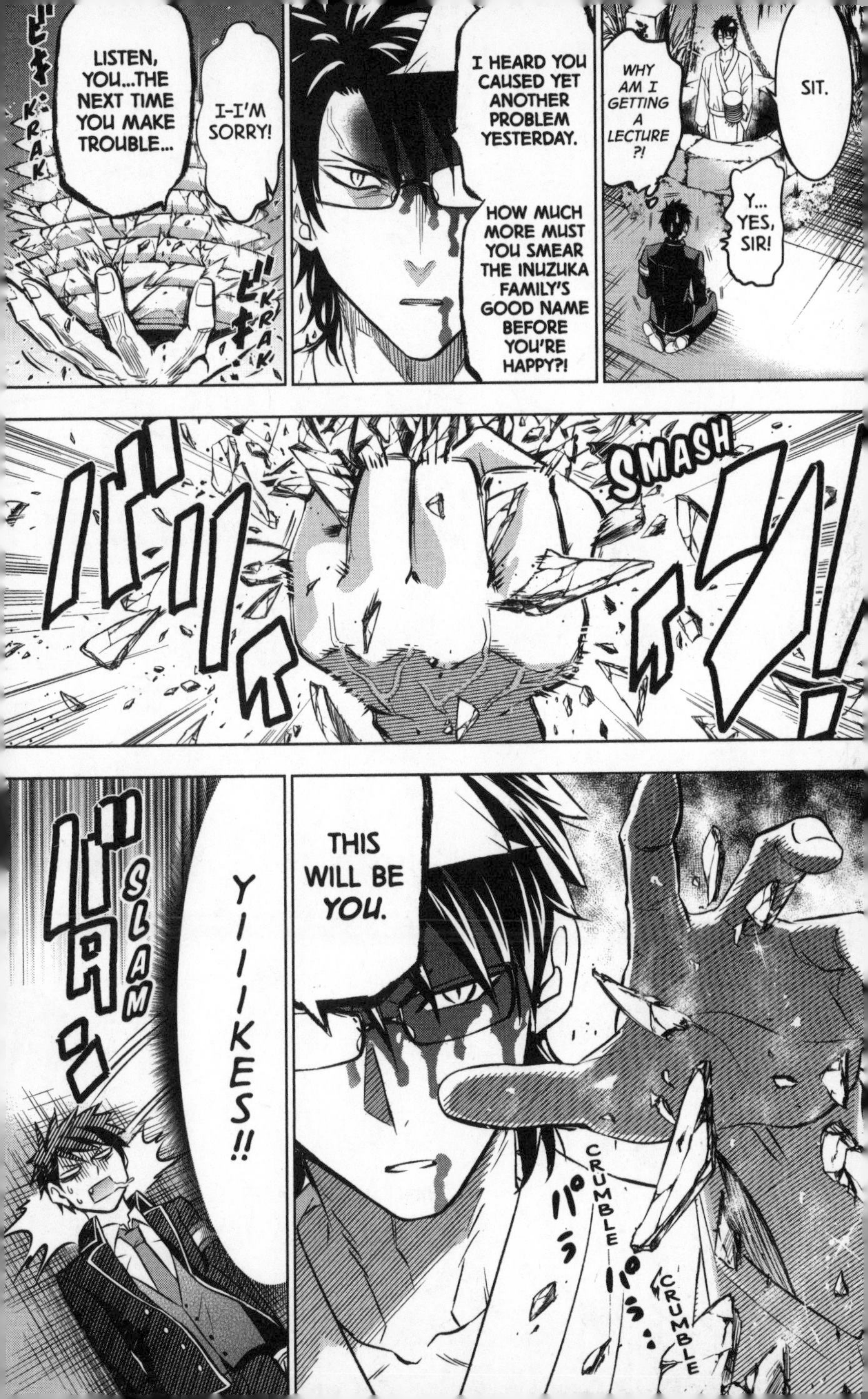
SIT.
Y... YES, SIR!
WHY AM I GETTING A LECTURE ?!
I HEARD YOU CAUSED YET ANOTHER PROBLEM YESTERDAY.
HOW MUCH MORE MUST YOU SMEAR THE INUZUKA FAMILY'S GOOD NAME BEFORE YOU'RE HAPPY?!
I-I'M SORRY!
LISTEN, YOU...THE NEXT TIME YOU MAKE TROUBLE...
KRAK
KRAK
SMASH
THIS WILL BE YOU.
CRUMBLE
CRUMBLE
YIIIIKES!!
SLAM

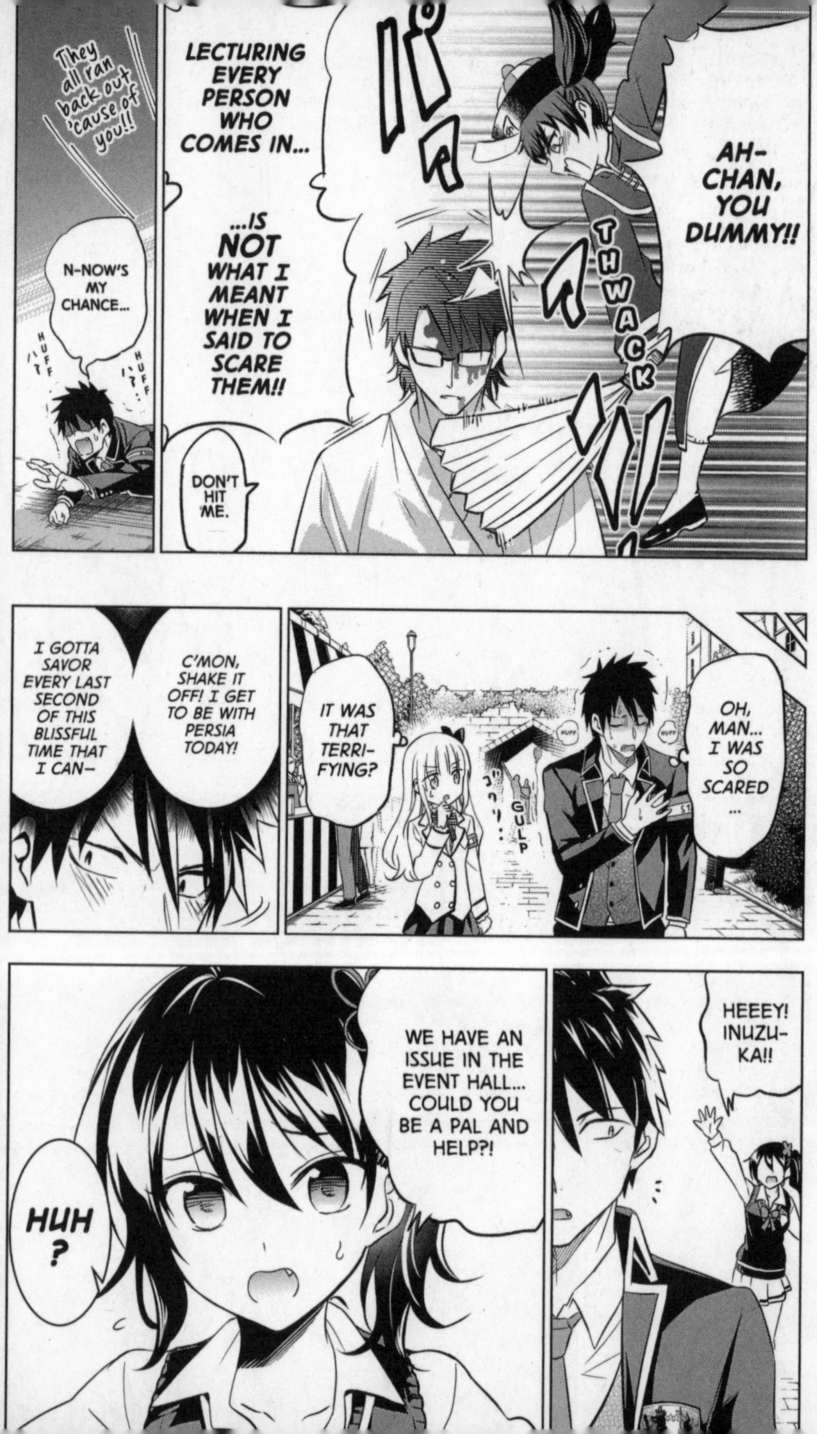
AH-CHAN, YOU DUMMY!!
THWACK
LECTURING EVERY PERSON WHO COMES IN...
...IS NOT WHAT I MEANT WHEN I SAID TO SCARE THEM!!
DON'T HIT ME.
They all ran back out 'cause of you!!
N-NOW'S MY CHANCE...
HUFF
HUFF
OH, MAN... I WAS SO SCARED ...
HUFF
HUFF
IT WAS THAT TERRI-FYING?
GULP
C'MON, SHAKE IT OFF! I GET TO BE WITH PERSIA TODAY!
I GOTTA SAVOR EVERY LAST SECOND OF THIS BLISSFUL TIME THAT I CAN–
HEEEY! INUZUKA!!
WE HAVE AN ISSUE IN THE EVENT HALL... COULD YOU BE A PAL AND HELP?!
HUH?

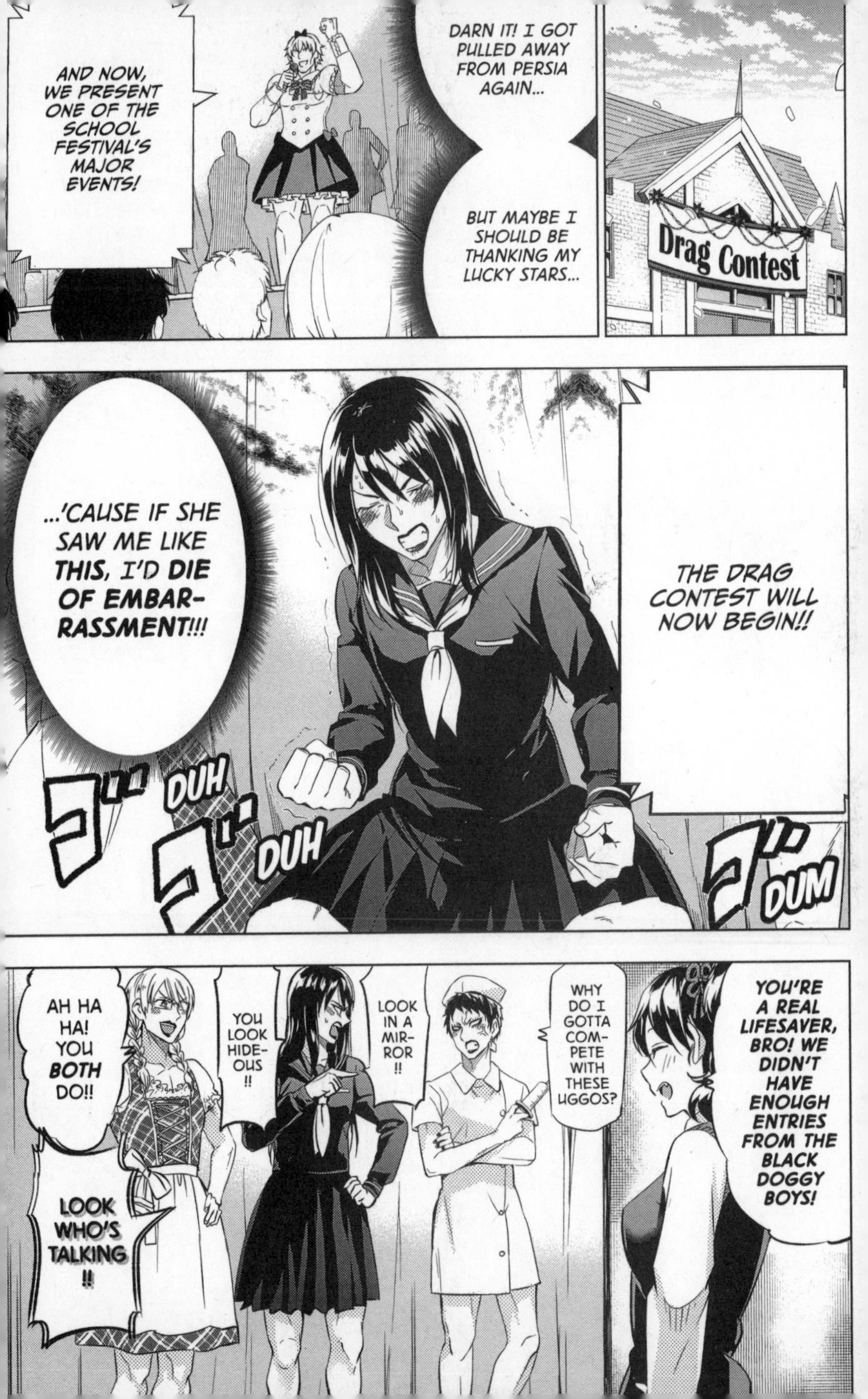
Drag Contest
DARN IT! I GOT PULLED AWAY FROM PERSIA AGAIN...
BUT MAYBE I SHOULD BE THANKING MY LUCKY STARS...
AND NOW, WE PRESENT ONE OF THE SCHOOL FESTIVAL'S MAJOR EVENTS!
THE DRAG CONTEST WILL NOW BEGIN!!
...'CAUSE IF SHE SAW ME LIKE THIS, I'D DIE OF EMBARRASSMENT!!!
DUM
DUH
DUH
YOU'RE A REAL LIFESAVER, BRO! WE DIDN'T HAVE ENOUGH ENTRIES FROM THE BLACK DOGGY BOYS!
WHY DO I GOTTA COMPETE WITH THESE UGGOS?
LOOK IN A MIRROR!!
YOU LOOK HIDEOUS!!
AH HA HA! YOU BOTH DO!!
LOOK WHO'S TALKING!!

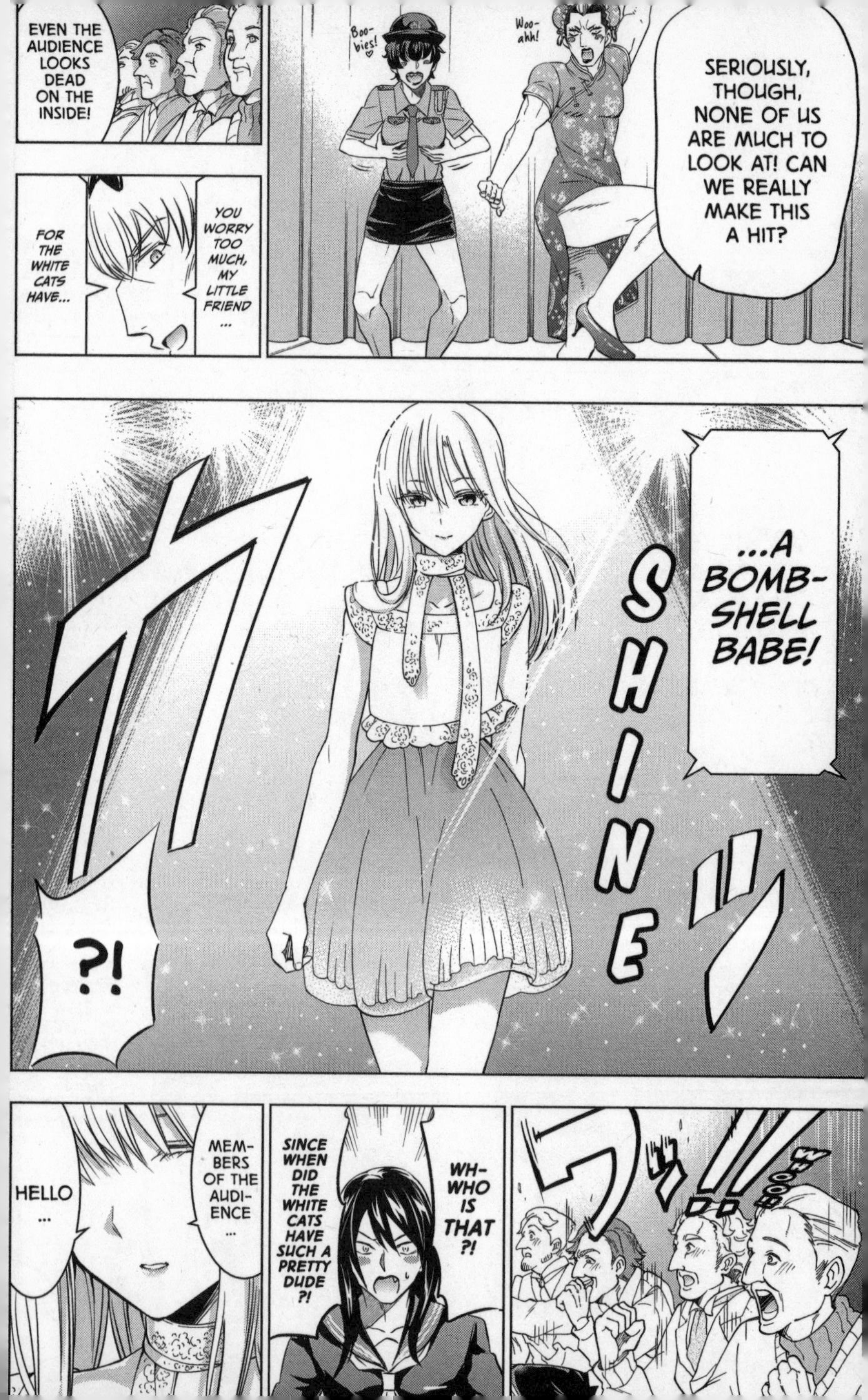
SERIOUSLY, THOUGH, NONE OF US ARE MUCH TO LOOK AT! CAN WE REALLY MAKE THIS A HIT?
Woo-ahh!
Boo-bies! ♡
EVEN THE AUDIENCE LOOKS DEAD ON THE INSIDE!
YOU WORRY TOO MUCH, MY LITTLE FRIEND...
FOR THE WHITE CATS HAVE...
...A BOMB-SHELL BABE!
SHINE
?!
WH-WHO IS THAT?!
SINCE WHEN DID THE WHITE CATS HAVE SUCH A PRETTY DUDE?!
MEM-BERS OF THE AUDI-ENCE...
HELLO...

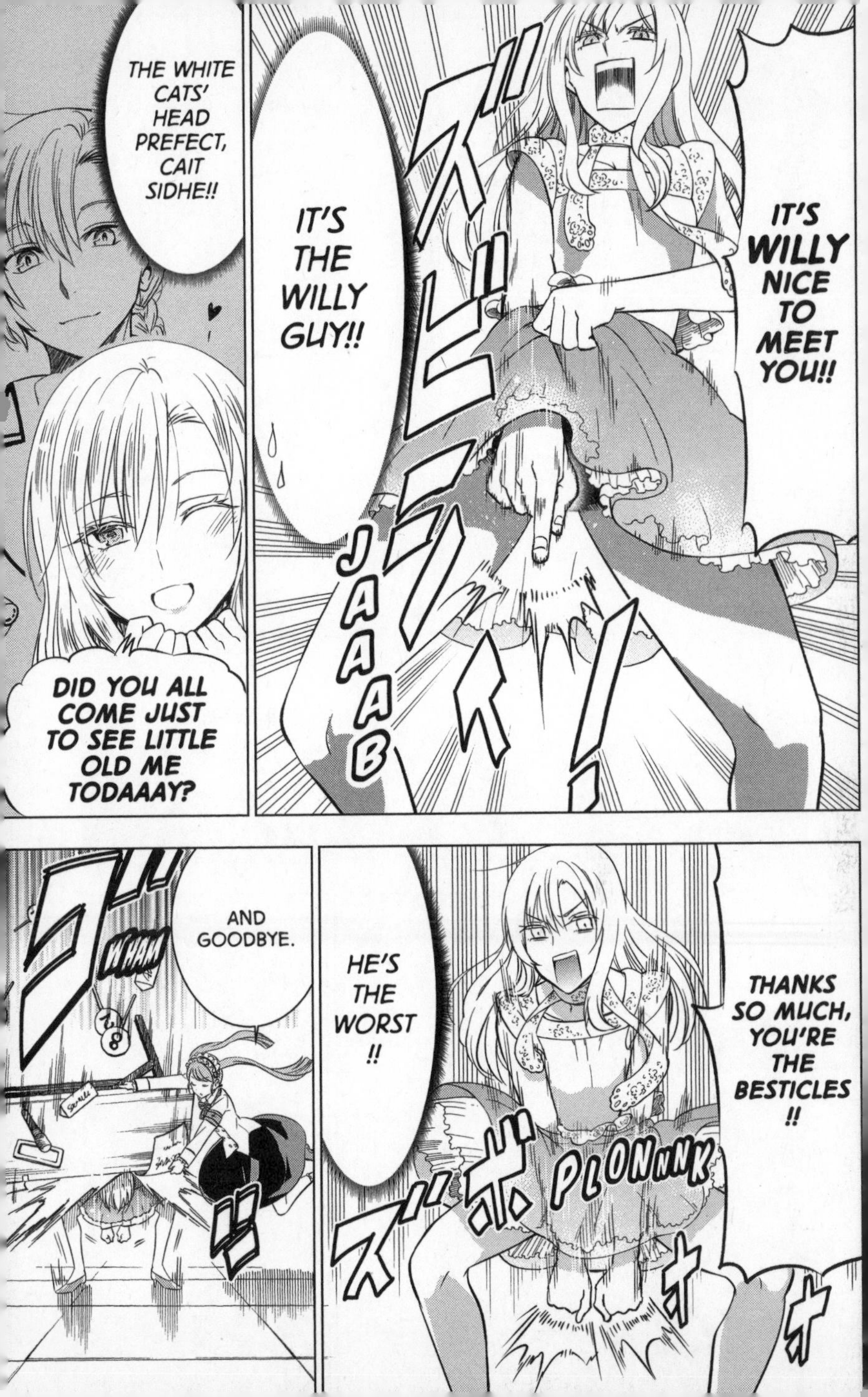
IT'S WILLY NICE TO MEET YOU!!
JAAAAB
IT'S THE WILLY GUY!!
THE WHITE CATS' HEAD PREFECT, CAIT SIDHE!!
DID YOU ALL COME JUST TO SEE LITTLE OLD ME TODAAAY?
THANKS SO MUCH, YOU'RE THE BESTICLES !!
PLONNNK
HE'S THE WORST !!
AND GOODBYE.
WHAM

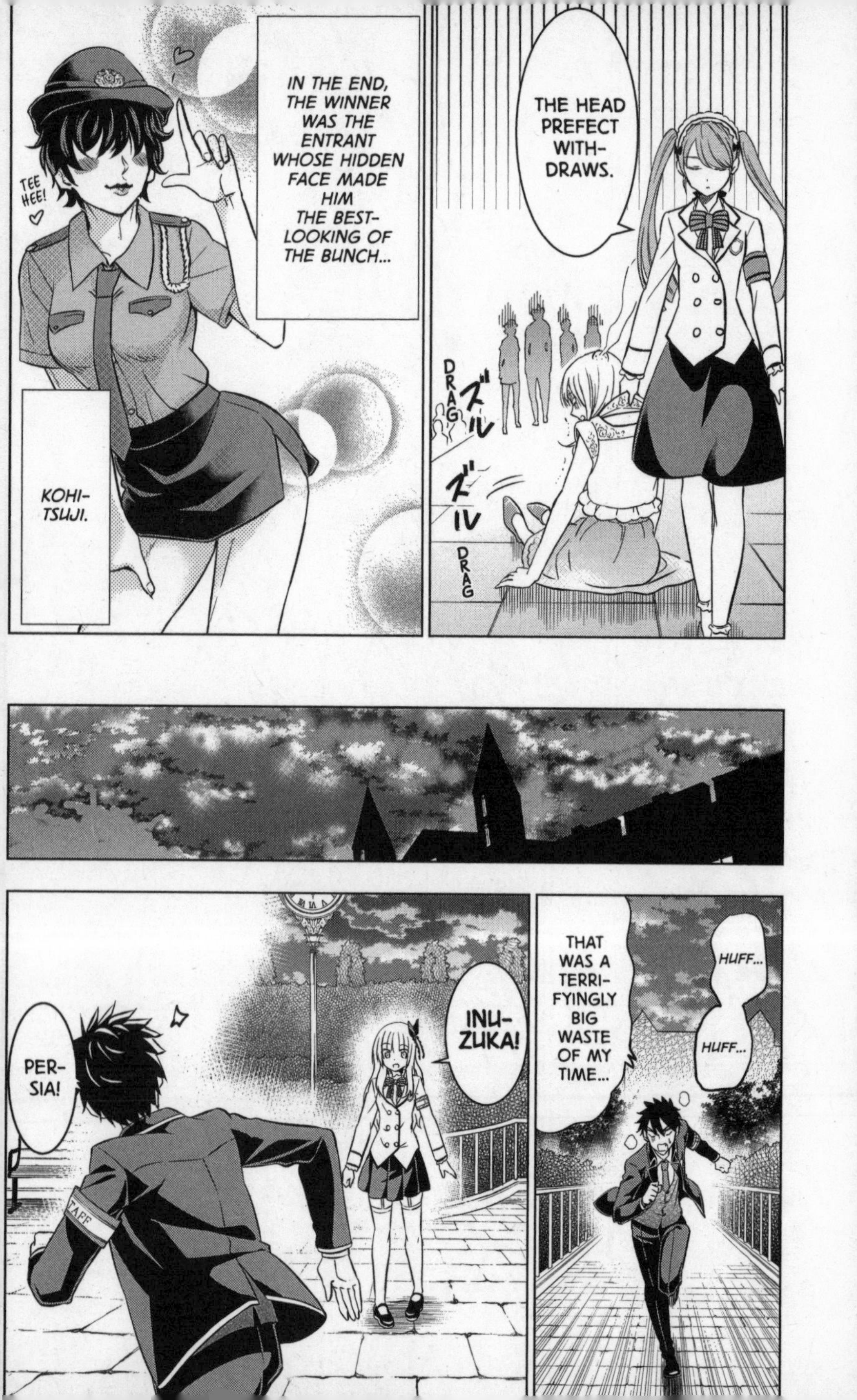
THE HEAD PREFECT WITH-DRAWS.
DRAG ズル
ズル DRAG
IN THE END, THE WINNER WAS THE ENTRANT WHOSE HIDDEN FACE MADE HIM THE BEST-LOOKING OF THE BUNCH...
TEE HEE! ♡
KOHI-TSUJI.
HUFF...
HUFF...
THAT WAS A TERRI-FYINGLY BIG WASTE OF MY TIME...
INU-ZUKA!
PER-SIA!

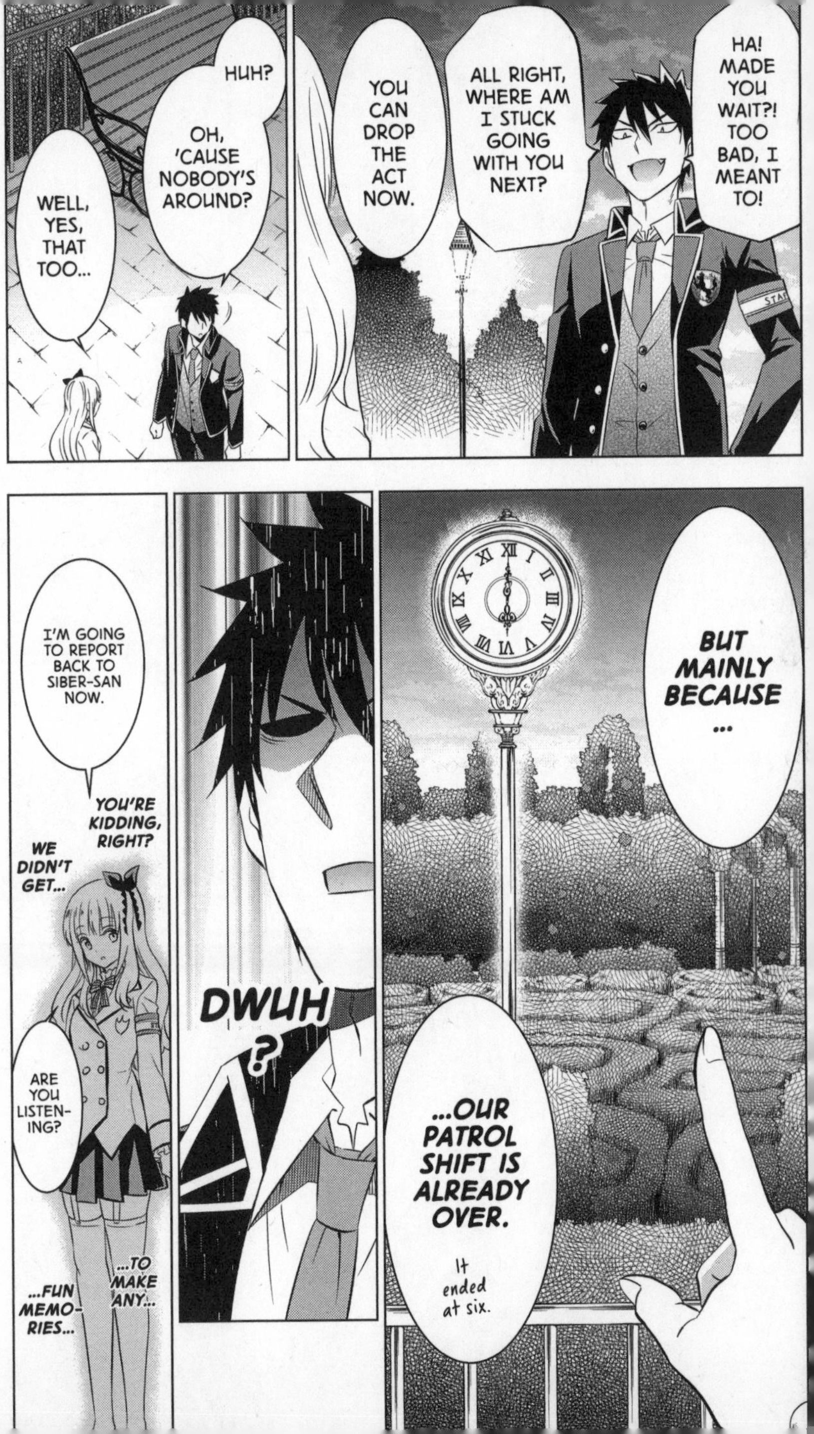
HA! MADE YOU WAIT?! TOO BAD, I MEANT TO!
ALL RIGHT, WHERE AM I STUCK GOING WITH YOU NEXT?
YOU CAN DROP THE ACT NOW.
HUH?
OH, 'CAUSE NOBODY'S AROUND?
WELL, YES, THAT TOO...
BUT MAINLY BECAUSE ...
...OUR PATROL SHIFT IS ALREADY OVER.
It ended at six.
DWUH ?
I'M GOING TO REPORT BACK TO SIBER-SAN NOW.
YOU'RE KIDDING, RIGHT?
WE DIDN'T GET...
ARE YOU LISTENING?
...TO MAKE ANY...
...FUN MEMORIES...

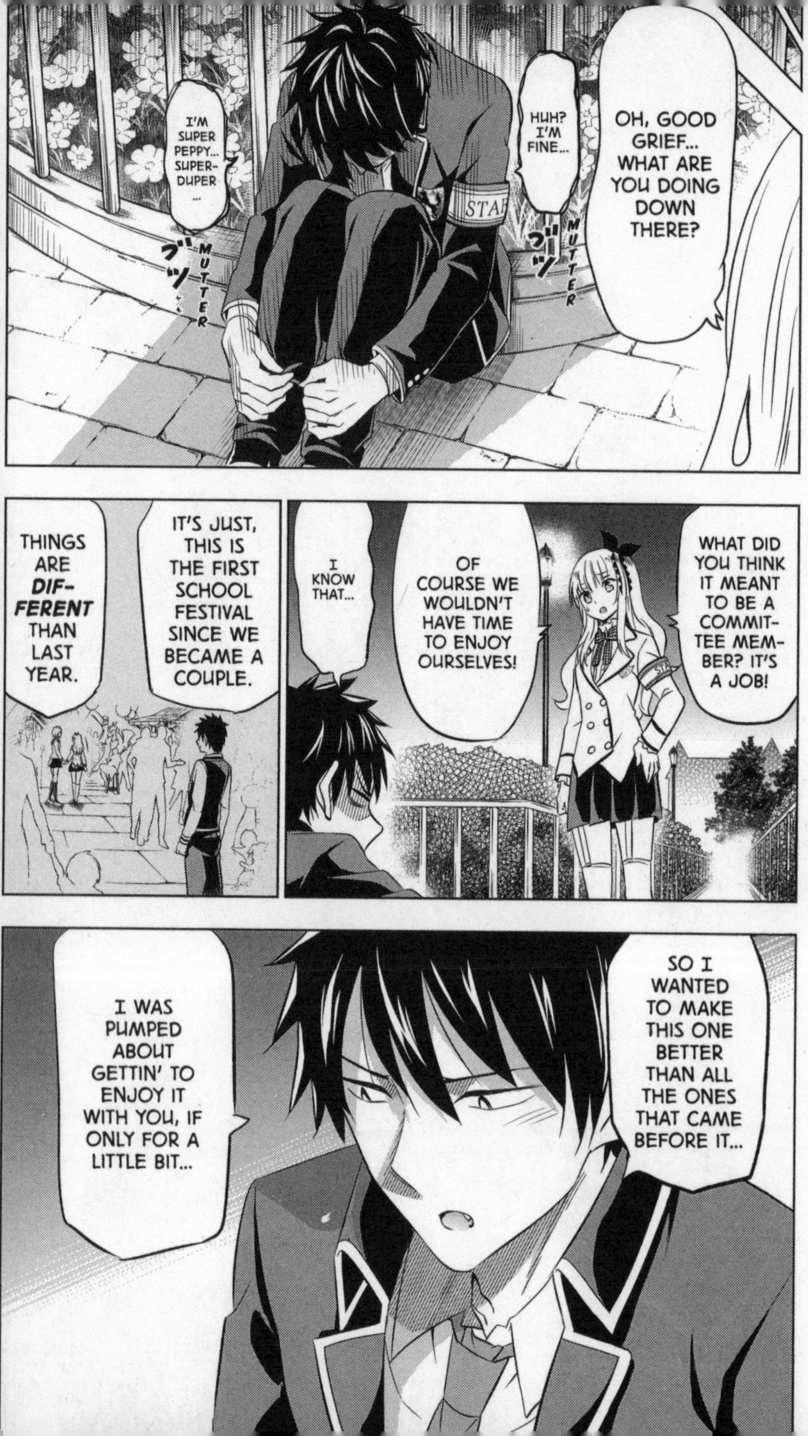
OH, GOOD GRIEF... WHAT ARE YOU DOING DOWN THERE?
HUH? I'M FINE...
MUTTER
I'M SUPER PEPPY... SUPER-DUPER ...
MUTTER
WHAT DID YOU THINK IT MEANT TO BE A COMMITTEE MEMBER? IT'S A JOB!
OF COURSE WE WOULDN'T HAVE TIME TO ENJOY OURSELVES!
I KNOW THAT...
IT'S JUST, THIS IS THE FIRST SCHOOL FESTIVAL SINCE WE BECAME A COUPLE.
THINGS ARE DIF-FERENT THAN LAST YEAR.
SO I WANTED TO MAKE THIS ONE BETTER THAN ALL THE ONES THAT CAME BEFORE IT...
I WAS PUMPED ABOUT GETTIN' TO ENJOY IT WITH YOU, IF ONLY FOR A LITTLE BIT...

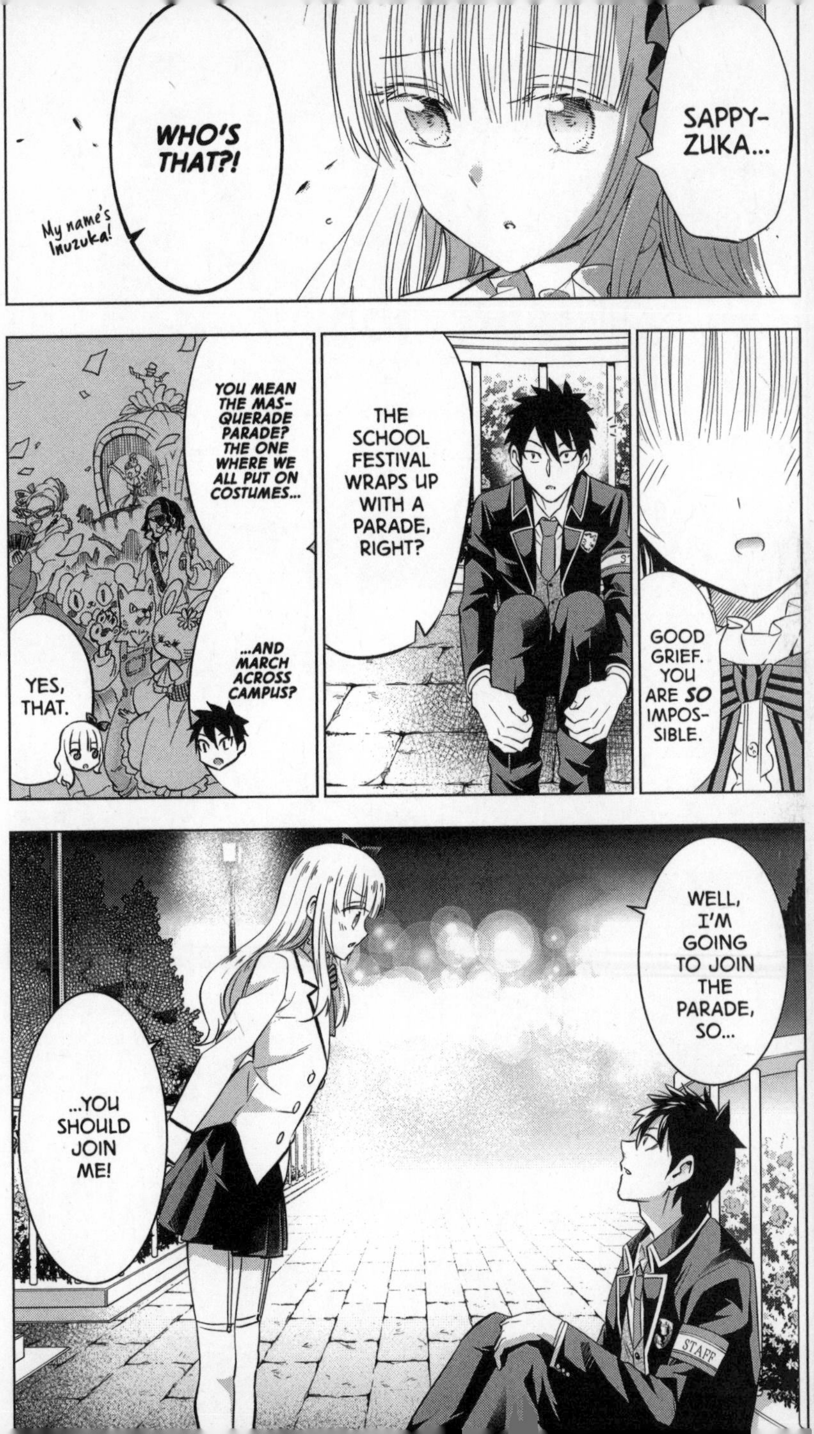
SAPPY-ZUKA...
WHO'S THAT?!
My name's Inuzuka!
GOOD GRIEF. YOU ARE SO IMPOSSIBLE.
THE SCHOOL FESTIVAL WRAPS UP WITH A PARADE, RIGHT?
YOU MEAN THE MAS-QUERADE PARADE? THE ONE WHERE WE ALL PUT ON COSTUMES...
...AND MARCH ACROSS CAMPUS?
YES, THAT.
WELL, I'M GOING TO JOIN THE PARADE, SO...
...YOU SHOULD JOIN ME!
STAFF

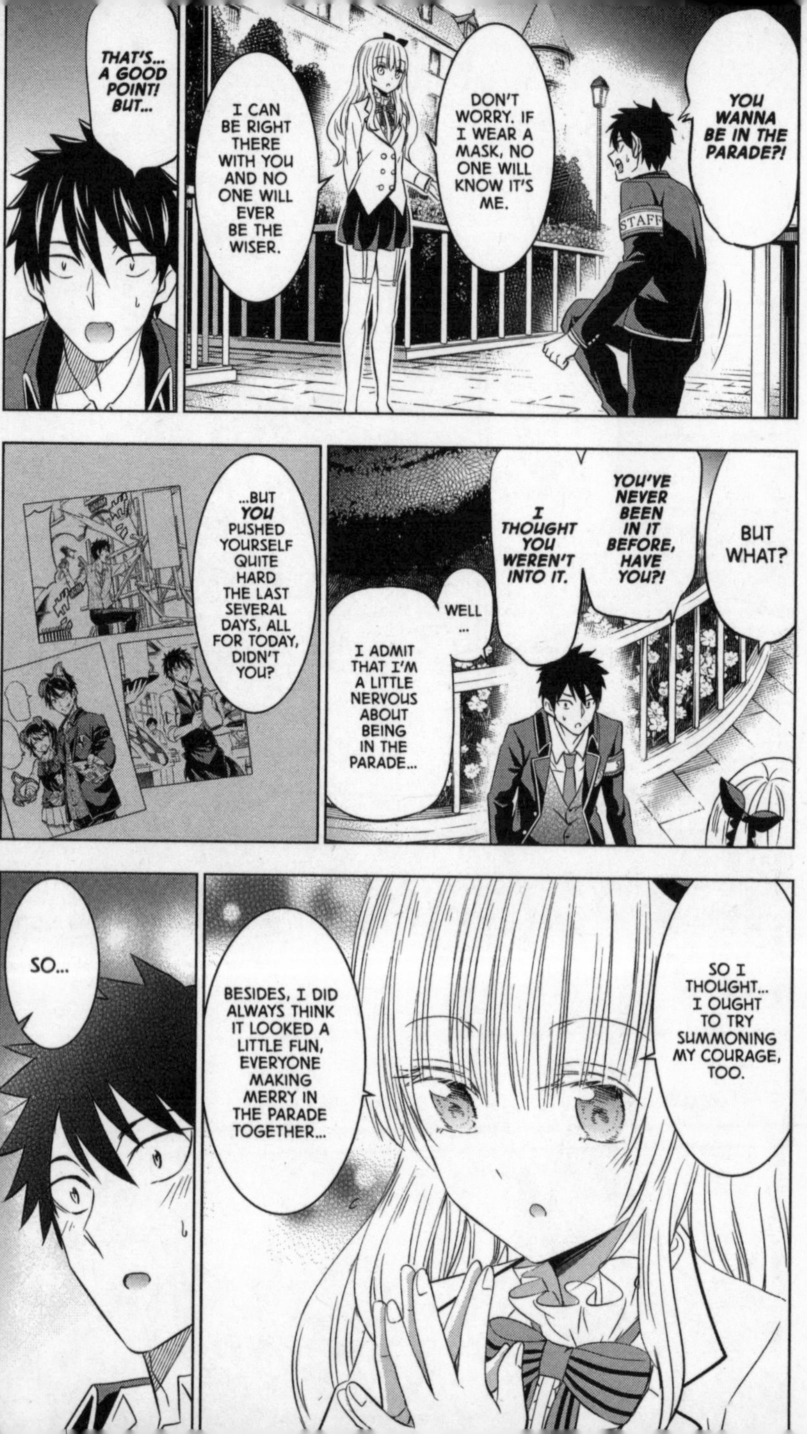
YOU WANNA BE IN THE PARADE?!
DON'T WORRY. IF I WEAR A MASK, NO ONE WILL KNOW IT'S ME.
I CAN BE RIGHT THERE WITH YOU AND NO ONE WILL EVER BE THE WISER.
THAT'S... A GOOD POINT! BUT...
BUT WHAT?
YOU'VE NEVER BEEN IN IT BEFORE, HAVE YOU?!
I THOUGHT YOU WEREN'T INTO IT.
WELL ...
I ADMIT THAT I'M A LITTLE NERVOUS ABOUT BEING IN THE PARADE...
...BUT YOU PUSHED YOURSELF QUITE HARD THE LAST SEVERAL DAYS, ALL FOR TODAY, DIDN'T YOU?
SO I THOUGHT... I OUGHT TO TRY SUMMONING MY COURAGE, TOO.
BESIDES, I DID ALWAYS THINK IT LOOKED A LITTLE FUN, EVERYONE MAKING MERRY IN THE PARADE TOGETHER...
SO...

COME ON, UP WITH YOU!

OR WE'LL LET THIS FUN MEMORY SLIP AWAY!

LET'S SQUARE AWAY OUR COSTUMES, AND THEN RENDEZVOUS.

YUP! SEE YA SOON!

OH, REALLY NOW? NEVER MIND THEN, I'LL GO WITH CHAR-CHAN.

I'M SORRY! LET ME GO WITH YOU!

SINCE YOU INSIST, I GUESS I'LL DO YOU A FAVOR AND GO WITH YOU!

A-ALL RIGHT, CAN'T SAY NO TO MY GIRL!

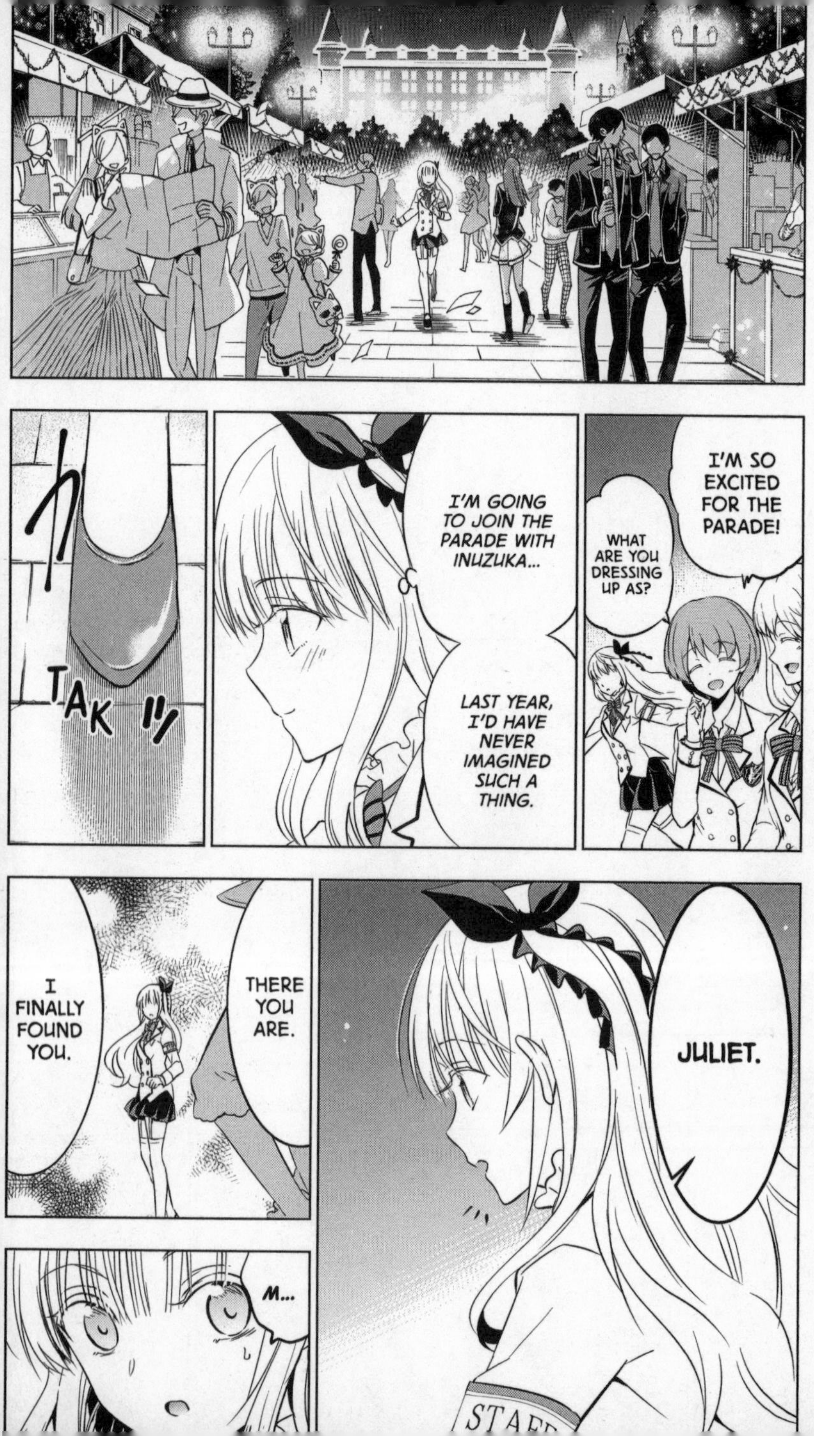
I'M SO EXCITED FOR THE PARADE!
WHAT ARE YOU DRESSING UP AS?
I'M GOING TO JOIN THE PARADE WITH INUZUKA...
LAST YEAR, I'D HAVE NEVER IMAGINED SUCH A THING.
TAK
JULIET.
THERE YOU ARE.
I FINALLY FOUND YOU.
M...

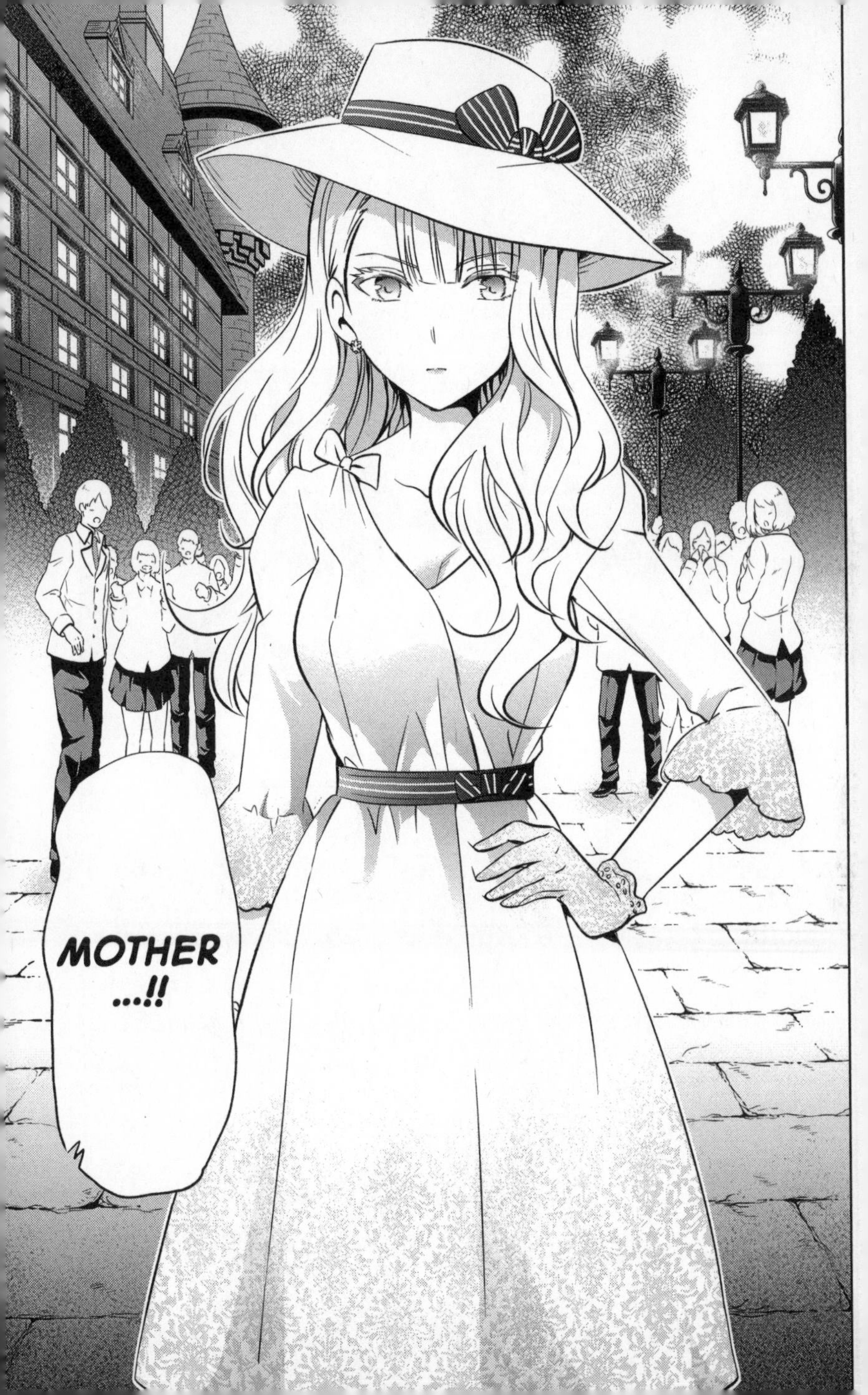
MOTHER
...!!

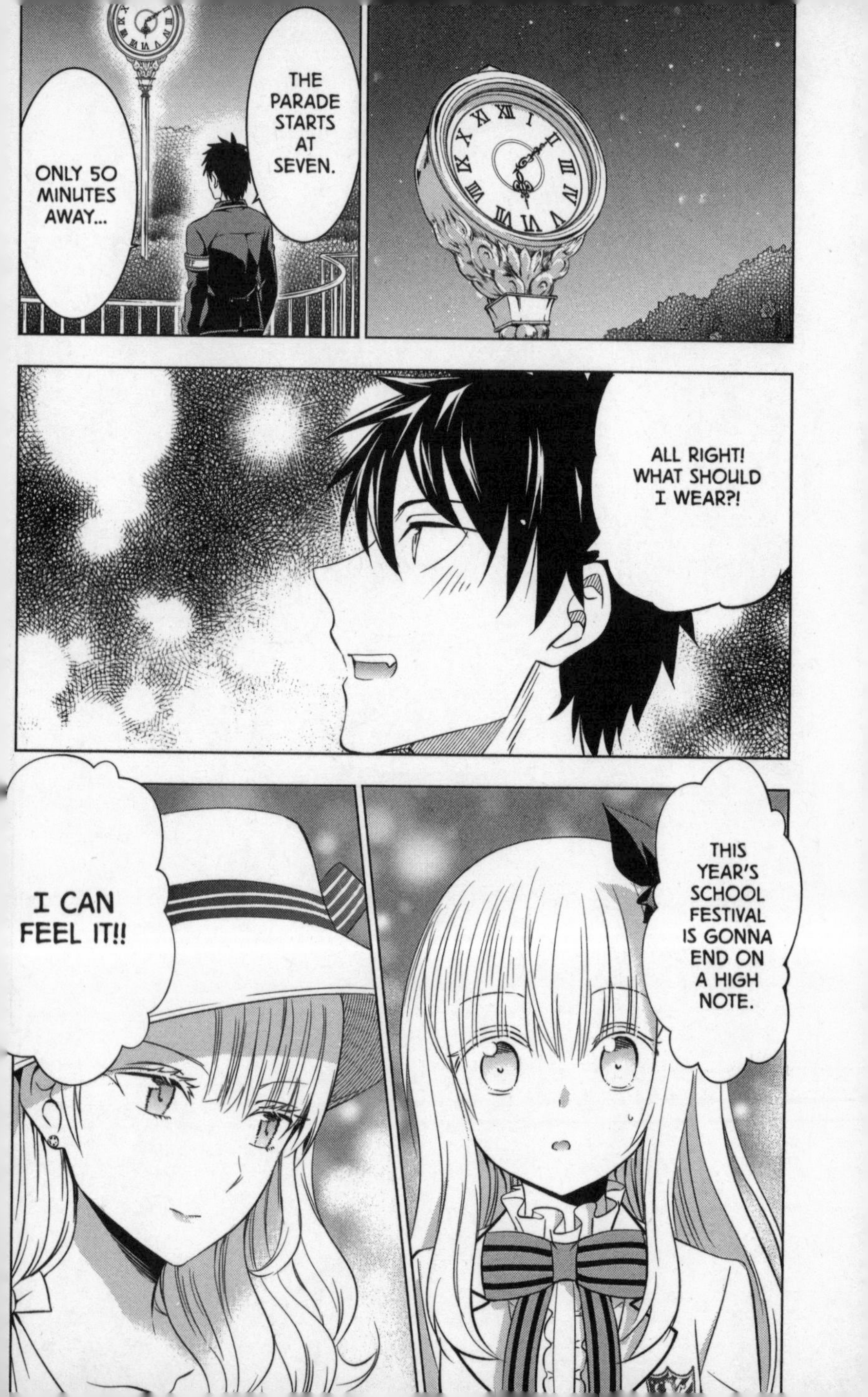
THE PARADE STARTS AT SEVEN.
ONLY 50 MINUTES AWAY...
ALL RIGHT! WHAT SHOULD I WEAR?!
THIS YEAR'S SCHOOL FESTIVAL IS GONNA END ON A HIGH NOTE.
I CAN FEEL IT!!

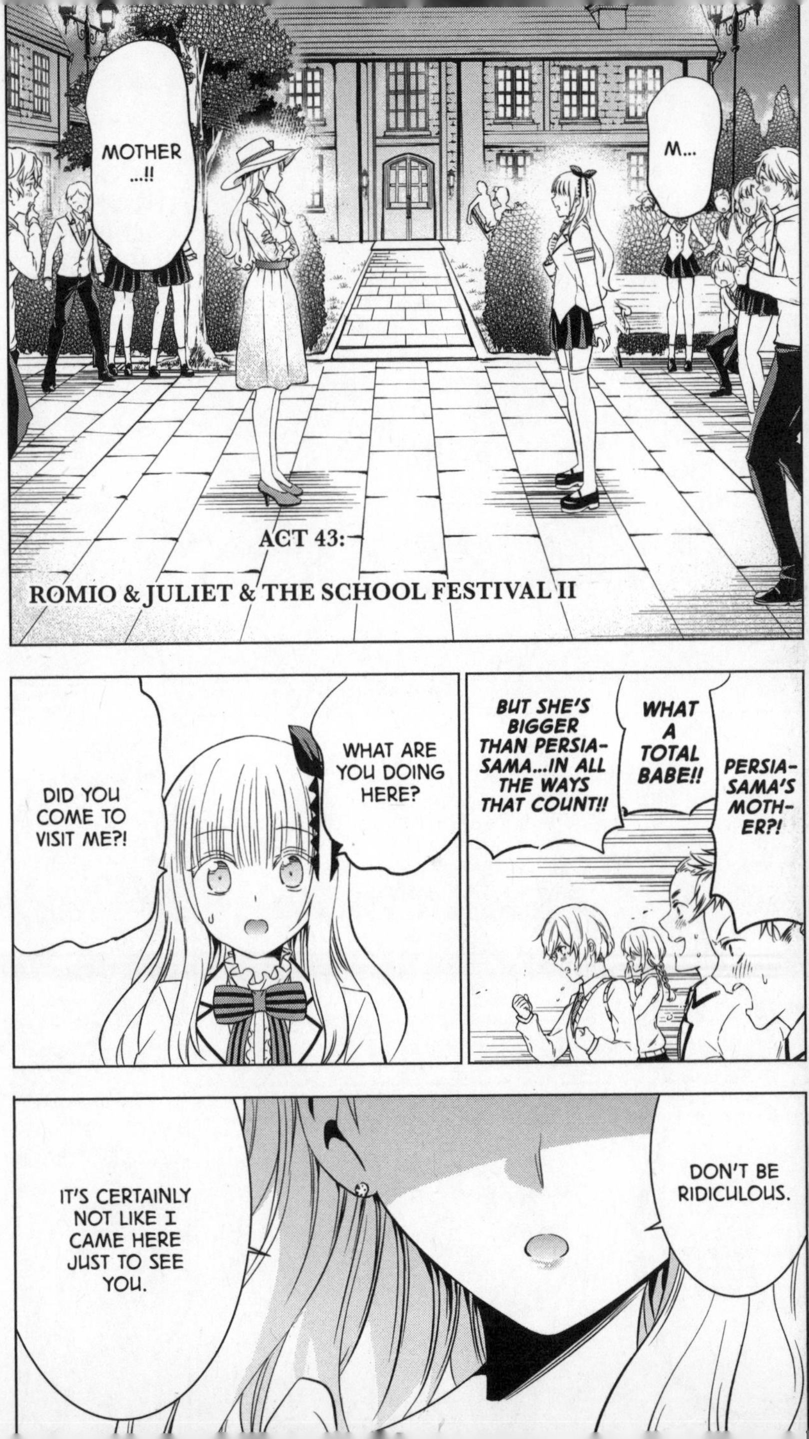
M...
MOTHER ...!!
ACT 43:
ROMIO & JULIET & THE SCHOOL FESTIVAL II
PERSIA-SAMA'S MOTHER?!
WHAT A TOTAL BABE!!
BUT SHE'S BIGGER THAN PERSIA-SAMA...IN ALL THE WAYS THAT COUNT!!
WHAT ARE YOU DOING HERE?
DID YOU COME TO VISIT ME?!
DON'T BE RIDICULOUS.
IT'S CERTAINLY NOT LIKE I CAME HERE JUST TO SEE YOU.

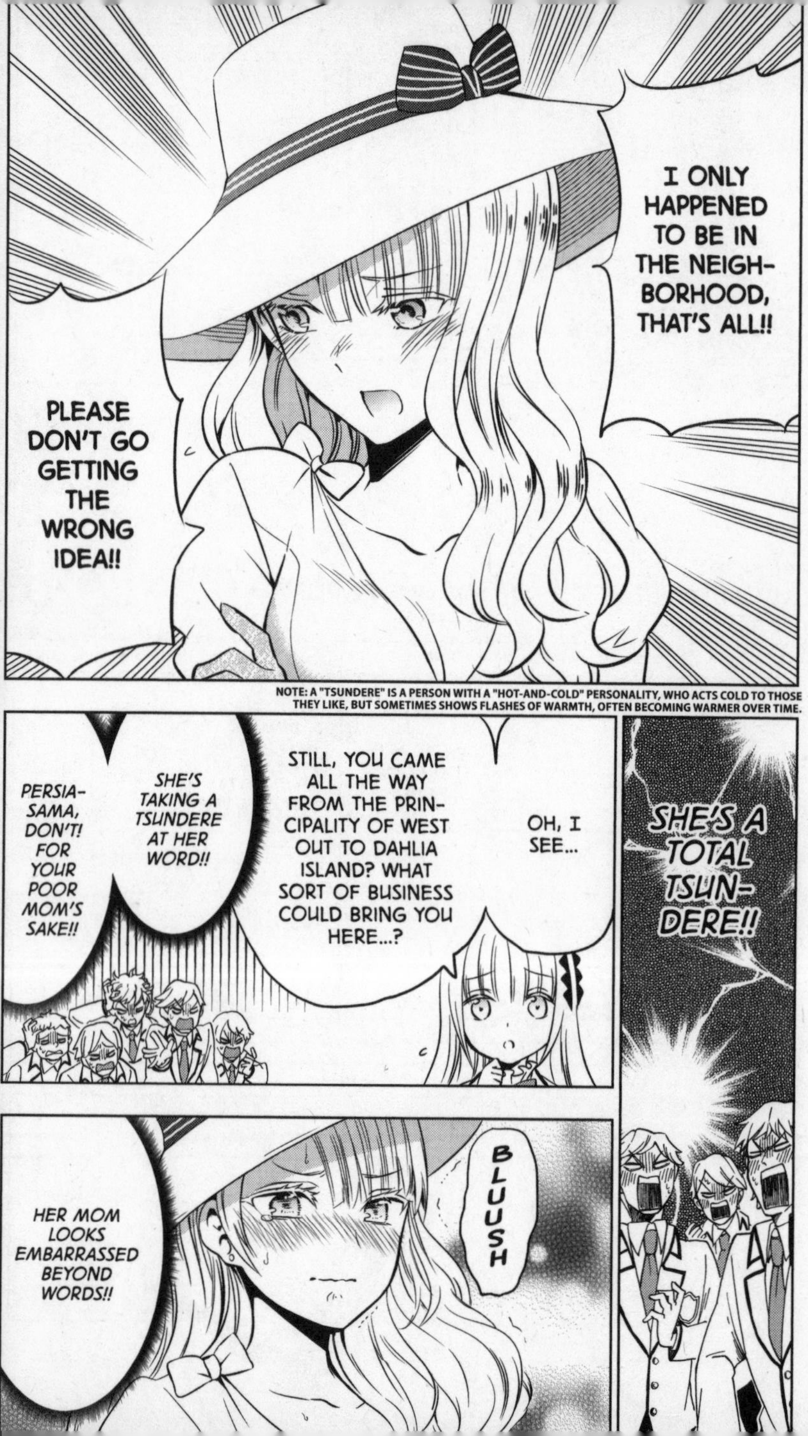
I ONLY HAPPENED TO BE IN THE NEIGH-BORHOOD, THAT'S ALL!!
PLEASE DON'T GO GETTING THE WRONG IDEA!!
SHE'S A TOTAL TSUN-DERE!!
OH, I SEE...
STILL, YOU CAME ALL THE WAY FROM THE PRIN-CIPALITY OF WEST OUT TO DAHLIA ISLAND? WHAT SORT OF BUSINESS COULD BRING YOU HERE...?
SHE'S TAKING A TSUNDERE AT HER WORD!!
PERSIA-SAMA, DON'T! FOR YOUR POOR MOM'S SAKE!!
BLUUSH
HER MOM LOOKS EMBARRASSED BEYOND WORDS!!
NOTE: A "TSUNDERE" IS A PERSON WITH A "HOT-AND-COLD" PERSONALITY, WHO ACTS COLD TO THOSE THEY LIKE, BUT SOMETIMES SHOWS FLASHES OF WARMTH, OFTEN BECOMING WARMER OVER TIME.

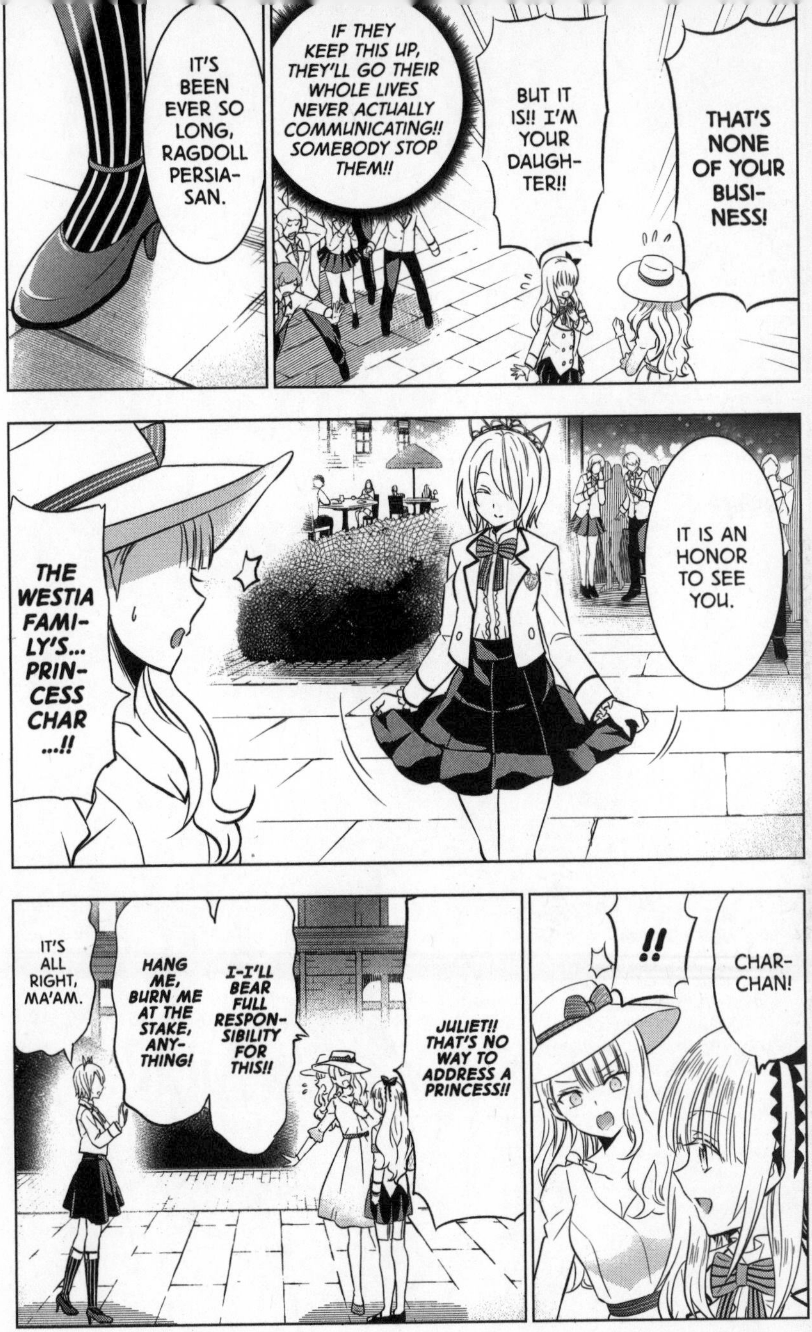
THAT'S NONE OF YOUR BUSINESS!
BUT IT IS!! I'M YOUR DAUGHTER!!
IF THEY KEEP THIS UP, THEY'LL GO THEIR WHOLE LIVES NEVER ACTUALLY COMMUNICATING!! SOMEBODY STOP THEM!!
IT'S BEEN EVER SO LONG, RAGDOLL PERSIA-SAN.
IT IS AN HONOR TO SEE YOU.
THE WESTIA FAMILY'S... PRINCESS CHAR...!!
CHAR-CHAN!
!!
JULIET!! THAT'S NO WAY TO ADDRESS A PRINCESS!!
I-I'LL BEAR FULL RESPONSIBILITY FOR THIS!!
HANG ME, BURN ME AT THE STAKE, ANYTHING!
IT'S ALL RIGHT, MA'AM.

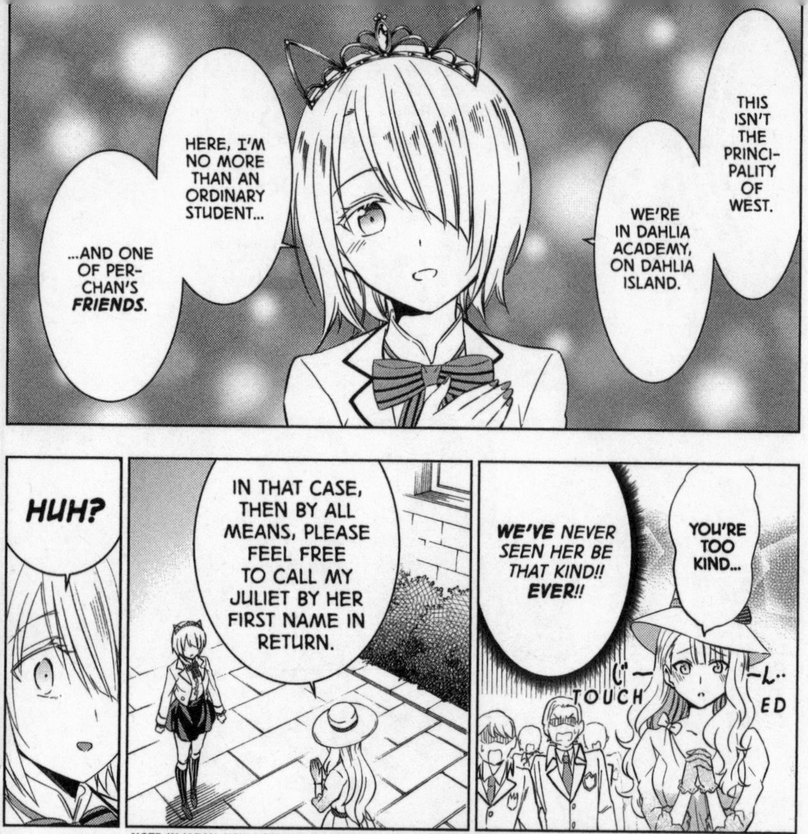
THIS ISN'T THE PRINCI-PALITY OF WEST.
WE'RE IN DAHLIA ACADEMY, ON DAHLIA ISLAND.
HERE, I'M NO MORE THAN AN ORDINARY STUDENT...
...AND ONE OF PER-CHAN'S FRIENDS.
YOU'RE TOO KIND...
TOUCHED
WE'VE NEVER SEEN HER BE THAT KIND!! EVER!!
IN THAT CASE, THEN BY ALL MEANS, PLEASE FEEL FREE TO CALL MY JULIET BY HER FIRST NAME IN RETURN.
HUH?

NOTE: IN JAPAN, USING SOMEONE'S GIVEN NAME CAN BE CONSIDERED A BIG STEP IN A RELATIONSHIP (AND IN THIS CASE, MAY HAVE ROMANTIC INSINUATIONS FOR CHARTREUX).

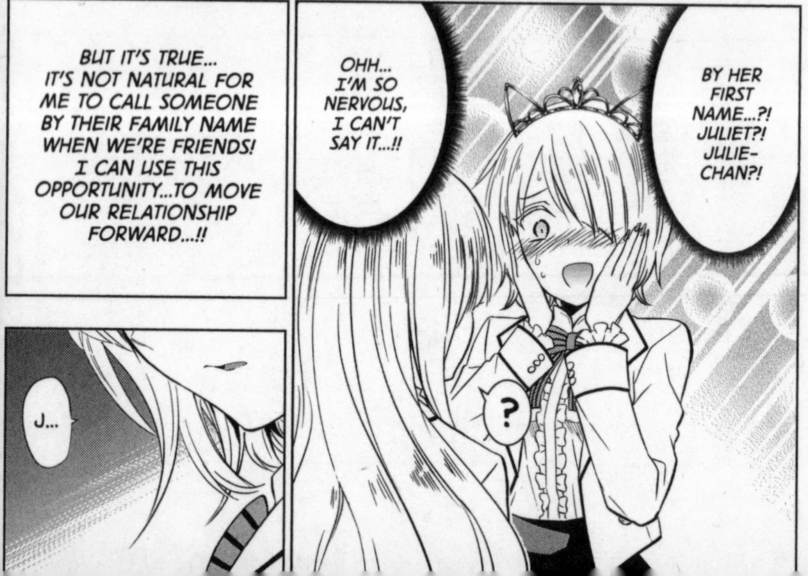
BY HER FIRST NAME...?! JULIET?! JULIE-CHAN?!
OHH... I'M SO NERVOUS, I CAN'T SAY IT...!!
?
BUT IT'S TRUE... IT'S NOT NATURAL FOR ME TO CALL SOMEONE BY THEIR FAMILY NAME WHEN WE'RE FRIENDS! I CAN USE THIS OPPORTUNITY...TO MOVE OUR RELATIONSHIP FORWARD...!!
J...

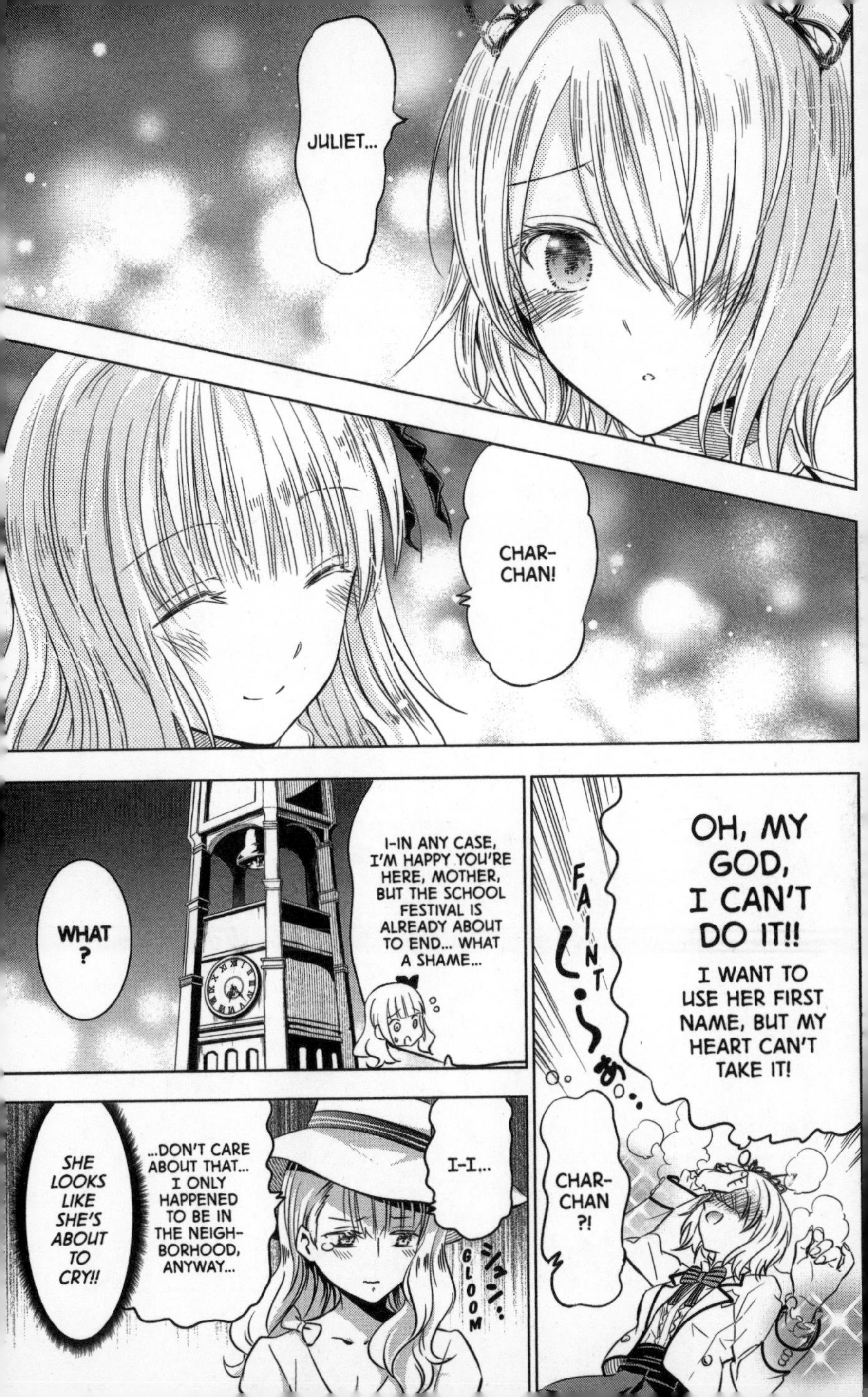
JULIET...
CHAR-CHAN!
OH, MY GOD, I CAN'T DO IT!!
I WANT TO USE HER FIRST NAME, BUT MY HEART CAN'T TAKE IT!
FAINT
CHAR-CHAN ?!
I-IN ANY CASE, I'M HAPPY YOU'RE HERE, MOTHER, BUT THE SCHOOL FESTIVAL IS ALREADY ABOUT TO END... WHAT A SHAME...
WHAT ?
I-I...
...DON'T CARE ABOUT THAT... I ONLY HAPPENED TO BE IN THE NEIGH-BORHOOD, ANYWAY...
SHE LOOKS LIKE SHE'S ABOUT TO CRY!!
GLOOM

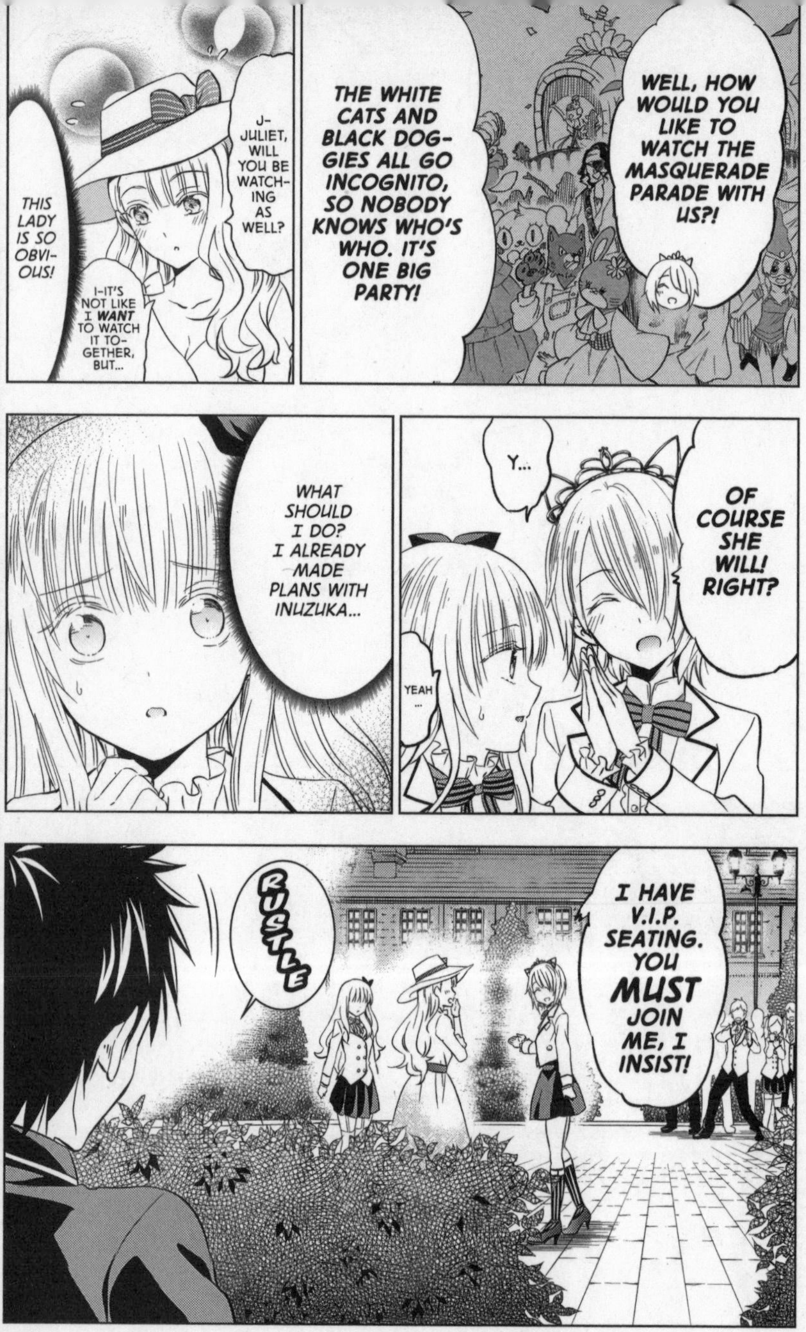
WELL, HOW WOULD YOU LIKE TO WATCH THE MASQUERADE PARADE WITH US?!
THE WHITE CATS AND BLACK DOG-GIES ALL GO INCOGNITO, SO NOBODY KNOWS WHO'S WHO. IT'S ONE BIG PARTY!
J-JULIET, WILL YOU BE WATCH-ING AS WELL?
I-IT'S NOT LIKE I WANT TO WATCH IT TO-GETHER, BUT...
THIS LADY IS SO OBVI-OUS!
OF COURSE SHE WILL! RIGHT?
Y...
YEAH...
WHAT SHOULD I DO? I ALREADY MADE PLANS WITH INUZUKA...
I HAVE V.I.P. SEATING. YOU MUST JOIN ME, I INSIST!
RUSTLE

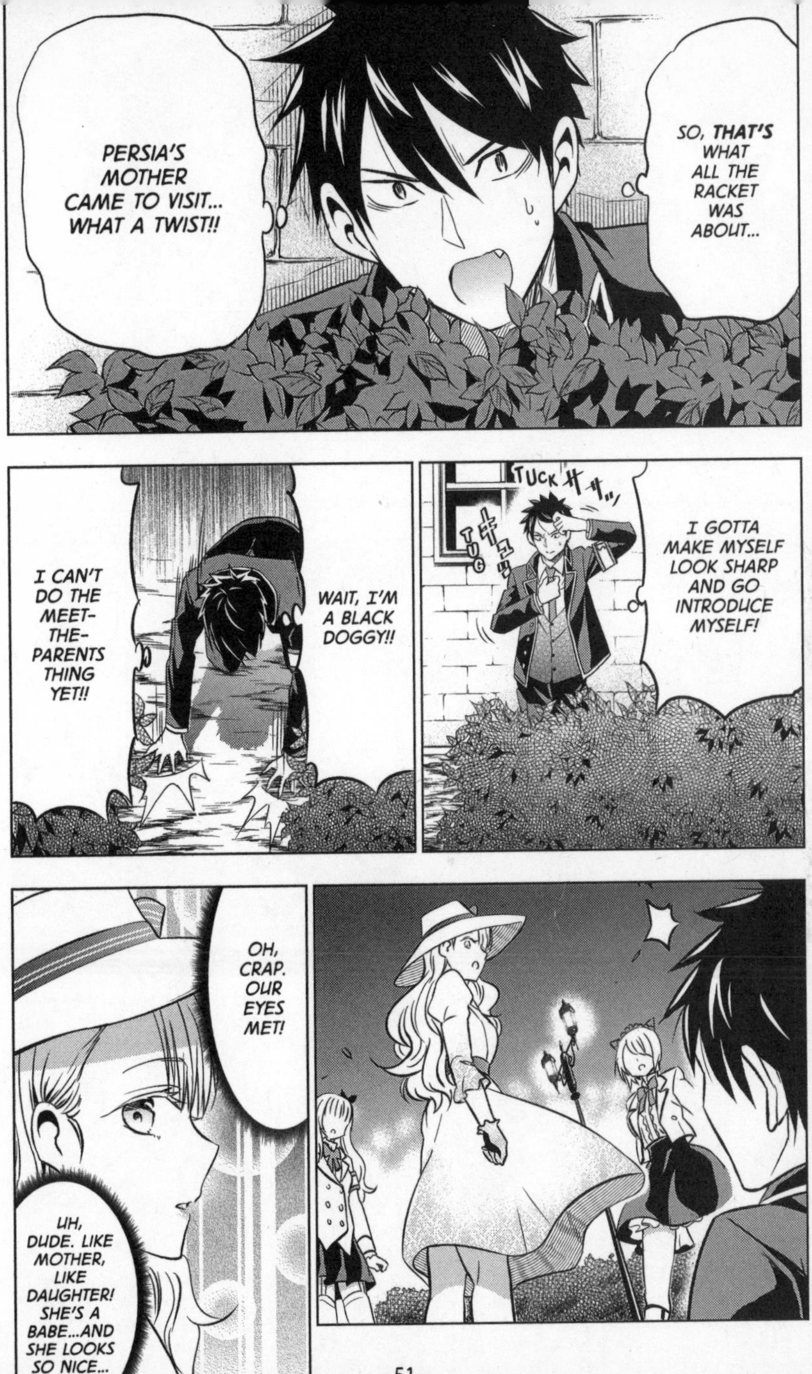
SO, THAT'S WHAT ALL THE RACKET WAS ABOUT...
PERSIA'S MOTHER CAME TO VISIT... WHAT A TWIST!!
TUCK
TUG
I GOTTA MAKE MYSELF LOOK SHARP AND GO INTRODUCE MYSELF!
WAIT, I'M A BLACK DOGGY!!
I CAN'T DO THE MEET-THE-PARENTS THING YET!!
OH, CRAP. OUR EYES MET!
UH, DUDE. LIKE MOTHER, LIKE DAUGHTER! SHE'S A BABE...AND SHE LOOKS SO NICE...

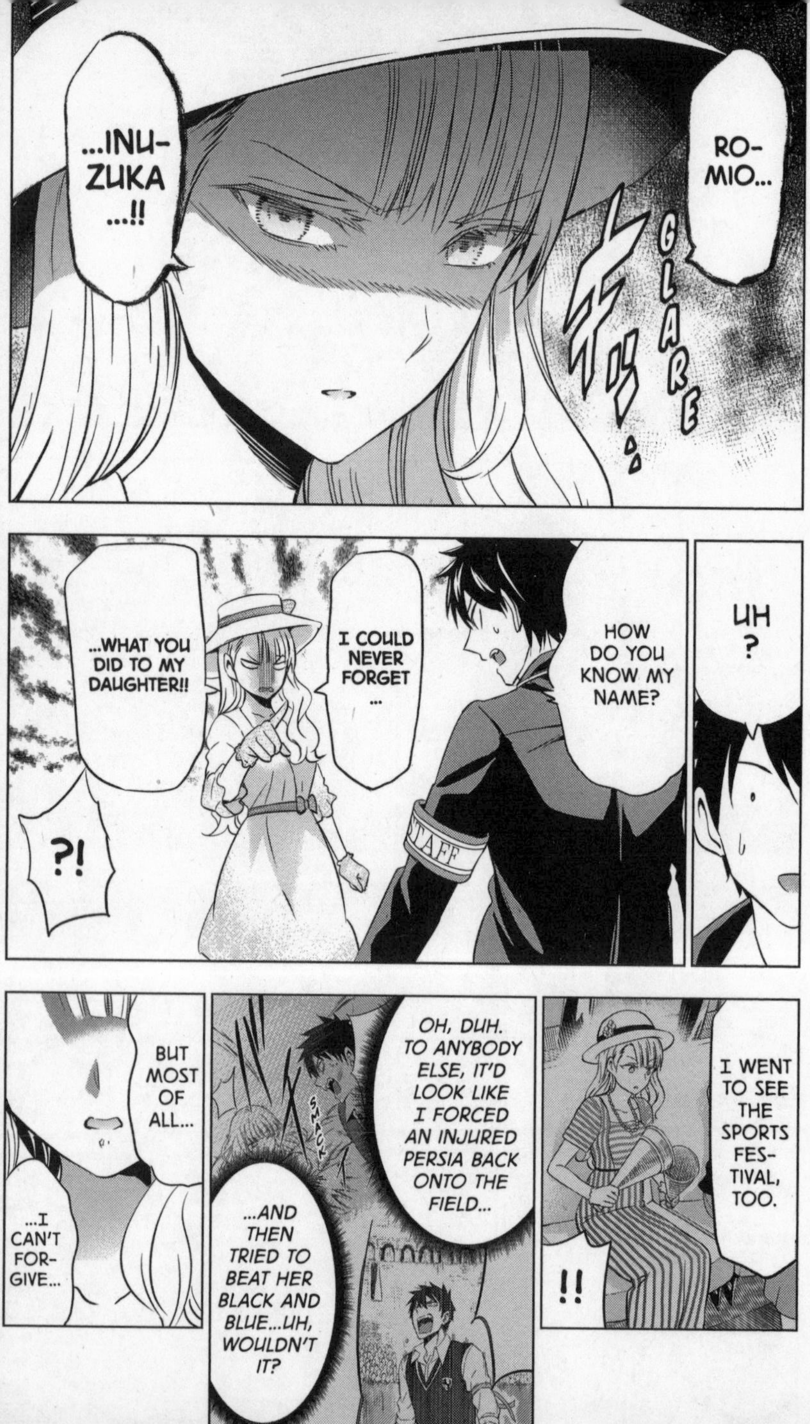

ROMIO...
GLARE
...INUZUKA...!!
UH?
HOW DO YOU KNOW MY NAME?
I COULD NEVER FORGET...
...WHAT YOU DID TO MY DAUGHTER!!
?!
I WENT TO SEE THE SPORTS FESTIVAL, TOO.
!!
OH, DUH. TO ANYBODY ELSE, IT'D LOOK LIKE I FORCED AN INJURED PERSIA BACK ONTO THE FIELD...
SMACK
...AND THEN TRIED TO BEAT HER BLACK AND BLUE...UH, WOULDN'T IT?
BUT MOST OF ALL...
...I CAN'T FORGIVE...

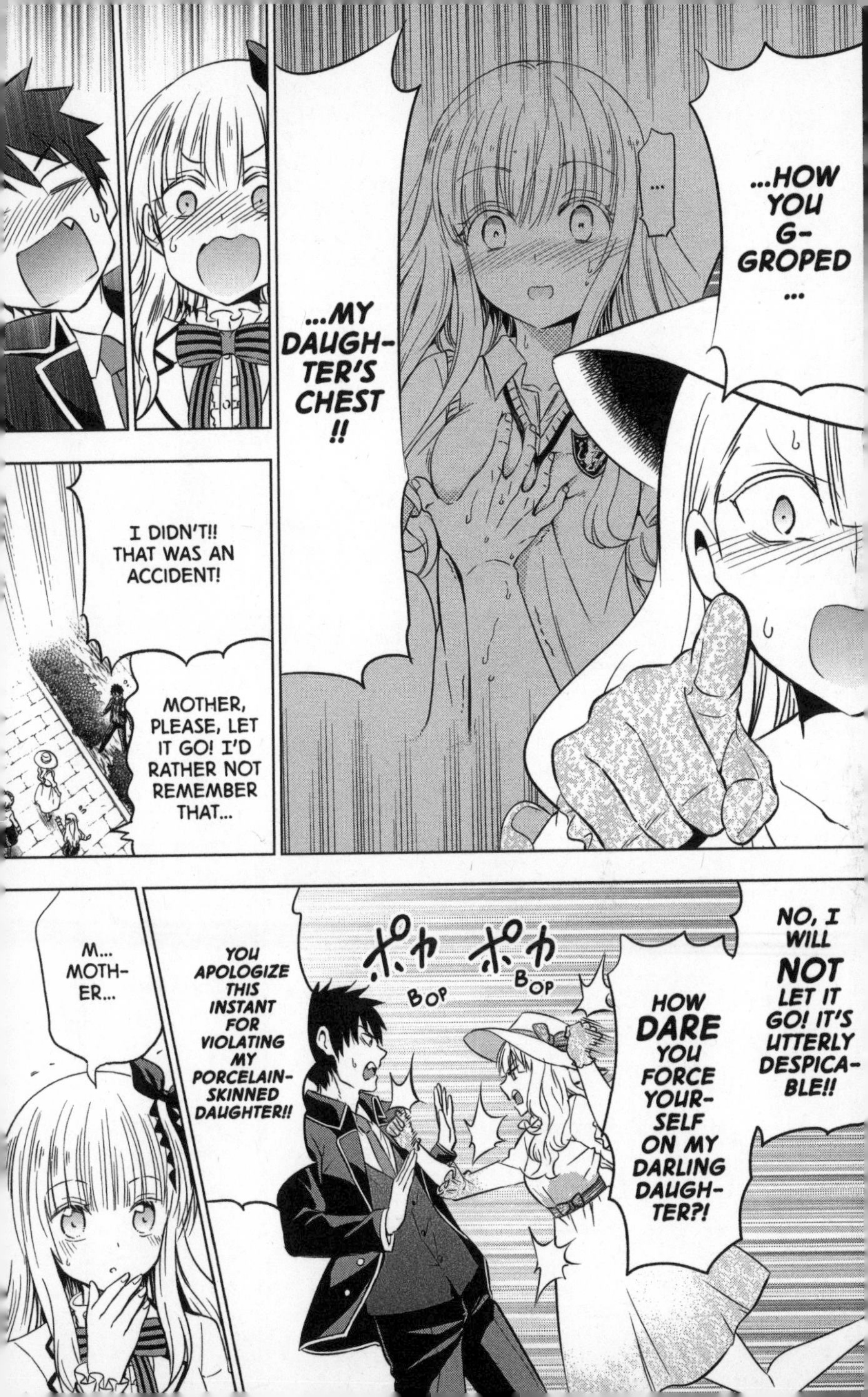
...HOW YOU G-GROPED ...
...
...MY DAUGHTER'S CHEST !!
I DIDN'T!! THAT WAS AN ACCIDENT!
MOTHER, PLEASE, LET IT GO! I'D RATHER NOT REMEMBER THAT...
NO, I WILL NOT LET IT GO! IT'S UTTERLY DESPICABLE!!
HOW DARE YOU FORCE YOURSELF ON MY DARLING DAUGHTER?!
ポカ BOP
ポカ BOP
YOU APOLOGIZE THIS INSTANT FOR VIOLATING MY PORCELAIN-SKINNED DAUGHTER!!
M... MOTHER...

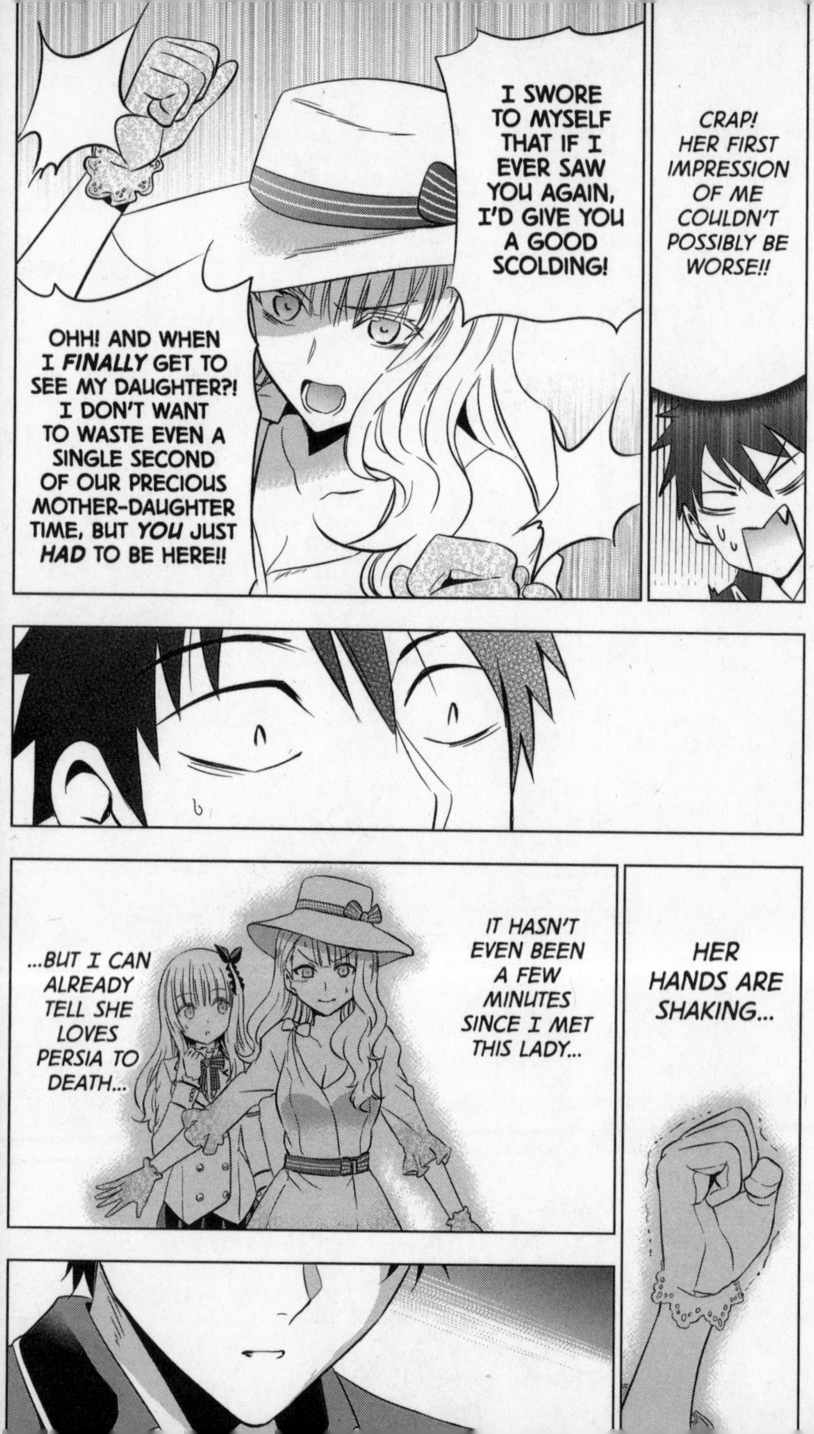
CRAP! HER FIRST IMPRESSION OF ME COULDN'T POSSIBLY BE WORSE!!
I SWORE TO MYSELF THAT IF I EVER SAW YOU AGAIN, I'D GIVE YOU A GOOD SCOLDING!
OHH! AND WHEN I *FINALLY* GET TO SEE MY DAUGHTER?! I DON'T WANT TO WASTE EVEN A SINGLE SECOND OF OUR PRECIOUS MOTHER-DAUGHTER TIME, BUT *YOU* JUST *HAD* TO BE HERE!!
HER HANDS ARE SHAKING...
IT HASN'T EVEN BEEN A FEW MINUTES SINCE I MET THIS LADY...
...BUT I CAN ALREADY TELL SHE LOVES PERSIA TO DEATH...

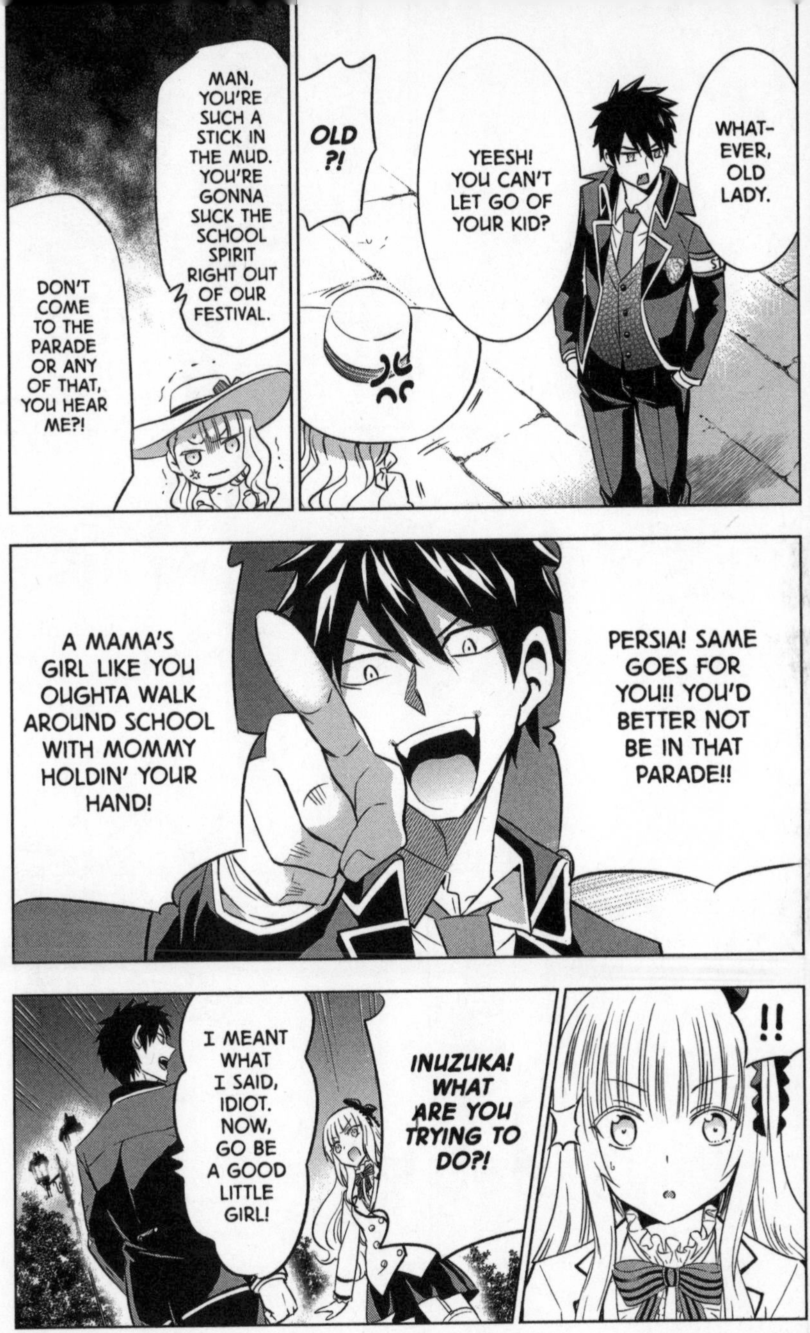

WHAT-EVER, OLD LADY.
YEESH! YOU CAN'T LET GO OF YOUR KID?
OLD ?!
MAN, YOU'RE SUCH A STICK IN THE MUD. YOU'RE GONNA SUCK THE SCHOOL SPIRIT RIGHT OUT OF OUR FESTIVAL.
DON'T COME TO THE PARADE OR ANY OF THAT, YOU HEAR ME?!
PERSIA! SAME GOES FOR YOU!! YOU'D BETTER NOT BE IN THAT PARADE!!
A MAMA'S GIRL LIKE YOU OUGHTA WALK AROUND SCHOOL WITH MOMMY HOLDIN' YOUR HAND!
!!
INUZUKA! WHAT ARE YOU TRYING TO DO?!
I MEANT WHAT I SAID, IDIOT. NOW, GO BE A GOOD LITTLE GIRL!

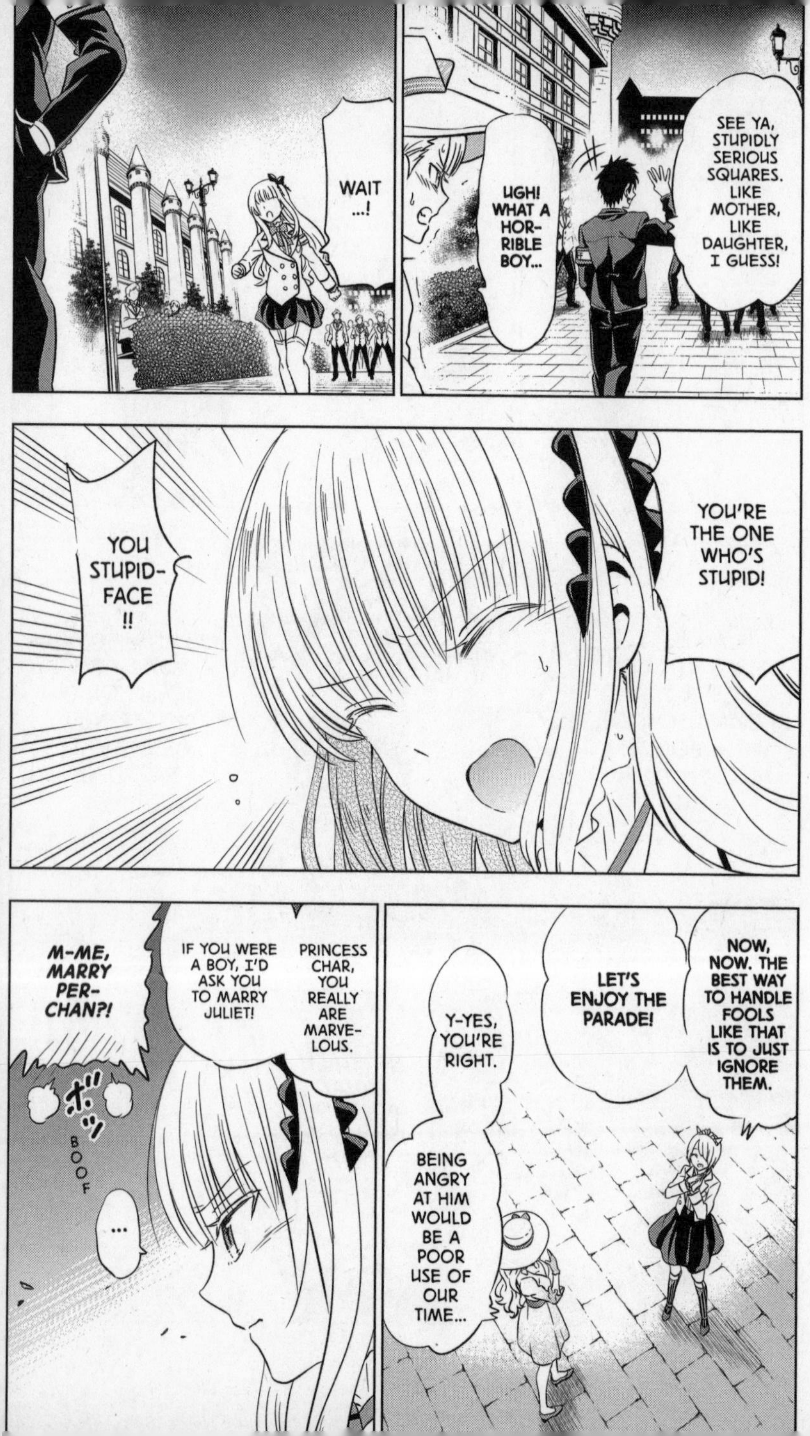
SEE YA, STUPIDLY SERIOUS SQUARES. LIKE MOTHER, LIKE DAUGHTER, I GUESS!
UGH! WHAT A HORRIBLE BOY...
WAIT ...!
YOU'RE THE ONE WHO'S STUPID!
YOU STUPID-FACE!!
NOW, NOW. THE BEST WAY TO HANDLE FOOLS LIKE THAT IS TO JUST IGNORE THEM.
LET'S ENJOY THE PARADE!
Y-YES, YOU'RE RIGHT.
BEING ANGRY AT HIM WOULD BE A POOR USE OF OUR TIME...
PRINCESS CHAR, YOU REALLY ARE MARVELOUS.
IF YOU WERE A BOY, I'D ASK YOU TO MARRY JULIET!
M-ME, MARRY PER-CHAN?!
ボッ
BOOF
...

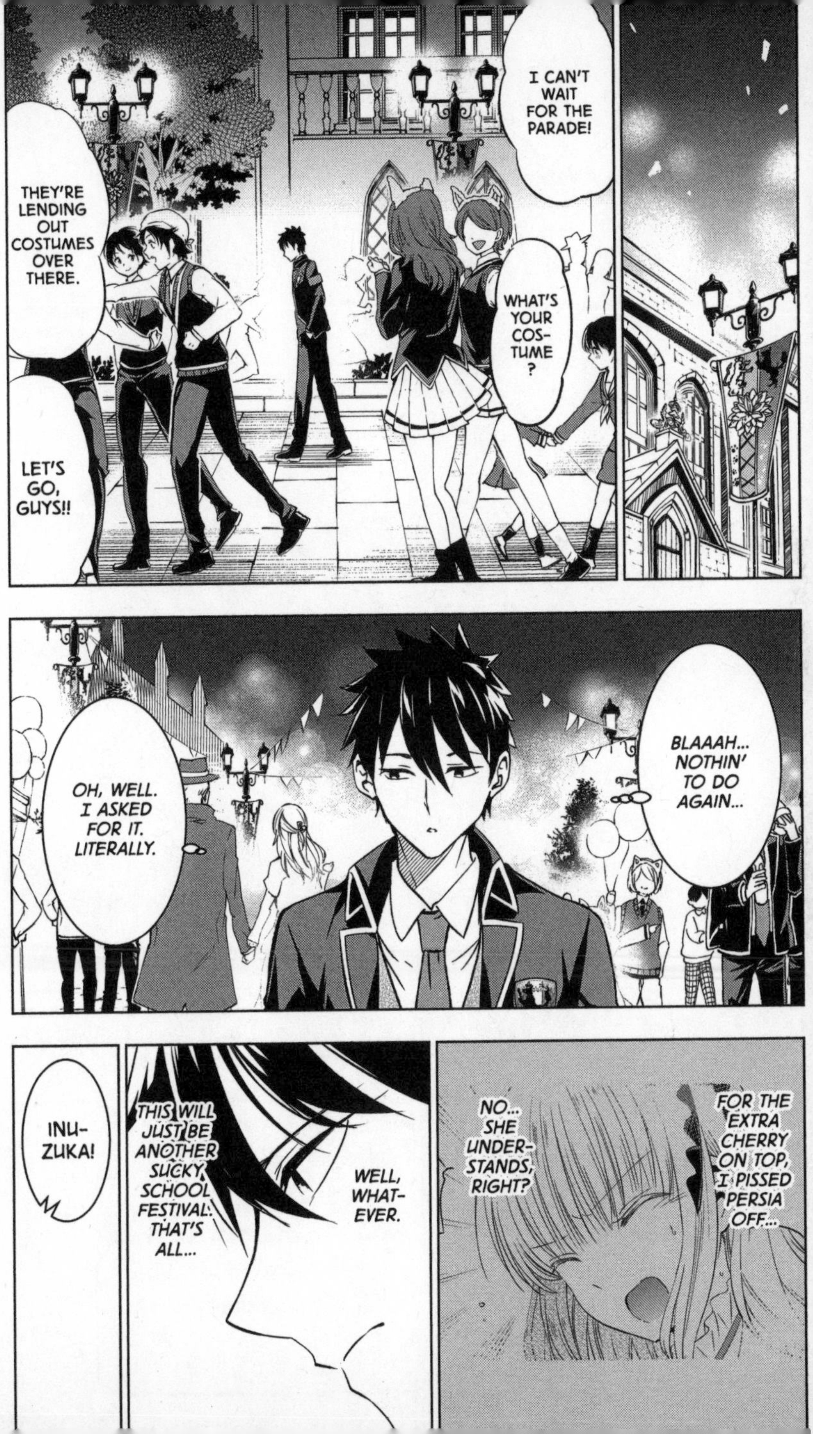
I CAN'T WAIT FOR THE PARADE!
WHAT'S YOUR COS-TUME?
THEY'RE LENDING OUT COSTUMES OVER THERE.
LET'S GO, GUYS!!
BLAAAH... NOTHIN' TO DO AGAIN...
OH, WELL. I ASKED FOR IT. LITERALLY.
FOR THE EXTRA CHERRY ON TOP, I PISSED PERSIA OFF...
NO... SHE UNDER-STANDS, RIGHT?
WELL, WHAT-EVER.
THIS WILL JUST BE ANOTHER SUCKY SCHOOL FESTIVAL. THAT'S ALL...
INU-ZUKA!

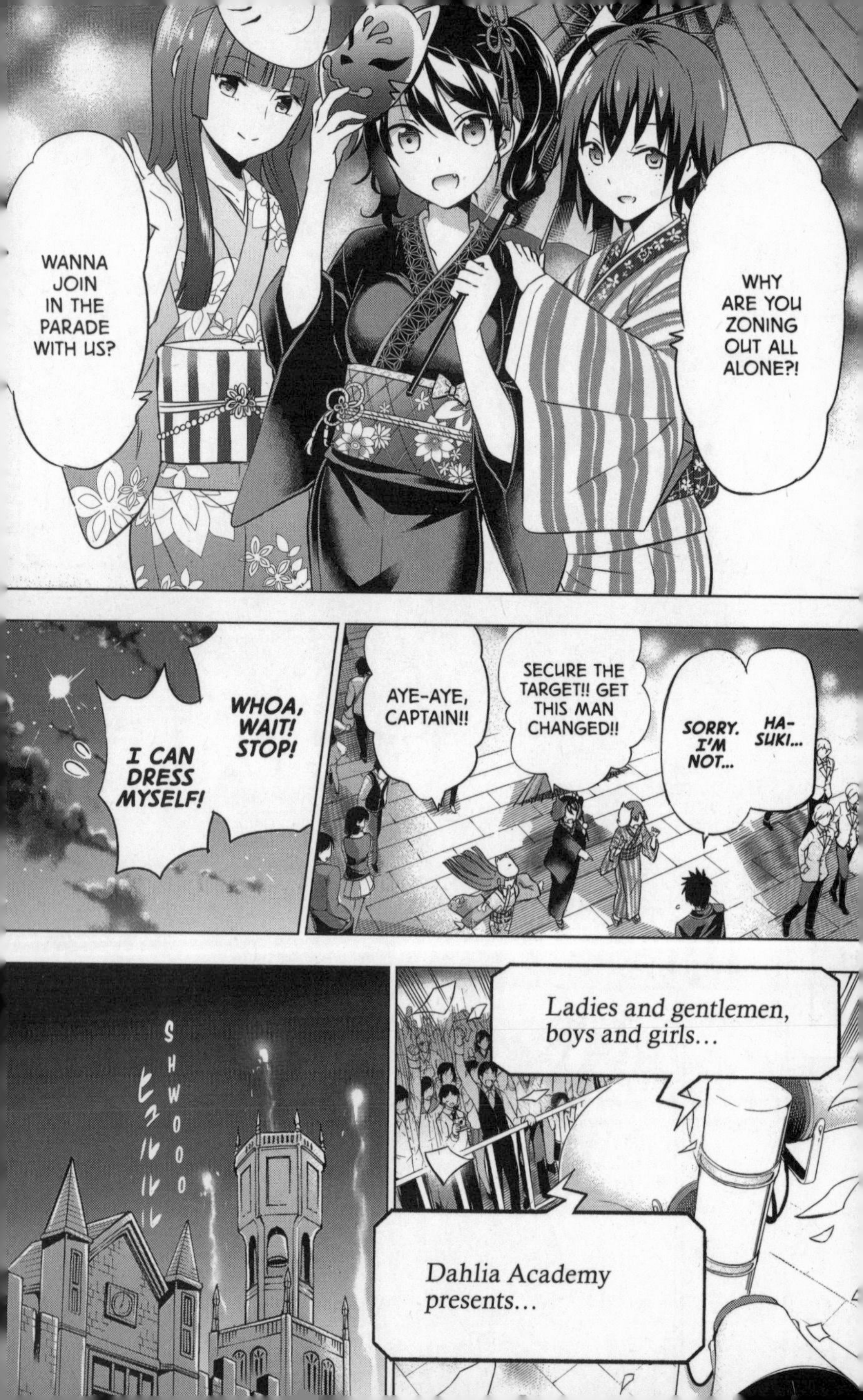
WHY ARE YOU ZONING OUT ALL ALONE?!
WANNA JOIN IN THE PARADE WITH US?
HA-SUKI...
SORRY. I'M NOT...
SECURE THE TARGET!! GET THIS MAN CHANGED!!
AYE-AYE, CAPTAIN!!
WHOA, WAIT! STOP!
I CAN DRESS MYSELF!
Ladies and gentlemen, boys and girls…
Dahlia Academy presents…
SHWOOO

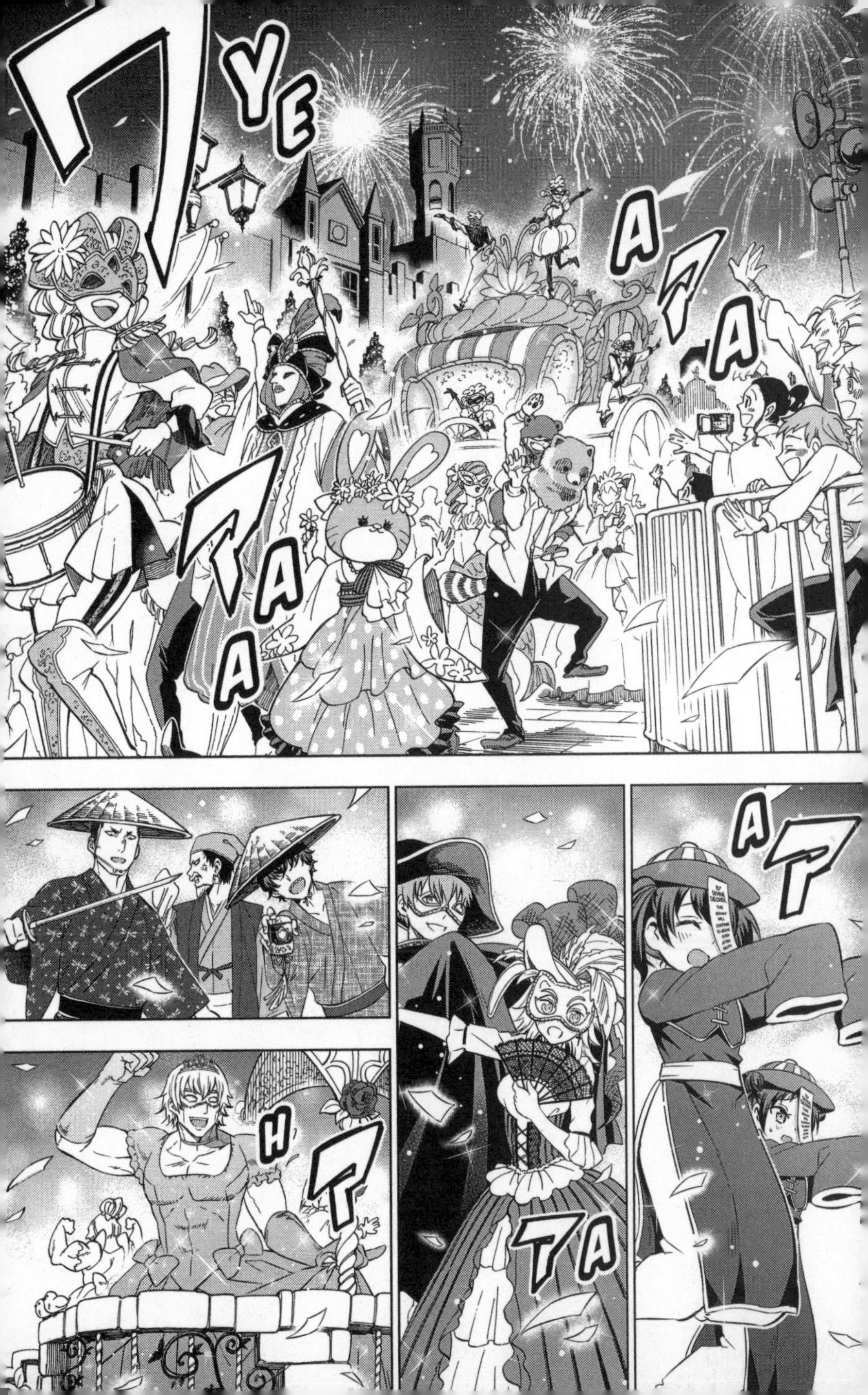
YE
A
A
A
A
A
A
A
T
TA
H
T

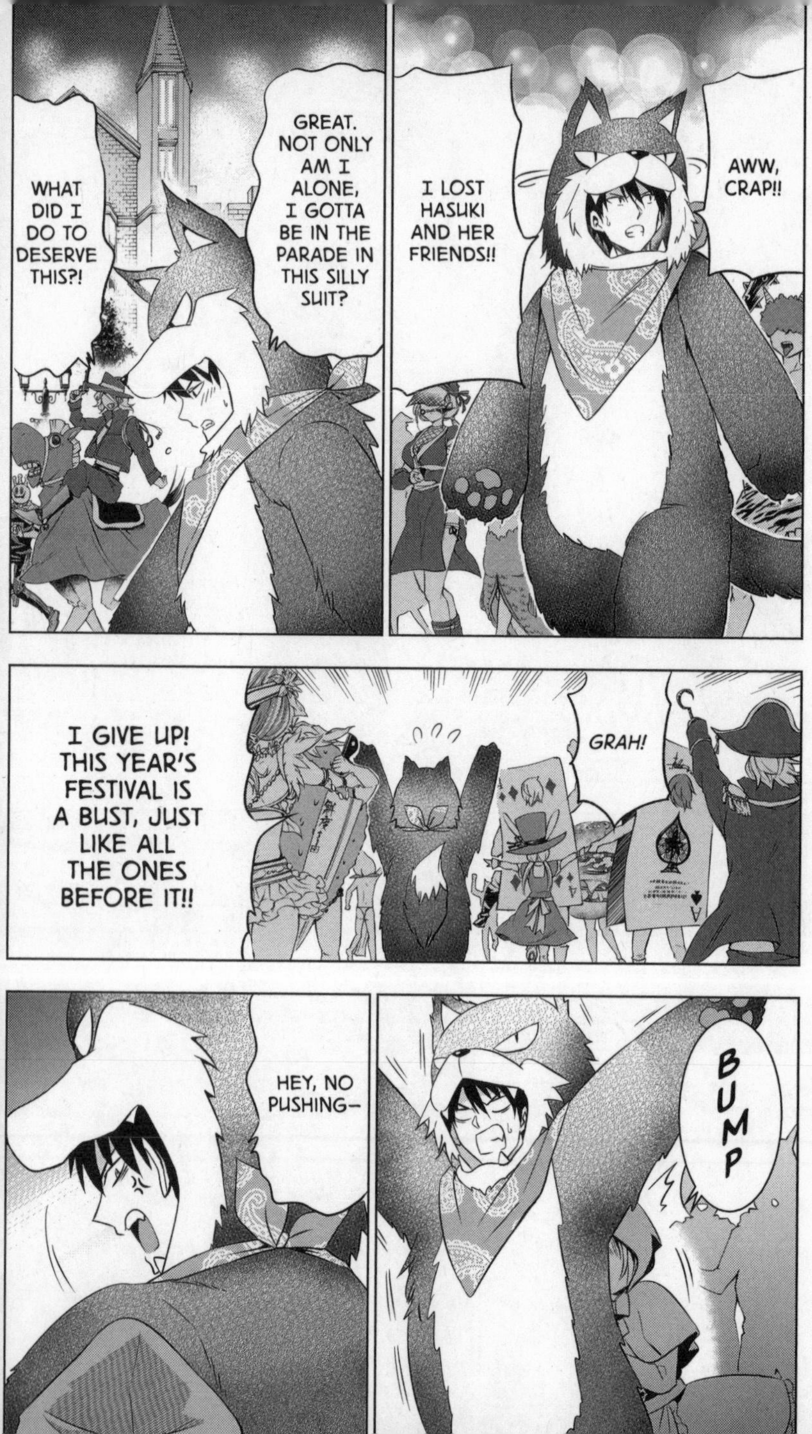
AWW, CRAP!!
I LOST HASUKI AND HER FRIENDS!!
GREAT. NOT ONLY AM I ALONE, I GOTTA BE IN THE PARADE IN THIS SILLY SUIT?
WHAT DID I DO TO DESERVE THIS?!
GRAH!
I GIVE UP! THIS YEAR'S FESTIVAL IS A BUST, JUST LIKE ALL THE ONES BEFORE IT!!
BUMP
HEY, NO PUSHING—

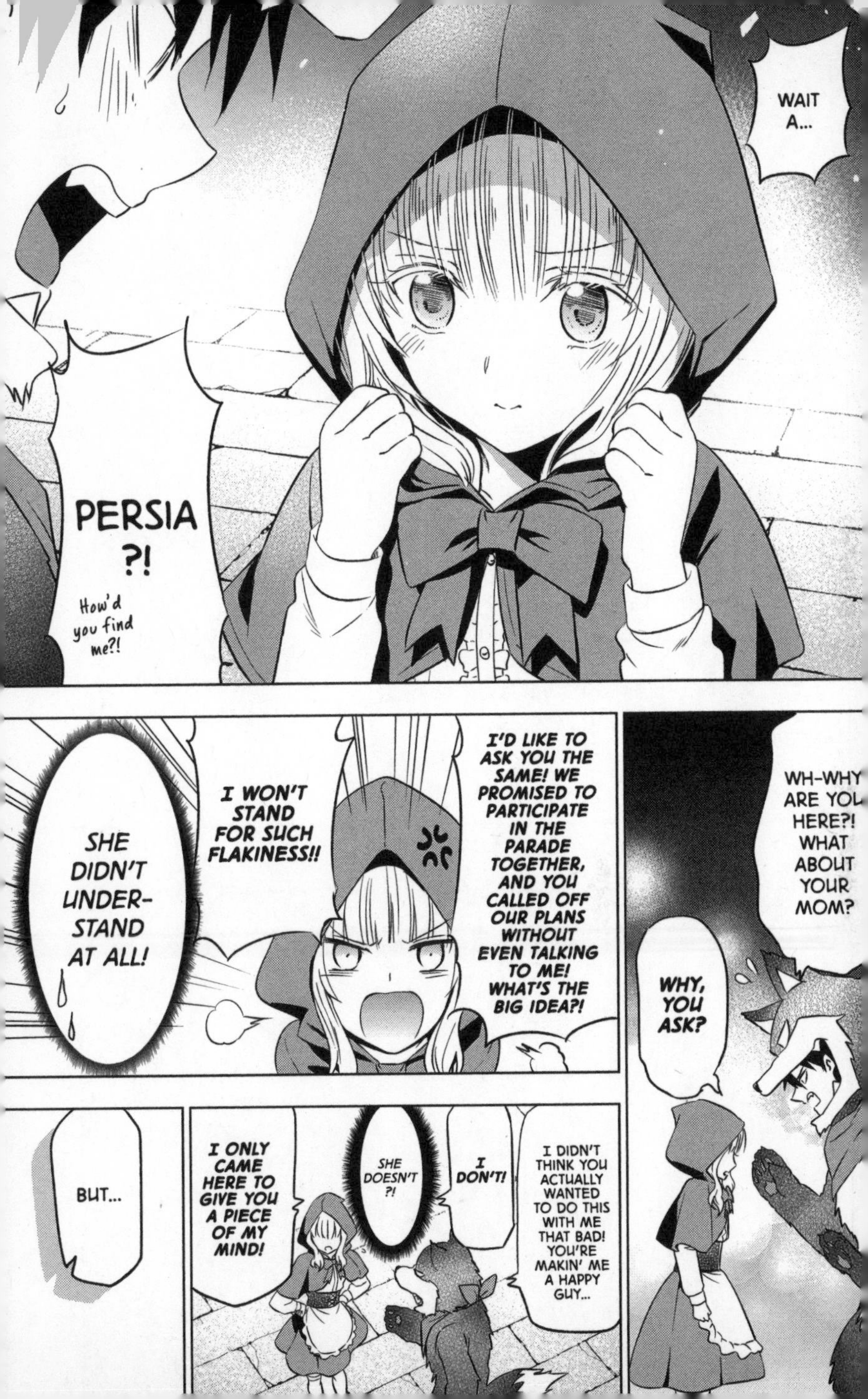
WAIT A...
PERSIA ?!
How'd you find me?!
WH-WHY ARE YOU HERE?! WHAT ABOUT YOUR MOM?
WHY, YOU ASK?
I'D LIKE TO ASK YOU THE SAME! WE PROMISED TO PARTICIPATE IN THE PARADE TOGETHER, AND YOU CALLED OFF OUR PLANS WITHOUT EVEN TALKING TO ME! WHAT'S THE BIG IDEA?!
I WON'T STAND FOR SUCH FLAKINESS!!
SHE DIDN'T UNDER-STAND AT ALL!
I DIDN'T THINK YOU ACTUALLY WANTED TO DO THIS WITH ME THAT BAD! YOU'RE MAKIN' ME A HAPPY GUY...
I DON'T!
SHE DOESN'T ?!
I ONLY CAME HERE TO GIVE YOU A PIECE OF MY MIND!
BUT...

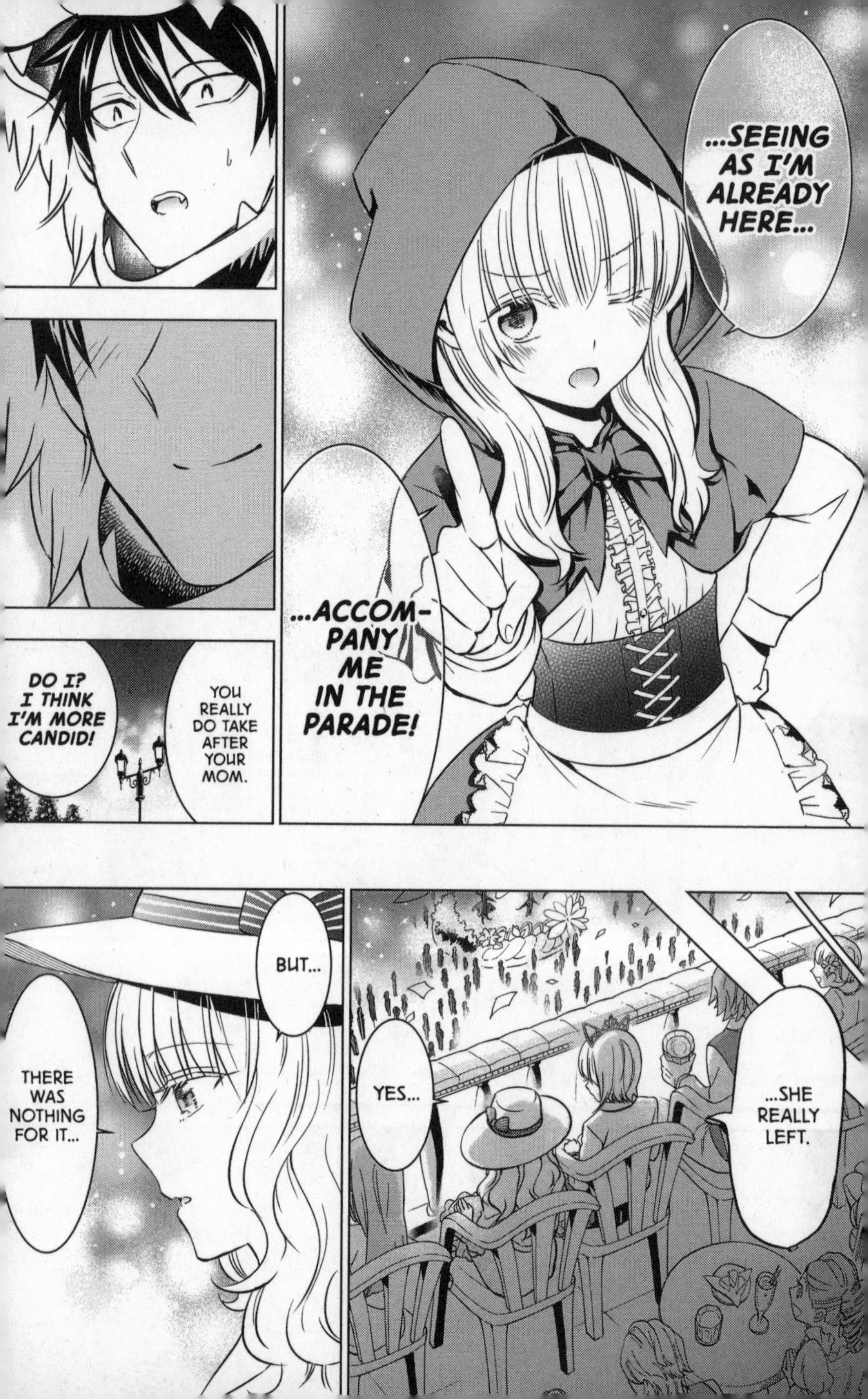
...SEEING AS I'M ALREADY HERE...
...ACCOMPANY ME IN THE PARADE!
YOU REALLY DO TAKE AFTER YOUR MOM.
DO I? I THINK I'M MORE CANDID!
...SHE REALLY LEFT.
YES...
BUT...
THERE WAS NOTHING FOR IT...

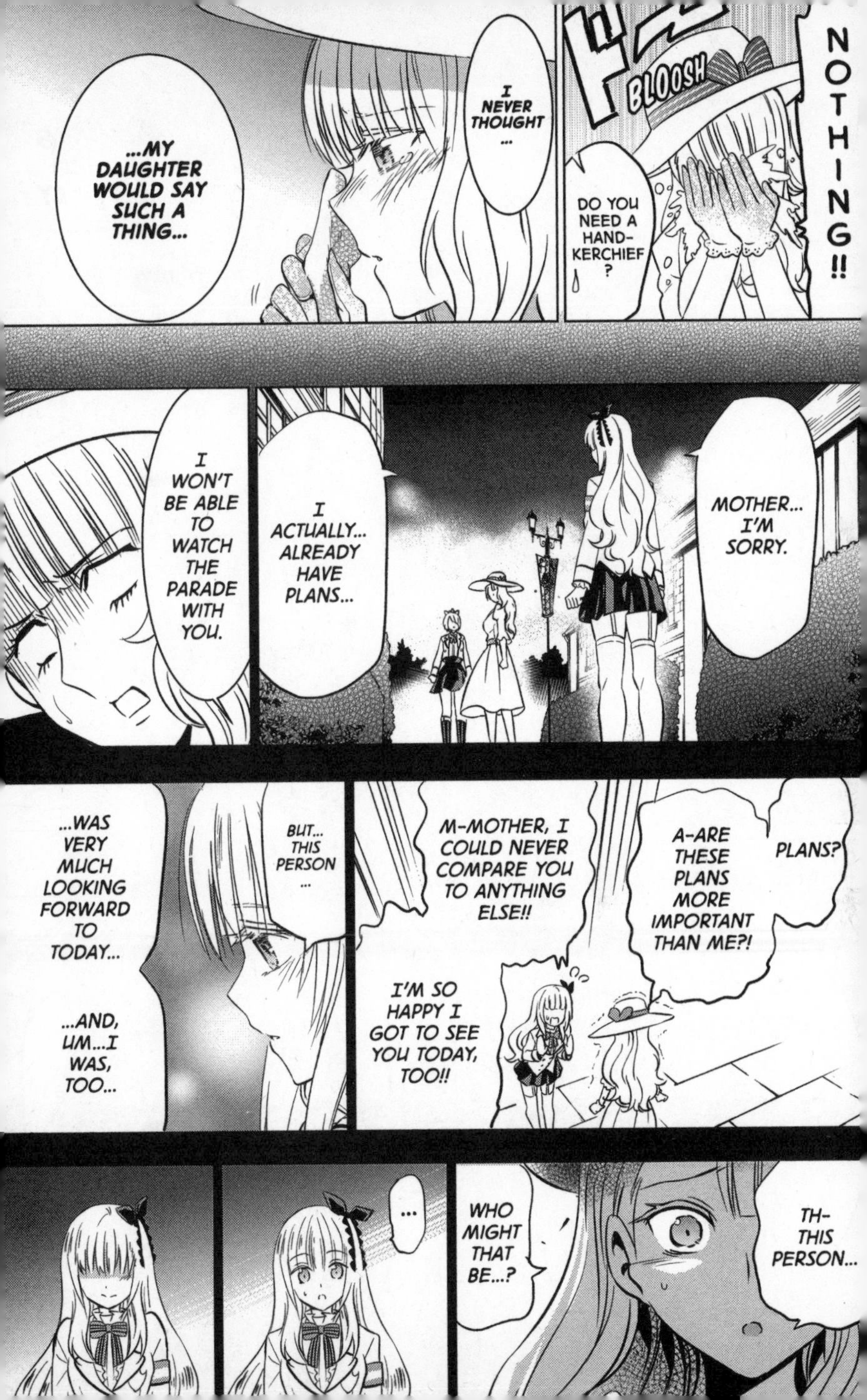
NOTHING!!
BLOOSH
DO YOU NEED A HANDKERCHIEF?
I NEVER THOUGHT...
...MY DAUGHTER WOULD SAY SUCH A THING...
MOTHER... I'M SORRY.
I ACTUALLY... ALREADY HAVE PLANS...
I WON'T BE ABLE TO WATCH THE PARADE WITH YOU.
PLANS?
A-ARE THESE PLANS MORE IMPORTANT THAN ME?!
M-MOTHER, I COULD NEVER COMPARE YOU TO ANYTHING ELSE!!
I'M SO HAPPY I GOT TO SEE YOU TODAY, TOO!!
BUT... THIS PERSON...
...WAS VERY MUCH LOOKING FORWARD TO TODAY...
...AND, UM...I WAS, TOO...
TH-THIS PERSON...
WHO MIGHT THAT BE...?
...

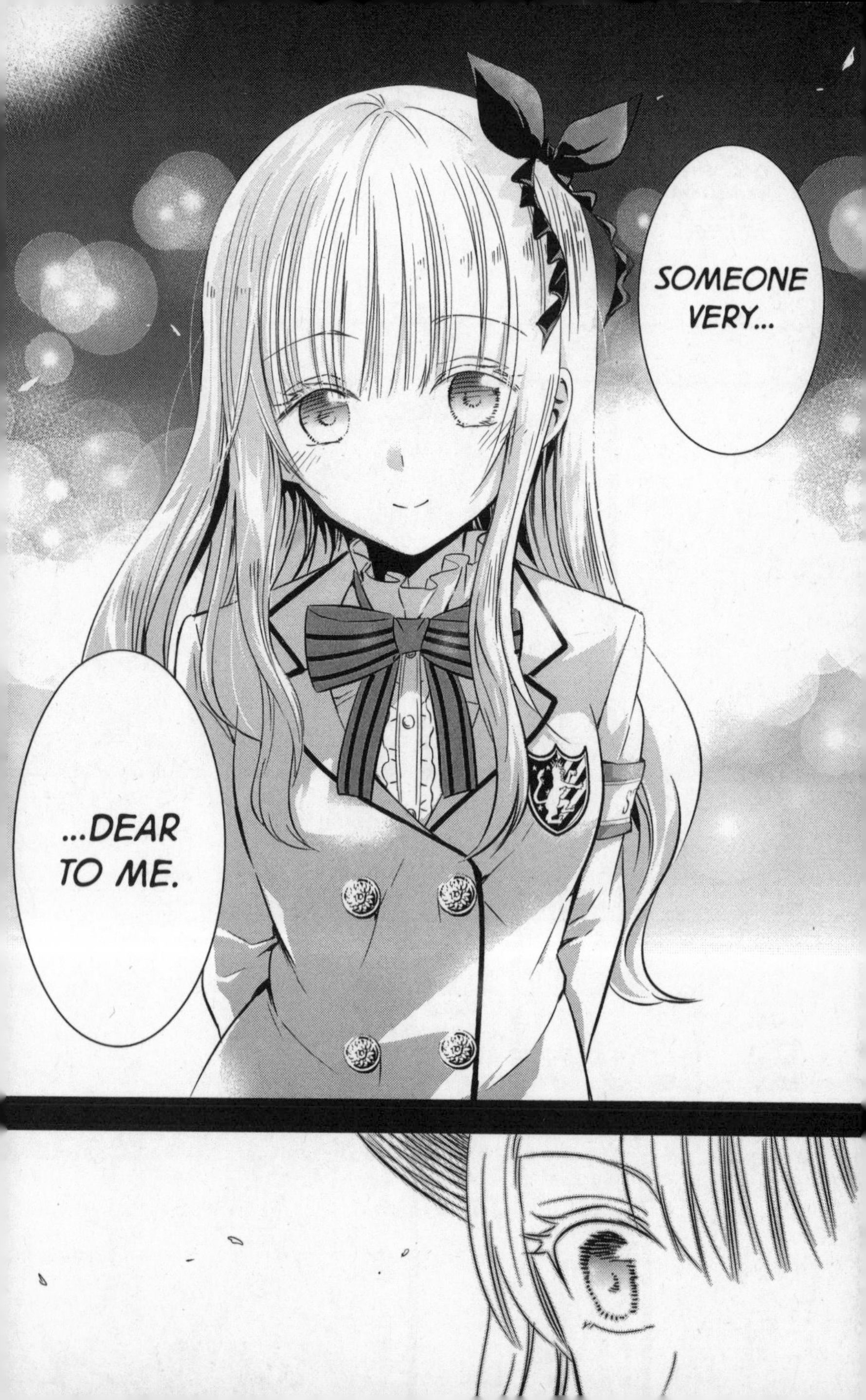
SOMEONE VERY...
...DEAR TO ME.

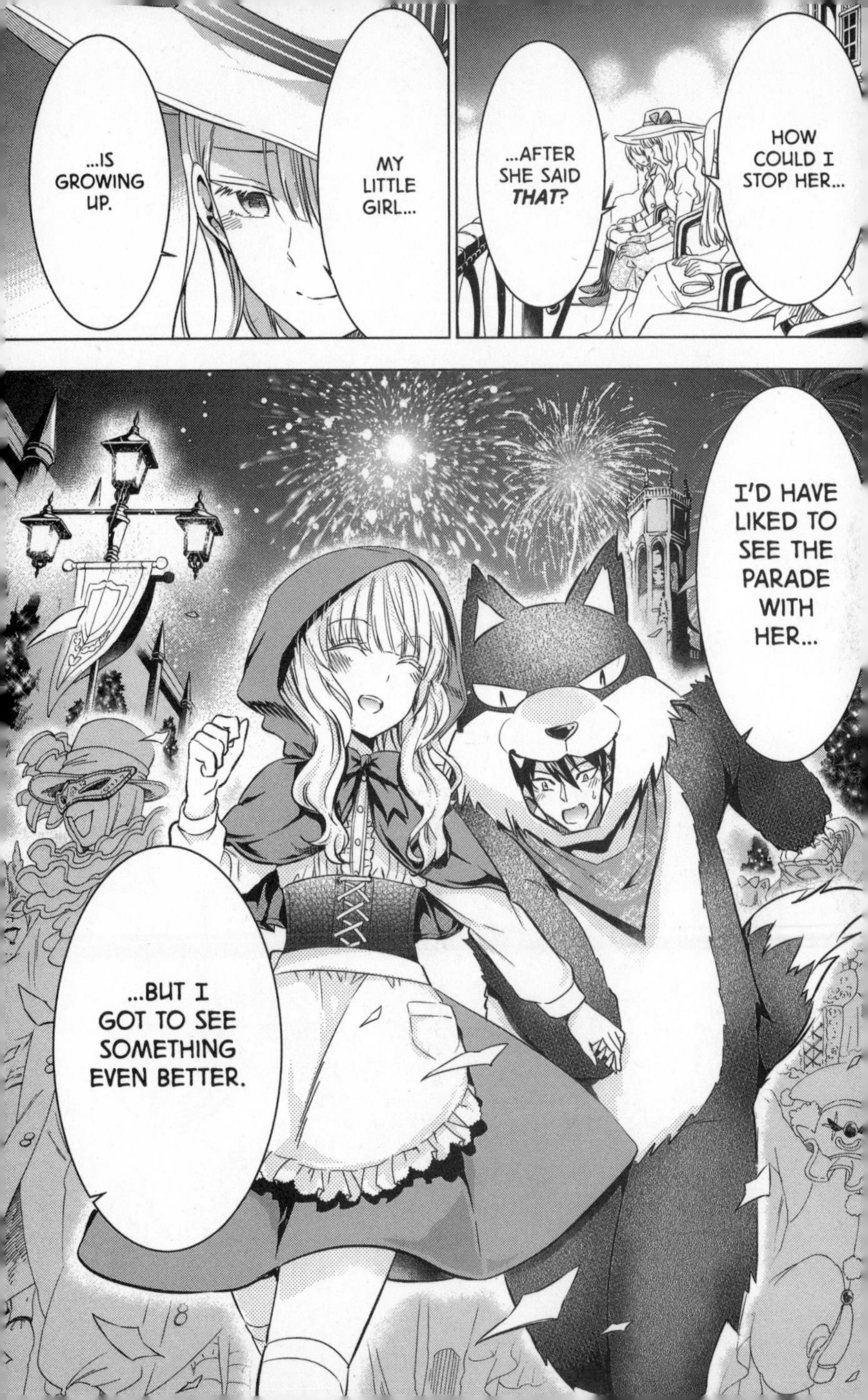
HOW COULD I STOP HER...
...AFTER SHE SAID *THAT*?
MY LITTLE GIRL...
...IS GROWING UP.
I'D HAVE LIKED TO SEE THE PARADE WITH HER...
...BUT I GOT TO SEE SOMETHING EVEN BETTER.

For the purposes of this manga, I made it easy to see Inuzuka and Persia's faces, but if this were real life, their faces would have been obscured, like this. To find Inuzuka despite that, Persia's sixth sense must be amazing.

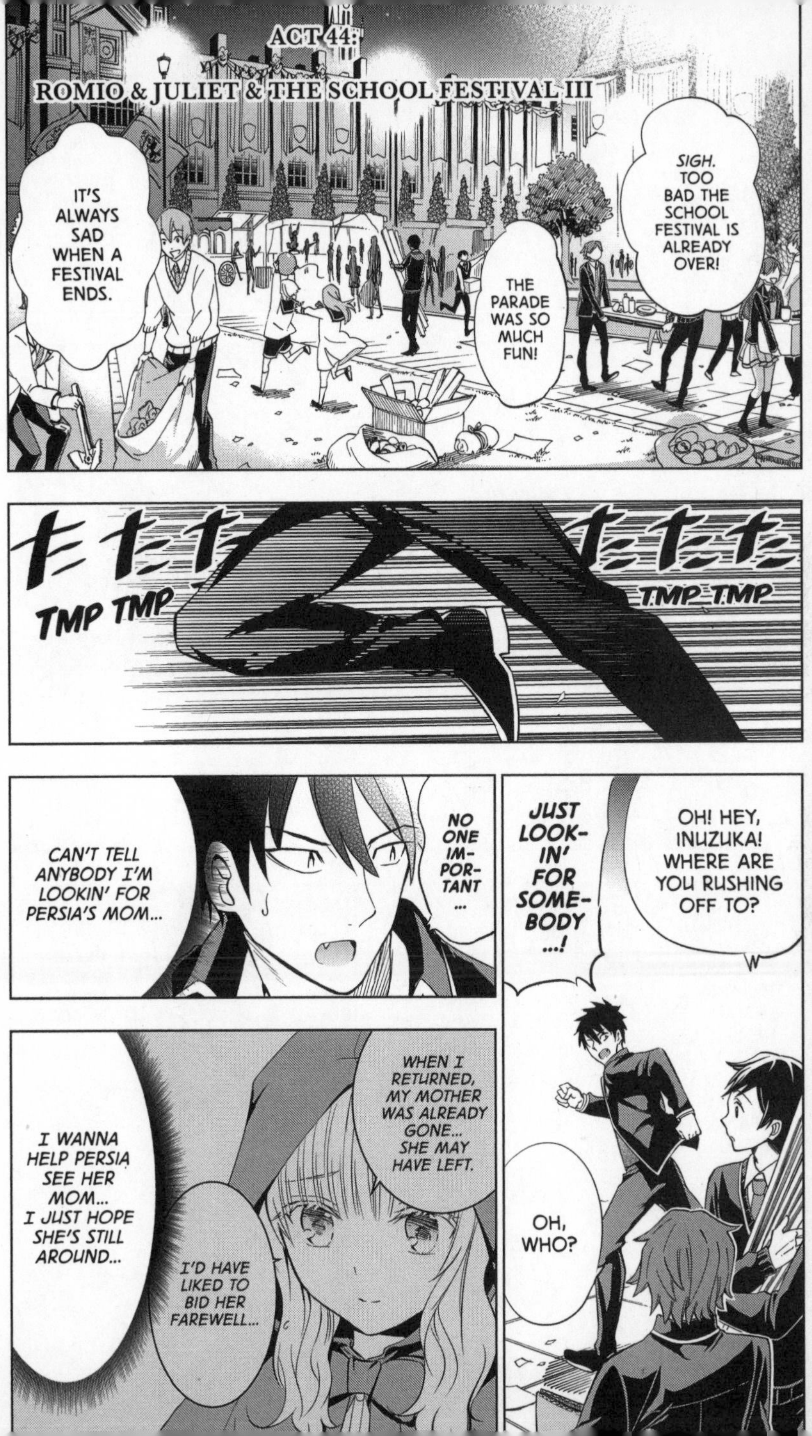
ACT 44:
ROMIO & JULIET & THE SCHOOL FESTIVAL III
SIGH. TOO BAD THE SCHOOL FESTIVAL IS ALREADY OVER!
THE PARADE WAS SO MUCH FUN!
IT'S ALWAYS SAD WHEN A FESTIVAL ENDS.
TMP TMP
TMP TMP
OH! HEY, INUZUKA! WHERE ARE YOU RUSHING OFF TO?
JUST LOOK-IN' FOR SOME-BODY ...!
OH, WHO?
NO ONE IM-POR-TANT ...
CAN'T TELL ANYBODY I'M LOOKIN' FOR PERSIA'S MOM...
WHEN I RETURNED, MY MOTHER WAS ALREADY GONE... SHE MAY HAVE LEFT.
I'D HAVE LIKED TO BID HER FAREWELL...
I WANNA HELP PERSIA SEE HER MOM... I JUST HOPE SHE'S STILL AROUND...

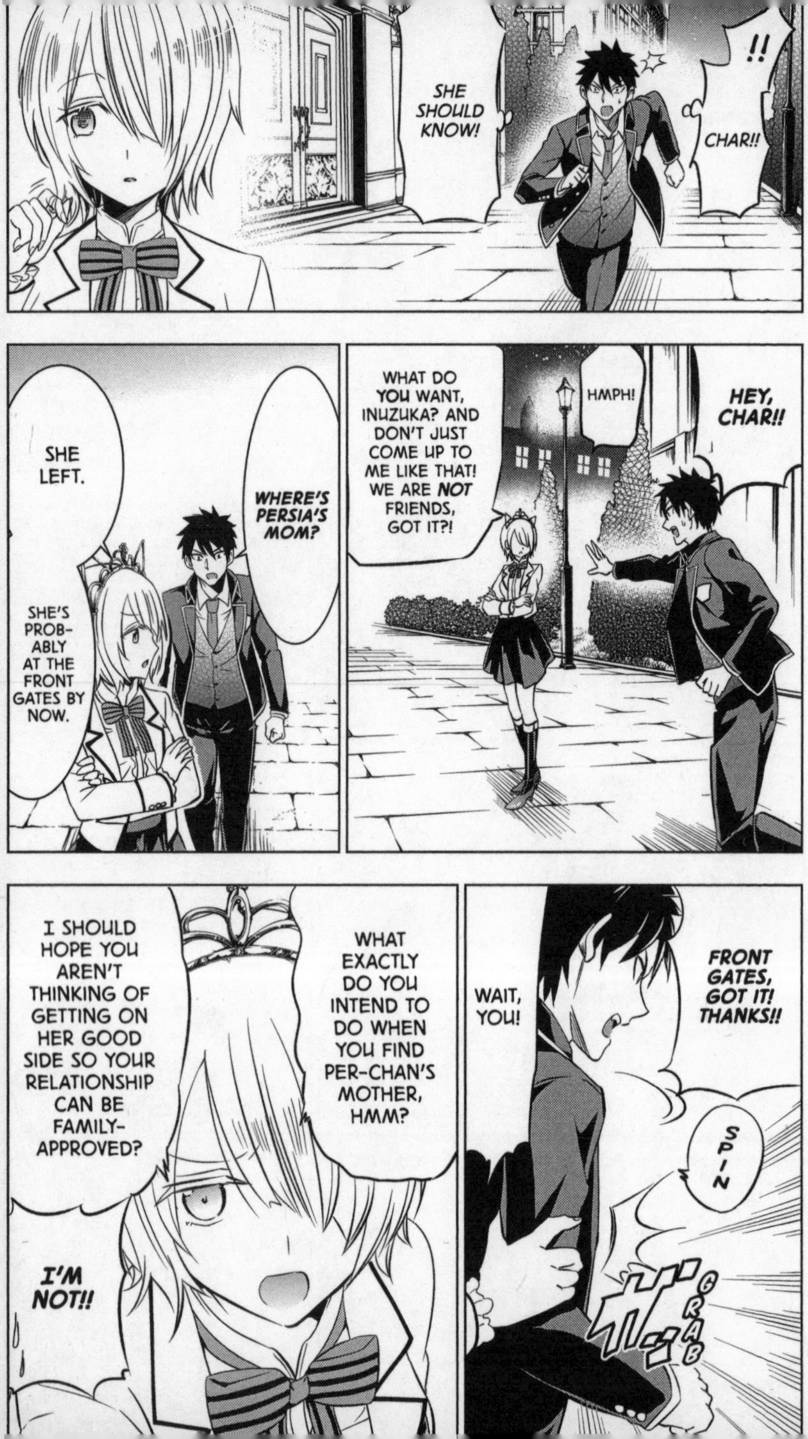
!!
CHAR!!
SHE SHOULD KNOW!
HEY, CHAR!!
HMPH!
WHAT DO YOU WANT, INUZUKA? AND DON'T JUST COME UP TO ME LIKE THAT! WE ARE NOT FRIENDS, GOT IT?!
WHERE'S PERSIA'S MOM?
SHE LEFT.
SHE'S PROB-ABLY AT THE FRONT GATES BY NOW.
FRONT GATES, GOT IT! THANKS!!
WAIT, YOU!
SPIN
GRAB
WHAT EXACTLY DO YOU INTEND TO DO WHEN YOU FIND PER-CHAN'S MOTHER, HMM?
I SHOULD HOPE YOU AREN'T THINKING OF GETTING ON HER GOOD SIDE SO YOUR RELATIONSHIP CAN BE FAMILY-APPROVED?
I'M NOT!!

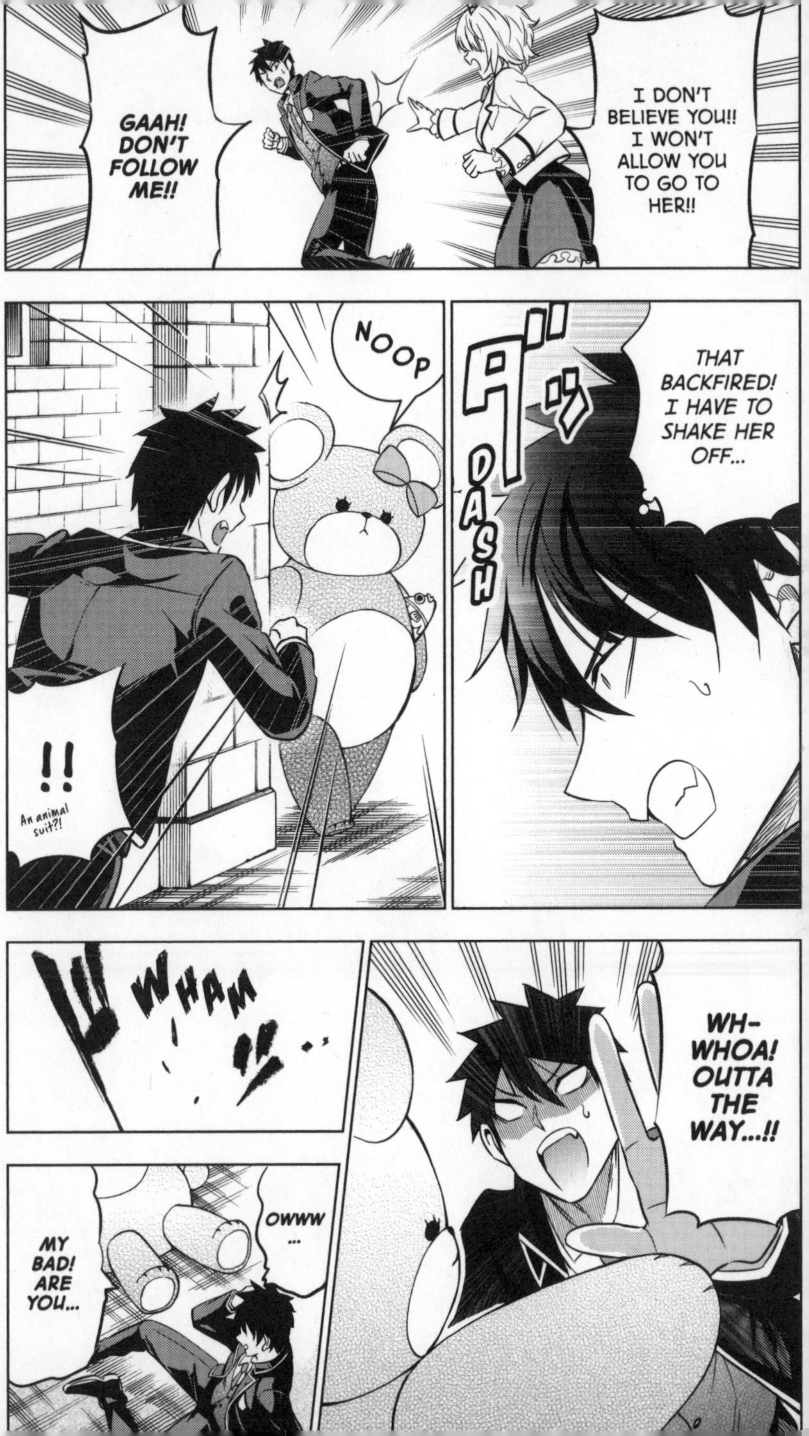
I DON'T BELIEVE YOU!! I WON'T ALLOW YOU TO GO TO HER!!
GAAH! DON'T FOLLOW ME!!
ダッ
DASH
THAT BACKFIRED! I HAVE TO SHAKE HER OFF...
NOOP
!!
An animal suit?!
WH-WHOA! OUTTA THE WAY...!!
WHAM
OWWW...
MY BAD! ARE YOU...

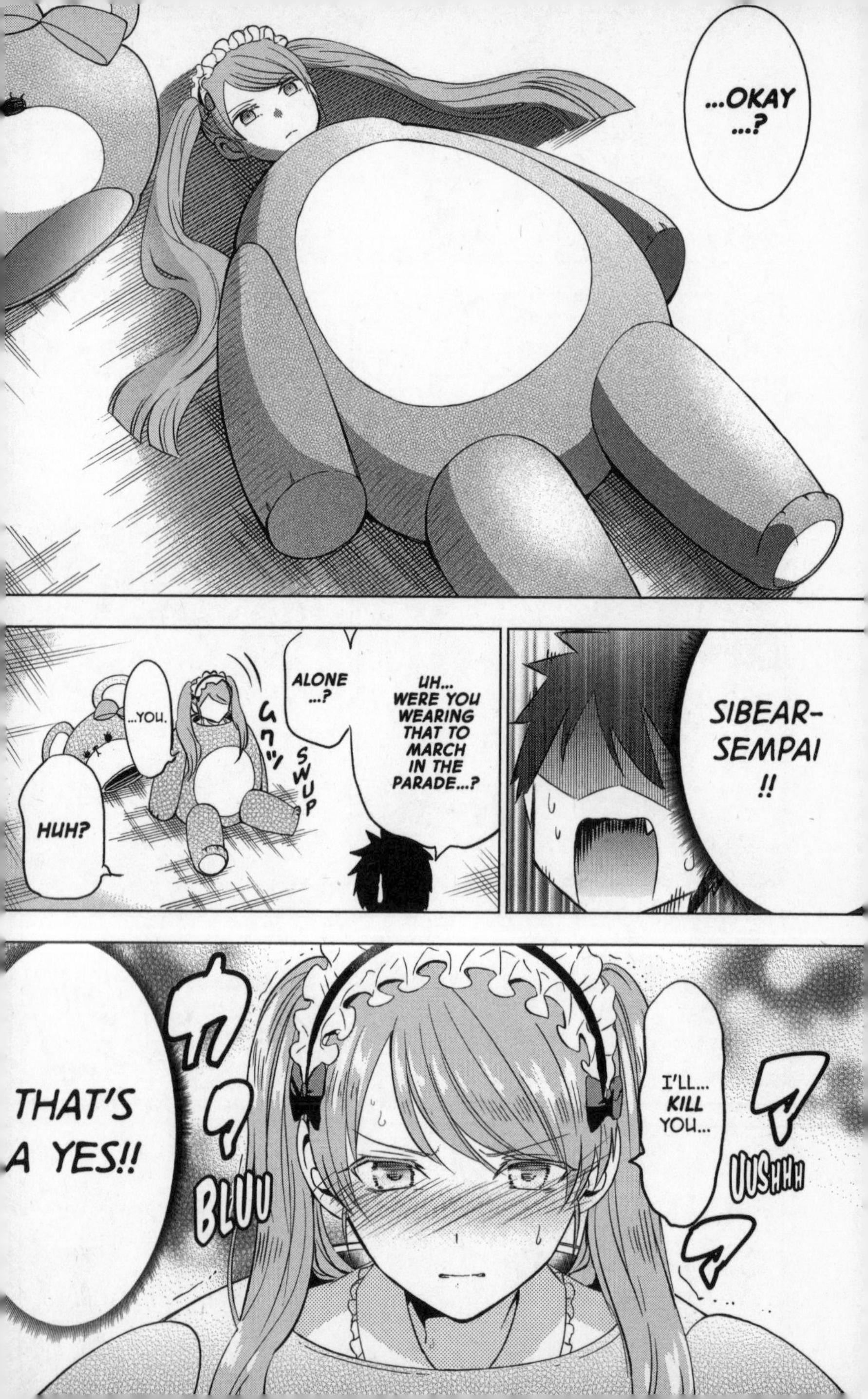

...OKAY ...?
SIBEAR-SEMPAI !!
UH... WERE YOU WEARING THAT TO MARCH IN THE PARADE...?
ALONE ...?
ムクッ
SWUP
...YOU.
HUH?
I'LL... KILL YOU...
UUSHHH
BLUU
THAT'S A YES!!

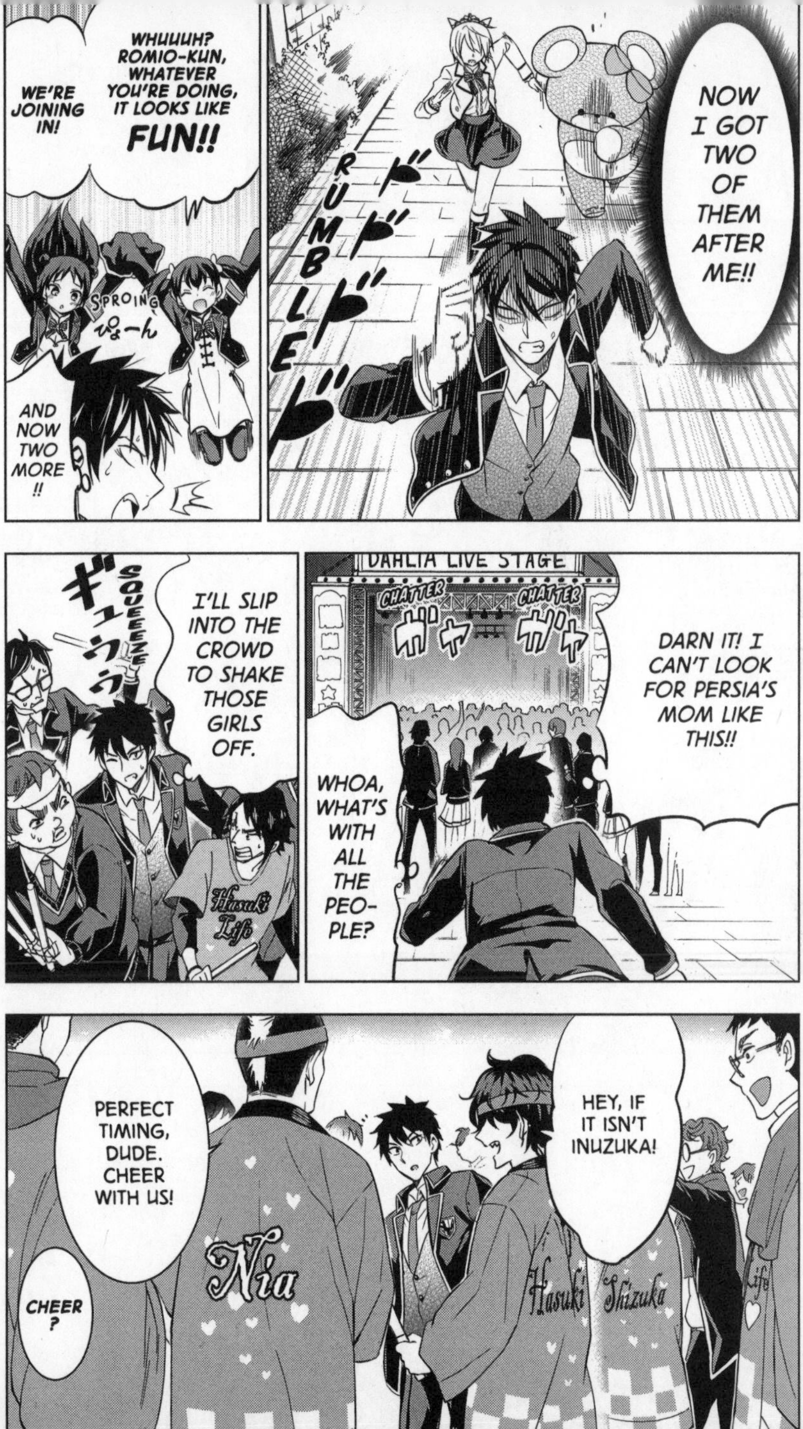
NOW I GOT TWO OF THEM AFTER ME!!
RUMBLE
ドドドド
WHUUUH? ROMIO-KUN, WHATEVER YOU'RE DOING, IT LOOKS LIKE FUN!!
WE'RE JOINING IN!
SPROING
ぴょーん
AND NOW TWO MORE !!
DAHLIA LIVE STAGE
CHATTER
ガヤ
CHATTER
ガヤ
DARN IT! I CAN'T LOOK FOR PERSIA'S MOM LIKE THIS!!
WHOA, WHAT'S WITH ALL THE PEOPLE?
I'LL SLIP INTO THE CROWD TO SHAKE THOSE GIRLS OFF.
SQUEEEZE
ギュウウ
Hasuki Life
HEY, IF IT ISN'T INUZUKA!
PERFECT TIMING, DUDE. CHEER WITH US!
CHEER?
Nia
Hasuki Shizuka
Life

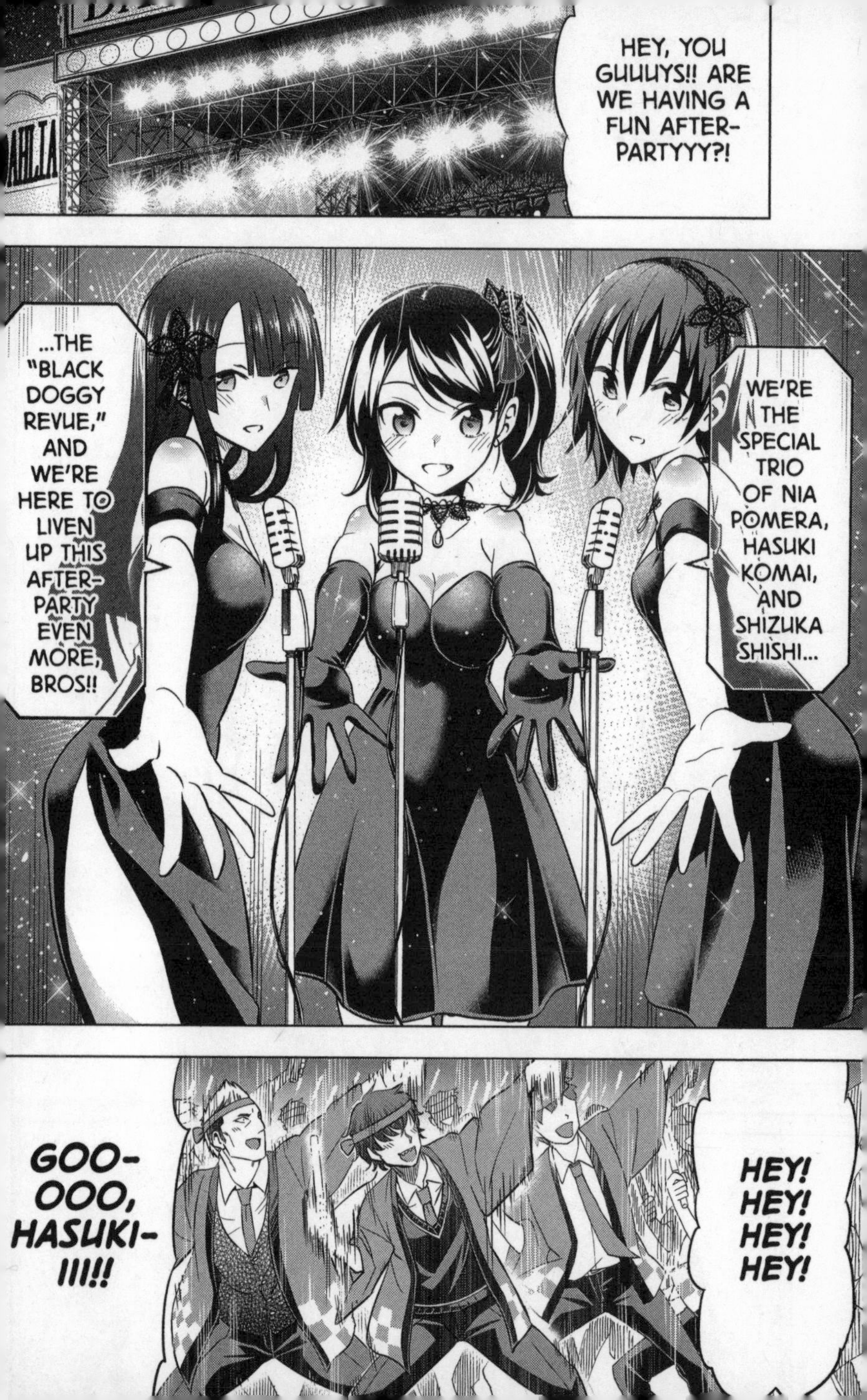
HEY, YOU GUUUYS!! ARE WE HAVING A FUN AFTER-PARTYYY?!
WE'RE THE SPECIAL TRIO OF NIA POMERA, HASUKI KOMAI, AND SHIZUKA SHISHI...
...THE "BLACK DOGGY REVUE," AND WE'RE HERE TO LIVEN UP THIS AFTER-PARTY EVEN MORE, BROS!!
HEY! HEY! HEY! HEY!
GOO-OOO, HASUKI-III!!

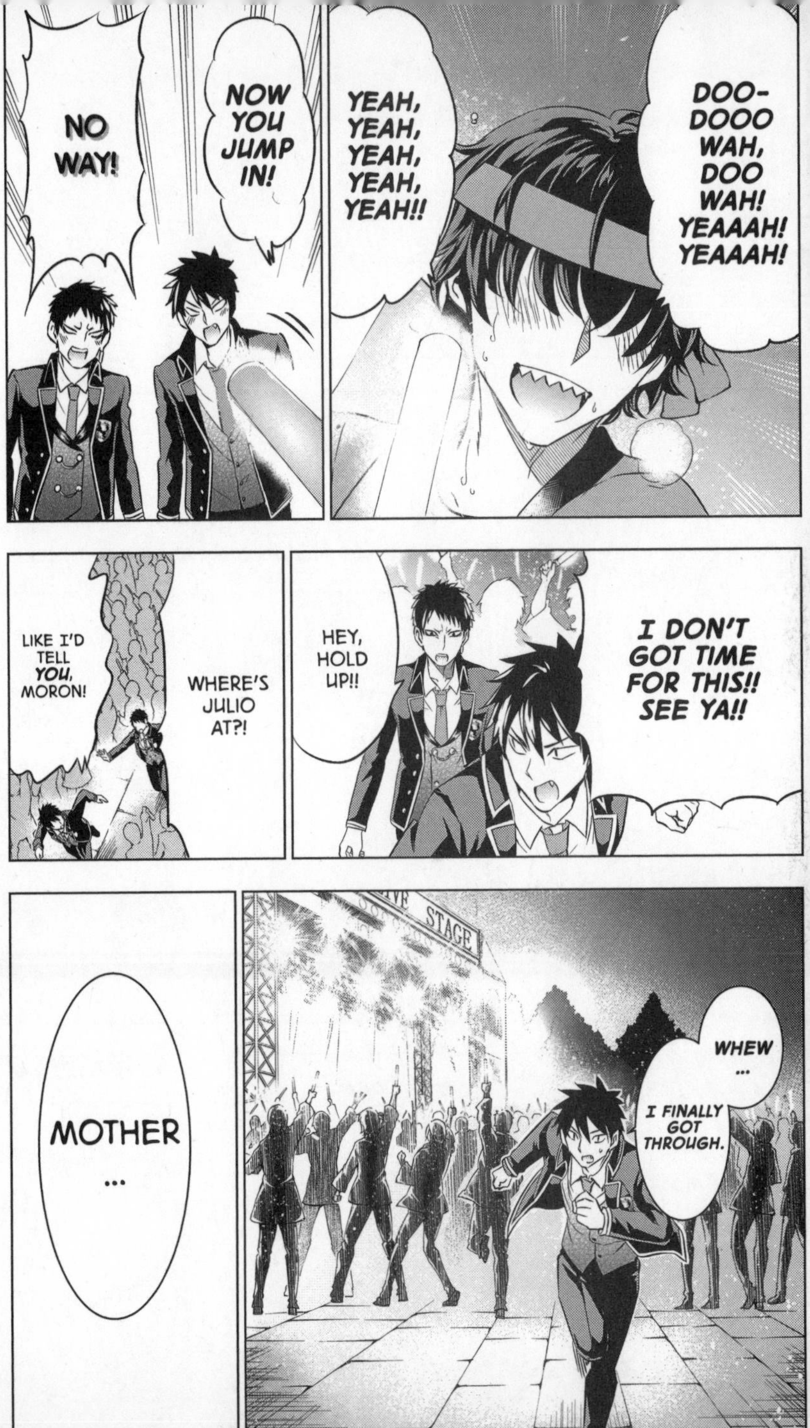
DOO-DOOO WAH, DOO WAH! YEAAAH! YEAAAH!
YEAH, YEAH, YEAH, YEAH, YEAH!!
NOW YOU JUMP IN!
NO WAY!
I DON'T GOT TIME FOR THIS!! SEE YA!!
HEY, HOLD UP!!
WHERE'S JULIO AT?!
LIKE I'D TELL *YOU*, MORON!
STAGE
WHEW ...
I FINALLY GOT THROUGH.
MOTHER ...

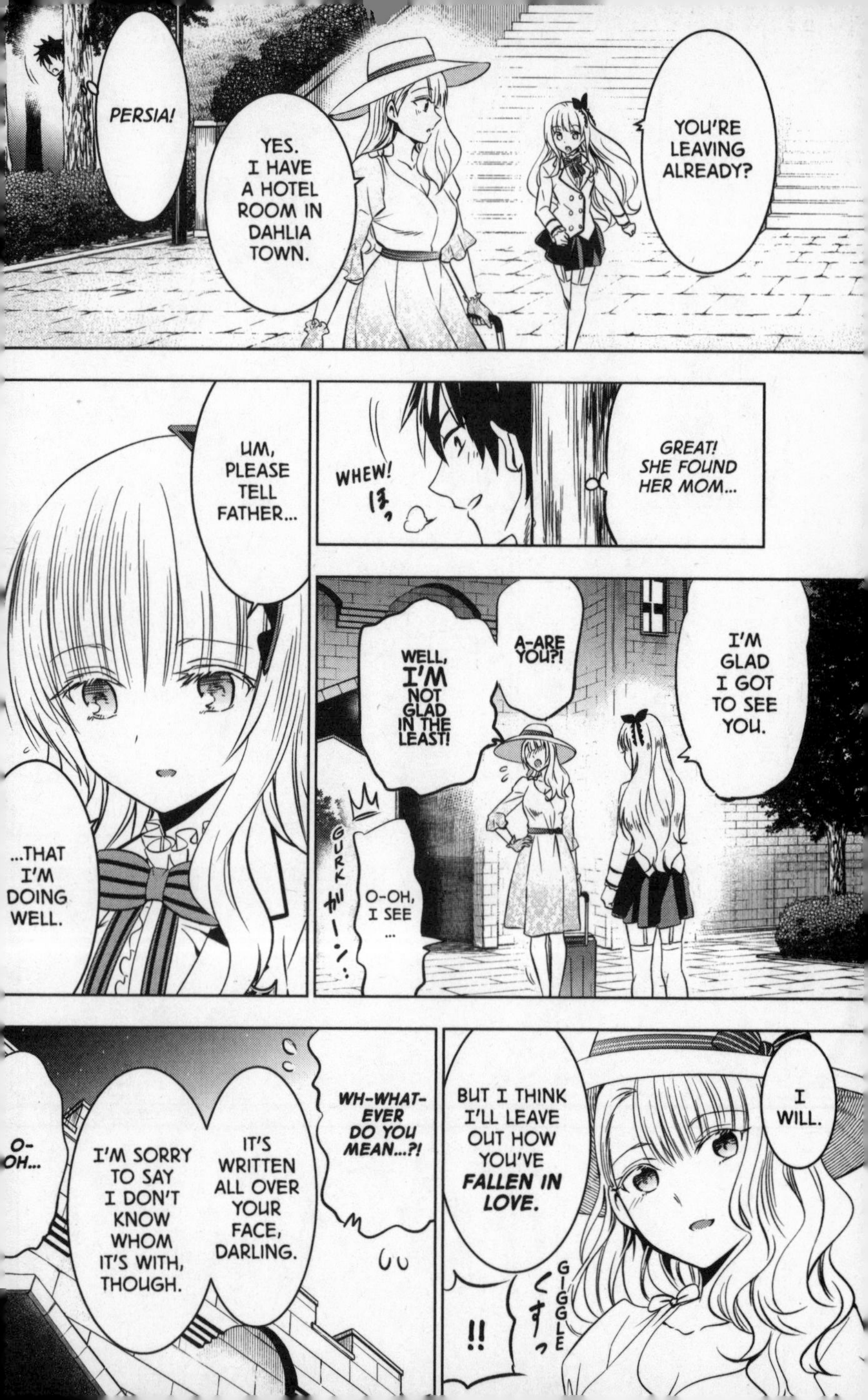
YOU'RE LEAVING ALREADY?
YES. I HAVE A HOTEL ROOM IN DAHLIA TOWN.
PERSIA!
GREAT! SHE FOUND HER MOM...
WHEW! ほっ
I'M GLAD I GOT TO SEE YOU.
A-ARE YOU?!
WELL, I'M NOT GLAD IN THE LEAST!
GURK
O-OH, I SEE...
UM, PLEASE TELL FATHER...
...THAT I'M DOING WELL.
I WILL.
BUT I THINK I'LL LEAVE OUT HOW YOU'VE FALLEN IN LOVE.
GIGGLE くすっ
!!
WH-WHAT-EVER DO YOU MEAN...?!
IT'S WRITTEN ALL OVER YOUR FACE, DARLING.
I'M SORRY TO SAY I DON'T KNOW WHOM IT'S WITH, THOUGH.
O-OH...

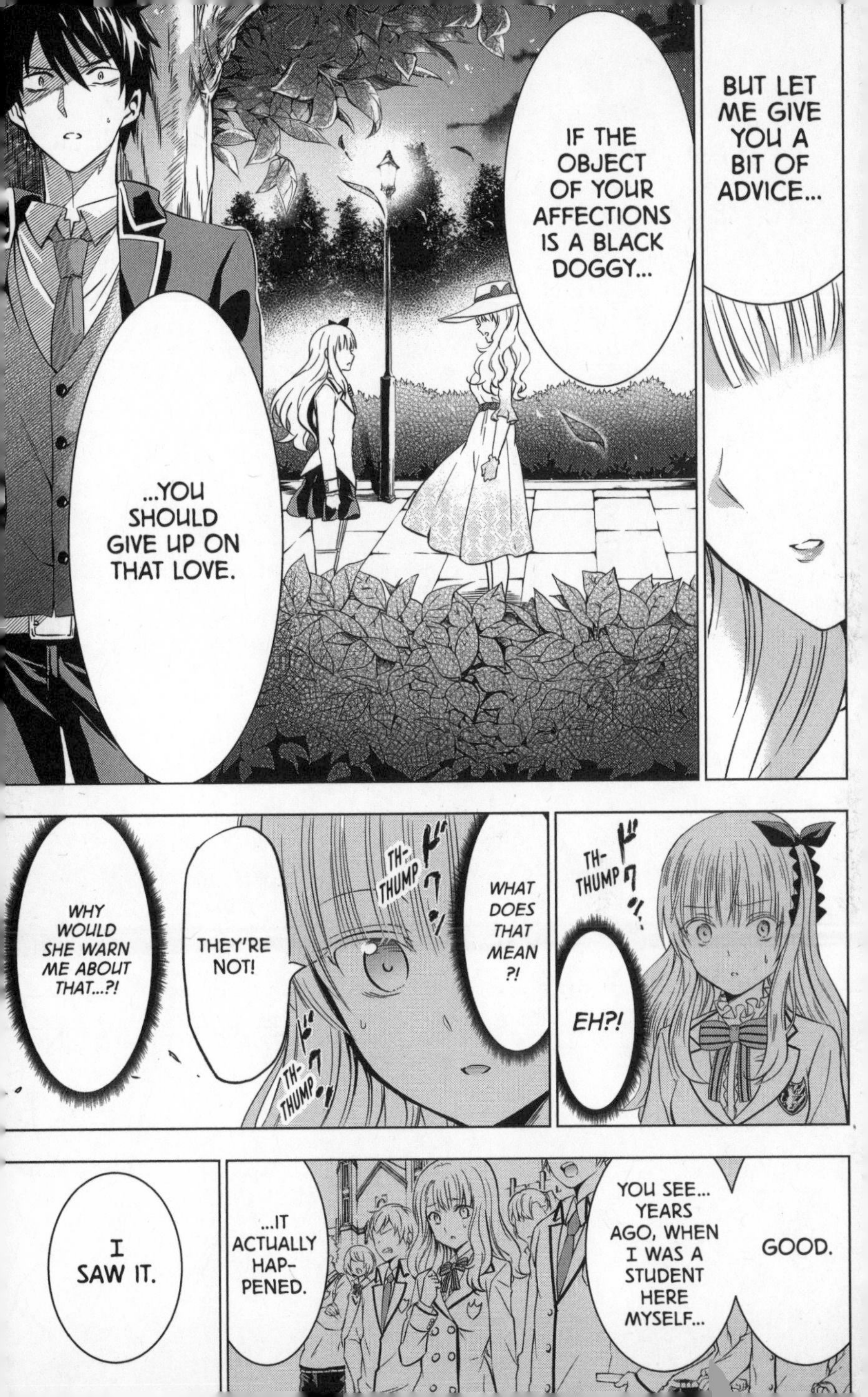
BUT LET ME GIVE YOU A BIT OF ADVICE...
IF THE OBJECT OF YOUR AFFECTIONS IS A BLACK DOGGY...
...YOU SHOULD GIVE UP ON THAT LOVE.
TH-THUMP
EH?!
WHAT DOES THAT MEAN ?!
TH-THUMP
THEY'RE NOT!
TH-THUMP
WHY WOULD SHE WARN ME ABOUT THAT...?!
GOOD.
YOU SEE... YEARS AGO, WHEN I WAS A STUDENT HERE MYSELF...
...IT ACTUALLY HAP-PENED.
I SAW IT.

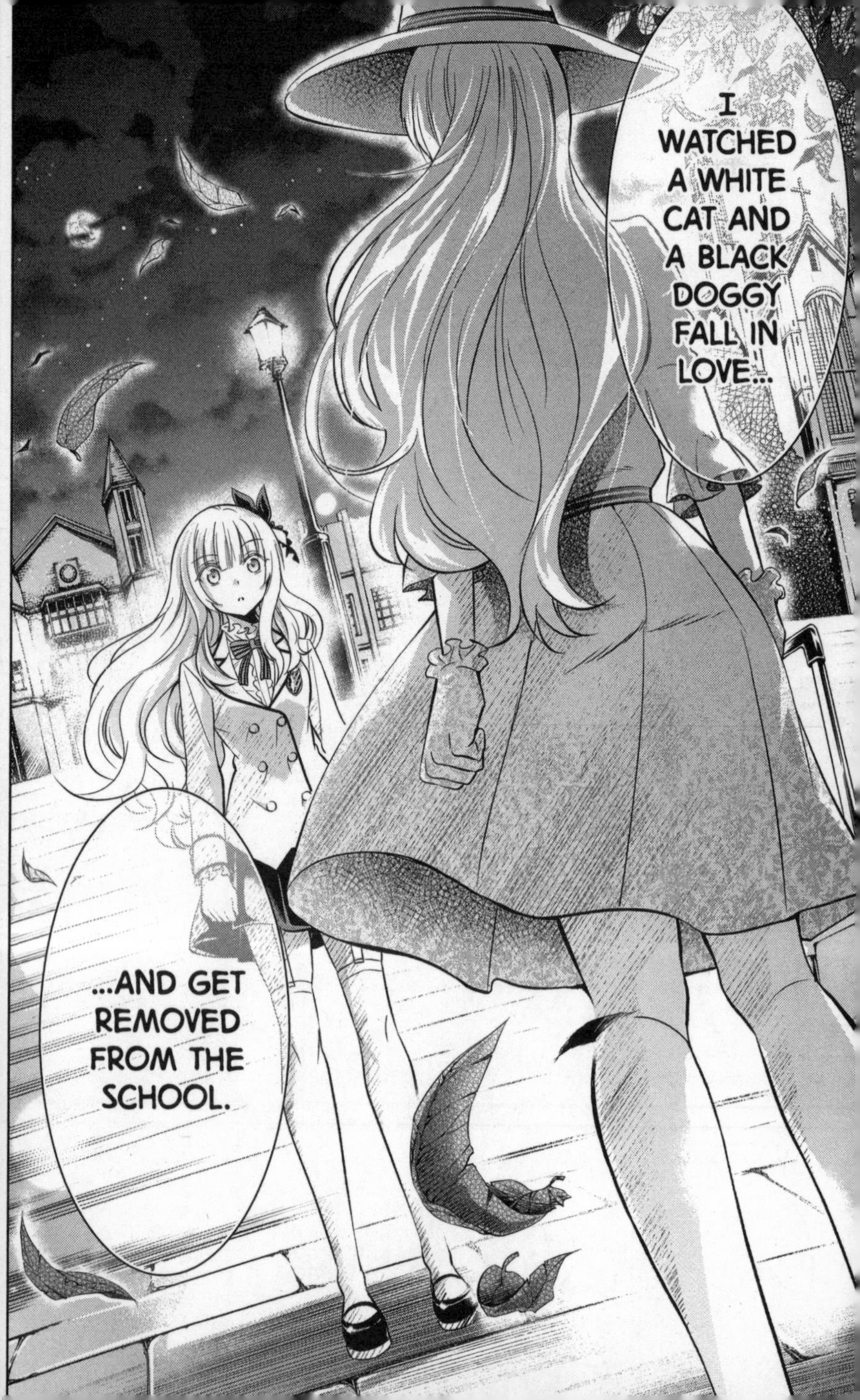
I WATCHED A WHITE CAT AND A BLACK DOGGY FALL IN LOVE...
...AND GET REMOVED FROM THE SCHOOL.

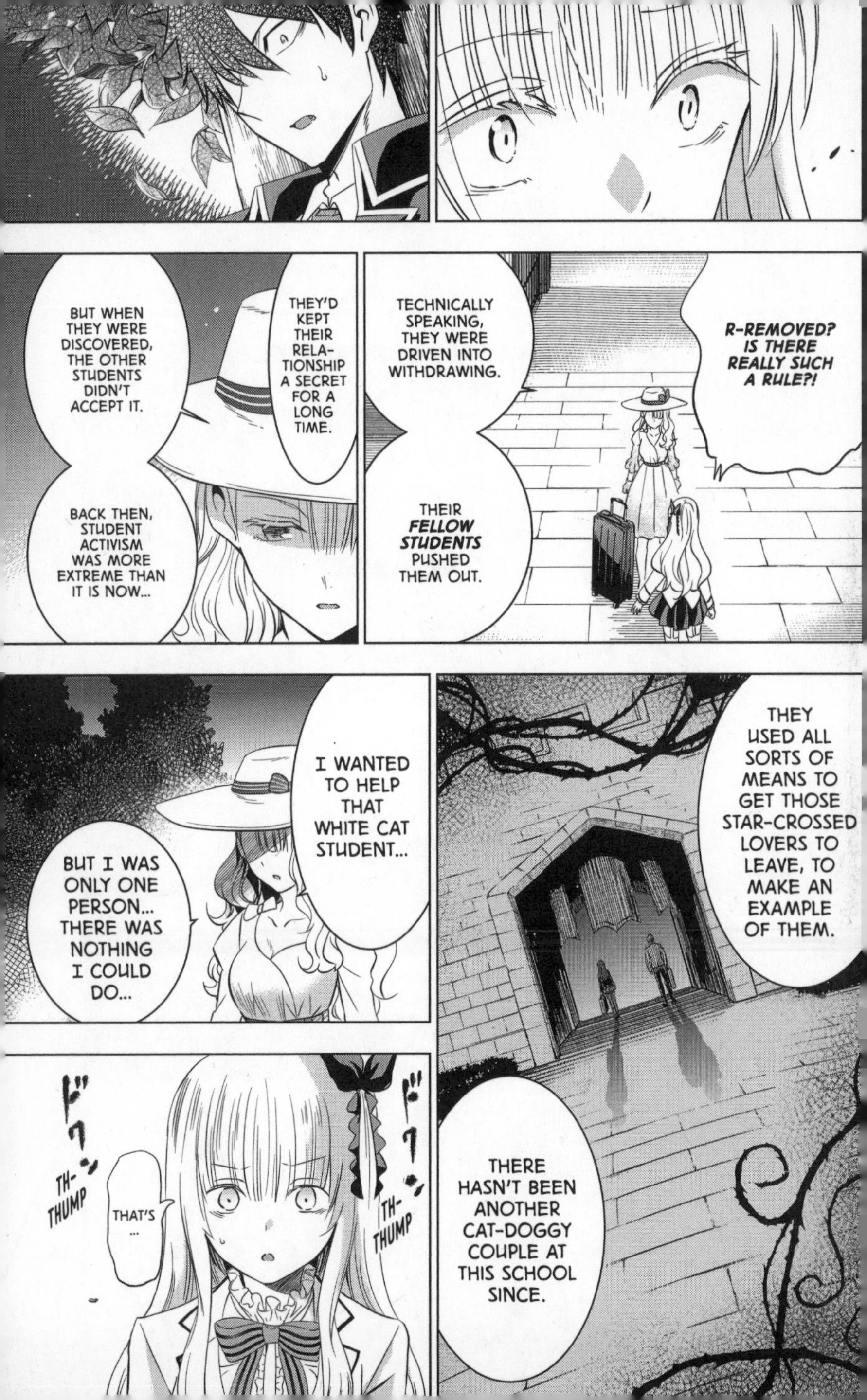
R-REMOVED? IS THERE REALLY SUCH A RULE?!
TECHNICALLY SPEAKING, THEY WERE DRIVEN INTO WITHDRAWING.
THEIR *FELLOW STUDENTS* PUSHED THEM OUT.
THEY'D KEPT THEIR RELA-TIONSHIP A SECRET FOR A LONG TIME.
BUT WHEN THEY WERE DISCOVERED, THE OTHER STUDENTS DIDN'T ACCEPT IT.
BACK THEN, STUDENT ACTIVISM WAS MORE EXTREME THAN IT IS NOW...
THEY USED ALL SORTS OF MEANS TO GET THOSE STAR-CROSSED LOVERS TO LEAVE, TO MAKE AN EXAMPLE OF THEM.
THERE HASN'T BEEN ANOTHER CAT-DOGGY COUPLE AT THIS SCHOOL SINCE.
I WANTED TO HELP THAT WHITE CAT STUDENT...
BUT I WAS ONLY ONE PERSON... THERE WAS NOTHING I COULD DO...
ドクン
TH-THUMP
THAT'S ...
ドクン
TH-THUMP

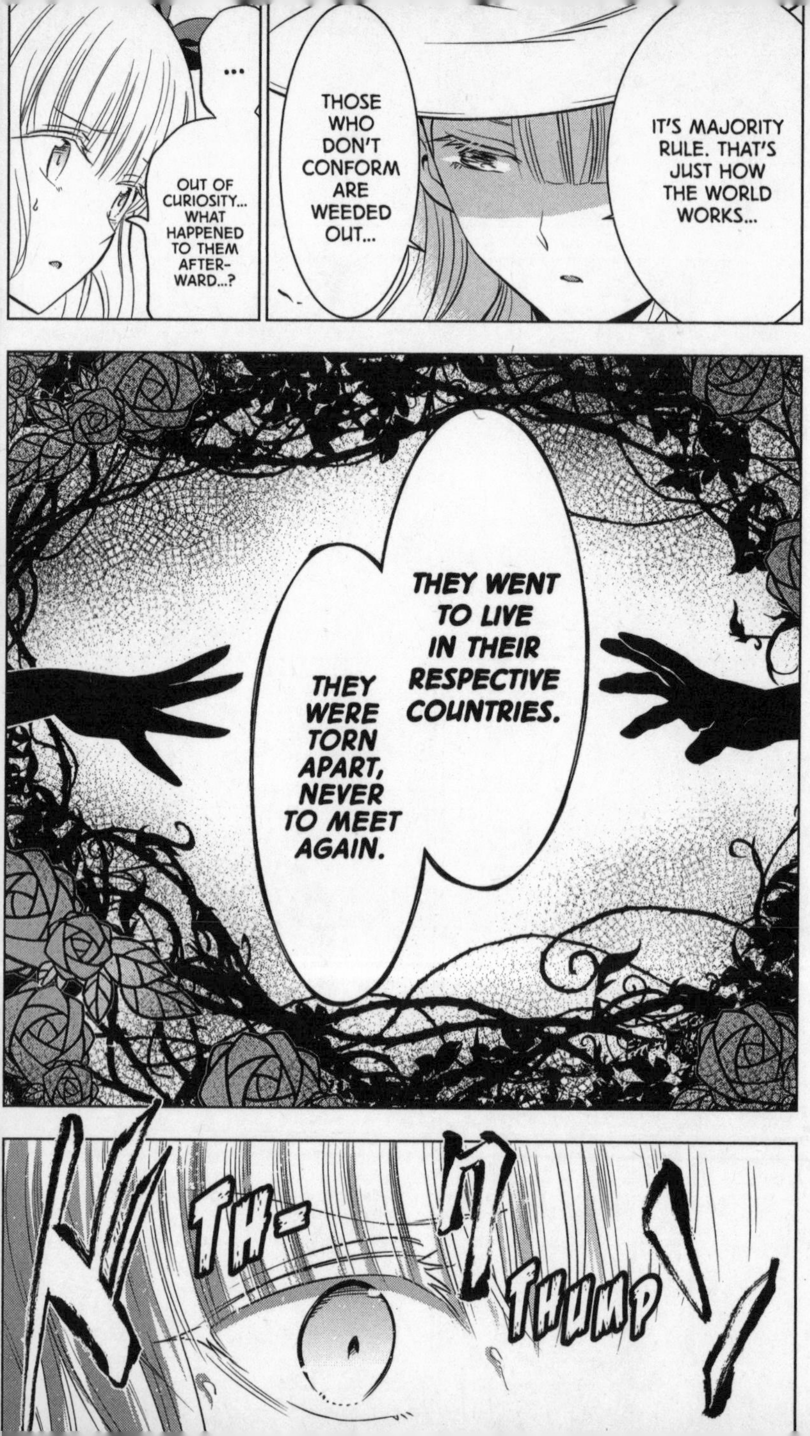
IT'S MAJORITY RULE. THAT'S JUST HOW THE WORLD WORKS...
THOSE WHO DON'T CONFORM ARE WEEDED OUT...
...
OUT OF CURIOSITY... WHAT HAPPENED TO THEM AFTER-WARD...?
THEY WENT TO LIVE IN THEIR RESPECTIVE COUNTRIES.
THEY WERE TORN APART, NEVER TO MEET AGAIN.
TH-
THUMP

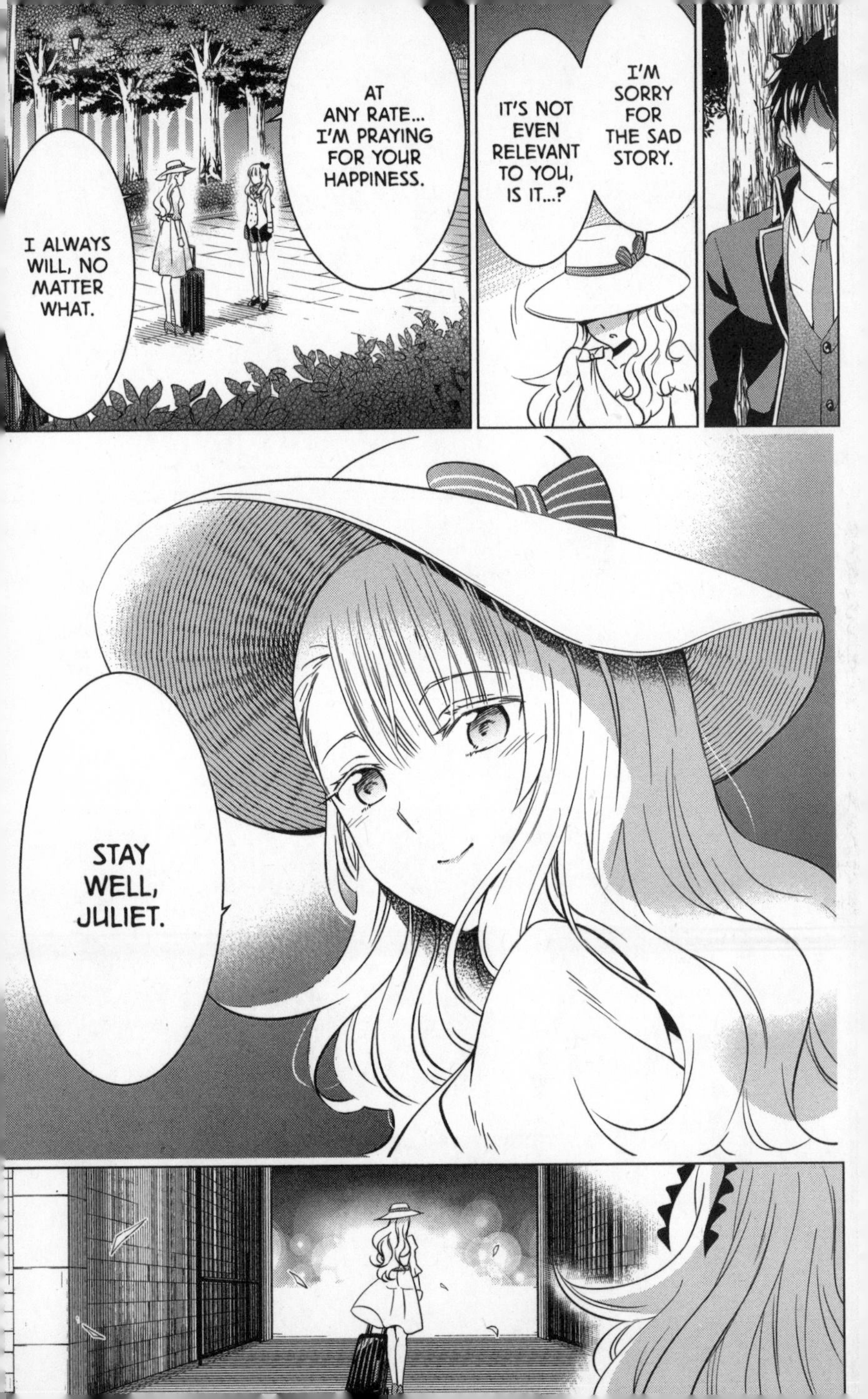
I'M SORRY FOR THE SAD STORY.
IT'S NOT EVEN RELEVANT TO YOU, IS IT...?
AT ANY RATE... I'M PRAYING FOR YOUR HAPPINESS.
I ALWAYS WILL, NO MATTER WHAT.
STAY WELL, JULIET.

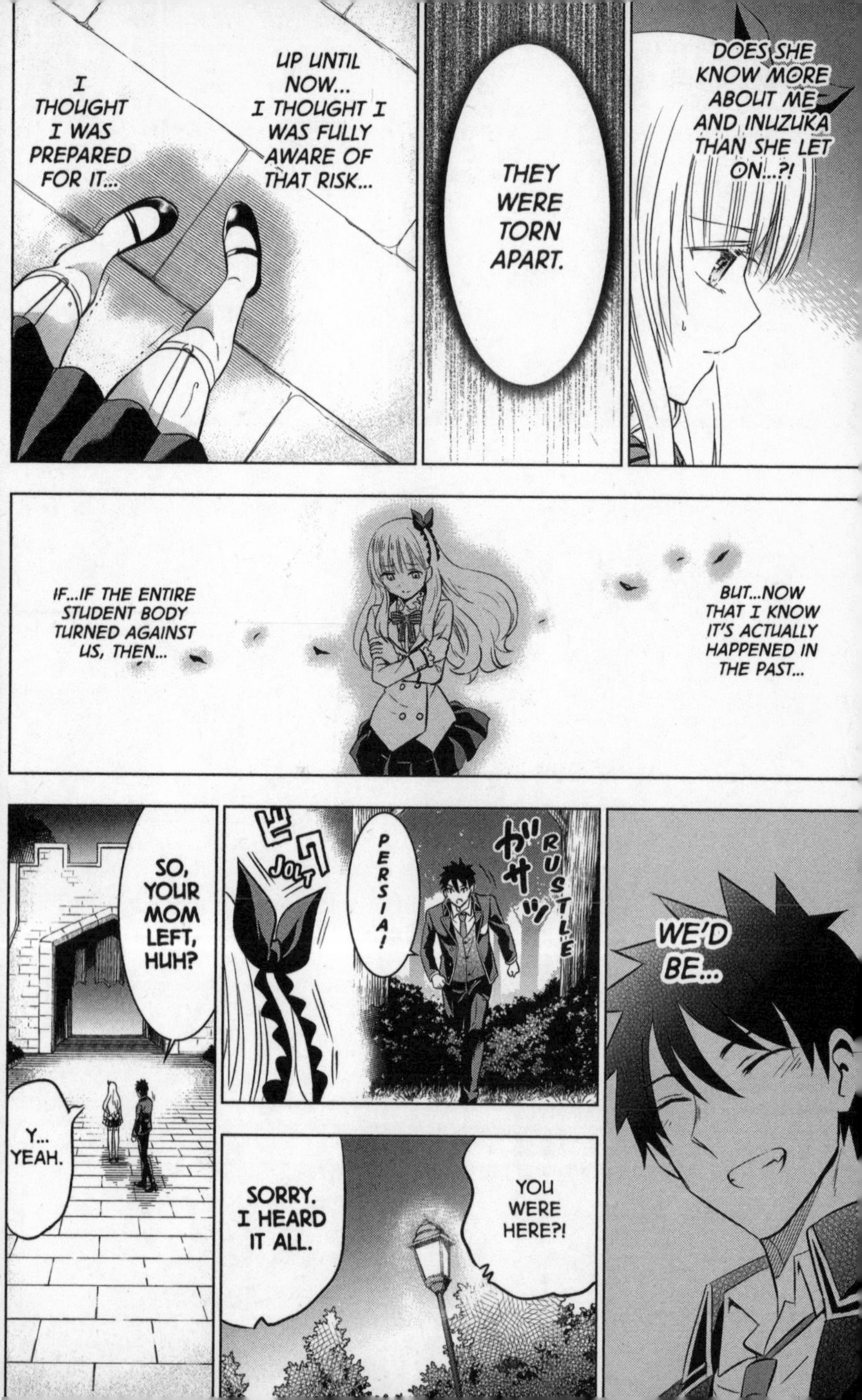
DOES SHE KNOW MORE ABOUT ME AND INUZUKA THAN SHE LET ON...?!
THEY WERE TORN APART.
UP UNTIL NOW... I THOUGHT I WAS FULLY AWARE OF THAT RISK...
I THOUGHT I WAS PREPARED FOR IT...
BUT...NOW THAT I KNOW IT'S ACTUALLY HAPPENED IN THE PAST...
IF...IF THE ENTIRE STUDENT BODY TURNED AGAINST US, THEN...
WE'D BE...
RUSTLE
PERSIA!
JOLT
YOU WERE HERE?!
SORRY. I HEARD IT ALL.
SO, YOUR MOM LEFT, HUH?
Y... YEAH.

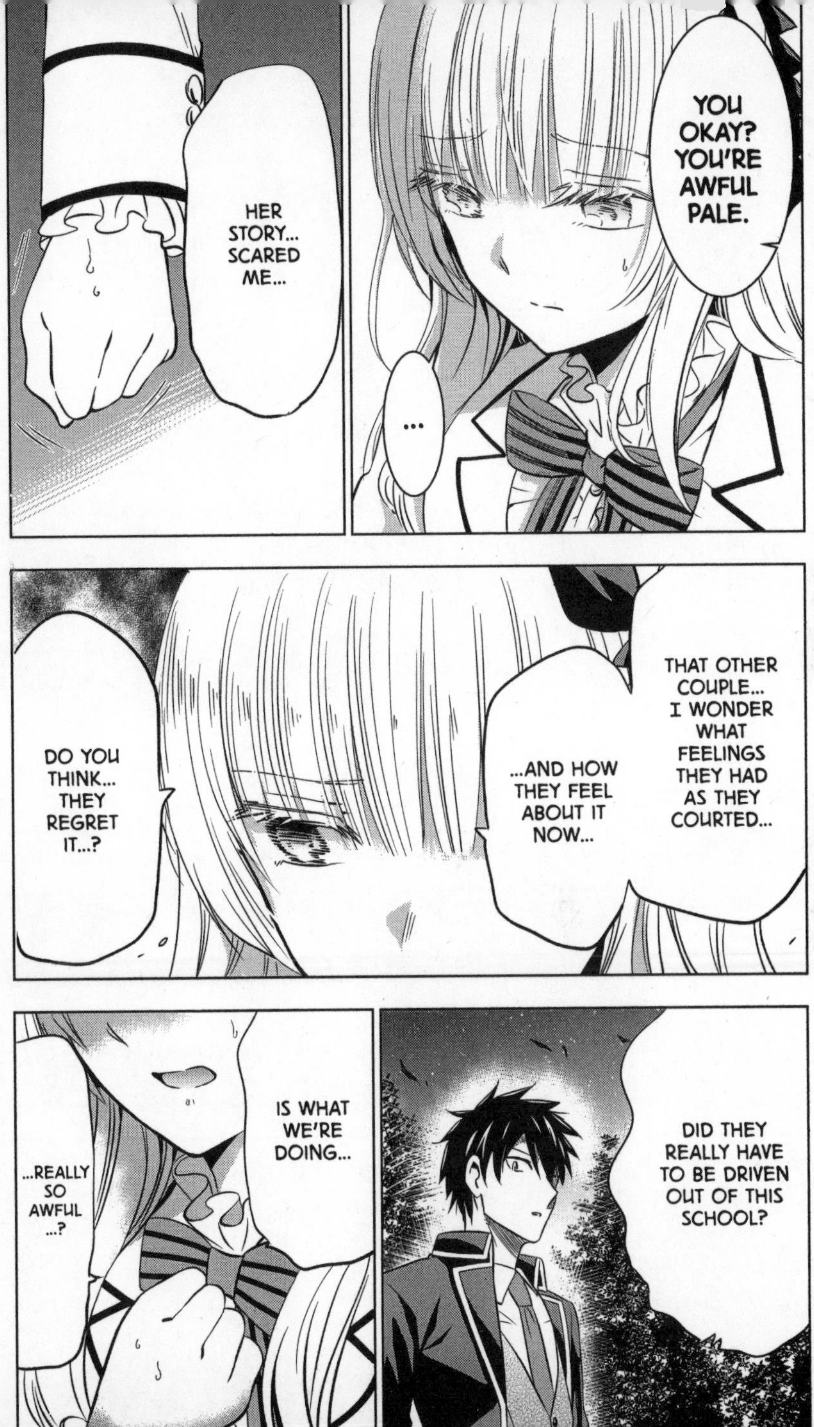
YOU OKAY? YOU'RE AWFUL PALE.
...
HER STORY... SCARED ME...
THAT OTHER COUPLE... I WONDER WHAT FEELINGS THEY HAD AS THEY COURTED...
...AND HOW THEY FEEL ABOUT IT NOW...
DO YOU THINK... THEY REGRET IT...?
DID THEY REALLY HAVE TO BE DRIVEN OUT OF THIS SCHOOL?
IS WHAT WE'RE DOING...
...REALLY SO AWFUL ...?

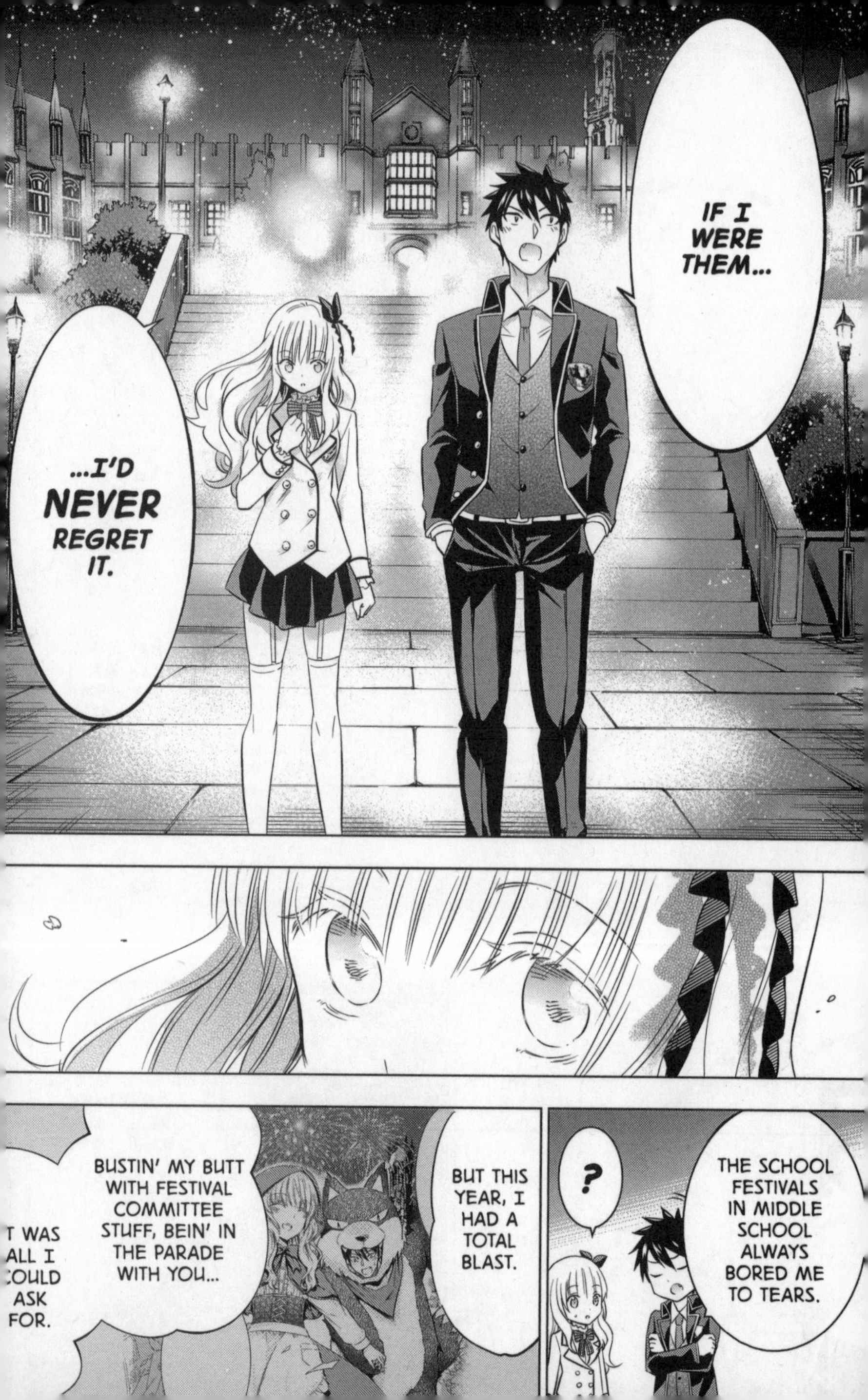
IF I WERE THEM...
...I'D NEVER REGRET IT.
THE SCHOOL FESTIVALS IN MIDDLE SCHOOL ALWAYS BORED ME TO TEARS.
?
BUT THIS YEAR, I HAD A TOTAL BLAST.
BUSTIN' MY BUTT WITH FESTIVAL COMMITTEE STUFF, BEIN' IN THE PARADE WITH YOU...
T WAS ALL I COULD ASK FOR.

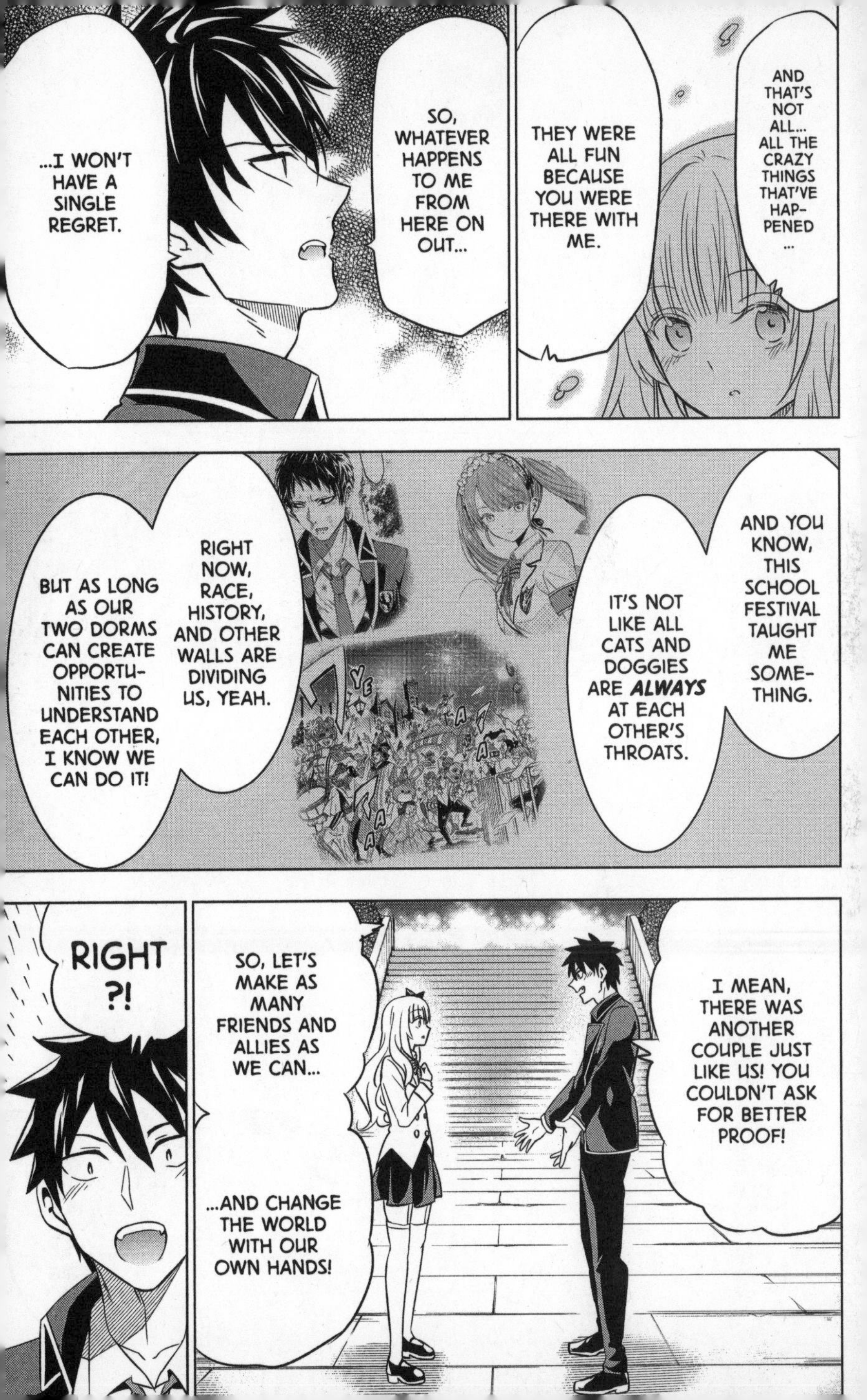
AND THAT'S NOT ALL... ALL THE CRAZY THINGS THAT'VE HAPPENED ...
THEY WERE ALL FUN BECAUSE YOU WERE THERE WITH ME.
SO, WHATEVER HAPPENS TO ME FROM HERE ON OUT...
...I WON'T HAVE A SINGLE REGRET.
AND YOU KNOW, THIS SCHOOL FESTIVAL TAUGHT ME SOMETHING.
IT'S NOT LIKE ALL CATS AND DOGGIES ARE *ALWAYS* AT EACH OTHER'S THROATS.
RIGHT NOW, RACE, HISTORY, AND OTHER WALLS ARE DIVIDING US, YEAH.
BUT AS LONG AS OUR TWO DORMS CAN CREATE OPPORTUNITIES TO UNDERSTAND EACH OTHER, I KNOW WE CAN DO IT!
I MEAN, THERE WAS ANOTHER COUPLE JUST LIKE US! YOU COULDN'T ASK FOR BETTER PROOF!
SO, LET'S MAKE AS MANY FRIENDS AND ALLIES AS WE CAN...
...AND CHANGE THE WORLD WITH OUR OWN HANDS!
RIGHT?!

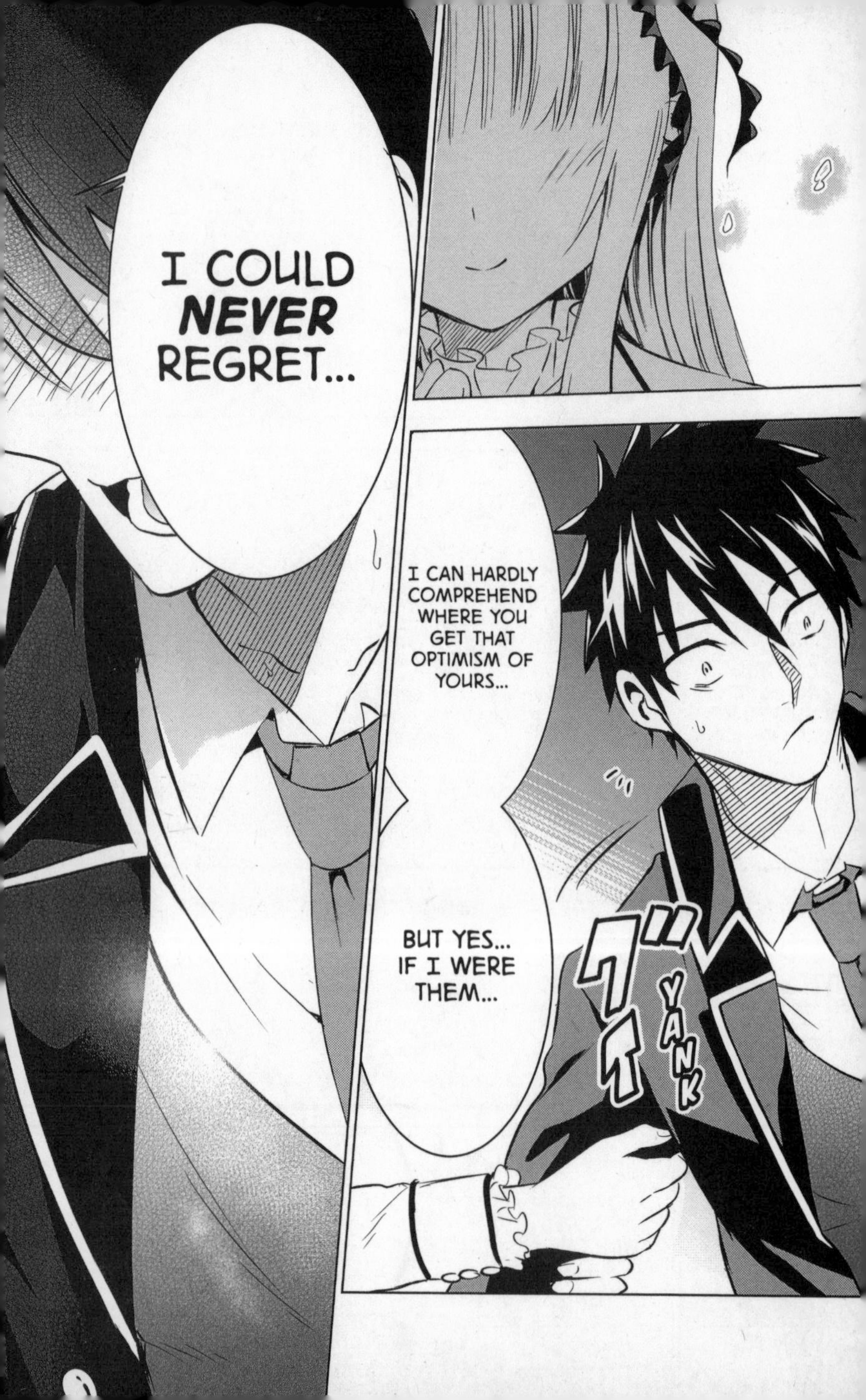
I CAN HARDLY COMPREHEND WHERE YOU GET THAT OPTIMISM OF YOURS...
BUT YES... IF I WERE THEM...
YANK
I COULD NEVER REGRET...

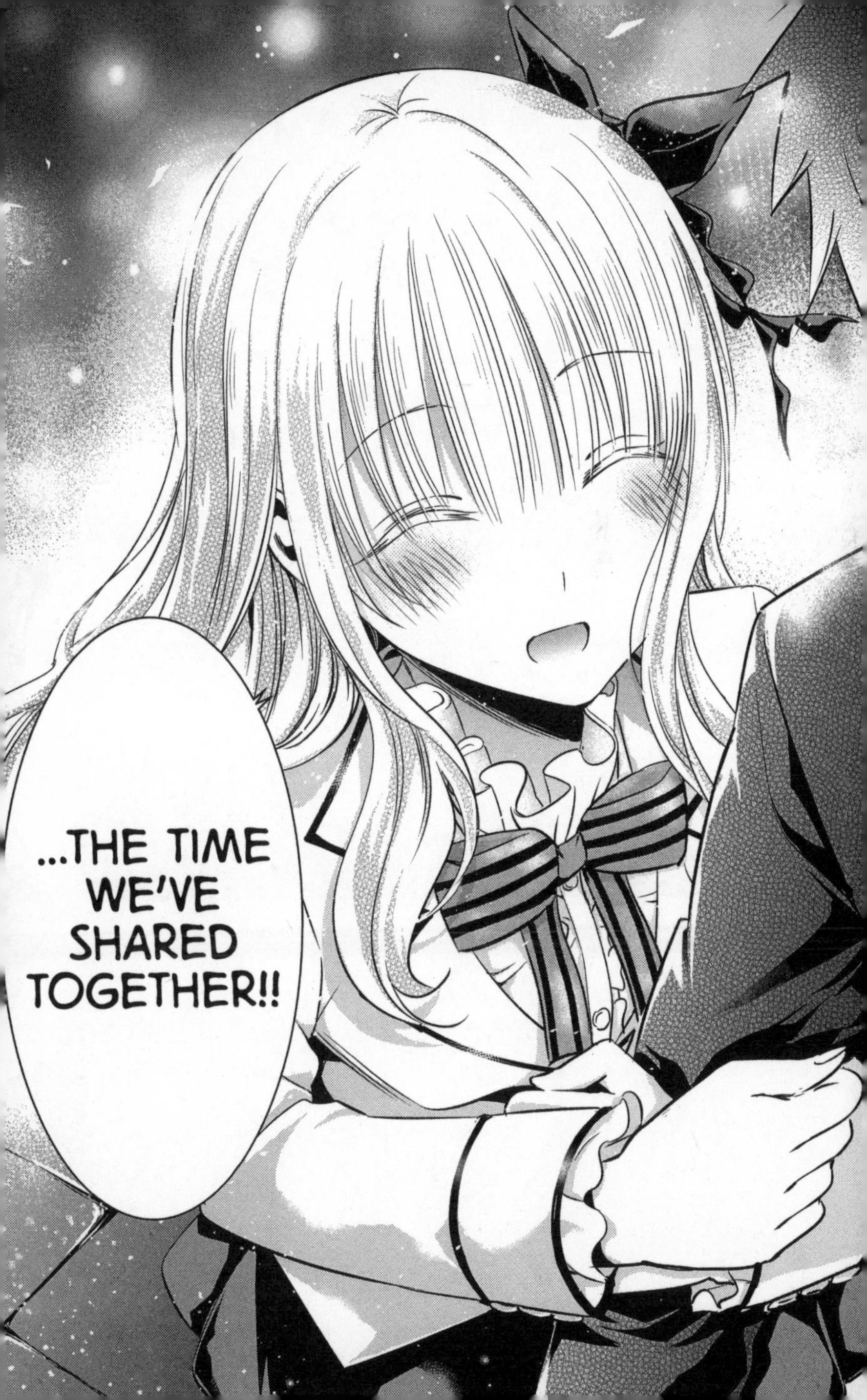
...THE TIME WE'VE SHARED TOGETHER!!

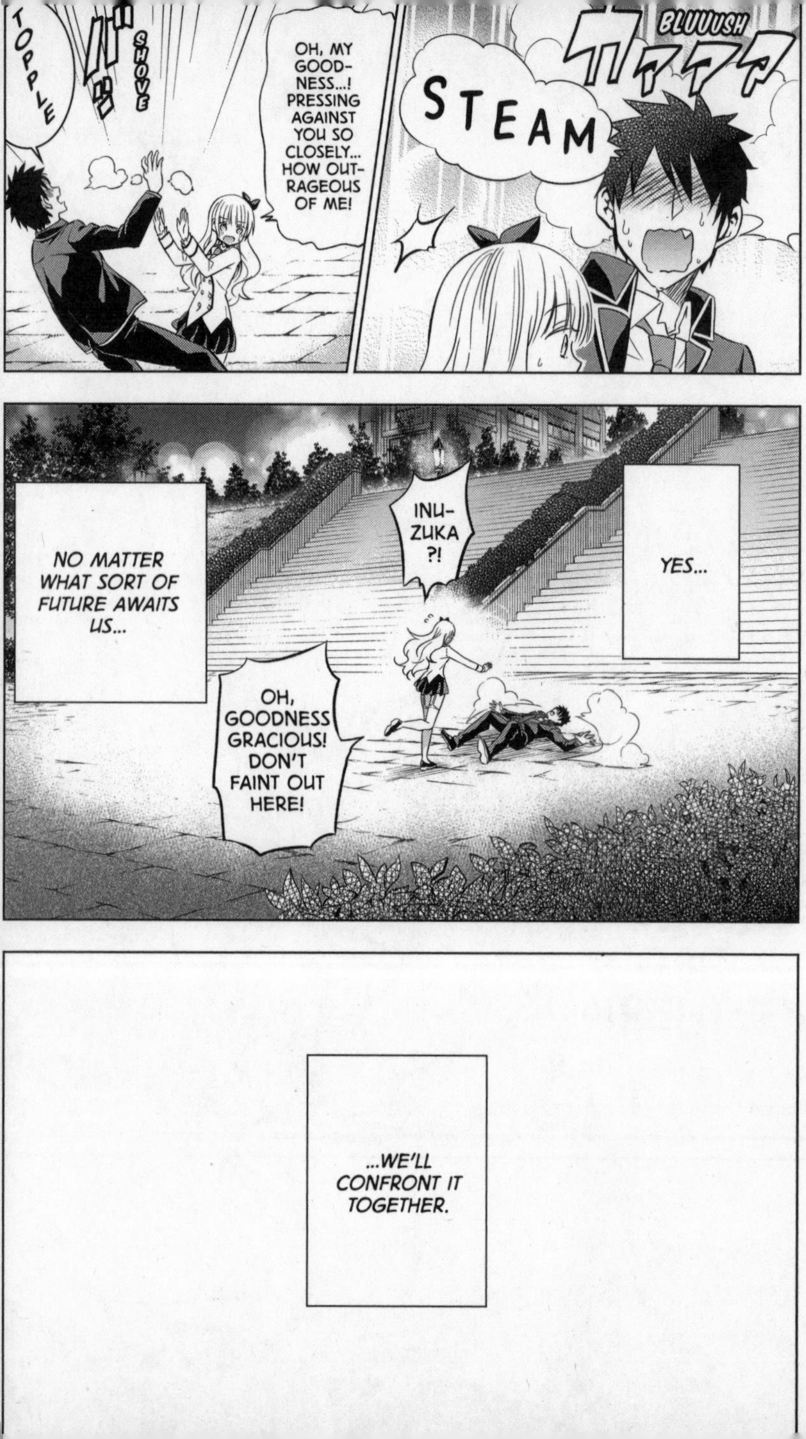
BLUUUSH
STEAM
OH, MY GOODNESS...! PRESSING AGAINST YOU SO CLOSELY... HOW OUTRAGEOUS OF ME!
SHOVE
TOPPLE
YES...
INUZUKA?!
NO MATTER WHAT SORT OF FUTURE AWAITS US...
OH, GOODNESS GRACIOUS! DON'T FAINT OUT HERE!
...WE'LL CONFRONT IT TOGETHER.

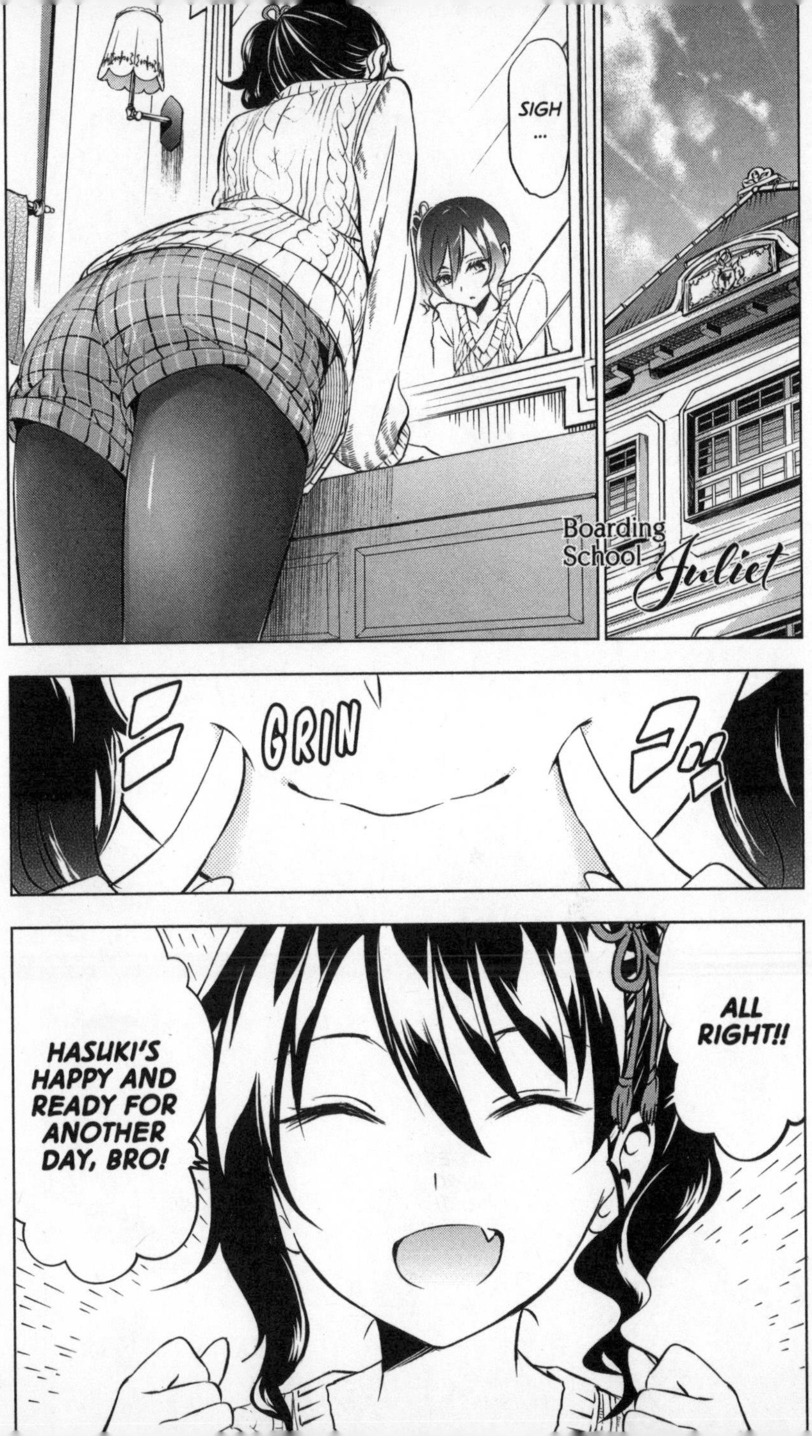
SIGH ...
Boarding School Juliet
GRIN
ALL RIGHT!!
HASUKI'S HAPPY AND READY FOR ANOTHER DAY, BRO!

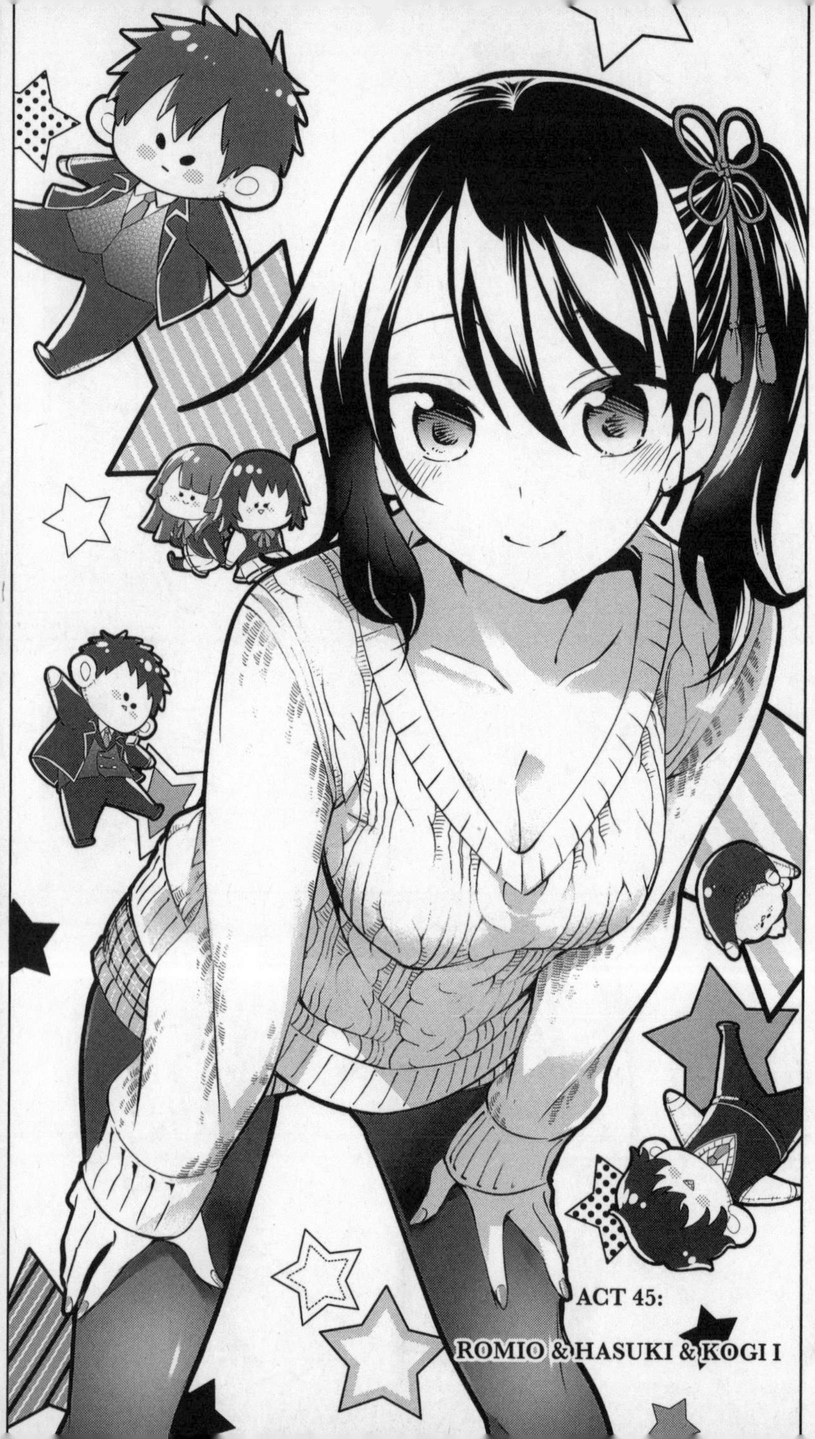
ACT 45:
ROMIO & HASUKI & KOGI I

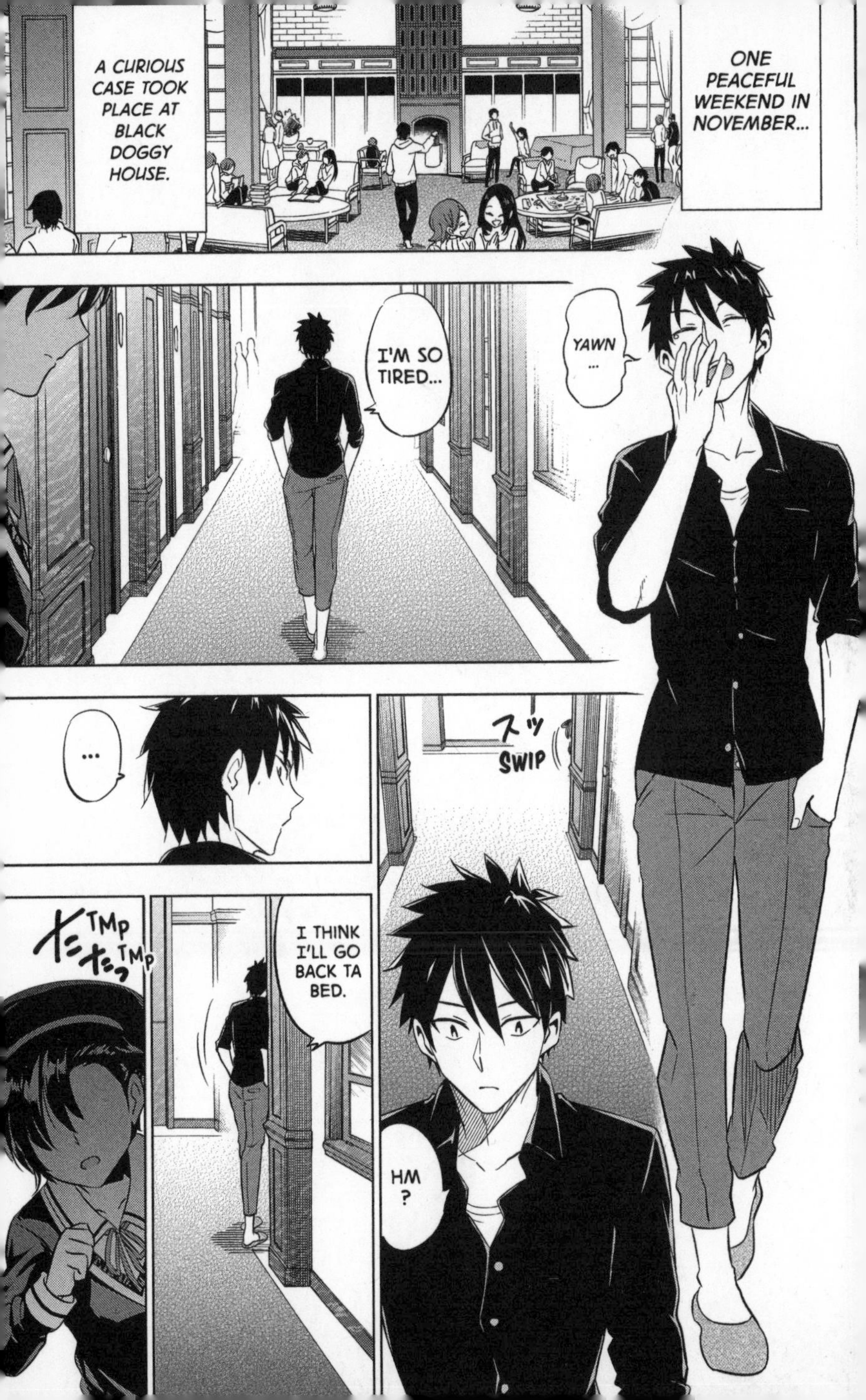
ONE PEACEFUL WEEKEND IN NOVEMBER...
A CURIOUS CASE TOOK PLACE AT BLACK DOGGY HOUSE.
YAWN ...
I'M SO TIRED...
スッ
SWIP
HM ?
...
I THINK I'LL GO BACK TA BED.
TMP TMP

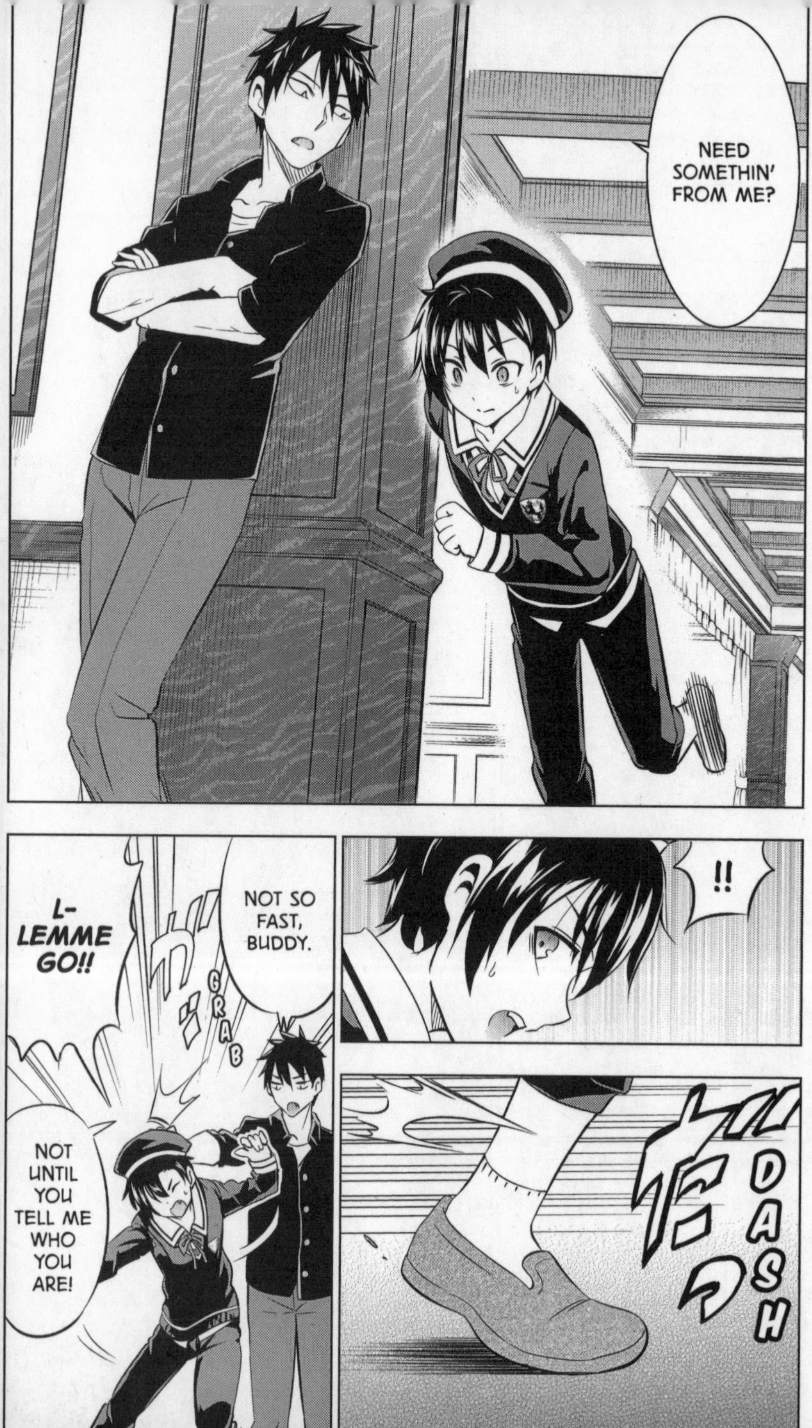
NEED SOMETHIN' FROM ME?
!!
DASH
NOT SO FAST, BUDDY.
GRAB
L-LEMME GO!!
NOT UNTIL YOU TELL ME WHO YOU ARE!

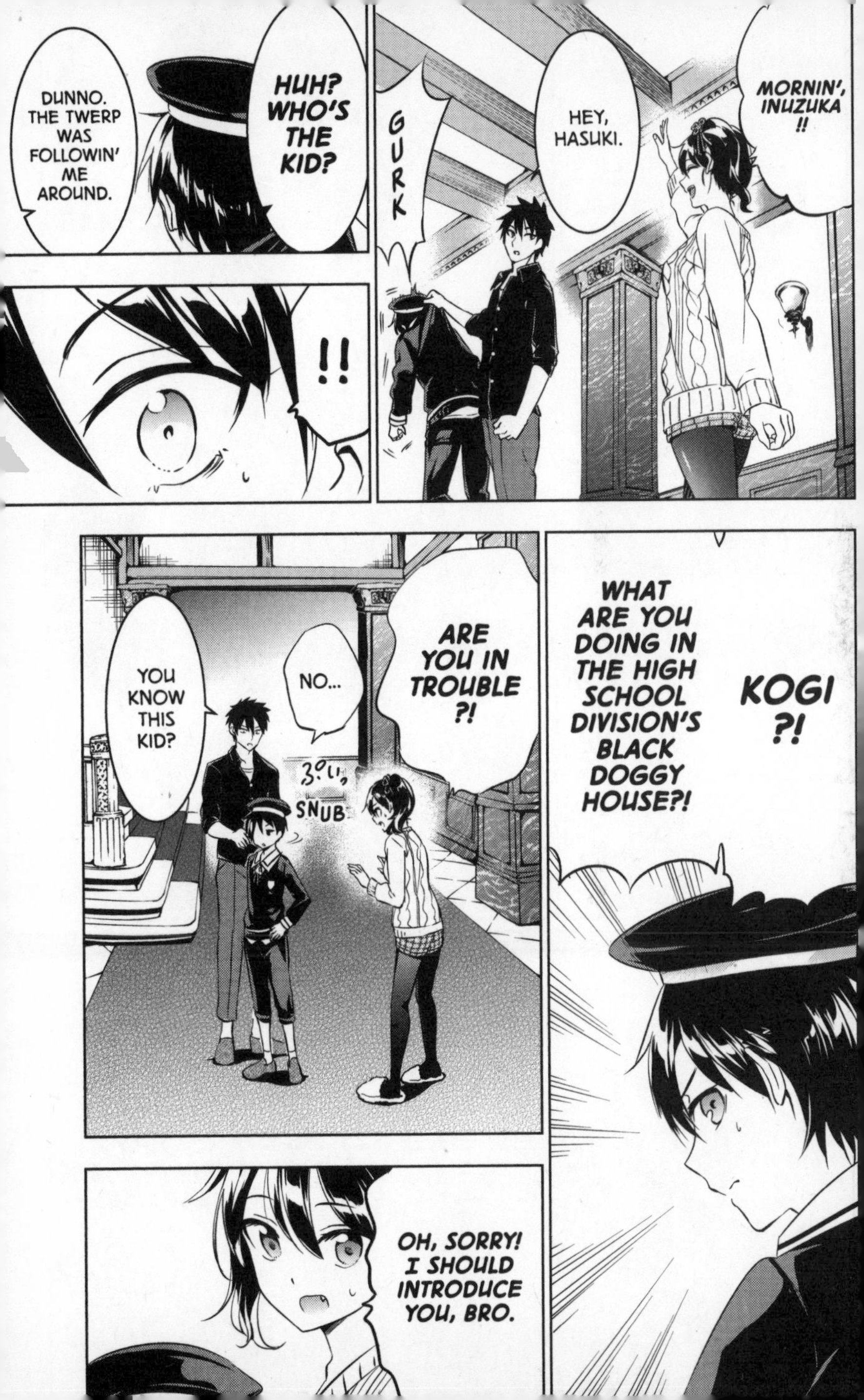
MORNIN', INUZUKA !!
HEY, HASUKI.
GURK
HUH? WHO'S THE KID?
DUNNO. THE TWERP WAS FOLLOWIN' ME AROUND.
!!
KOGI ?!
WHAT ARE YOU DOING IN THE HIGH SCHOOL DIVISION'S BLACK DOGGY HOUSE?!
ARE YOU IN TROUBLE ?!
NO...
YOU KNOW THIS KID?
SNUB
OH, SORRY! I SHOULD INTRODUCE YOU, BRO.

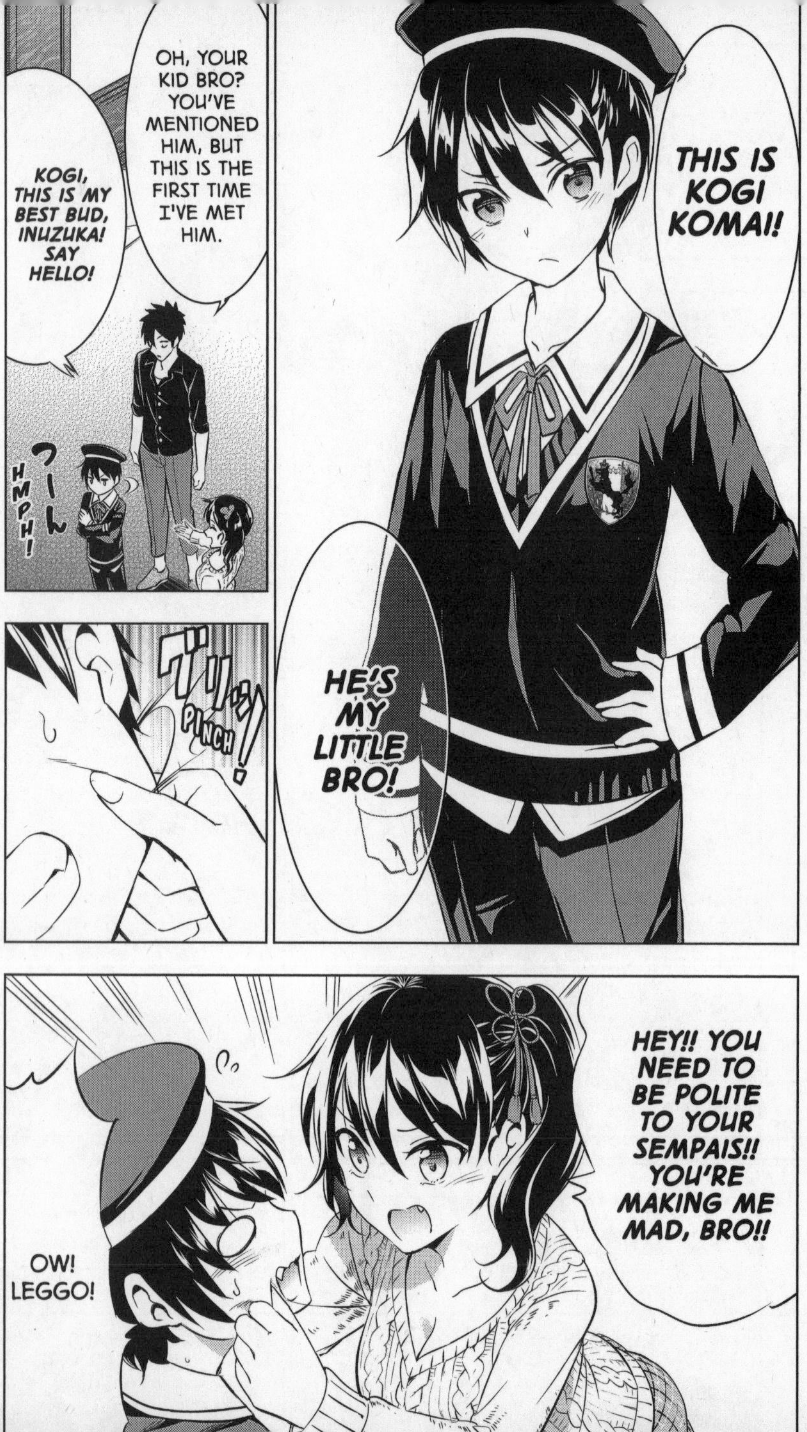
THIS IS KOGI KOMAI!
HE'S MY LITTLE BRO!
OH, YOUR KID BRO? YOU'VE MENTIONED HIM, BUT THIS IS THE FIRST TIME I'VE MET HIM.
KOGI, THIS IS MY BEST BUD, INUZUKA! SAY HELLO!
HMPH!
PINCH
HEY!! YOU NEED TO BE POLITE TO YOUR SEMPAIS!! YOU'RE MAKING ME MAD, BRO!!
OW! LEGGO!

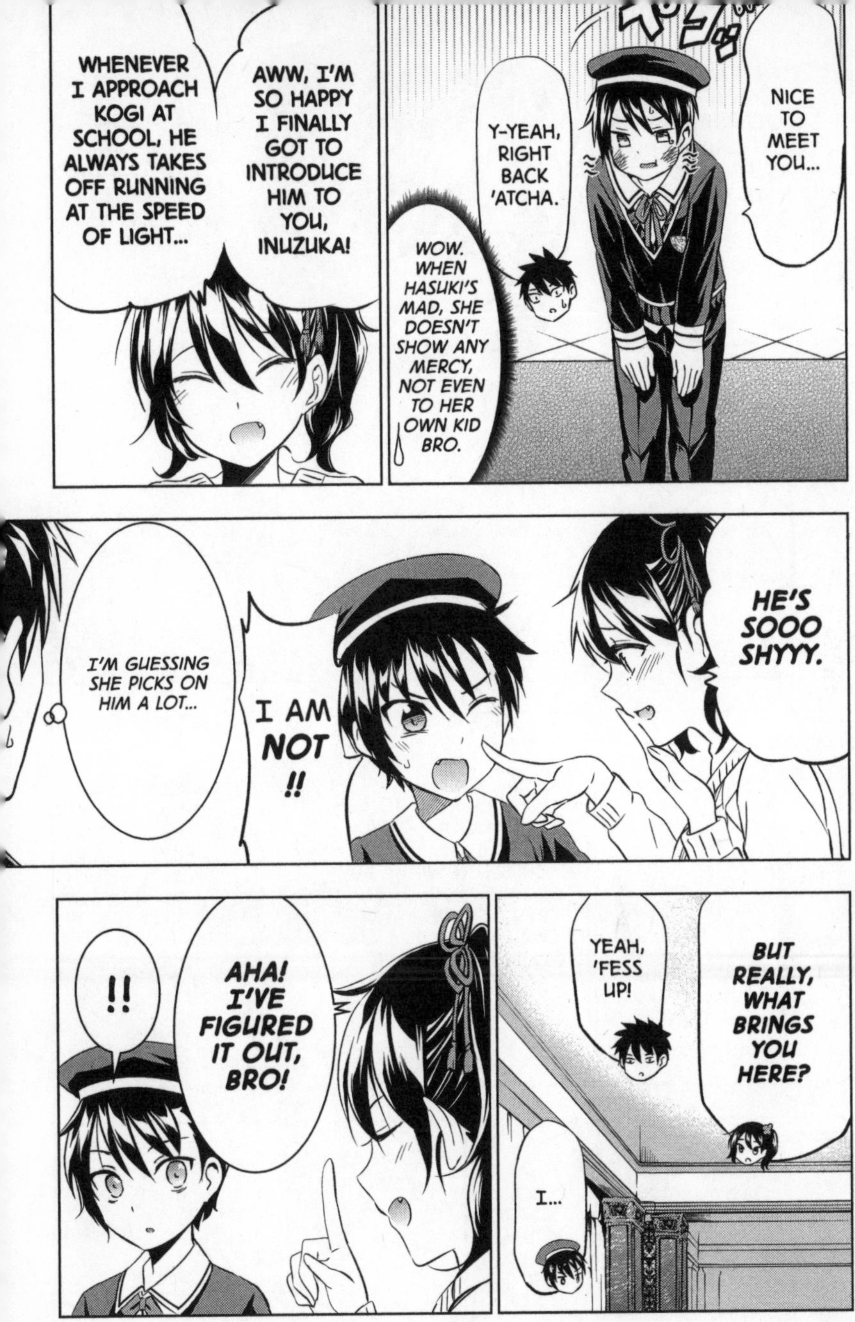
NICE TO MEET YOU...
Y-YEAH, RIGHT BACK 'ATCHA.
WOW. WHEN HASUKI'S MAD, SHE DOESN'T SHOW ANY MERCY, NOT EVEN TO HER OWN KID BRO.
AWW, I'M SO HAPPY I FINALLY GOT TO INTRODUCE HIM TO YOU, INUZUKA!
WHENEVER I APPROACH KOGI AT SCHOOL, HE ALWAYS TAKES OFF RUNNING AT THE SPEED OF LIGHT...
HE'S SOOO SHYYY.
I AM NOT !!
I'M GUESSING SHE PICKS ON HIM A LOT...
BUT REALLY, WHAT BRINGS YOU HERE?
YEAH, 'FESS UP!
I...
AHA! I'VE FIGURED IT OUT, BRO!
!!

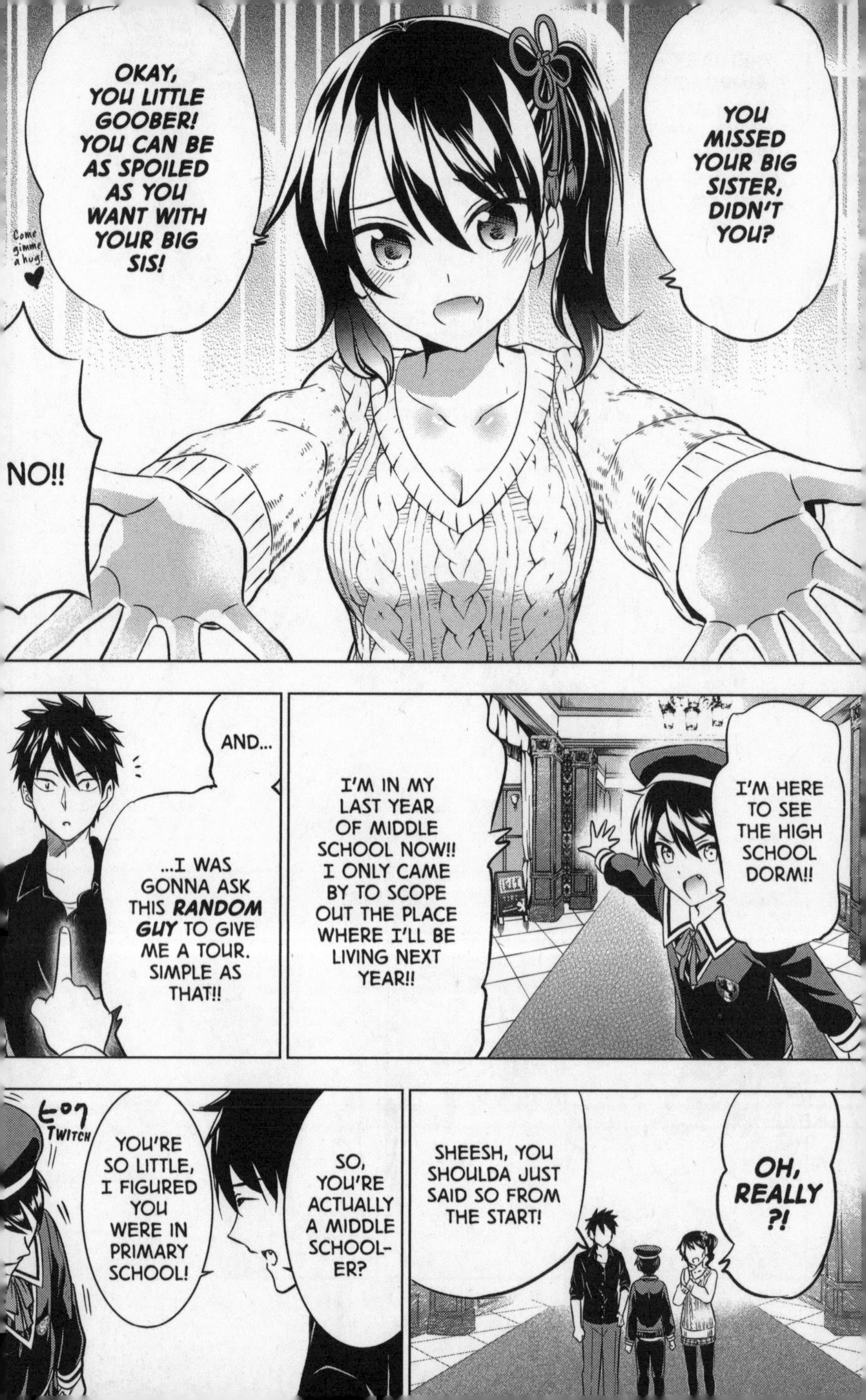
YOU MISSED YOUR BIG SISTER, DIDN'T YOU?
OKAY, YOU LITTLE GOOBER! YOU CAN BE AS SPOILED AS YOU WANT WITH YOUR BIG SIS!
Come gimme a hug! ♥
NO!!
I'M HERE TO SEE THE HIGH SCHOOL DORM!!
I'M IN MY LAST YEAR OF MIDDLE SCHOOL NOW!! I ONLY CAME BY TO SCOPE OUT THE PLACE WHERE I'LL BE LIVING NEXT YEAR!!
AND...
...I WAS GONNA ASK THIS ***RANDOM GUY*** TO GIVE ME A TOUR. SIMPLE AS THAT!!
OH, REALLY?!
SHEESH, YOU SHOULDA JUST SAID SO FROM THE START!
SO, YOU'RE ACTUALLY A MIDDLE SCHOOL-ER?
TWITCH
YOU'RE SO LITTLE, I FIGURED YOU WERE IN PRIMARY SCHOOL!

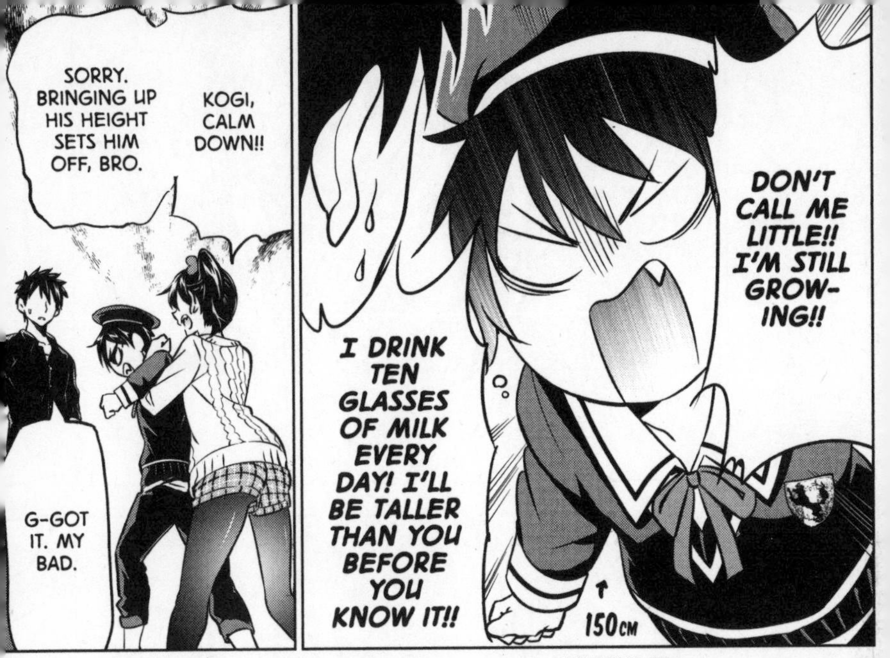
DON'T CALL ME LITTLE!! I'M STILL GROW-ING!!
I DRINK TEN GLASSES OF MILK EVERY DAY! I'LL BE TALLER THAN YOU BEFORE YOU KNOW IT!!
150CM
KOGI, CALM DOWN!!
SORRY. BRINGING UP HIS HEIGHT SETS HIM OFF, BRO.
G-GOT IT. MY BAD.

NOTE: APPROX. 4'9"

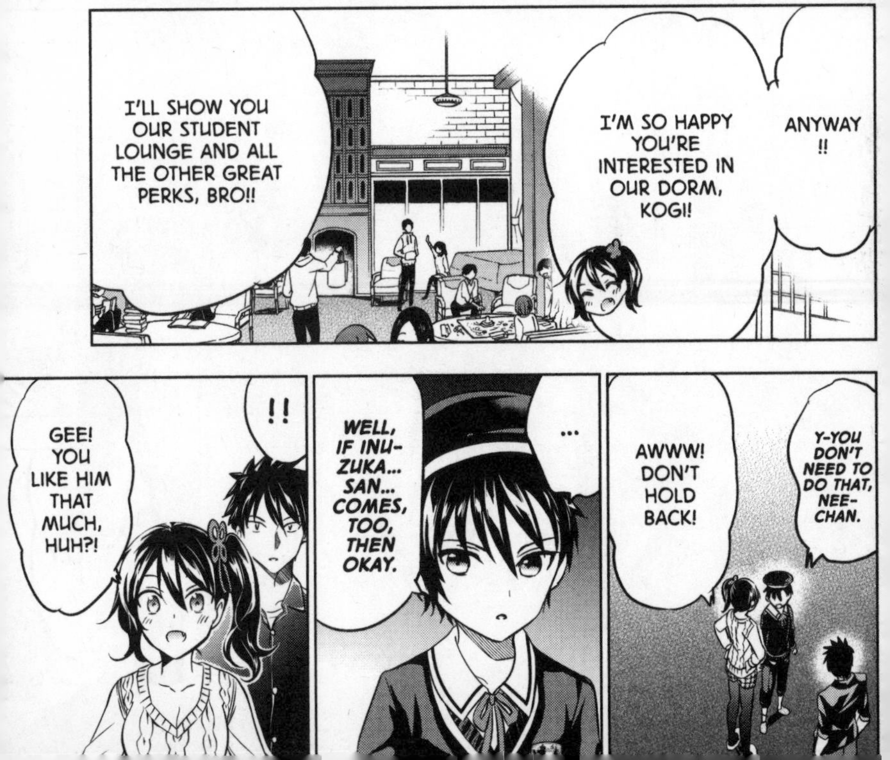
ANYWAY!!
I'M SO HAPPY YOU'RE INTERESTED IN OUR DORM, KOGI!
I'LL SHOW YOU OUR STUDENT LOUNGE AND ALL THE OTHER GREAT PERKS, BRO!!
Y-YOU DON'T NEED TO DO THAT, NEE-CHAN.
AWWW! DON'T HOLD BACK!
...
WELL, IF INUZUKA... SAN... COMES, TOO, THEN OKAY.
!!
GEE! YOU LIKE HIM THAT MUCH, HUH?!

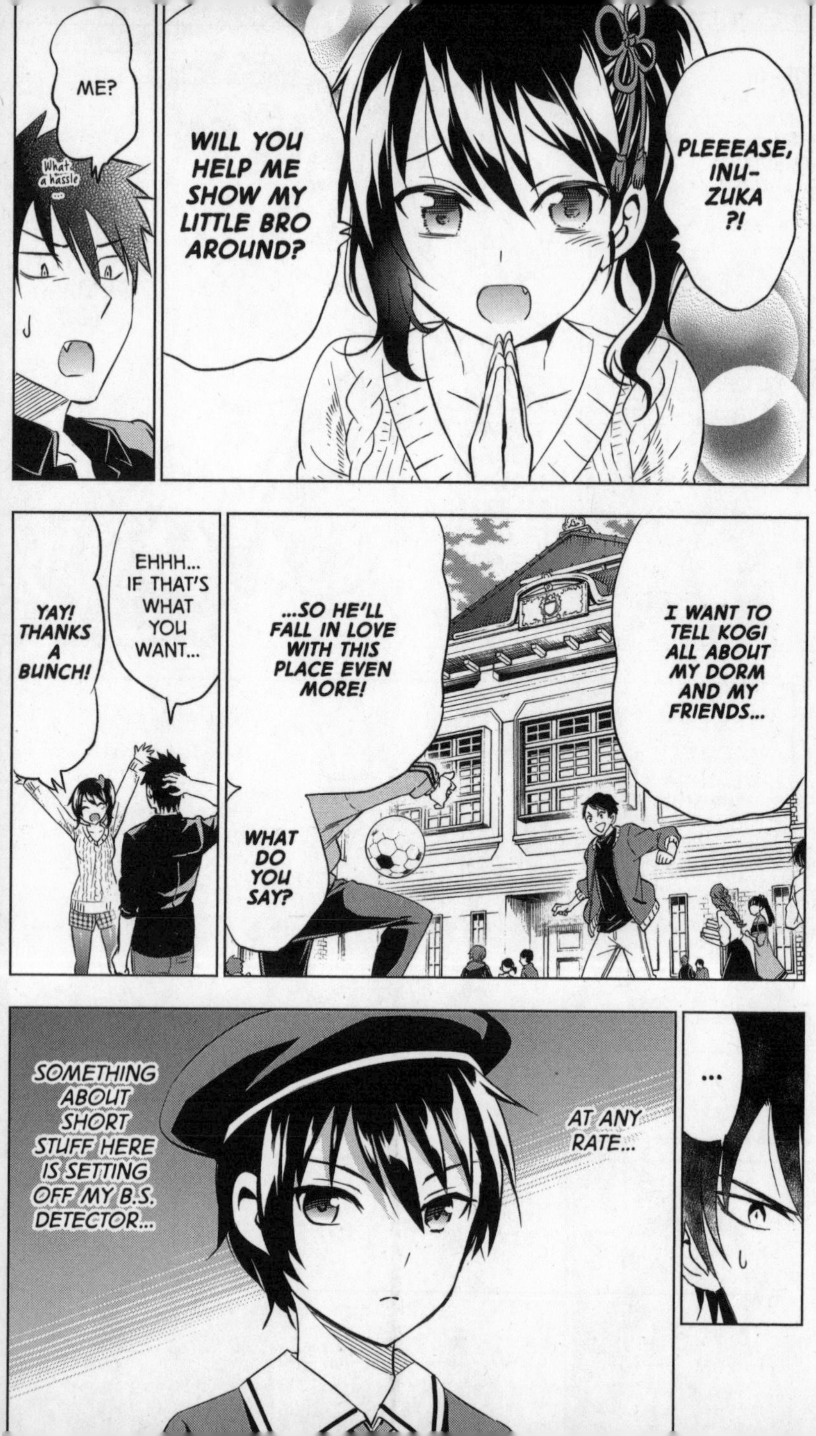
PLEEEASE, INU-ZUKA?!
WILL YOU HELP ME SHOW MY LITTLE BRO AROUND?
ME?
What a hassle...
I WANT TO TELL KOGI ALL ABOUT MY DORM AND MY FRIENDS...
...SO HE'LL FALL IN LOVE WITH THIS PLACE EVEN MORE!
WHAT DO YOU SAY?
EHHH... IF THAT'S WHAT YOU WANT...
YAY! THANKS A BUNCH!
...
AT ANY RATE...
SOMETHING ABOUT SHORT STUFF HERE IS SETTING OFF MY B.S. DETECTOR...

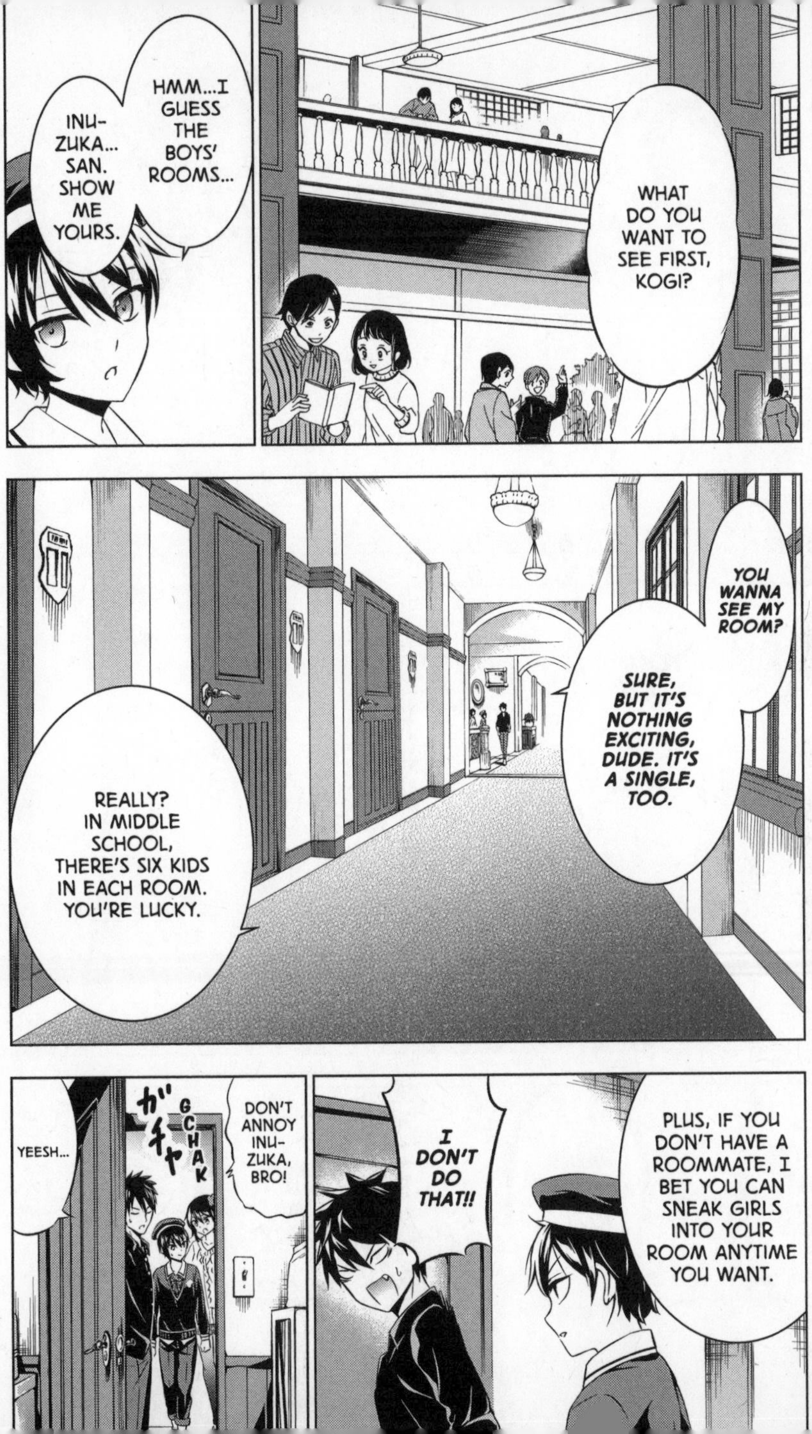
WHAT DO YOU WANT TO SEE FIRST, KOGI?
HMM...I GUESS THE BOYS' ROOMS...
INU-ZUKA... SAN. SHOW ME YOURS.
YOU WANNA SEE MY ROOM?
SURE, BUT IT'S NOTHING EXCITING, DUDE. IT'S A SINGLE, TOO.
REALLY? IN MIDDLE SCHOOL, THERE'S SIX KIDS IN EACH ROOM. YOU'RE LUCKY.
PLUS, IF YOU DON'T HAVE A ROOMMATE, I BET YOU CAN SNEAK GIRLS INTO YOUR ROOM ANYTIME YOU WANT.
I DON'T DO THAT!!
DON'T ANNOY INU-ZUKA, BRO!
ガチャ
GCHAK
YEESH...

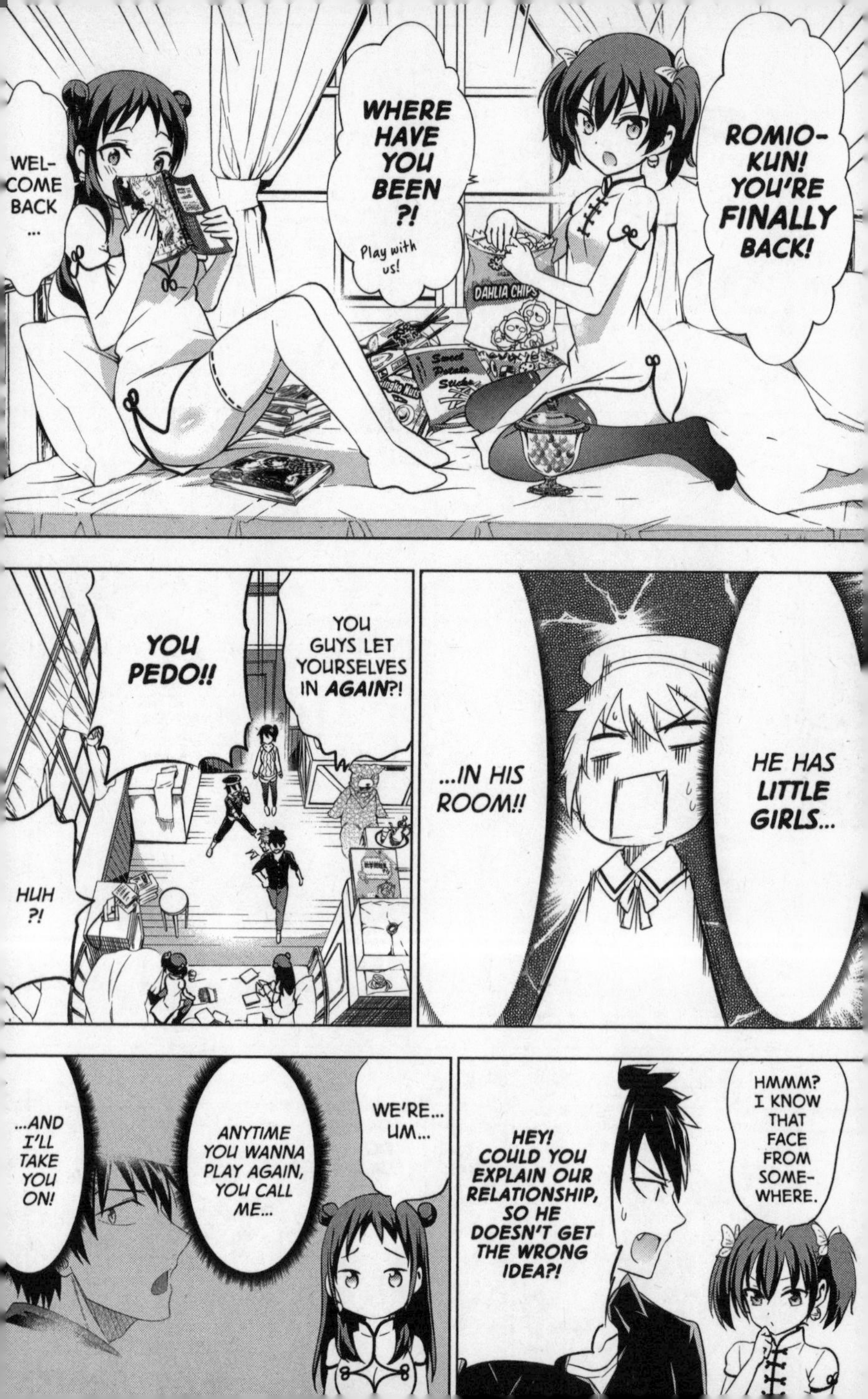
ROMIO-KUN! YOU'RE FINALLY BACK!
WHERE HAVE YOU BEEN?!
Play with us!
DAHLIA CHIPS
WEL-COME BACK ...
HE HAS LITTLE GIRLS...
...IN HIS ROOM!!
YOU GUYS LET YOURSELVES IN AGAIN?!
YOU PEDO!!
HUH?!
HMMM? I KNOW THAT FACE FROM SOME-WHERE.
HEY! COULD YOU EXPLAIN OUR RELATIONSHIP, SO HE DOESN'T GET THE WRONG IDEA?!
WE'RE... UM...
ANYTIME YOU WANNA PLAY AGAIN, YOU CALL ME...
...AND I'LL TAKE YOU ON!

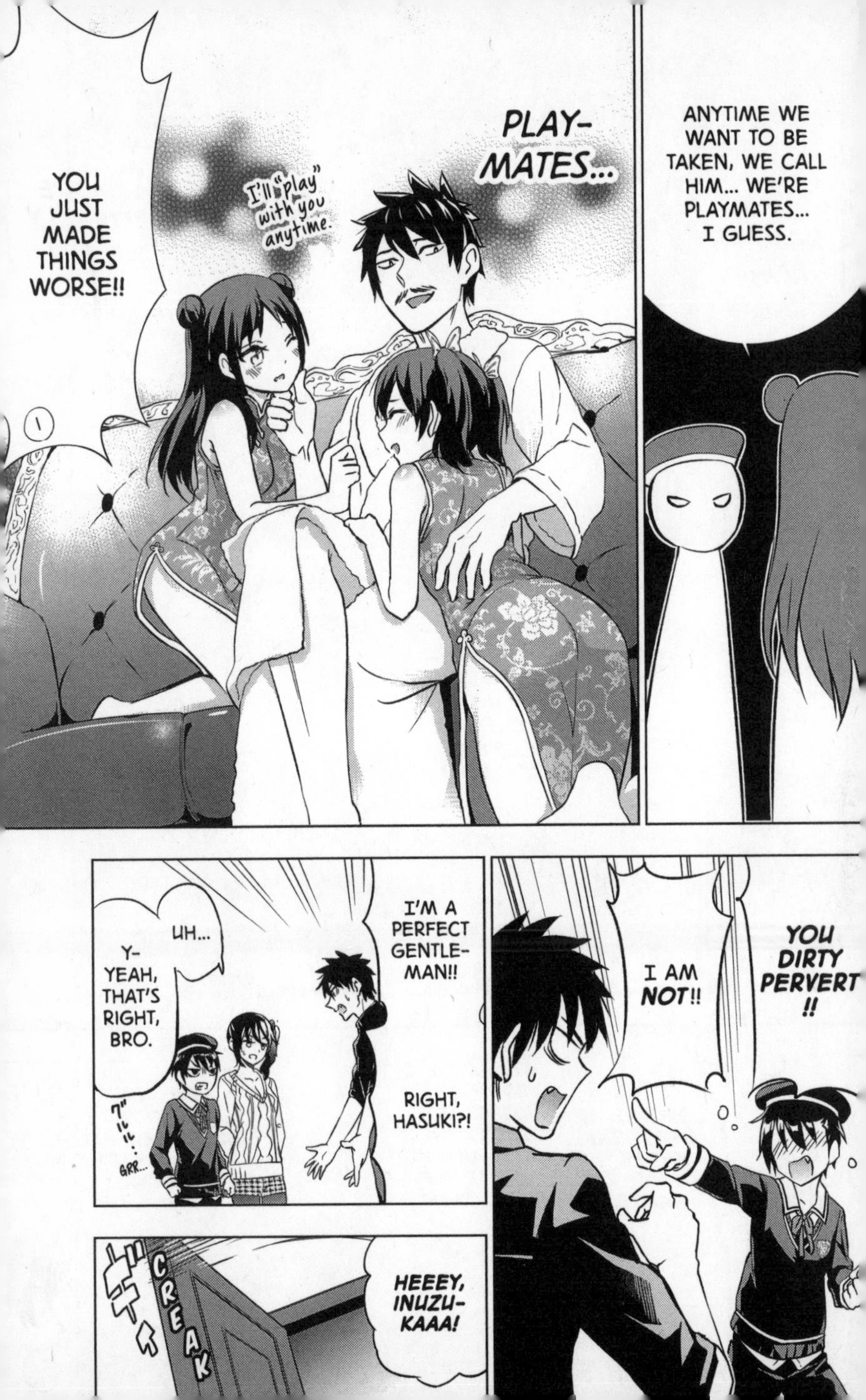
ANYTIME WE WANT TO BE TAKEN, WE CALL HIM... WE'RE PLAYMATES... I GUESS.
PLAY-MATES...
I'll "play" with you anytime.
YOU JUST MADE THINGS WORSE!!
YOU DIRTY PERVERT!!
I AM NOT!!
I'M A PERFECT GENTLE-MAN!!
RIGHT, HASUKI?!
UH...
Y-YEAH, THAT'S RIGHT, BRO.
GRR...
HEEEY, INUZU-KAAA!
CREAK

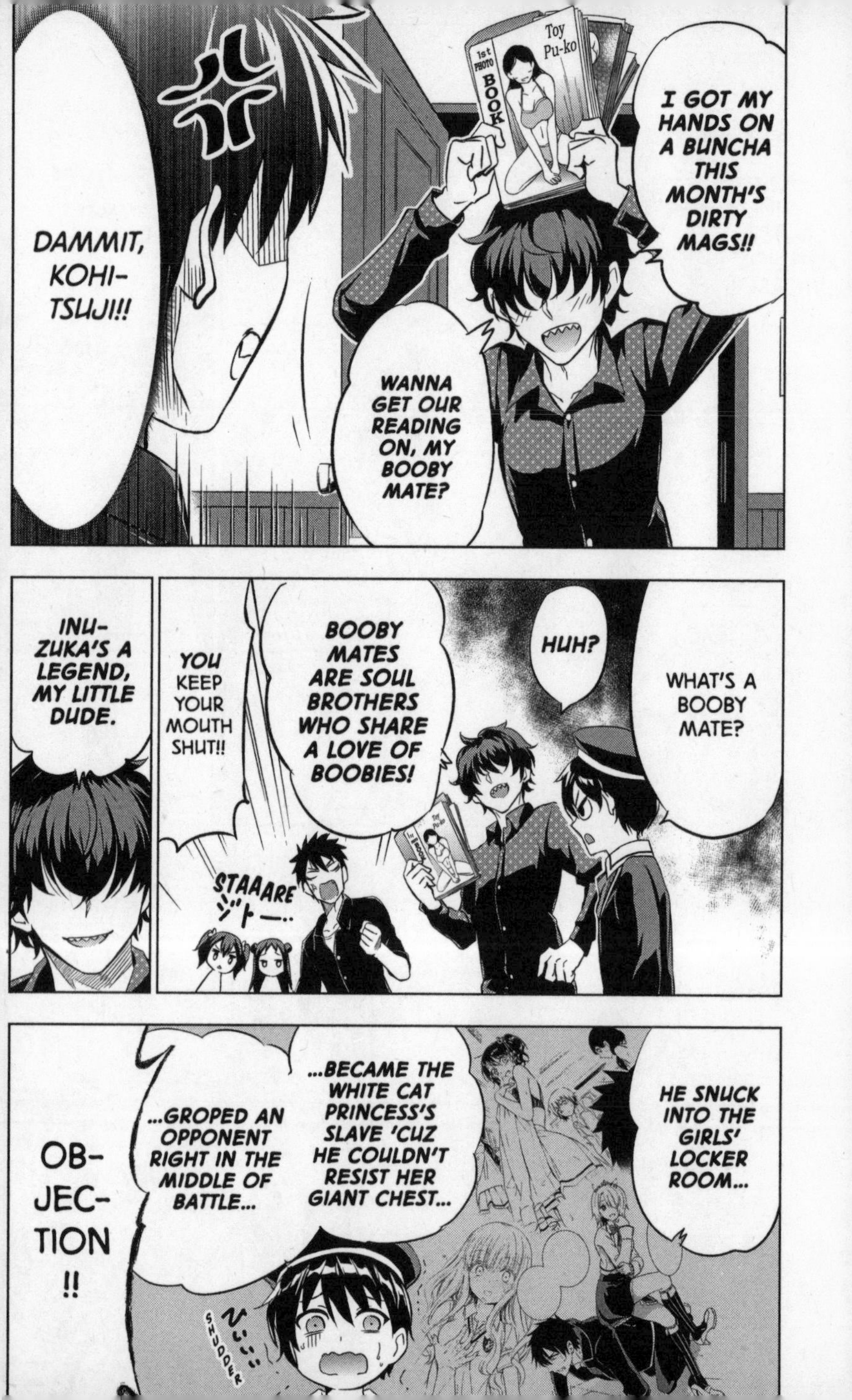
I GOT MY HANDS ON A BUNCHA THIS MONTH'S DIRTY MAGS!!
Toy Pu-ko
1st PHOTO BOOK
WANNA GET OUR READING ON, MY BOOBY MATE?
DAMMIT, KOHI-TSUJI!!
WHAT'S A BOOBY MATE?
HUH?
BOOBY MATES ARE SOUL BROTHERS WHO SHARE A LOVE OF BOOBIES!
YOU KEEP YOUR MOUTH SHUT!!
STAAARE
ジトー…
INU-ZUKA'S A LEGEND, MY LITTLE DUDE.
HE SNUCK INTO THE GIRLS' LOCKER ROOM...
...BECAME THE WHITE CAT PRINCESS'S SLAVE 'CUZ HE COULDN'T RESIST HER GIANT CHEST...
...GROPED AN OPPONENT RIGHT IN THE MIDDLE OF BATTLE...
OB-JEC-TION!!
SHUDDER

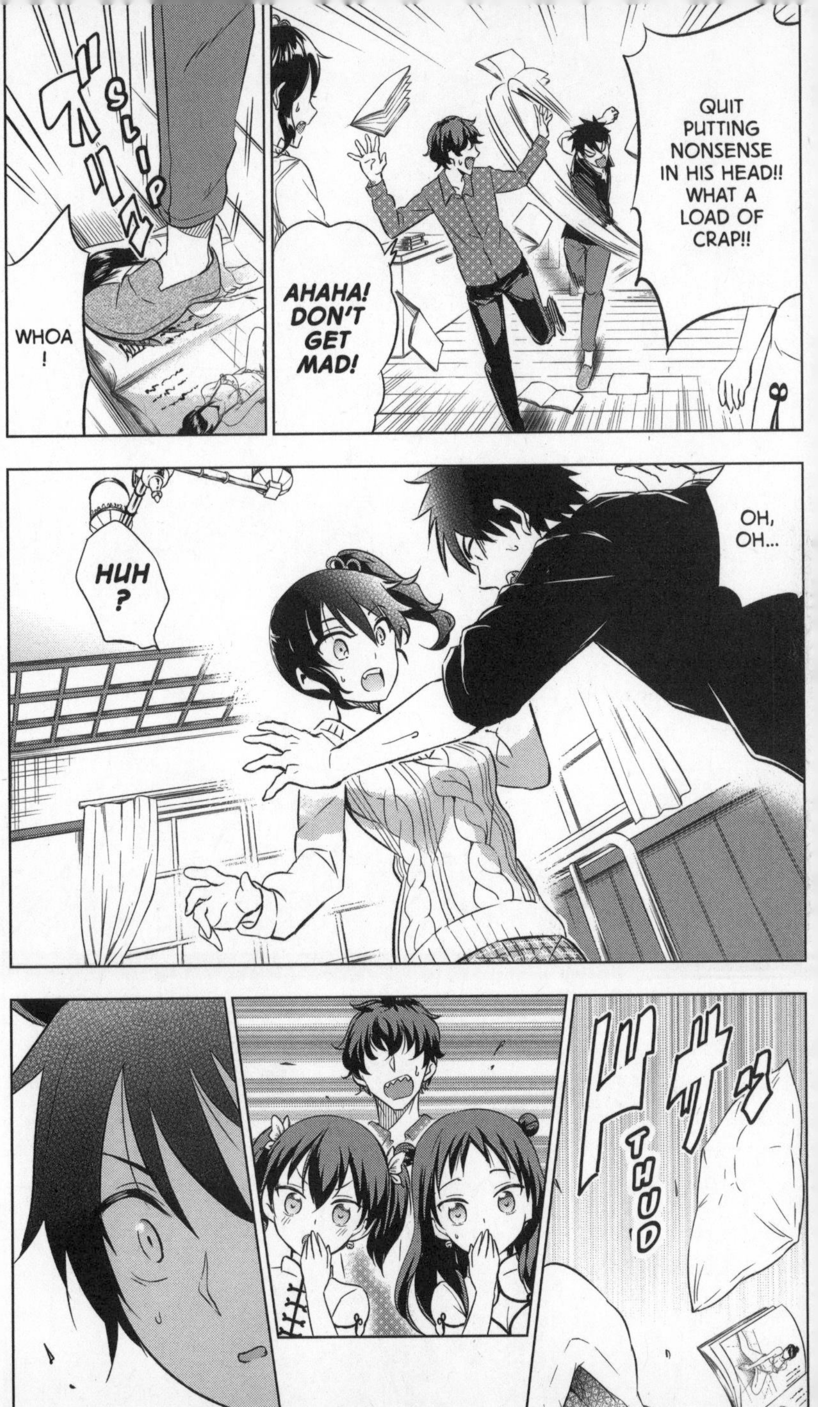
QUIT PUTTING NONSENSE IN HIS HEAD!! WHAT A LOAD OF CRAP!!
AHAHA! DON'T GET MAD!
SLIP
WHOA!
OH, OH...
HUH?
THUD

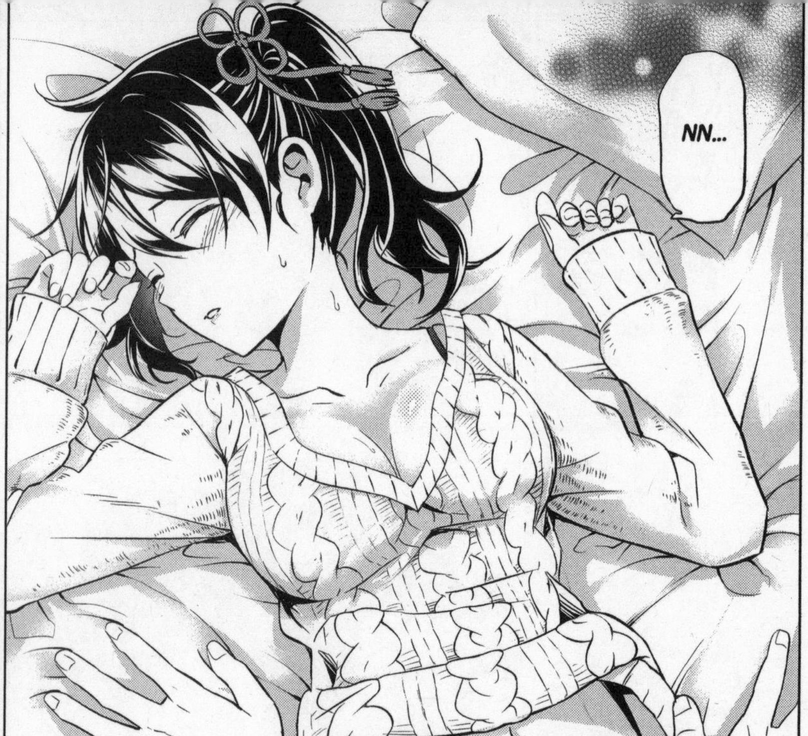
NN...

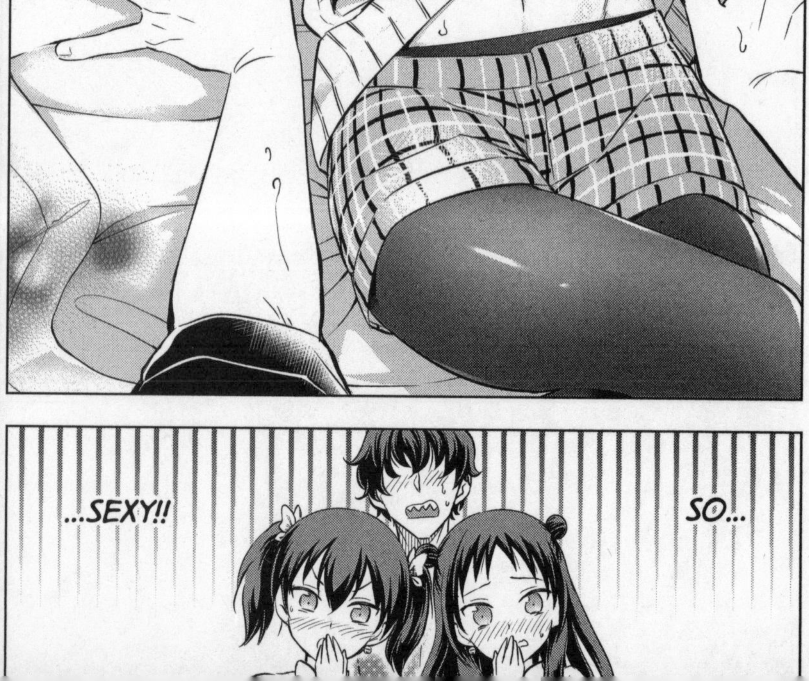
SO...
...SEXY!!

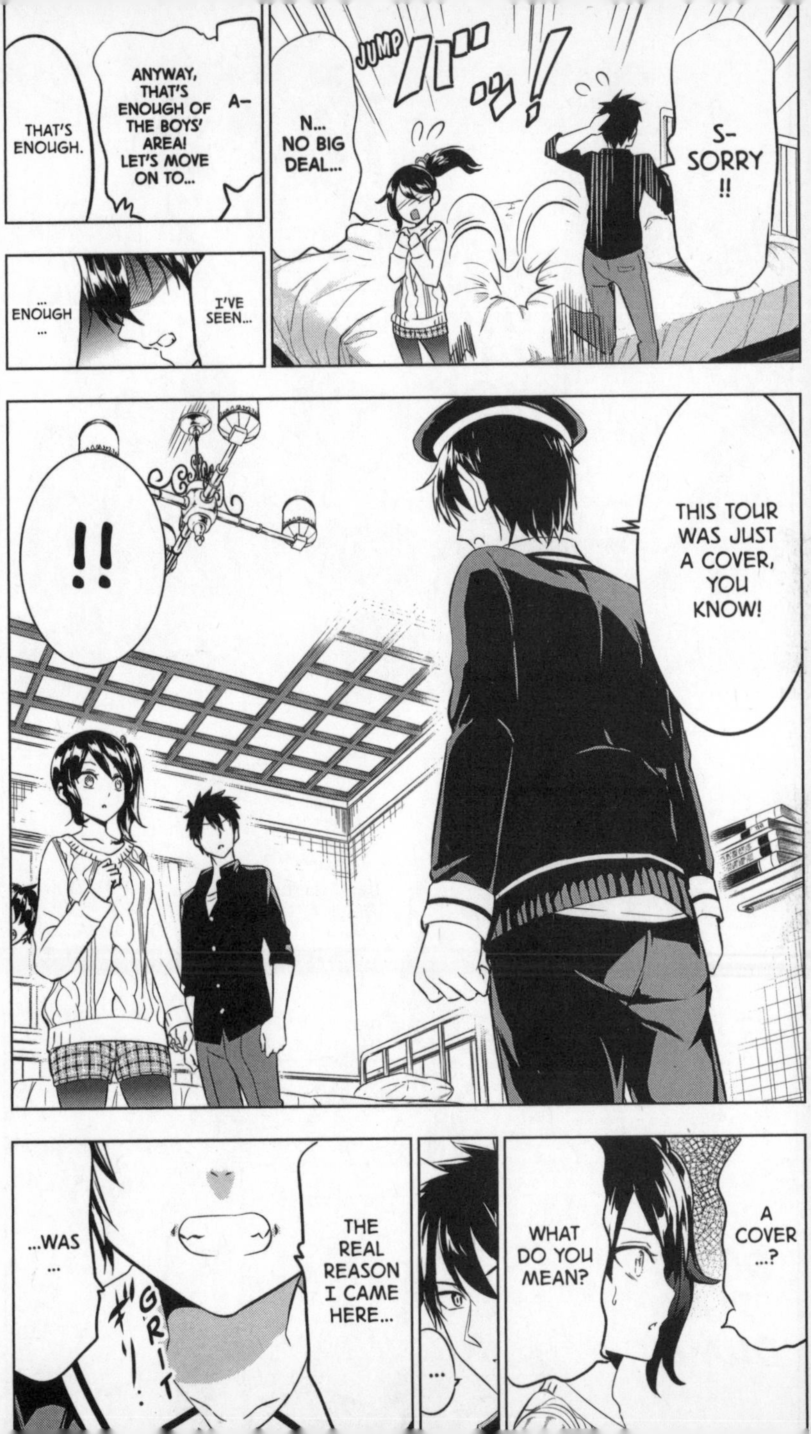
S-SORRY!!
JUMP
N... NO BIG DEAL...
A-
ANYWAY, THAT'S ENOUGH OF THE BOYS' AREA! LET'S MOVE ON TO...
THAT'S ENOUGH.
I'VE SEEN...
...ENOUGH...
THIS TOUR WAS JUST A COVER, YOU KNOW!
!!
A COVER...?
WHAT DO YOU MEAN?
...
THE REAL REASON I CAME HERE...
...WAS...
GRIT

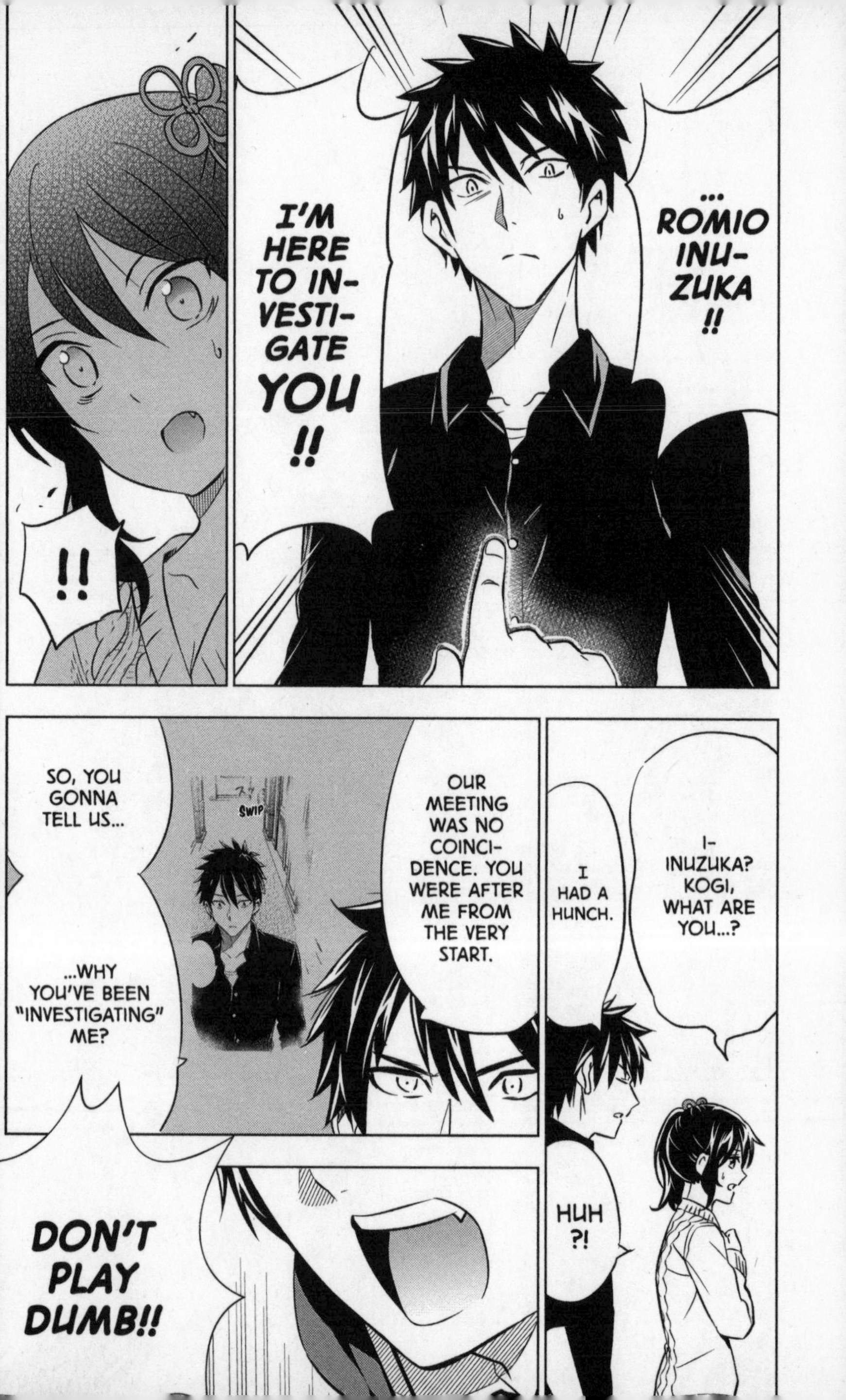
...ROMIO INUZUKA!!
I'M HERE TO INVESTIGATE YOU!!
!!
I-INUZUKA? KOGI, WHAT ARE YOU...?
I HAD A HUNCH.
OUR MEETING WAS NO COINCIDENCE. YOU WERE AFTER ME FROM THE VERY START.
SO, YOU GONNA TELL US...
SWIP
...WHY YOU'VE BEEN "INVESTIGATING" ME?
HUH?!
DON'T PLAY DUMB!!

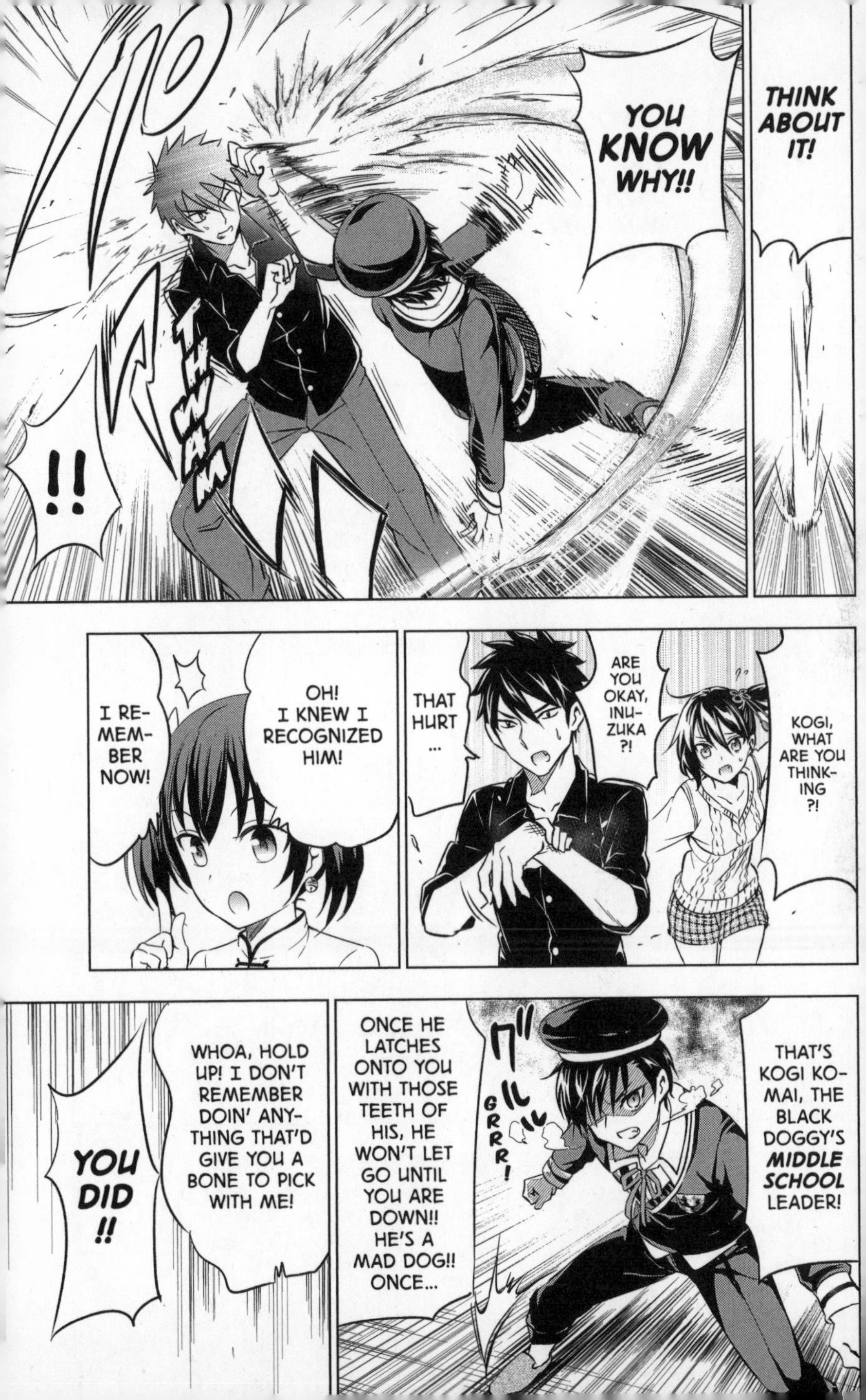
THINK ABOUT IT!
YOU KNOW WHY!!
THWAM
!!
KOGI, WHAT ARE YOU THINKING?!
ARE YOU OKAY, INUZUKA?!
THAT HURT ...
OH! I KNEW I RECOGNIZED HIM!
I REMEMBER NOW!
THAT'S KOGI KOMAI, THE BLACK DOGGY'S MIDDLE SCHOOL LEADER!
GRRR!
ONCE HE LATCHES ONTO YOU WITH THOSE TEETH OF HIS, HE WON'T LET GO UNTIL YOU ARE DOWN!! HE'S A MAD DOG!! ONCE...
WHOA, HOLD UP! I DON'T REMEMBER DOIN' ANYTHING THAT'D GIVE YOU A BONE TO PICK WITH ME!
YOU DID!!

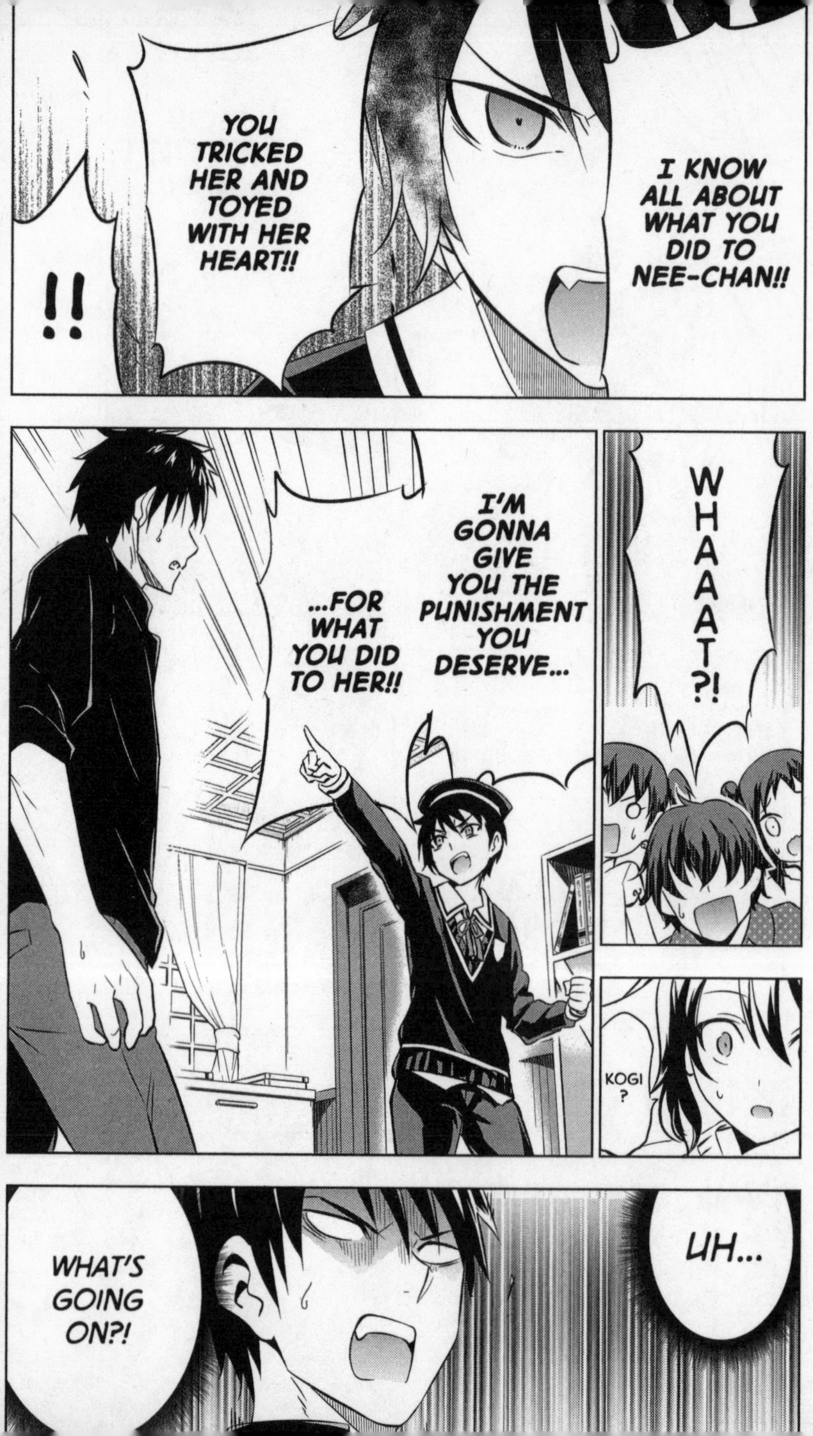

I KNOW ALL ABOUT WHAT YOU DID TO NEE-CHAN!!
YOU TRICKED HER AND TOYED WITH HER HEART!!
!!
WHAAAT?!
KOGI?
I'M GONNA GIVE YOU THE PUNISHMENT YOU DESERVE...
...FOR WHAT YOU DID TO HER!!
UH...
WHAT'S GOING ON?!

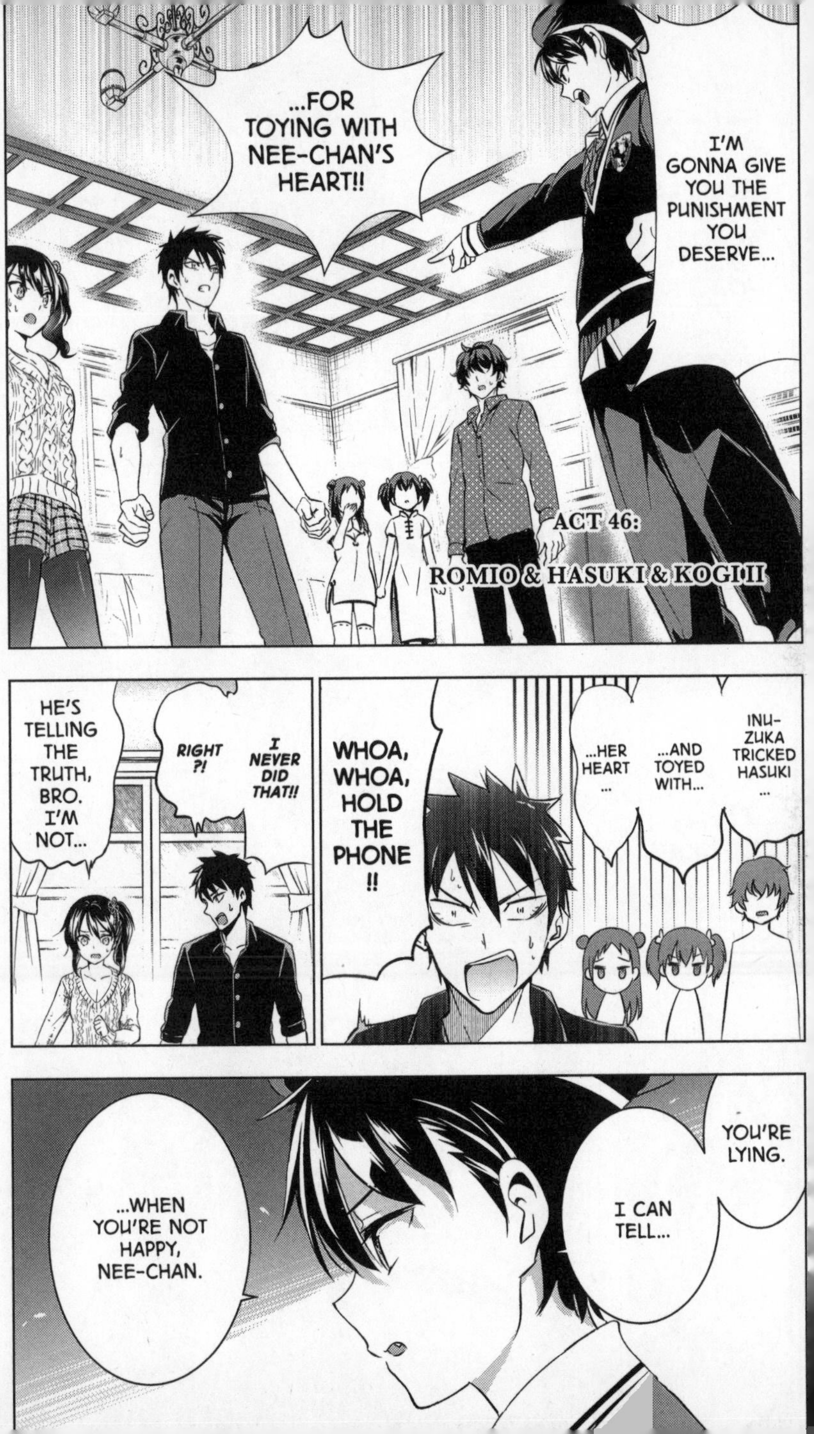
I'M GONNA GIVE YOU THE PUNISHMENT YOU DESERVE...
...FOR TOYING WITH NEE-CHAN'S HEART!!
ACT 46:
ROMIO & HASUKI & KOGI II
INU-ZUKA TRICKED HASUKI ...
...AND TOYED WITH...
...HER HEART ...
WHOA, WHOA, HOLD THE PHONE !!
I NEVER DID THAT!!
RIGHT ?!
HE'S TELLING THE TRUTH, BRO. I'M NOT...
YOU'RE LYING.
I CAN TELL...
...WHEN YOU'RE NOT HAPPY, NEE-CHAN.

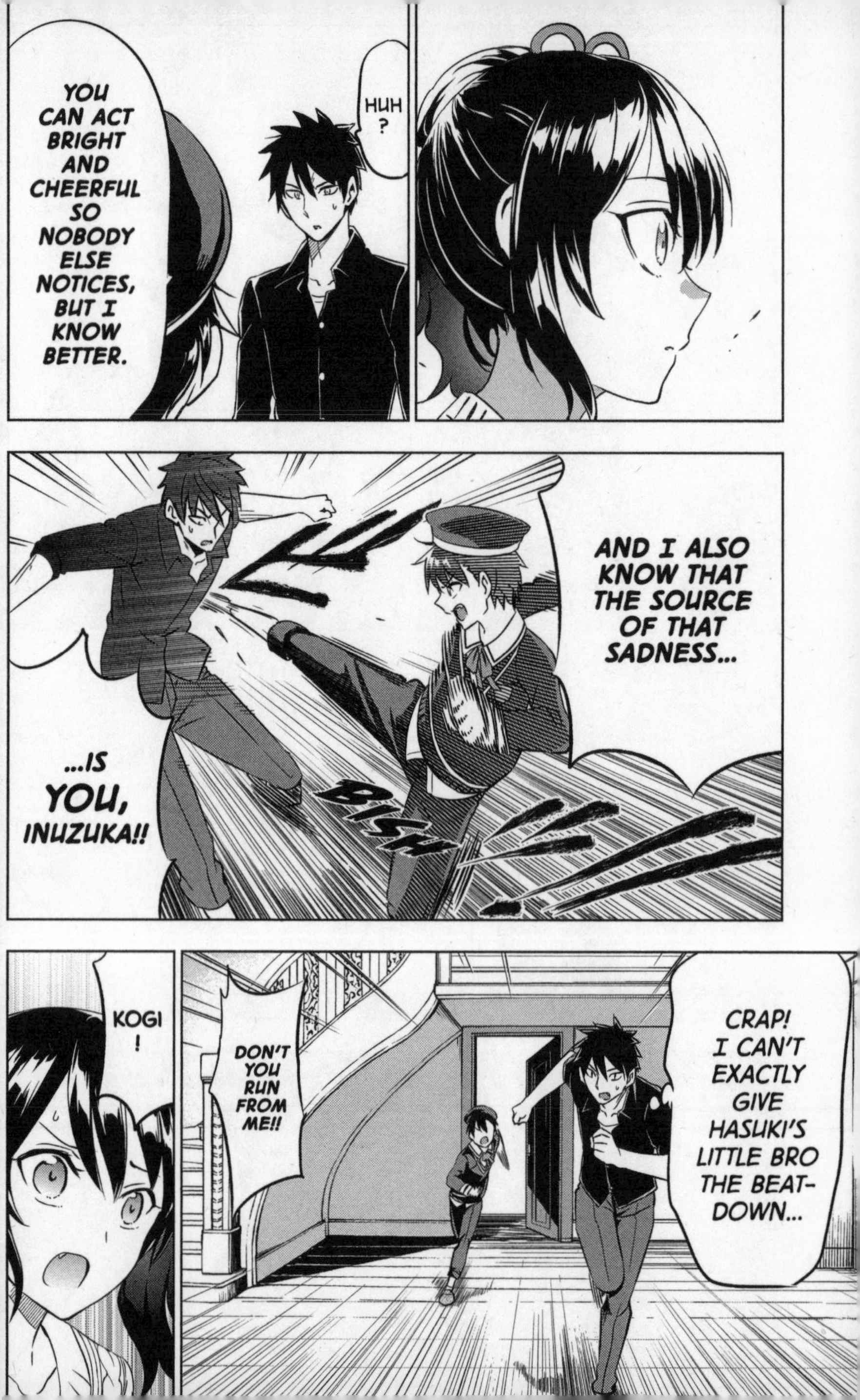
HUH?
YOU CAN ACT BRIGHT AND CHEERFUL SO NOBODY ELSE NOTICES, BUT I KNOW BETTER.
AND I ALSO KNOW THAT THE SOURCE OF THAT SADNESS...
...IS YOU, INUZUKA!!
BISH
CRAP! I CAN'T EXACTLY GIVE HASUKI'S LITTLE BRO THE BEAT-DOWN...
DON'T YOU RUN FROM ME!!
KOGI!

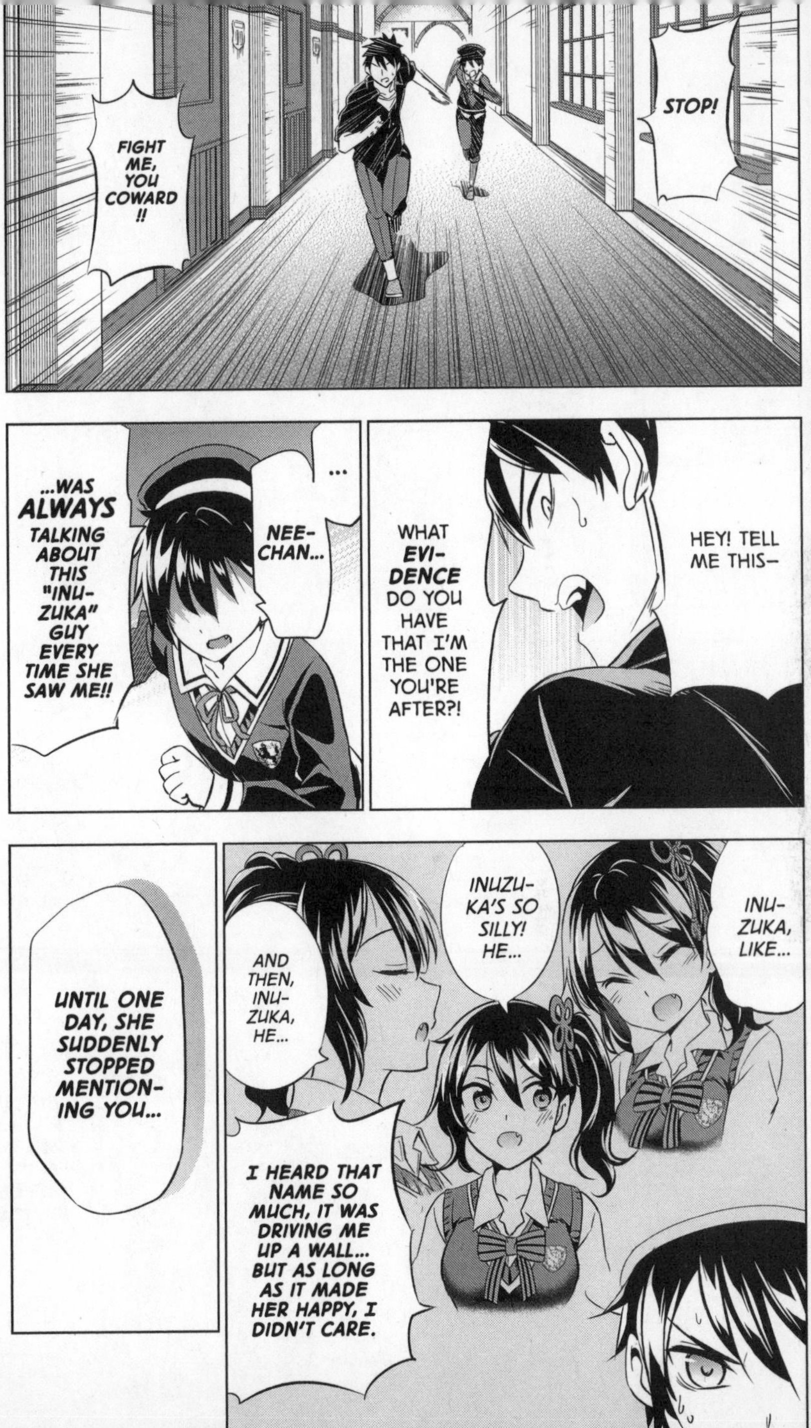
STOP!
FIGHT ME, YOU COWARD!!
HEY! TELL ME THIS—
WHAT EVI-DENCE DO YOU HAVE THAT I'M THE ONE YOU'RE AFTER?!
...
NEE-CHAN...
...WAS ALWAYS TALKING ABOUT THIS "INU-ZUKA" GUY EVERY TIME SHE SAW ME!!
INU-ZUKA, LIKE...
INUZU-KA'S SO SILLY! HE...
AND THEN, INU-ZUKA, HE...
I HEARD THAT NAME SO MUCH, IT WAS DRIVING ME UP A WALL... BUT AS LONG AS IT MADE HER HAPPY, I DIDN'T CARE.
UNTIL ONE DAY, SHE SUDDENLY STOPPED MENTION-ING YOU...

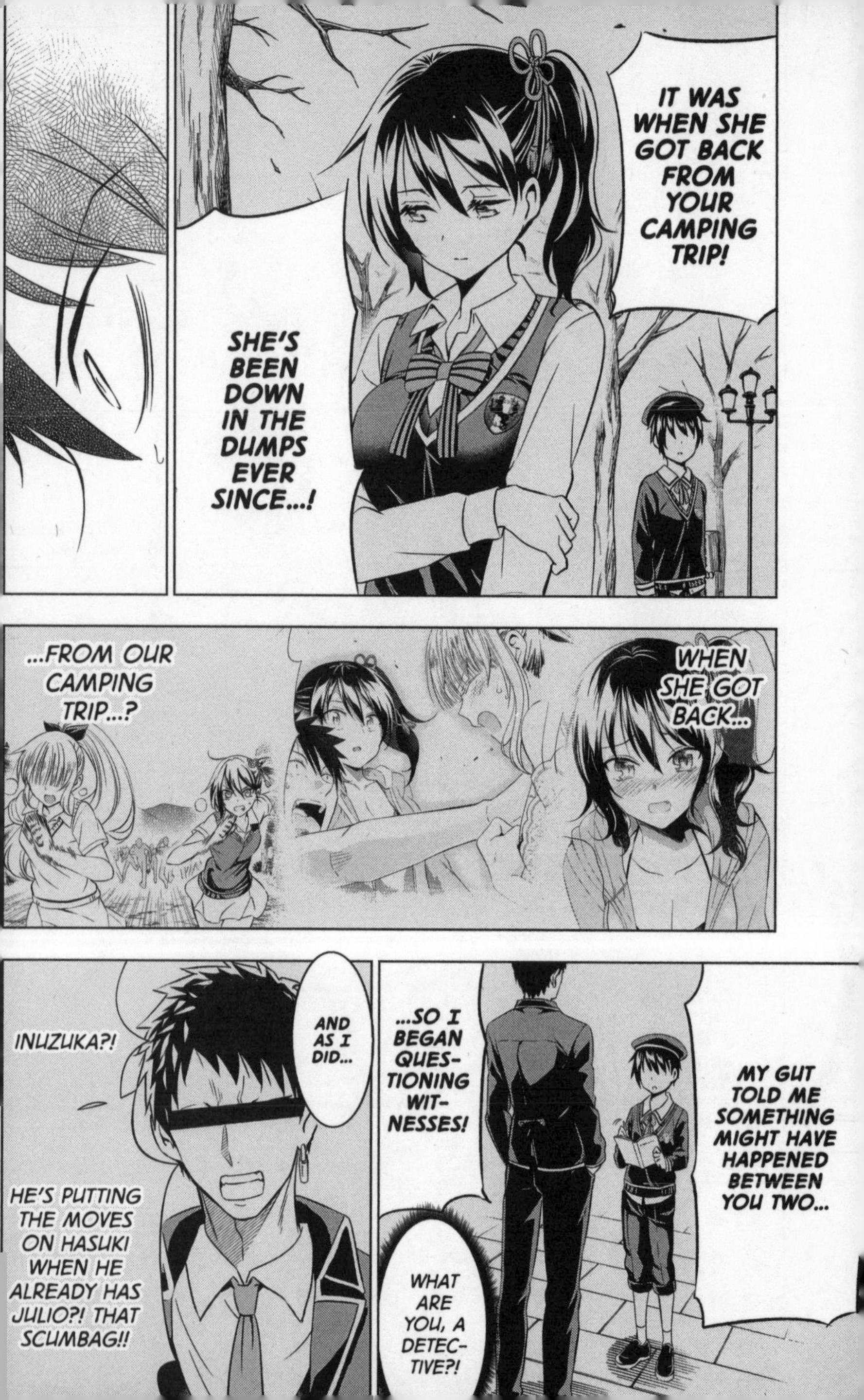
IT WAS WHEN SHE GOT BACK FROM YOUR CAMPING TRIP!
SHE'S BEEN DOWN IN THE DUMPS EVER SINCE...!
WHEN SHE GOT BACK...
...FROM OUR CAMPING TRIP...?
MY GUT TOLD ME SOMETHING MIGHT HAVE HAPPENED BETWEEN YOU TWO...
...SO I BEGAN QUESTIONING WITNESSES!
WHAT ARE YOU, A DETECTIVE?!
AND AS I DID...
INUZUKA?!
HE'S PUTTING THE MOVES ON HASUKI WHEN HE ALREADY HAS JULIO?! THAT SCUMBAG!!

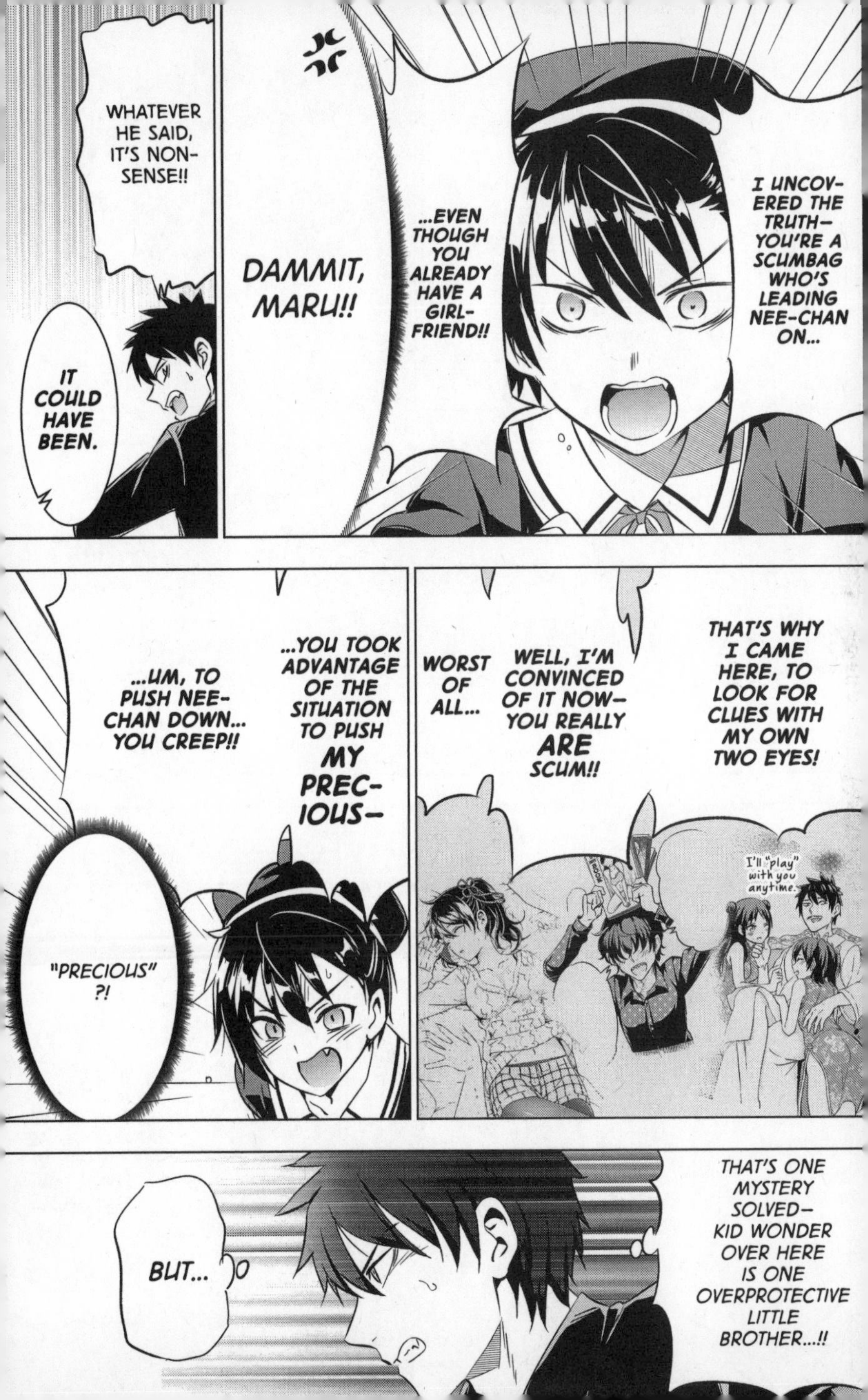
I UNCOVERED THE TRUTH— YOU'RE A SCUMBAG WHO'S LEADING NEE-CHAN ON...
...EVEN THOUGH YOU ALREADY HAVE A GIRLFRIEND!!
DAMMIT, MARU!!
WHATEVER HE SAID, IT'S NONSENSE!!
IT COULD HAVE BEEN.
THAT'S WHY I CAME HERE, TO LOOK FOR CLUES WITH MY OWN TWO EYES!
WELL, I'M CONVINCED OF IT NOW— YOU REALLY ARE SCUM!!
WORST OF ALL...
I'll "play" with you anytime.
...YOU TOOK ADVANTAGE OF THE SITUATION TO PUSH MY PRECIOUS—
...UM, TO PUSH NEE-CHAN DOWN... YOU CREEP!!
"PRECIOUS"?!
THAT'S ONE MYSTERY SOLVED— KID WONDER OVER HERE IS ONE OVERPROTECTIVE LITTLE BROTHER...!!
BUT...

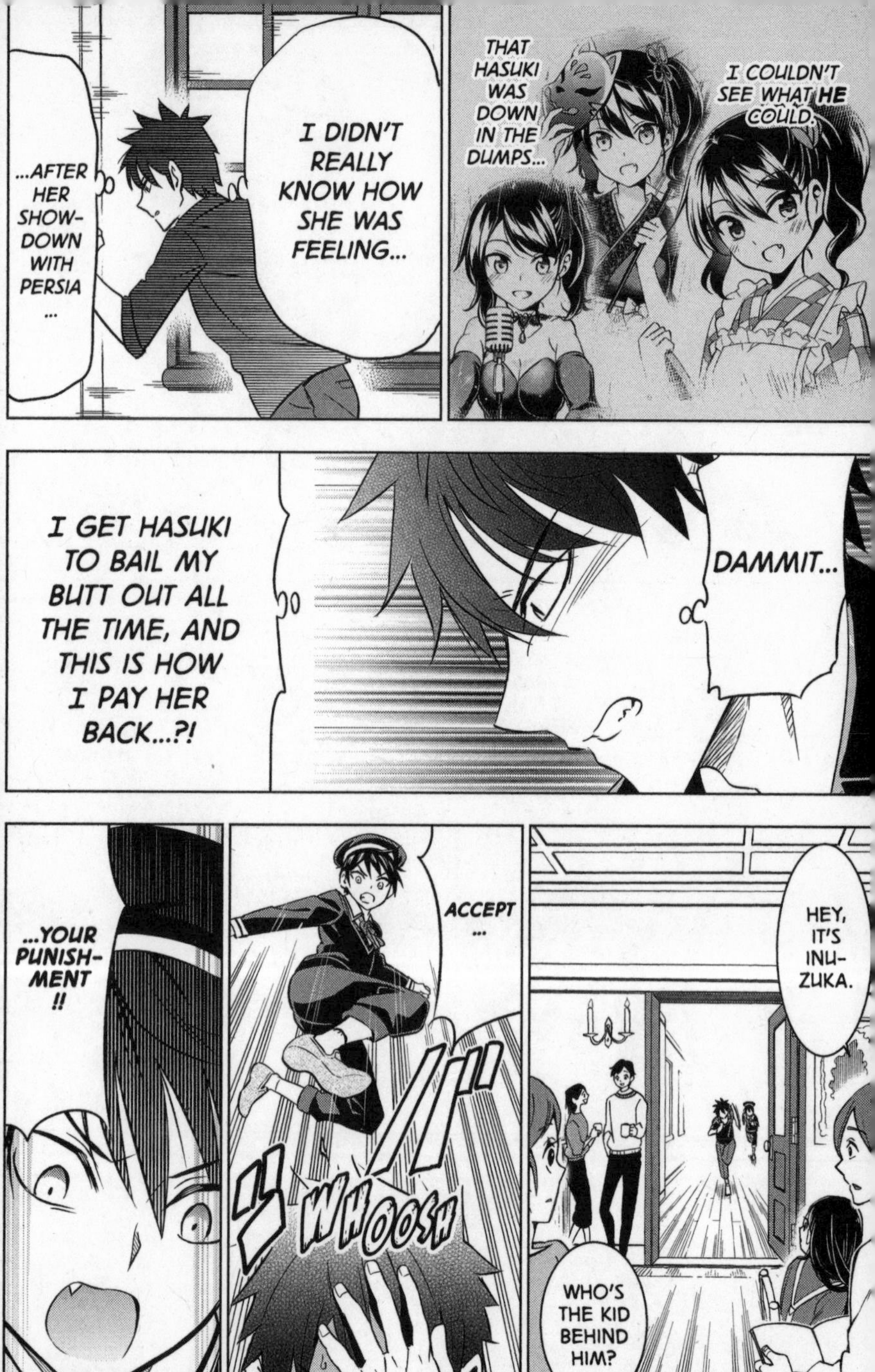
I COULDN'T SEE WHAT HE COULD.
THAT HASUKI WAS DOWN IN THE DUMPS...
I DIDN'T REALLY KNOW HOW SHE WAS FEELING...
...AFTER HER SHOWDOWN WITH PERSIA...
DAMMIT...
I GET HASUKI TO BAIL MY BUTT OUT ALL THE TIME, AND THIS IS HOW I PAY HER BACK...?!
HEY, IT'S INUZUKA.
WHO'S THE KID BEHIND HIM?
ACCEPT...
WHOOSH
...YOUR PUNISHMENT!!

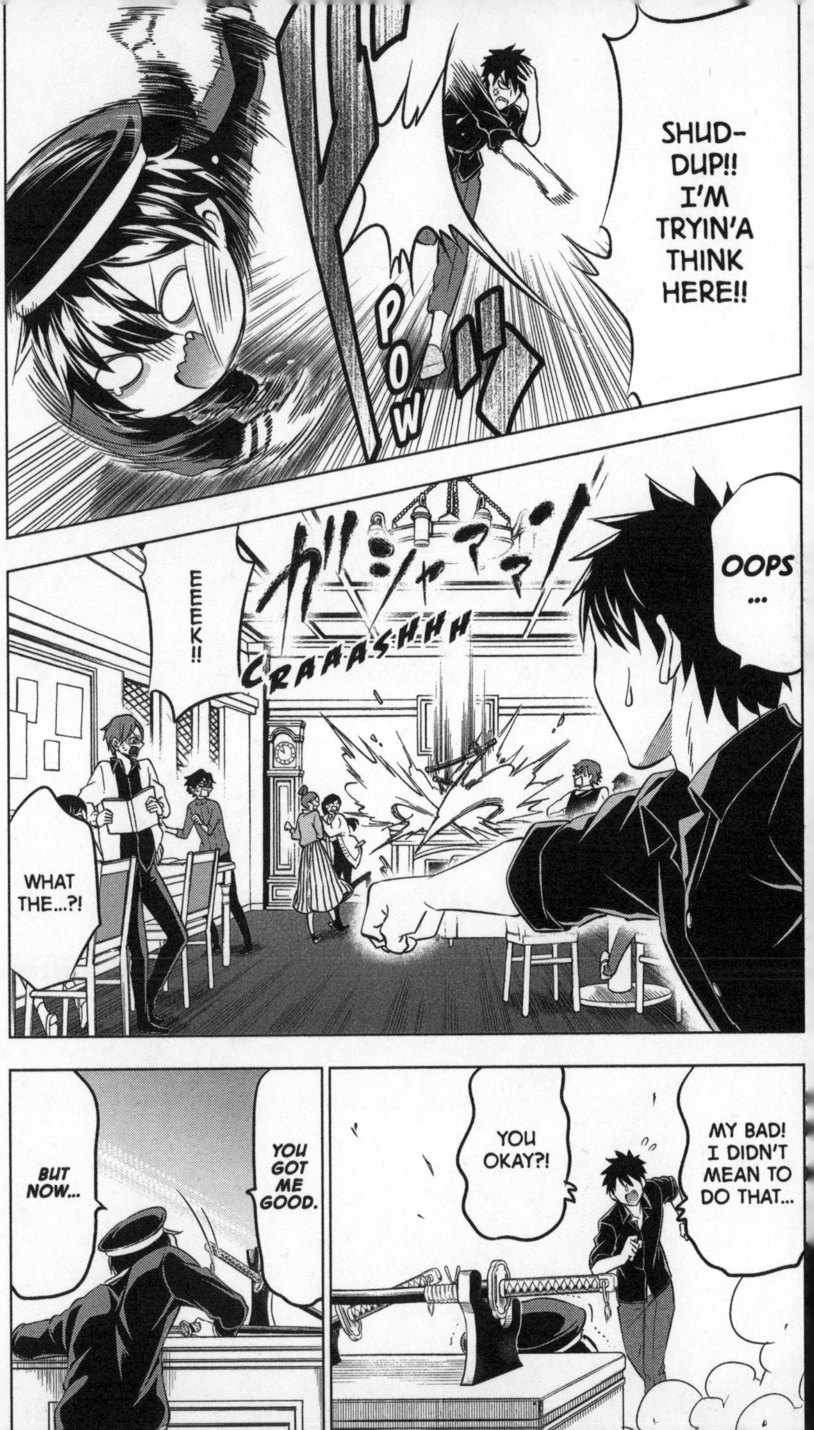
SHUD-DUP!! I'M TRYIN'A THINK HERE!!
POW
OOPS...
CRAAASHHH
EEEK!!
WHAT THE...?!
MY BAD! I DIDN'T MEAN TO DO THAT...
YOU OKAY?!
YOU GOT ME GOOD.
BUT NOW...

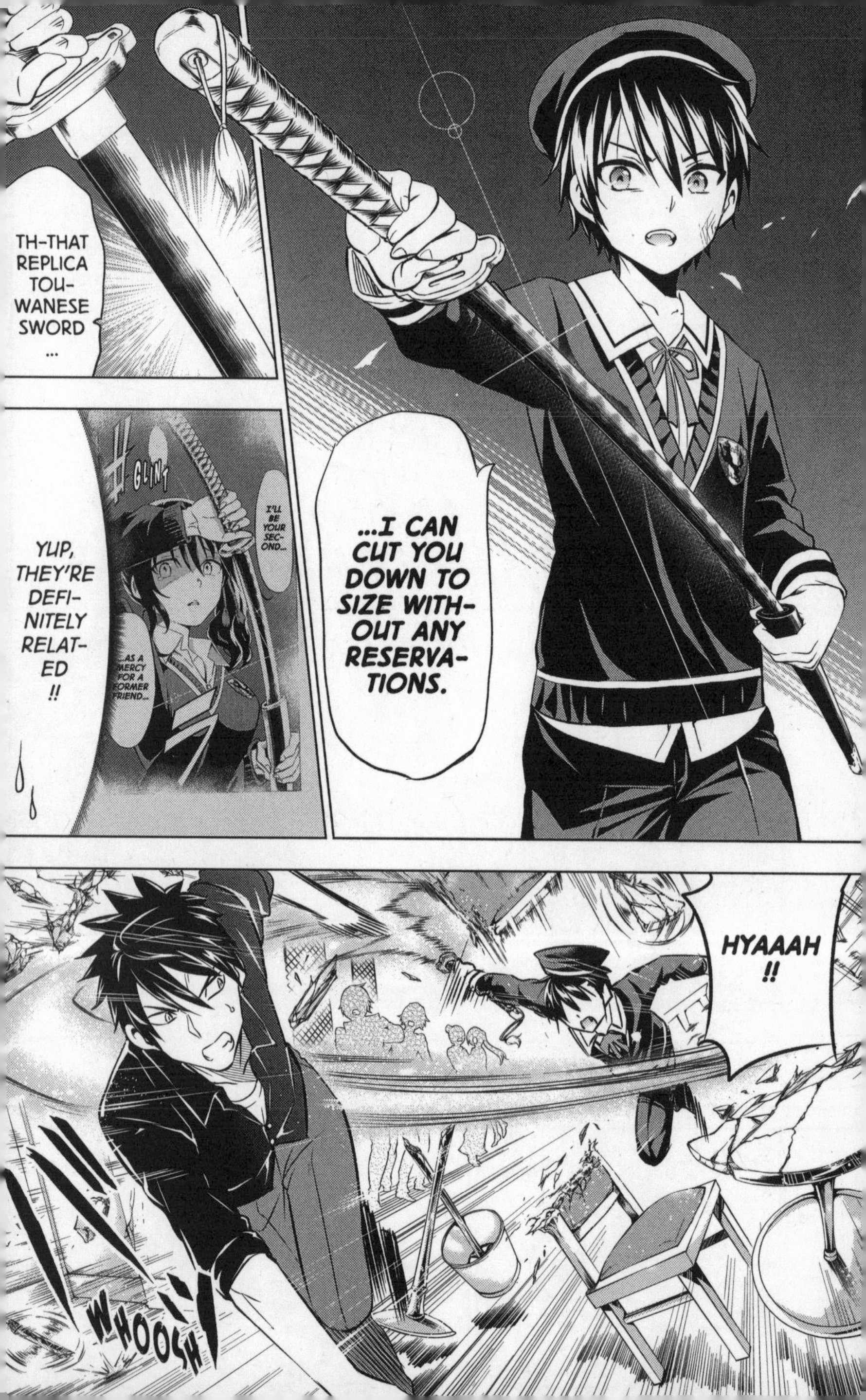

...I CAN CUT YOU DOWN TO SIZE WITHOUT ANY RESERVATIONS.
TH-THAT REPLICA TOUWANESE SWORD ...
GLINT
I'LL BE YOUR SECOND...
...AS A MERCY FOR A FORMER FRIEND...
YUP, THEY'RE DEFINITELY RELATED !!
HYAAAH !!
WHOOSH

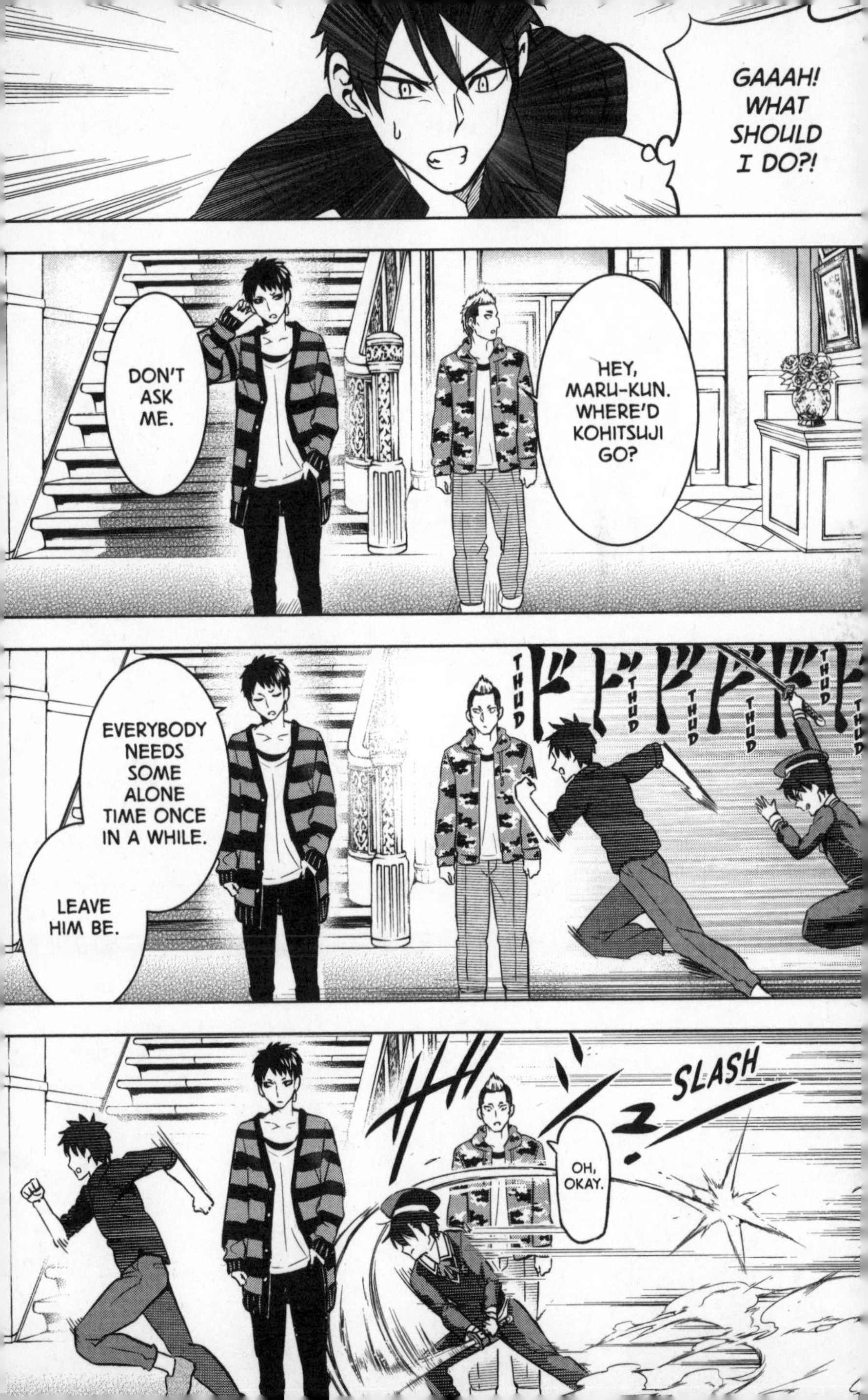
GAAAH! WHAT SHOULD I DO?!
HEY, MARU-KUN. WHERE'D KOHITSUJI GO?
DON'T ASK ME.
THUD THUD THUD THUD THUD THUD THUD
EVERYBODY NEEDS SOME ALONE TIME ONCE IN A WHILE.
LEAVE HIM BE.
SLASH
OH, OKAY.

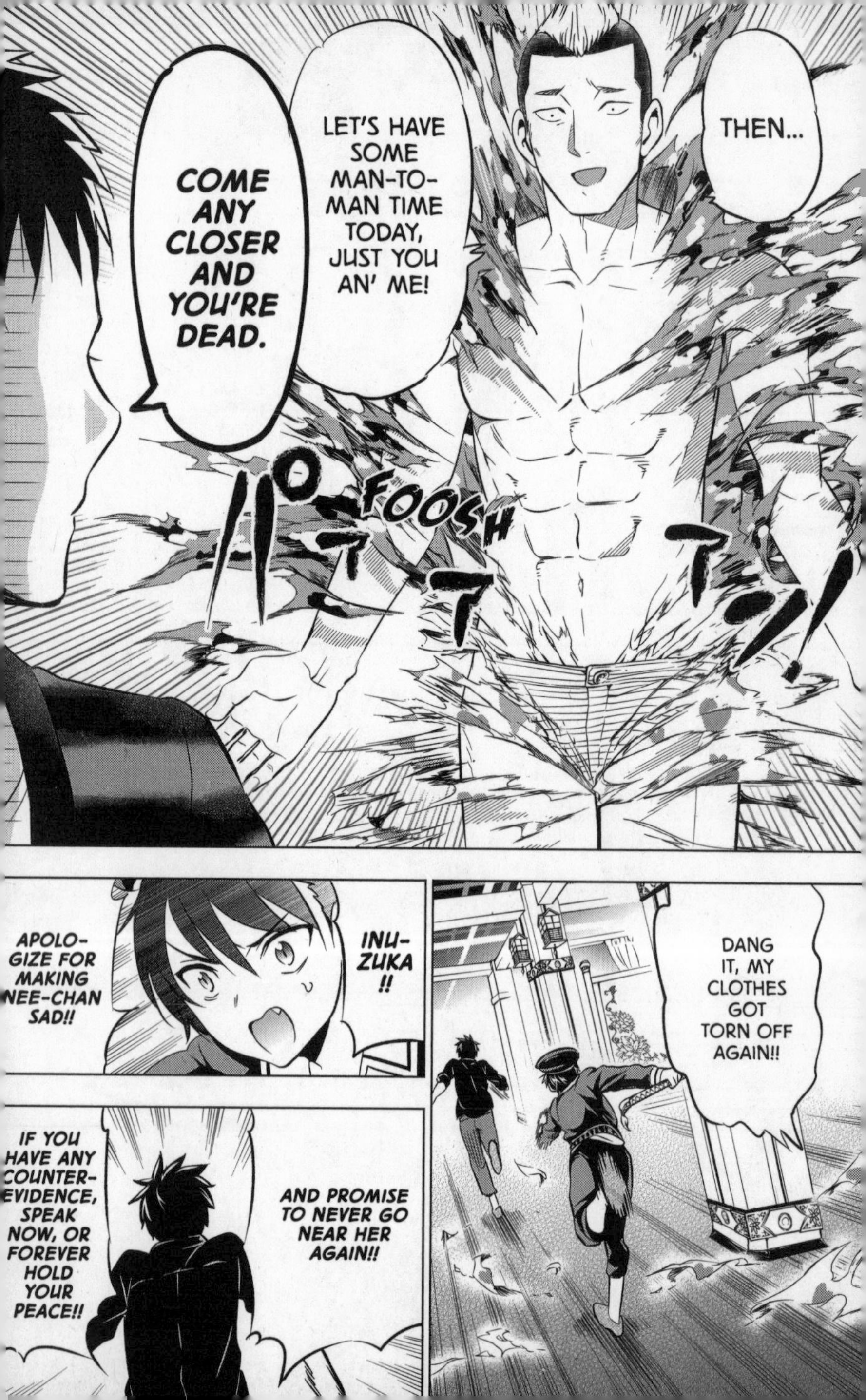
THEN...
LET'S HAVE SOME MAN-TO-MAN TIME TODAY, JUST YOU AN' ME!
COME ANY CLOSER AND YOU'RE DEAD.
FOOSH
DANG IT, MY CLOTHES GOT TORN OFF AGAIN!!
INU-ZUKA!!
APOLO-GIZE FOR MAKING NEE-CHAN SAD!!
AND PROMISE TO NEVER GO NEAR HER AGAIN!!
IF YOU HAVE ANY COUNTER-EVIDENCE, SPEAK NOW, OR FOREVER HOLD YOUR PEACE!!

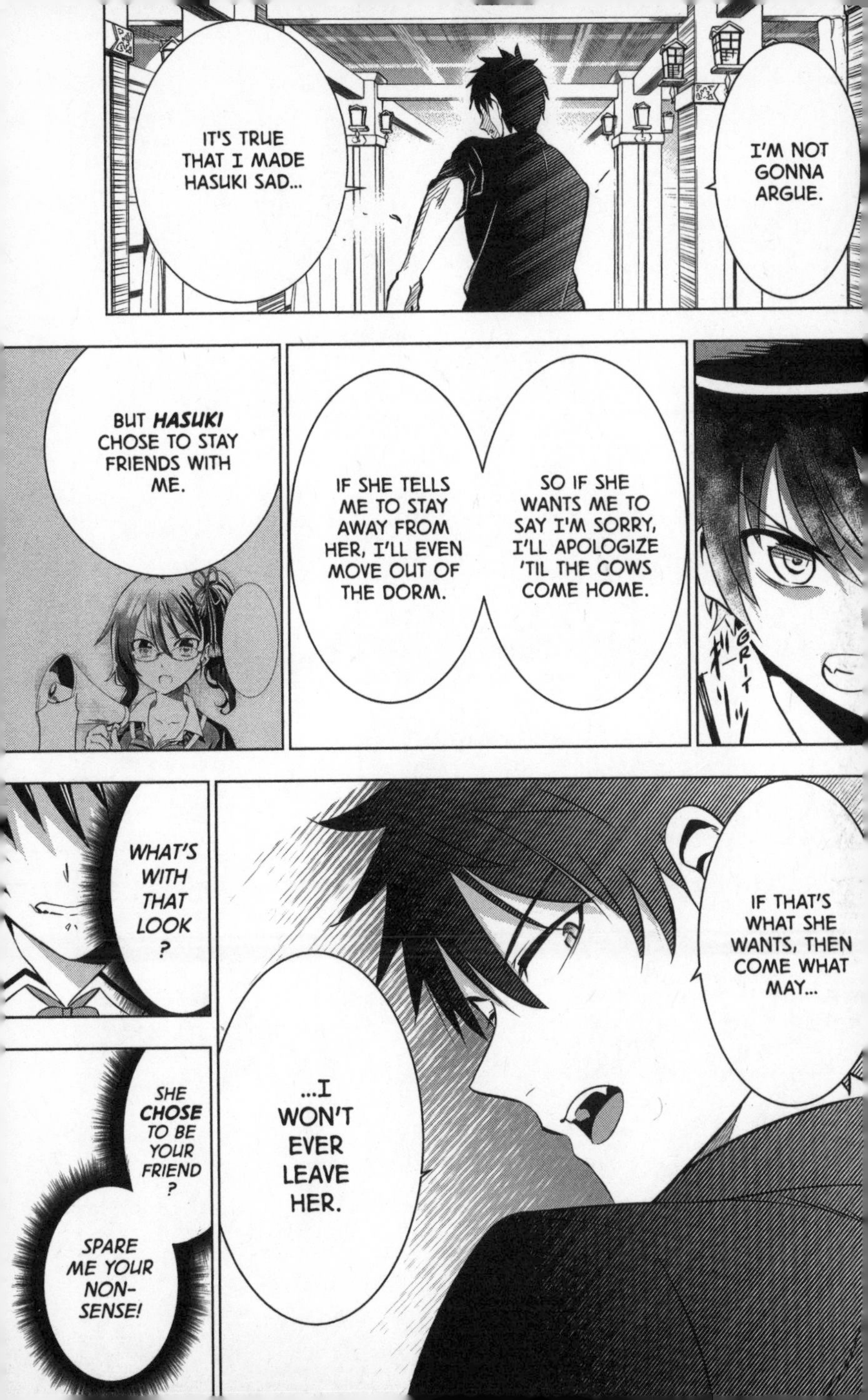
I'M NOT GONNA ARGUE.
IT'S TRUE THAT I MADE HASUKI SAD...
GRIT
SO IF SHE WANTS ME TO SAY I'M SORRY, I'LL APOLOGIZE 'TIL THE COWS COME HOME.
IF SHE TELLS ME TO STAY AWAY FROM HER, I'LL EVEN MOVE OUT OF THE DORM.
BUT **HASUKI** CHOSE TO STAY FRIENDS WITH ME.
IF THAT'S WHAT SHE WANTS, THEN COME WHAT MAY...
...I WON'T EVER LEAVE HER.
WHAT'S WITH THAT LOOK?
*SHE **CHOSE** TO BE YOUR FRIEND?*
SPARE ME YOUR NON-SENSE!

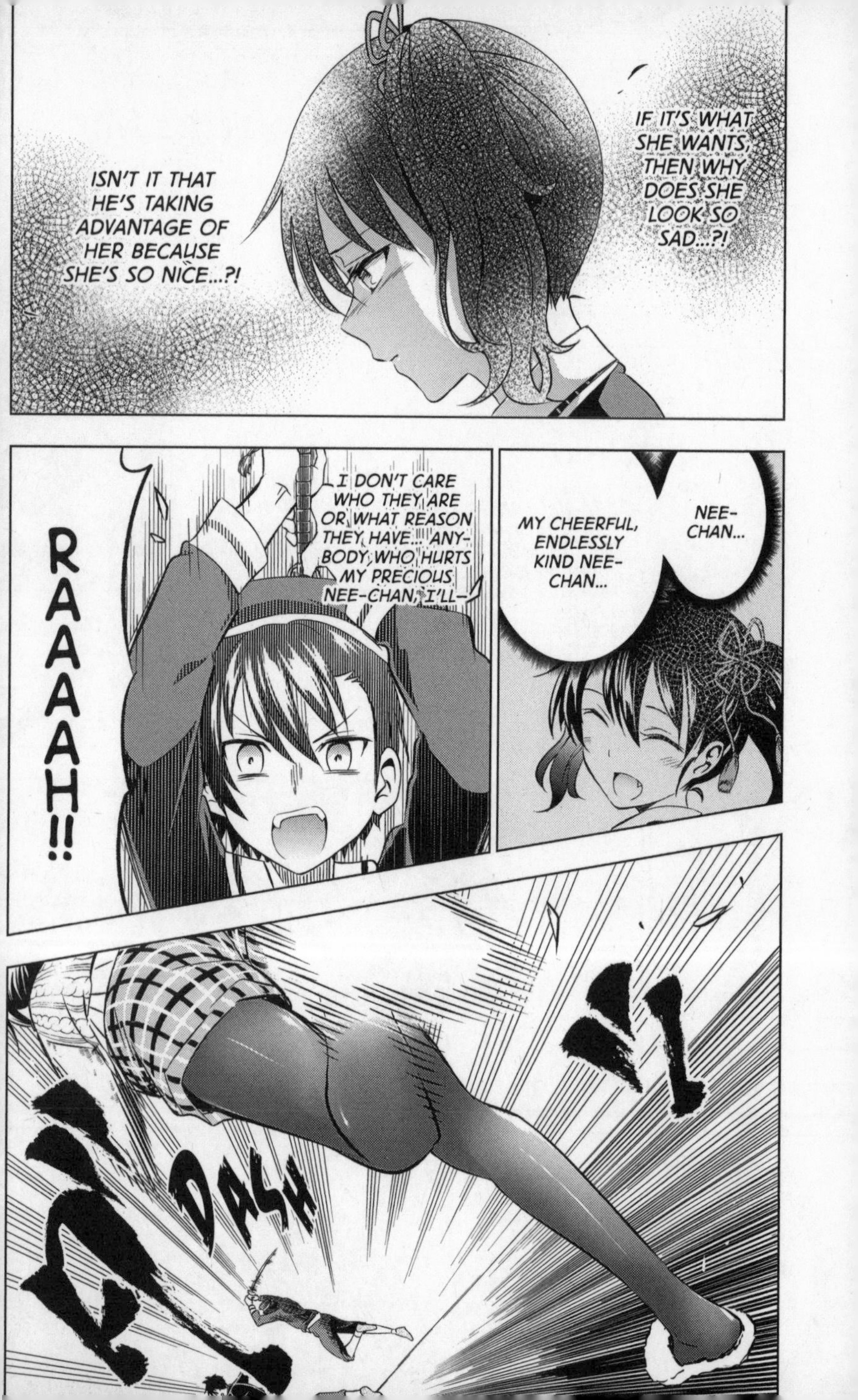
IF IT'S WHAT SHE WANTS, THEN WHY DOES SHE LOOK SO SAD...?!
ISN'T IT THAT HE'S TAKING ADVANTAGE OF HER BECAUSE SHE'S SO NICE...?!
NEE-CHAN...
MY CHEERFUL, ENDLESSLY KIND NEE-CHAN...
I DON'T CARE WHO THEY ARE OR WHAT REASON THEY HAVE... ANYBODY WHO HURTS MY PRECIOUS NEE-CHAN, I'LL—
RAAAAAH!!
DASH

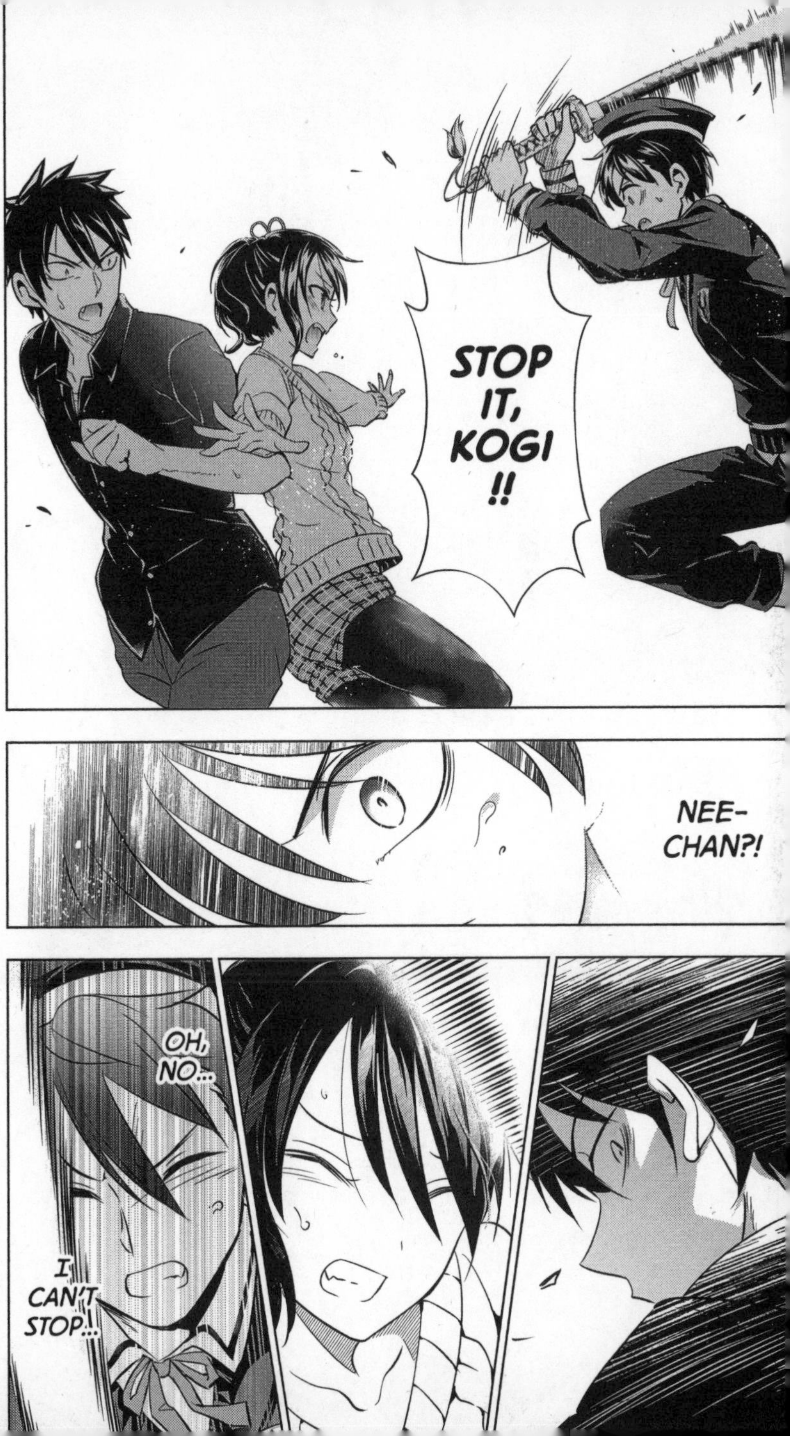
STOP IT, KOGI !!
NEE-CHAN?!
OH, NO...
I CAN'T STOP...

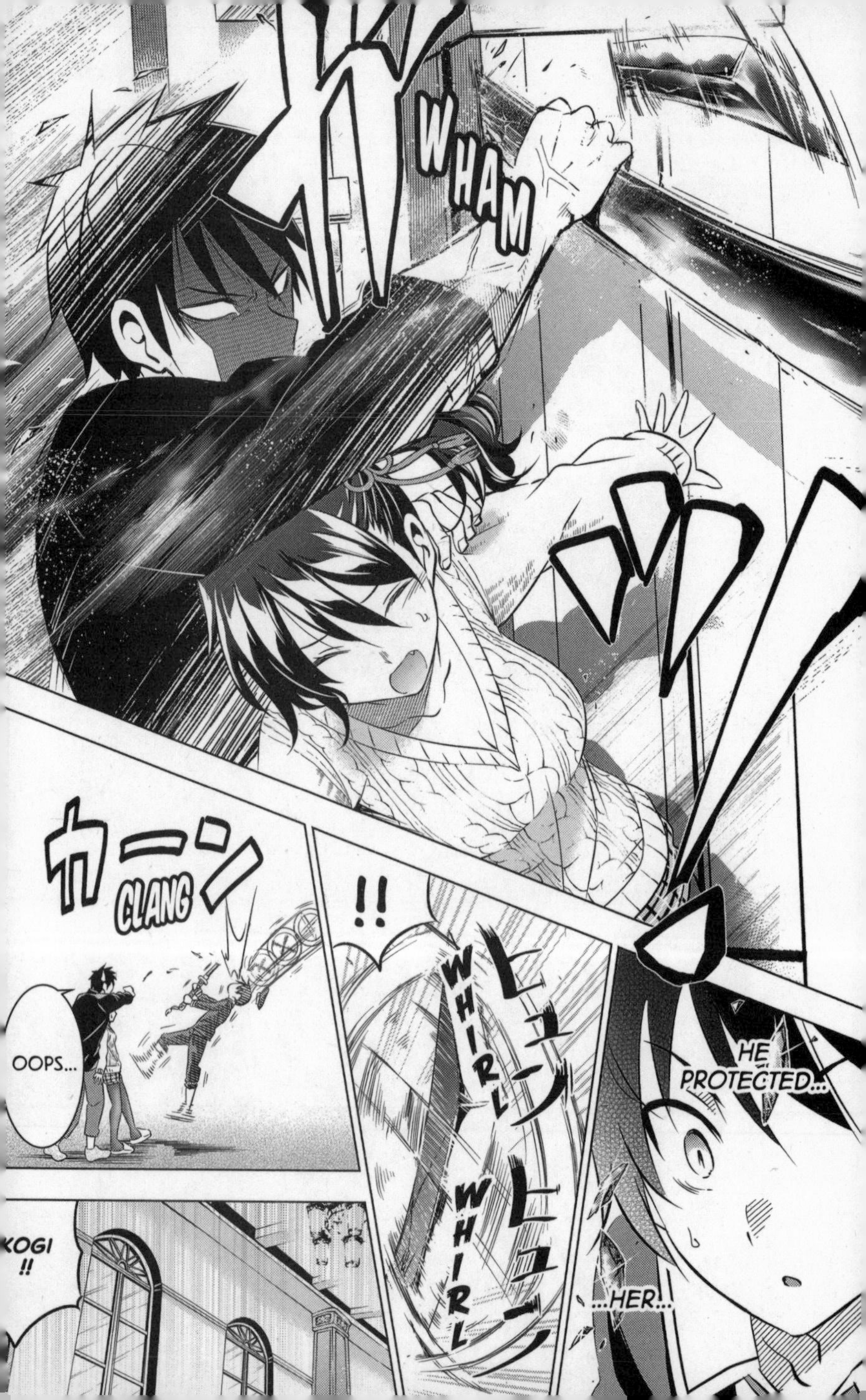
WHAM
カーン
CLANG
OOPS...
!!
ヒューンヒューン
WHIRL
WHIRL
HE PROTECTED...
...HER...
KOGI !!

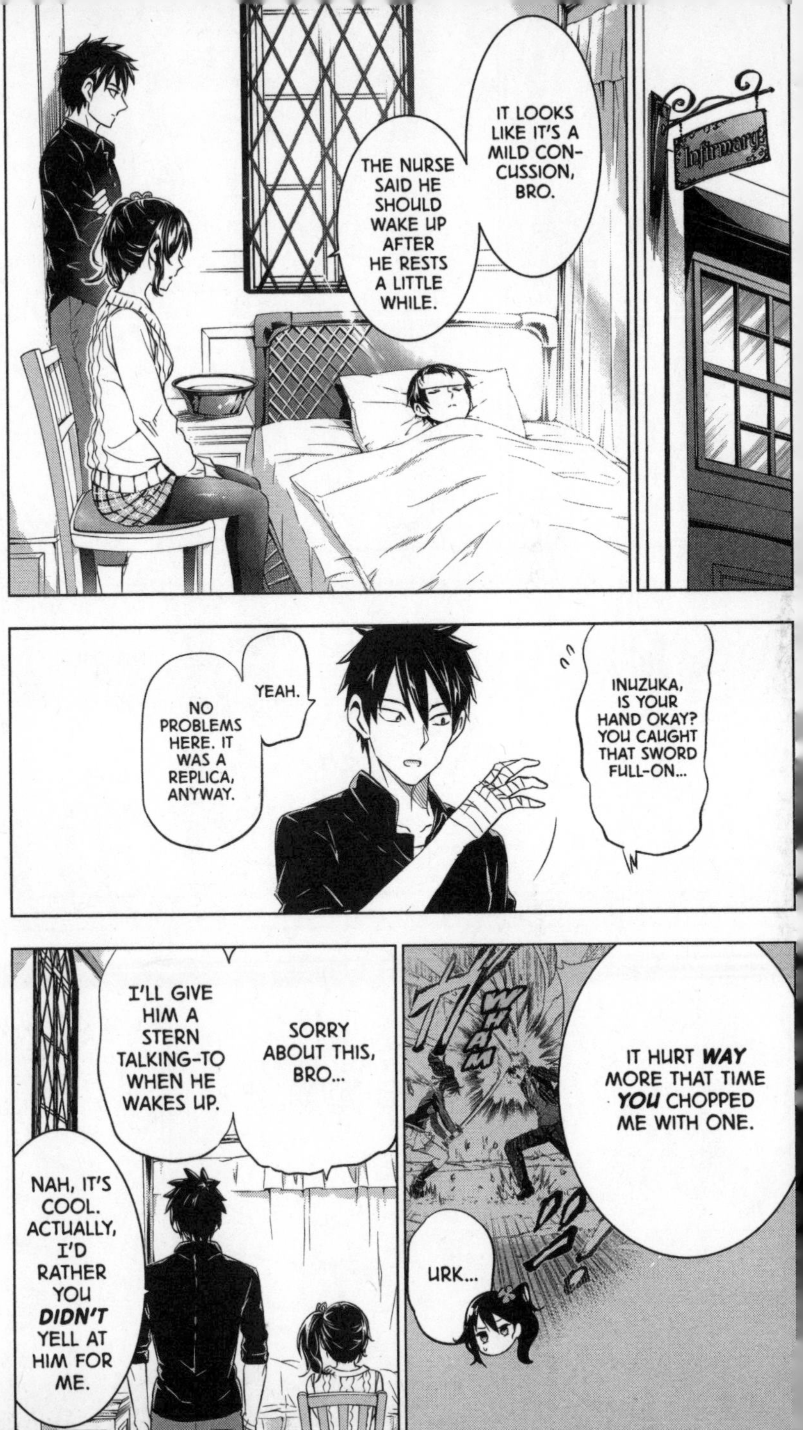
Infirmary
IT LOOKS LIKE IT'S A MILD CON-CUSSION, BRO.
THE NURSE SAID HE SHOULD WAKE UP AFTER HE RESTS A LITTLE WHILE.
INUZUKA, IS YOUR HAND OKAY? YOU CAUGHT THAT SWORD FULL-ON...
YEAH.
NO PROBLEMS HERE. IT WAS A REPLICA, ANYWAY.
WHAM
IT HURT WAY MORE THAT TIME YOU CHOPPED ME WITH ONE.
URK...
SORRY ABOUT THIS, BRO...
I'LL GIVE HIM A STERN TALKING-TO WHEN HE WAKES UP.
NAH, IT'S COOL. ACTUALLY, I'D RATHER YOU DIDN'T YELL AT HIM FOR ME.

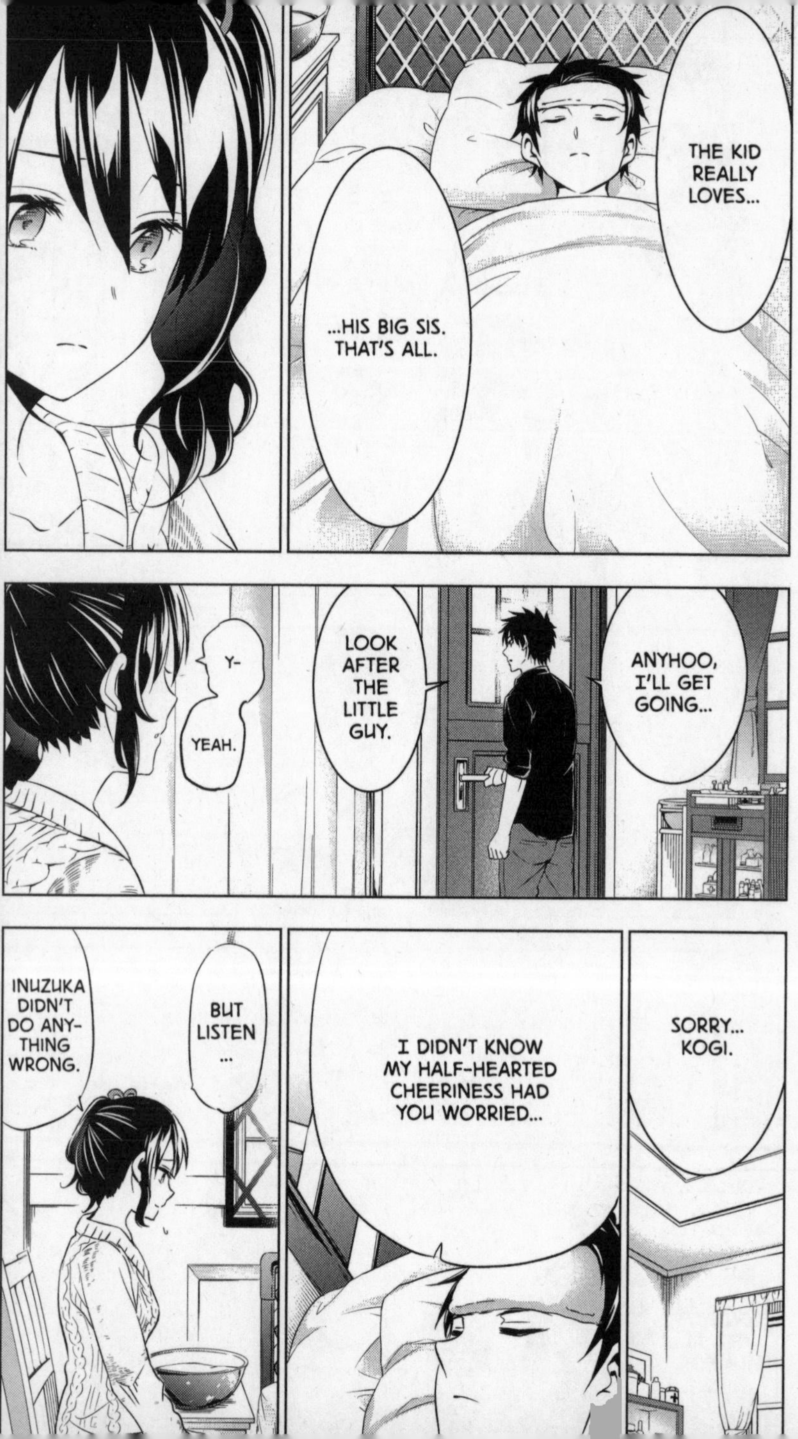
THE KID REALLY LOVES...
...HIS BIG SIS. THAT'S ALL.
ANYHOO, I'LL GET GOING...
LOOK AFTER THE LITTLE GUY.
Y-
YEAH.
SORRY... KOGI.
I DIDN'T KNOW MY HALF-HEARTED CHEERINESS HAD YOU WORRIED...
BUT LISTEN ...
INUZUKA DIDN'T DO ANY-THING WRONG.

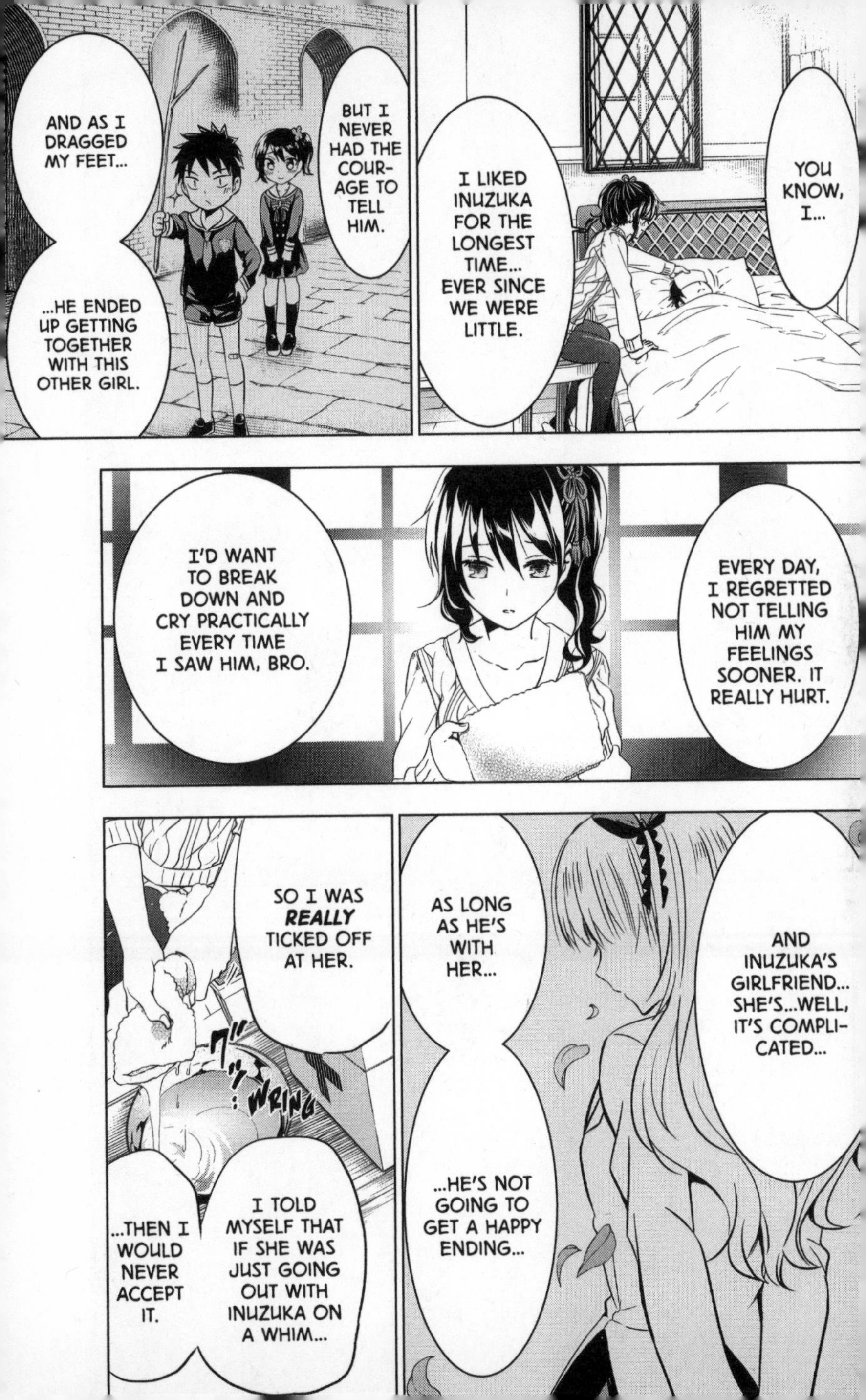
YOU KNOW, I...
I LIKED INUZUKA FOR THE LONGEST TIME... EVER SINCE WE WERE LITTLE.
BUT I NEVER HAD THE COURAGE TO TELL HIM.
AND AS I DRAGGED MY FEET...
...HE ENDED UP GETTING TOGETHER WITH THIS OTHER GIRL.
EVERY DAY, I REGRETTED NOT TELLING HIM MY FEELINGS SOONER. IT REALLY HURT.
I'D WANT TO BREAK DOWN AND CRY PRACTICALLY EVERY TIME I SAW HIM, BRO.
AND INUZUKA'S GIRLFRIEND... SHE'S...WELL, IT'S COMPLICATED...
AS LONG AS HE'S WITH HER...
...HE'S NOT GOING TO GET A HAPPY ENDING...
SO I WAS *REALLY* TICKED OFF AT HER.
WRING
I TOLD MYSELF THAT IF SHE WAS JUST GOING OUT WITH INUZUKA ON A WHIM...
...THEN I WOULD NEVER ACCEPT IT.

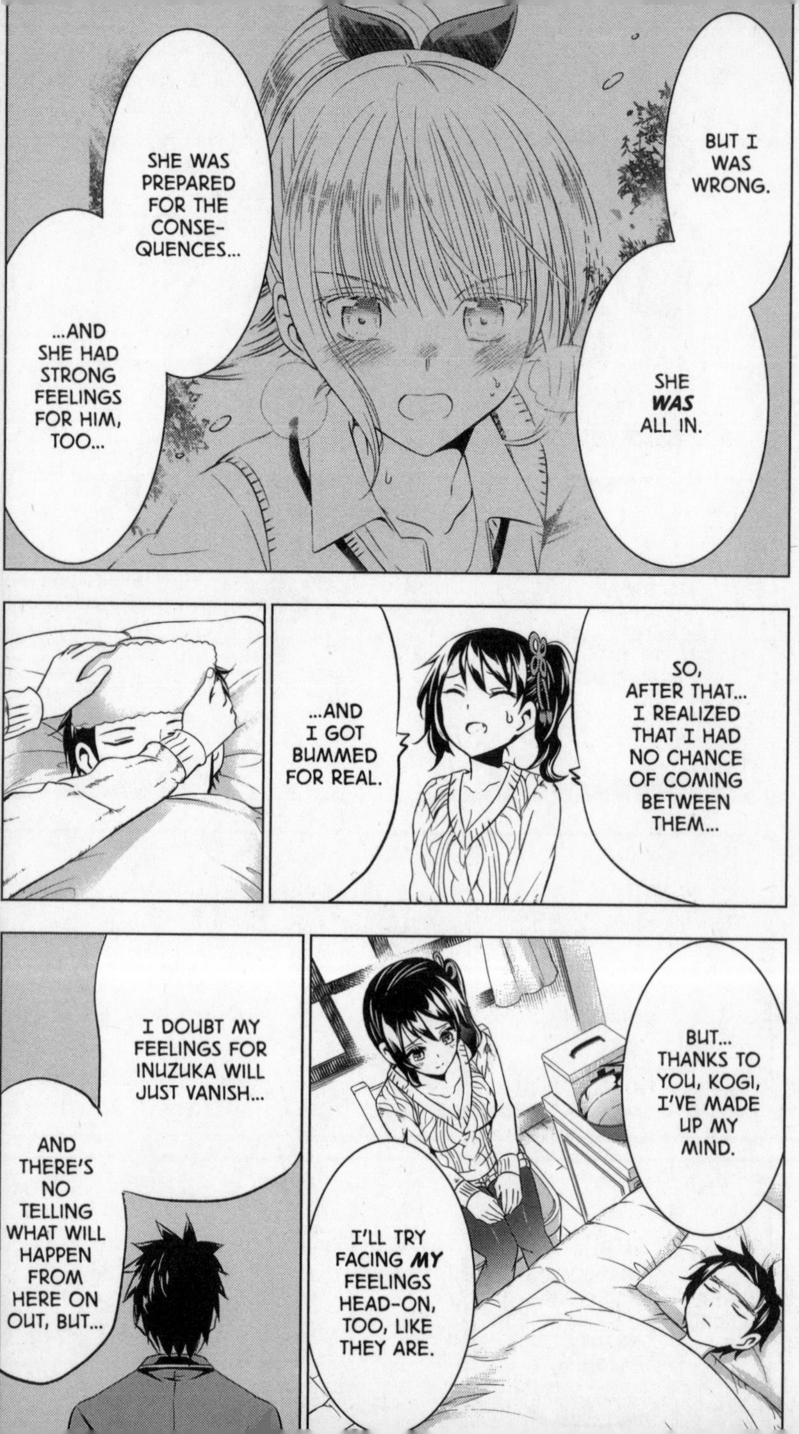
BUT I WAS WRONG.
SHE WAS PREPARED FOR THE CONSE-QUENCES...
SHE ***WAS*** ALL IN.
...AND SHE HAD STRONG FEELINGS FOR HIM, TOO...
SO, AFTER THAT... I REALIZED THAT I HAD NO CHANCE OF COMING BETWEEN THEM...
...AND I GOT BUMMED FOR REAL.
BUT... THANKS TO YOU, KOGI, I'VE MADE UP MY MIND.
I'LL TRY FACING ***MY*** FEELINGS HEAD-ON, TOO, LIKE THEY ARE.
I DOUBT MY FEELINGS FOR INUZUKA WILL JUST VANISH...
AND THERE'S NO TELLING WHAT WILL HAPPEN FROM HERE ON OUT, BUT...

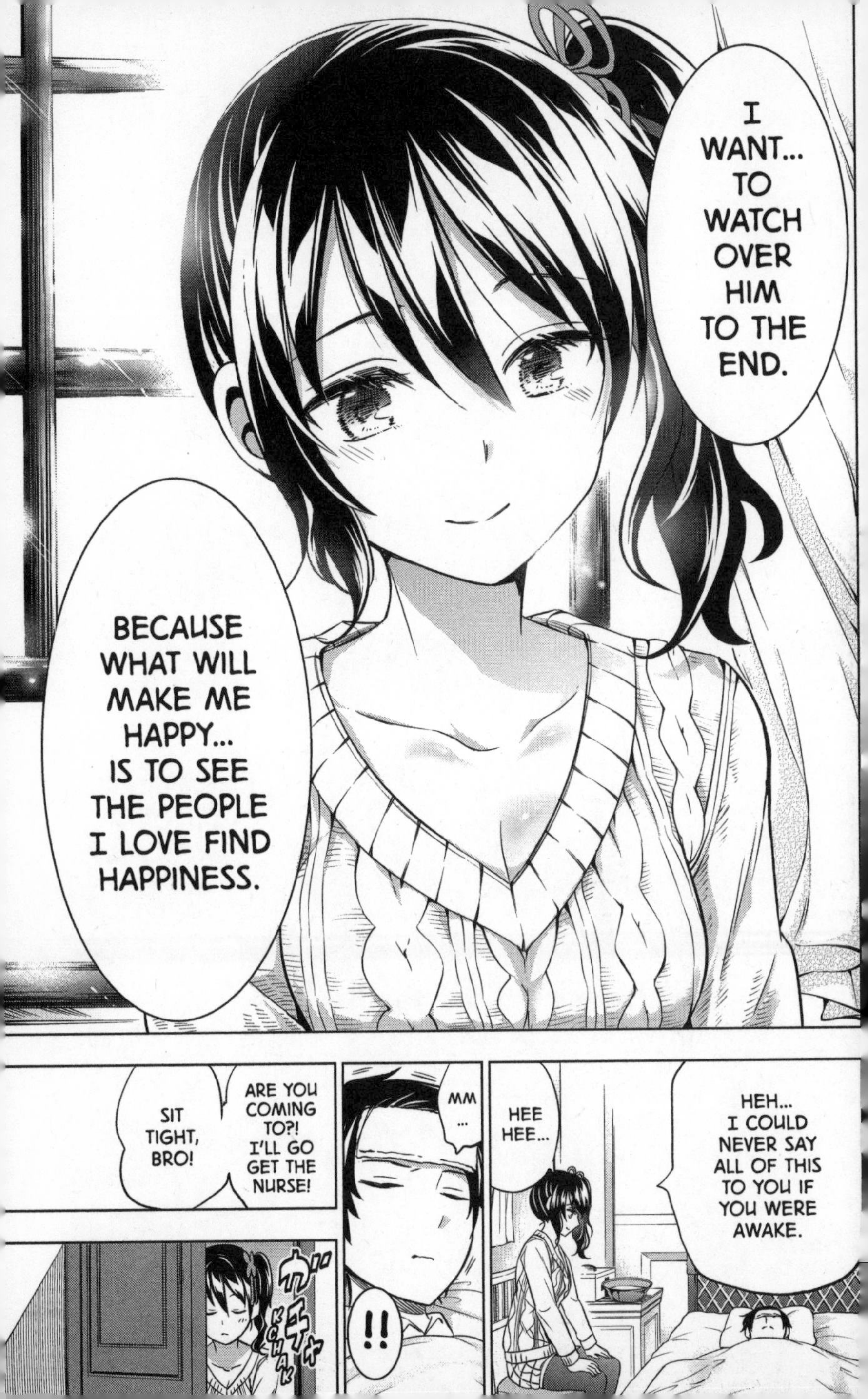
I WANT... TO WATCH OVER HIM TO THE END.
BECAUSE WHAT WILL MAKE ME HAPPY... IS TO SEE THE PEOPLE I LOVE FIND HAPPINESS.
HEH... I COULD NEVER SAY ALL OF THIS TO YOU IF YOU WERE AWAKE.
HEE HEE...
MM ...
!!
ARE YOU COMING TO?! I'LL GO GET THE NURSE!
SIT TIGHT, BRO!
KCHAK

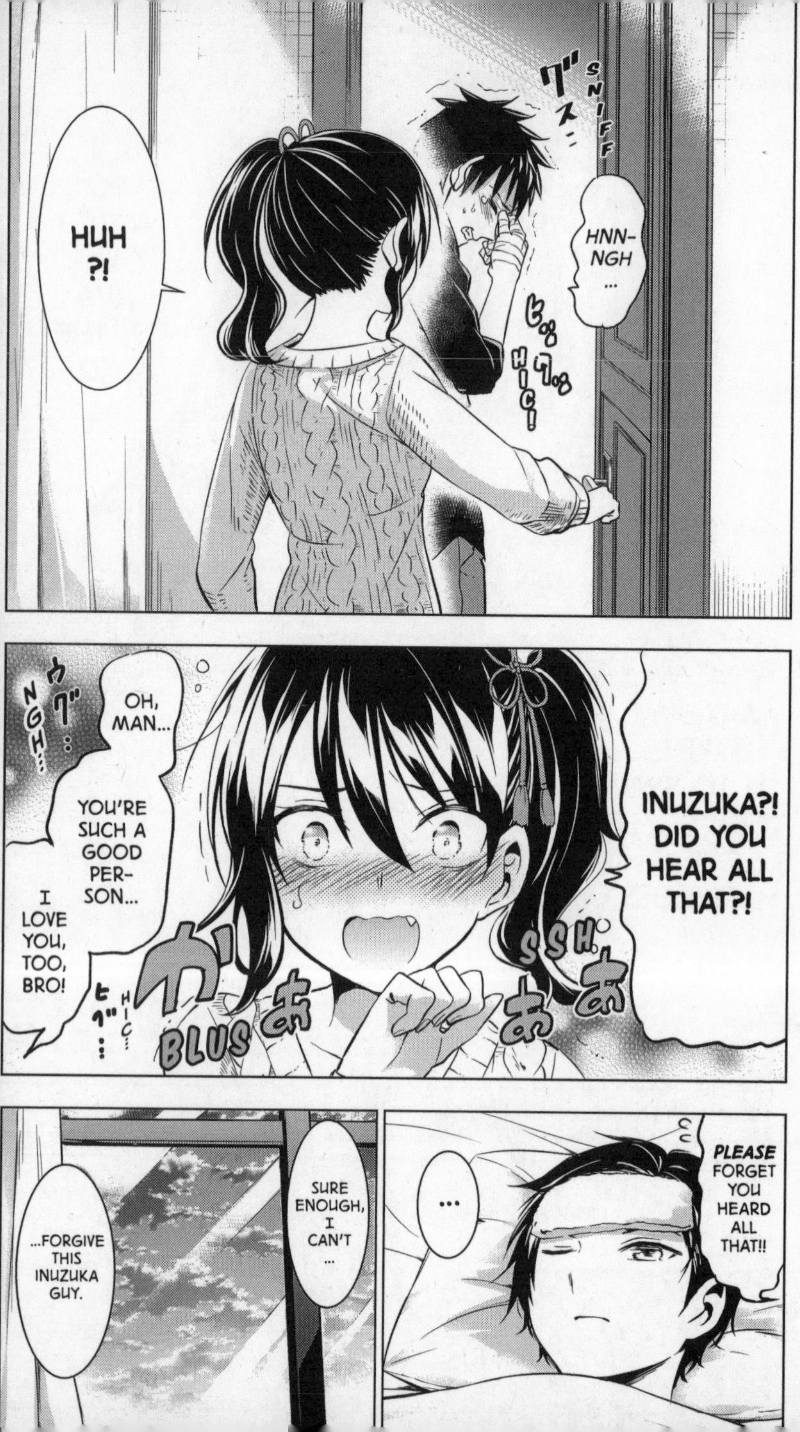
SNIFF
HNN-NGH...
HIC!
HUH?!
INUZUKA?! DID YOU HEAR ALL THAT?!
SSH
BLUS
OH, MAN...
YOU'RE SUCH A GOOD PERSON...
I LOVE YOU, TOO, BRO!
NGH...
HIC...
PLEASE FORGET YOU HEARD ALL THAT!!
...
SURE ENOUGH, I CAN'T...
...FORGIVE THIS INUZUKA GUY.

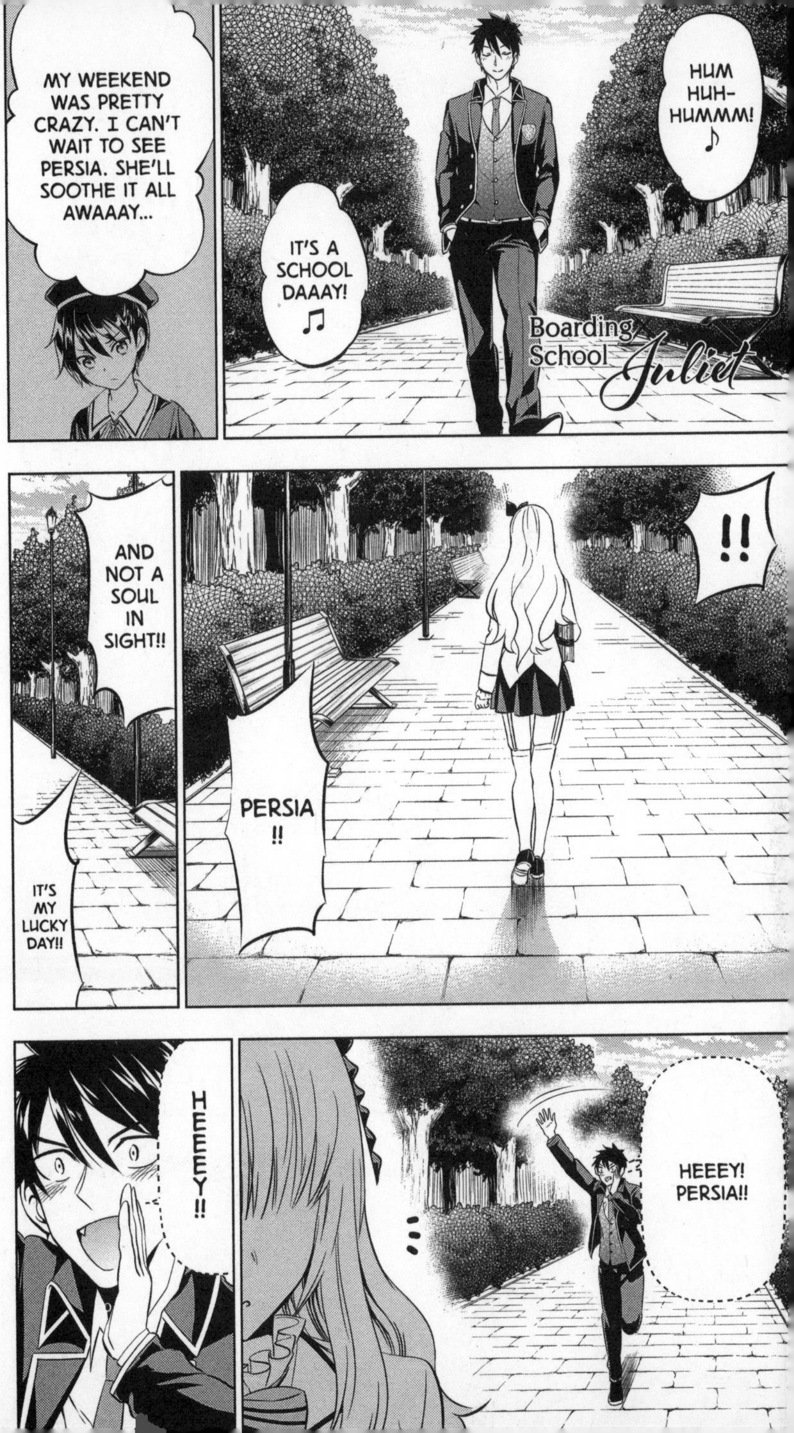
HUM HUH-HUMMM! ♪
IT'S A SCHOOL DAAAY! ♫
Boarding School Juliet
MY WEEKEND WAS PRETTY CRAZY. I CAN'T WAIT TO SEE PERSIA. SHE'LL SOOTHE IT ALL AWAAAY...
!!
PERSIA !!
AND NOT A SOUL IN SIGHT!!
IT'S MY LUCKY DAY!!
HEEEY! PERSIA!!
HEEEY!!

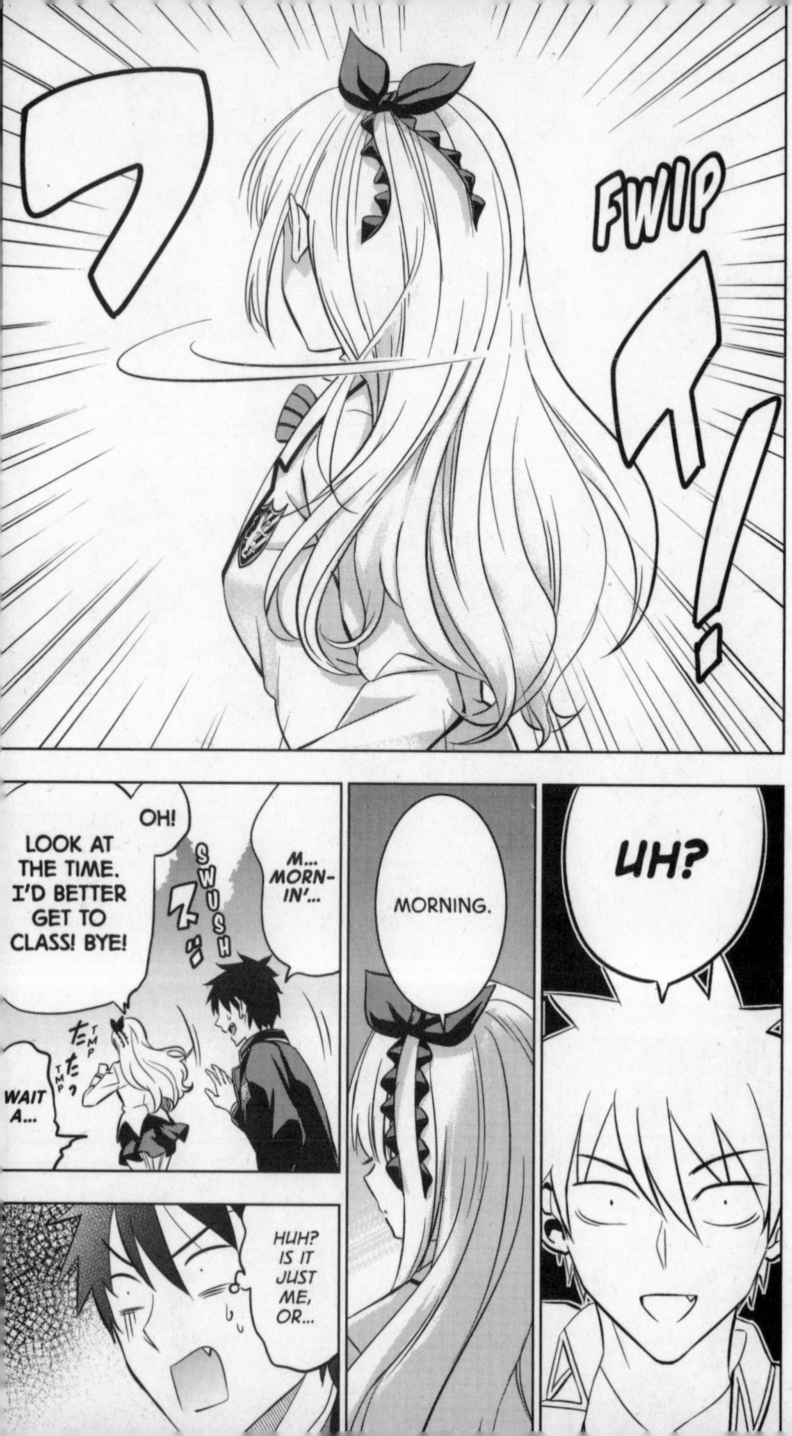
FWIP
UH?
MORNING.
M... MORNIN'...
OH!
LOOK AT THE TIME. I'D BETTER GET TO CLASS! BYE!
SWUSH
TMP TMP
WAIT A...
HUH? IS IT JUST ME, OR...

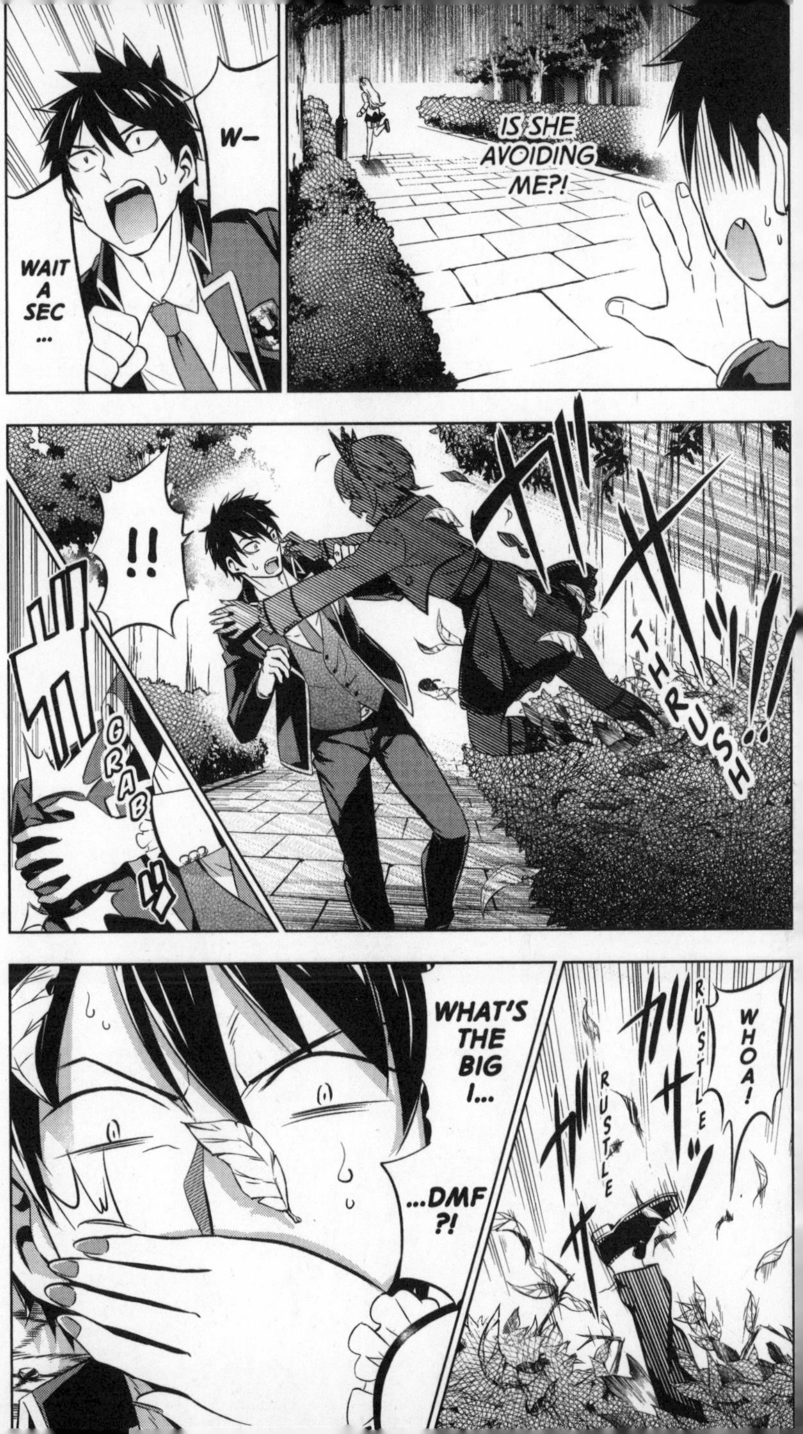
IS SHE AVOIDING ME?!
W—
WAIT A SEC...
THRUSH
!!
GRAB
WHOA!
RUSTLE
RUSTLE
WHAT'S THE BIG I...
...DMF?!

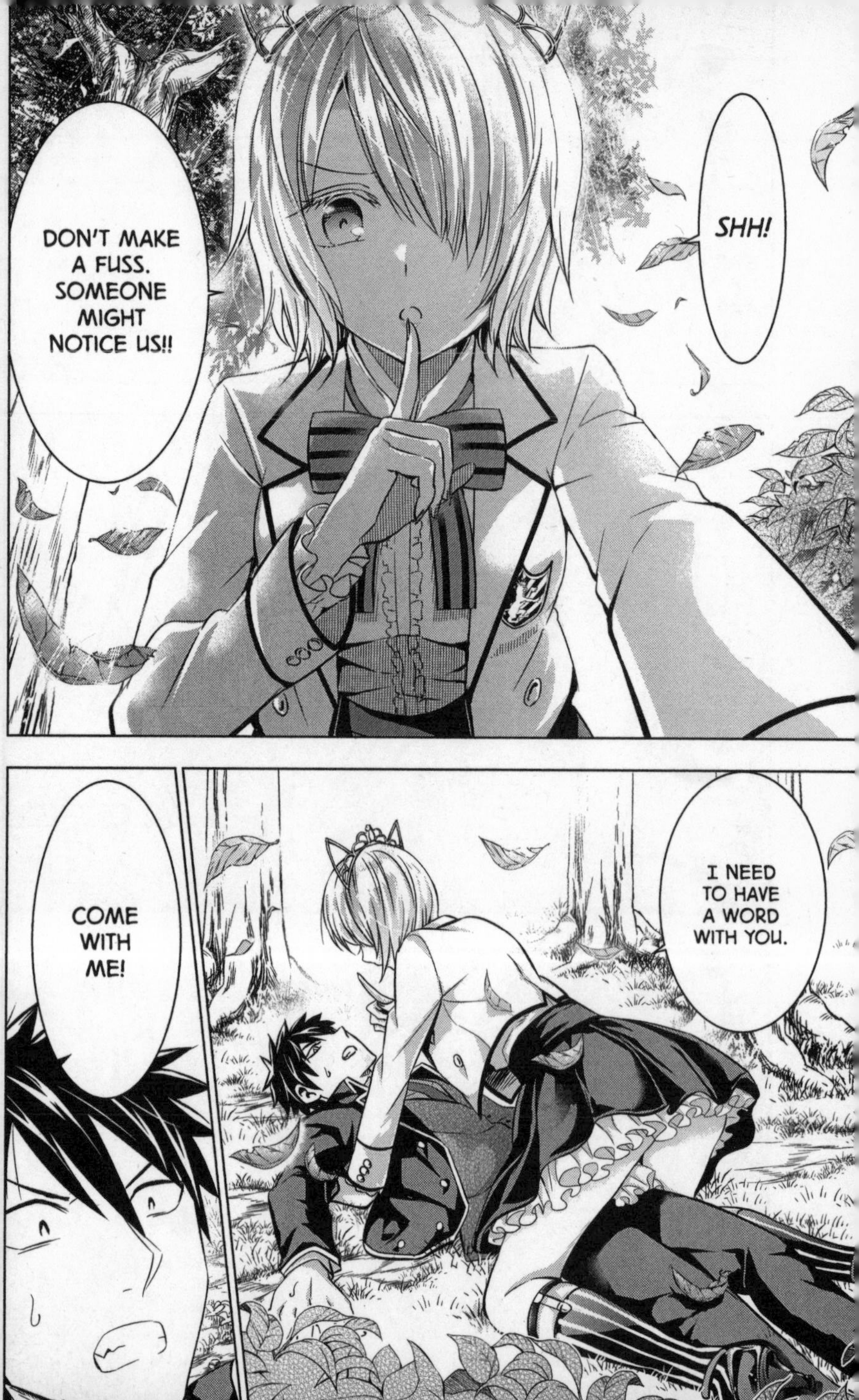
SHH!
DON'T MAKE A FUSS. SOMEONE MIGHT NOTICE US!!
I NEED TO HAVE A WORD WITH YOU.
COME WITH ME!

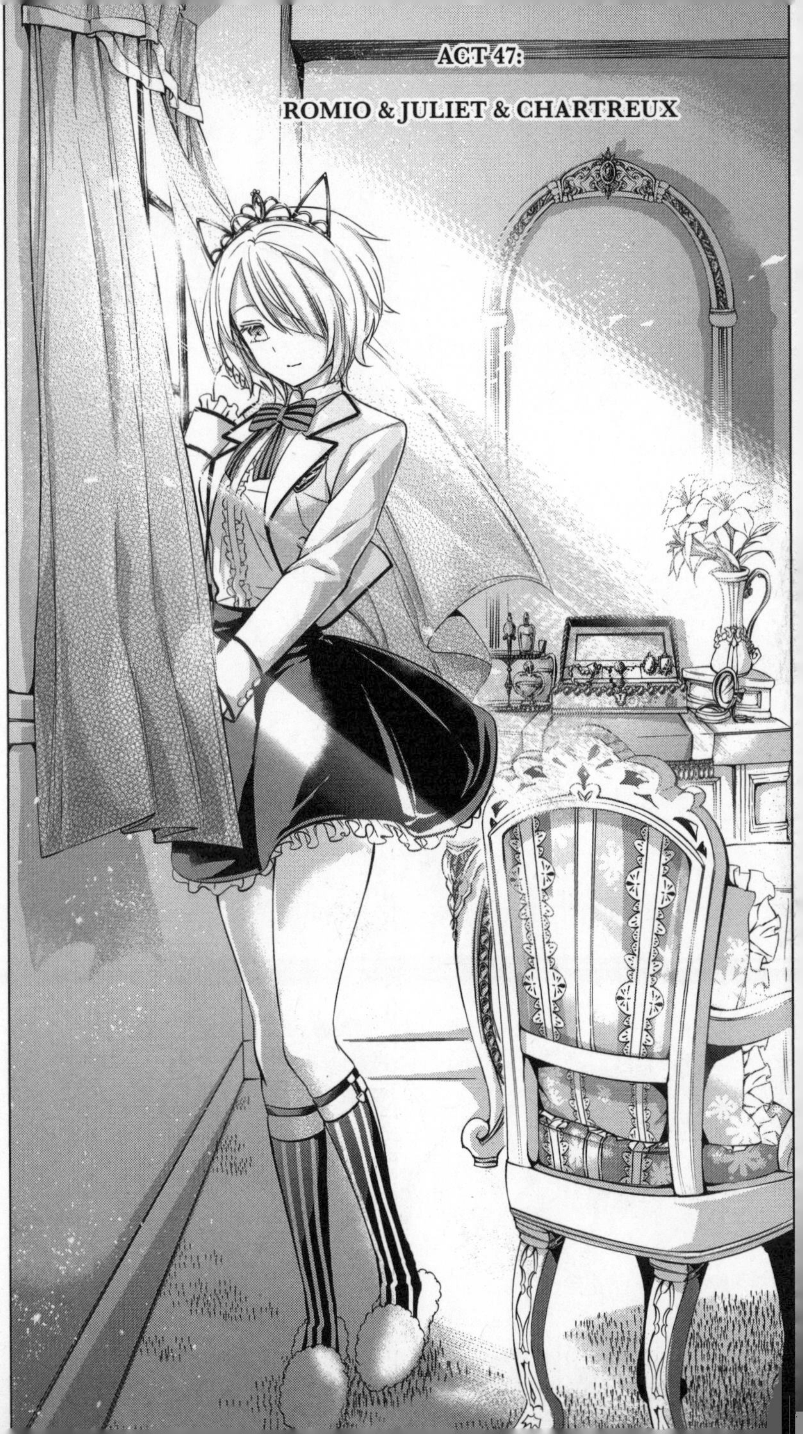
ACT 47:
ROMIO & JULIET & CHARTREUX

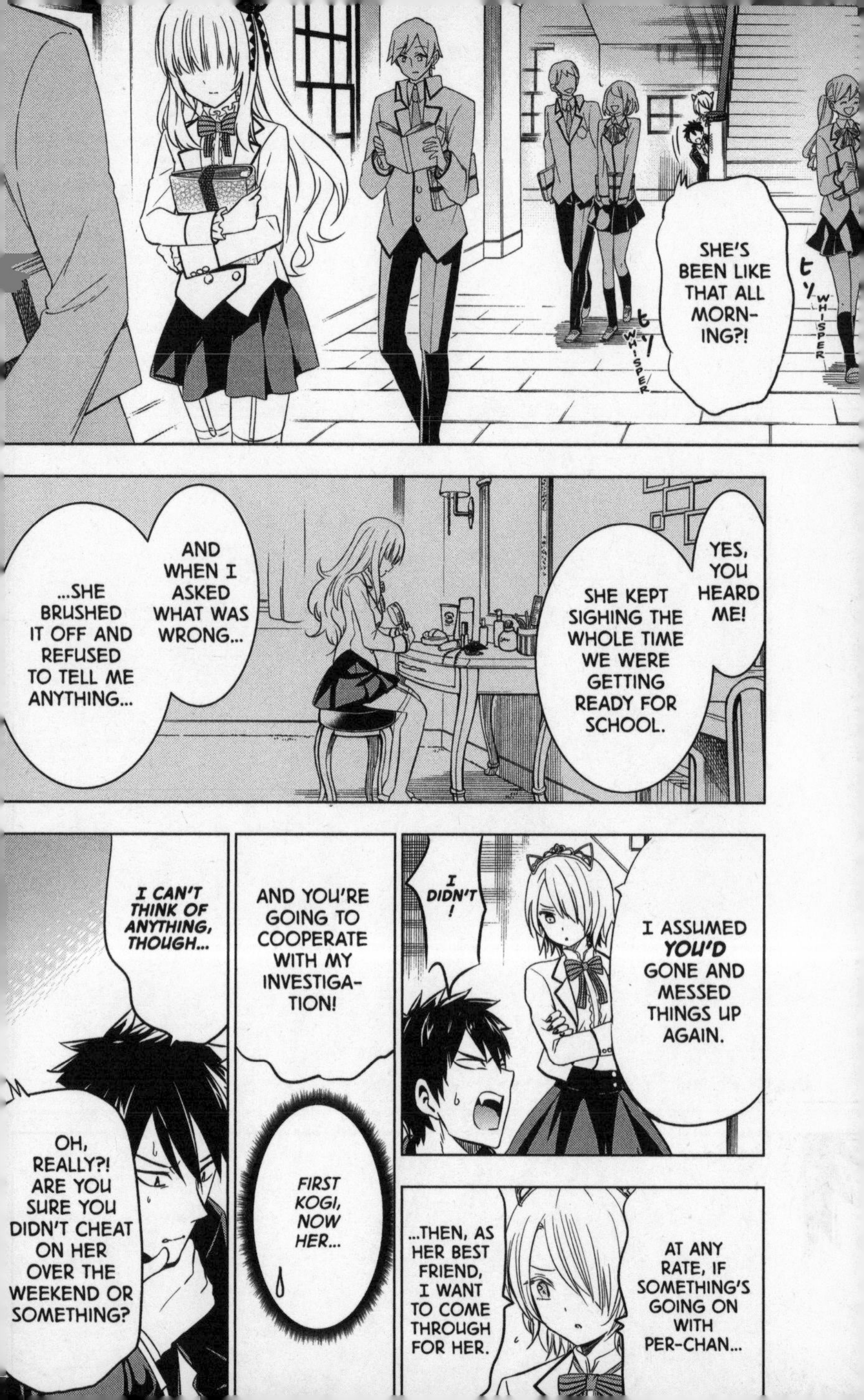
ヒソ
WHISPER
SHE'S BEEN LIKE THAT ALL MORNING?!
ヒソ
WHISPER
YES, YOU HEARD ME!
SHE KEPT SIGHING THE WHOLE TIME WE WERE GETTING READY FOR SCHOOL.
AND WHEN I ASKED WHAT WAS WRONG...
...SHE BRUSHED IT OFF AND REFUSED TO TELL ME ANYTHING...
I ASSUMED *YOU'D* GONE AND MESSED THINGS UP AGAIN.
I DIDN'T!
AT ANY RATE, IF SOMETHING'S GOING ON WITH PER-CHAN...
...THEN, AS HER BEST FRIEND, I WANT TO COME THROUGH FOR HER.
AND YOU'RE GOING TO COOPERATE WITH MY INVESTIGATION!
FIRST KOGI, NOW HER...
I CAN'T THINK OF ANYTHING, THOUGH...
OH, REALLY?! ARE YOU SURE YOU DIDN'T CHEAT ON HER OVER THE WEEKEND OR SOMETHING?

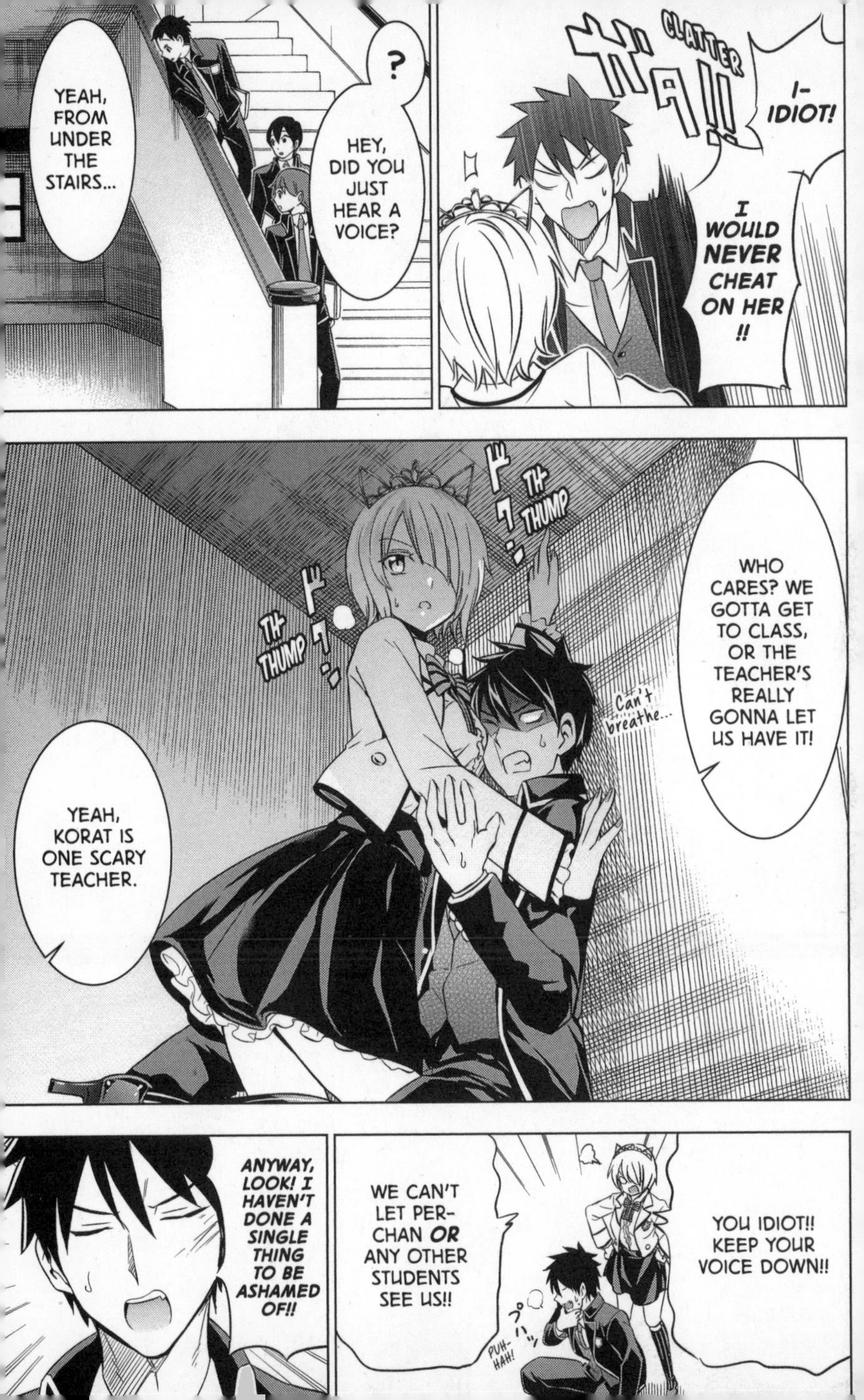
CLATTER
I- IDIOT!
I WOULD NEVER CHEAT ON HER!!
?
HEY, DID YOU JUST HEAR A VOICE?
YEAH, FROM UNDER THE STAIRS...
WHO CARES? WE GOTTA GET TO CLASS, OR THE TEACHER'S REALLY GONNA LET US HAVE IT!
TH-THUMP
Can't breathe...
TH-THUMP
YEAH, KORAT IS ONE SCARY TEACHER.
YOU IDIOT!! KEEP YOUR VOICE DOWN!!
PUH-HAH!
WE CAN'T LET PER-CHAN **OR** ANY OTHER STUDENTS SEE US!!
ANYWAY, LOOK! I HAVEN'T DONE A SINGLE THING TO BE ASHAMED OF!!

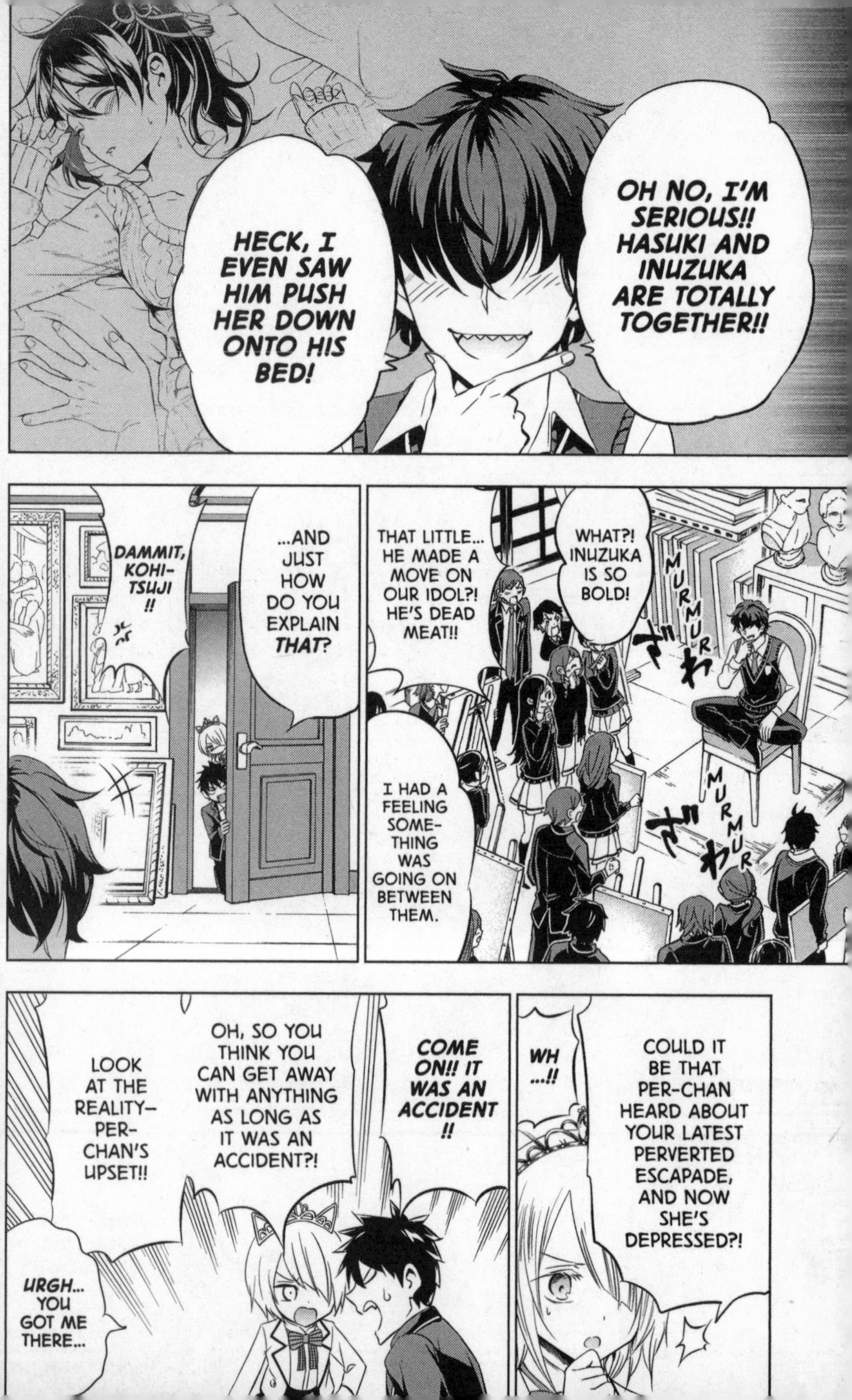
OH NO, I'M SERIOUS!! HASUKI AND INUZUKA ARE TOTALLY TOGETHER!!
HECK, I EVEN SAW HIM PUSH HER DOWN ONTO HIS BED!
WHAT?! INUZUKA IS SO BOLD!
MURMUR
THAT LITTLE... HE MADE A MOVE ON OUR IDOL?! HE'S DEAD MEAT!!
I HAD A FEELING SOMETHING WAS GOING ON BETWEEN THEM.
MURMUR
...AND JUST HOW DO YOU EXPLAIN *THAT*?
DAMMIT, KOHITSUJI!!
COULD IT BE THAT PER-CHAN HEARD ABOUT YOUR LATEST PERVERTED ESCAPADE, AND NOW SHE'S DEPRESSED?!
WH...!!
COME ON!! IT WAS AN ACCIDENT!!
OH, SO YOU THINK YOU CAN GET AWAY WITH ANYTHING AS LONG AS IT WAS AN ACCIDENT?!
LOOK AT THE REALITY—PER-CHAN'S UPSET!!
URGH... YOU GOT ME THERE...

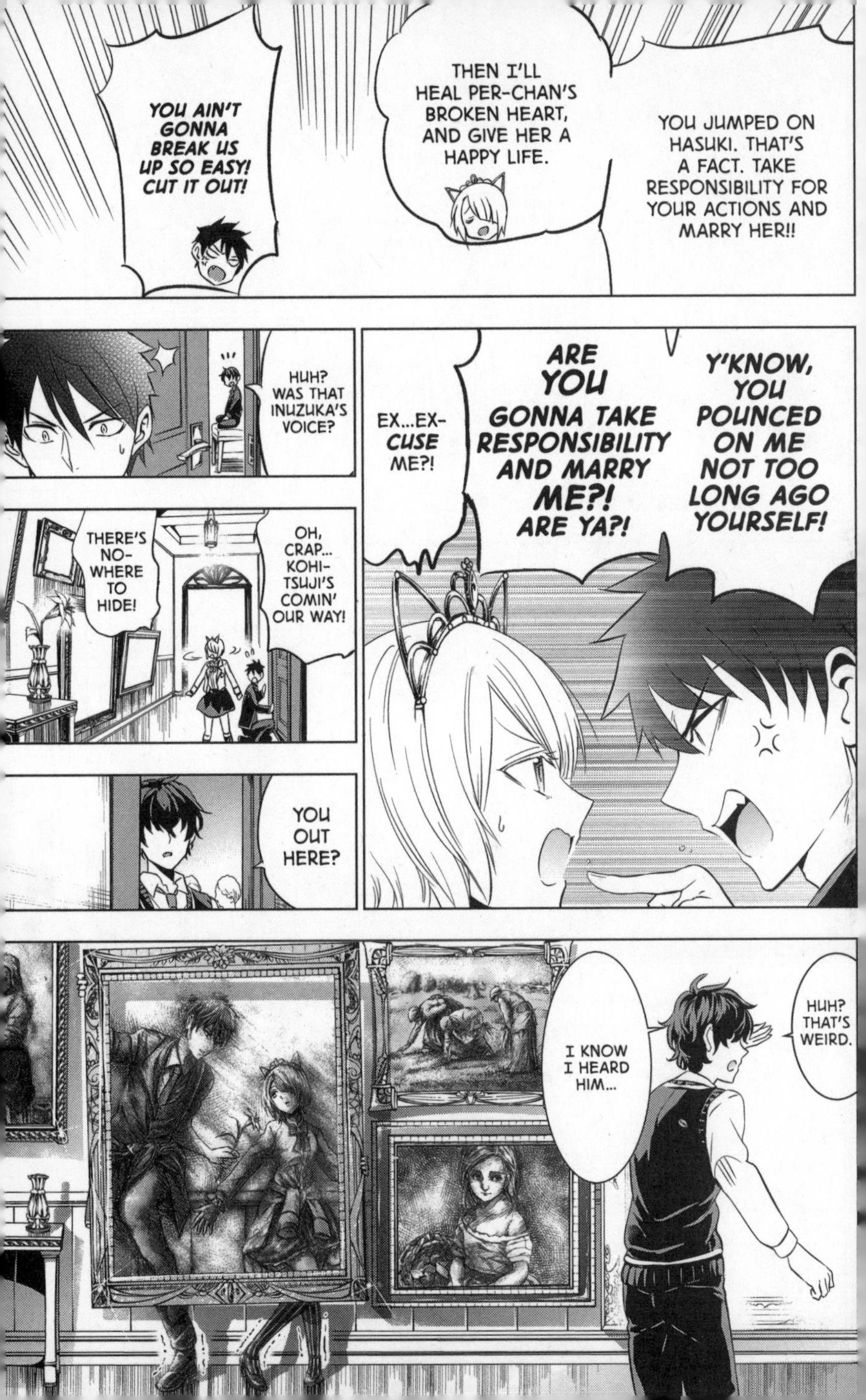
YOU JUMPED ON HASUKI. THAT'S A FACT. TAKE RESPONSIBILITY FOR YOUR ACTIONS AND MARRY HER!!
THEN I'LL HEAL PER-CHAN'S BROKEN HEART, AND GIVE HER A HAPPY LIFE.
YOU AIN'T GONNA BREAK US UP SO EASY! CUT IT OUT!
Y'KNOW, YOU POUNCED ON ME NOT TOO LONG AGO YOURSELF!
ARE YOU GONNA TAKE RESPONSIBILITY AND MARRY ME?! ARE YA?!
EX...EX-CUSE ME?!
HUH? WAS THAT INUZUKA'S VOICE?
OH, CRAP... KOHI-TSUJI'S COMIN' OUR WAY!
THERE'S NO-WHERE TO HIDE!
YOU OUT HERE?
HUH? THAT'S WEIRD.
I KNOW I HEARD HIM...

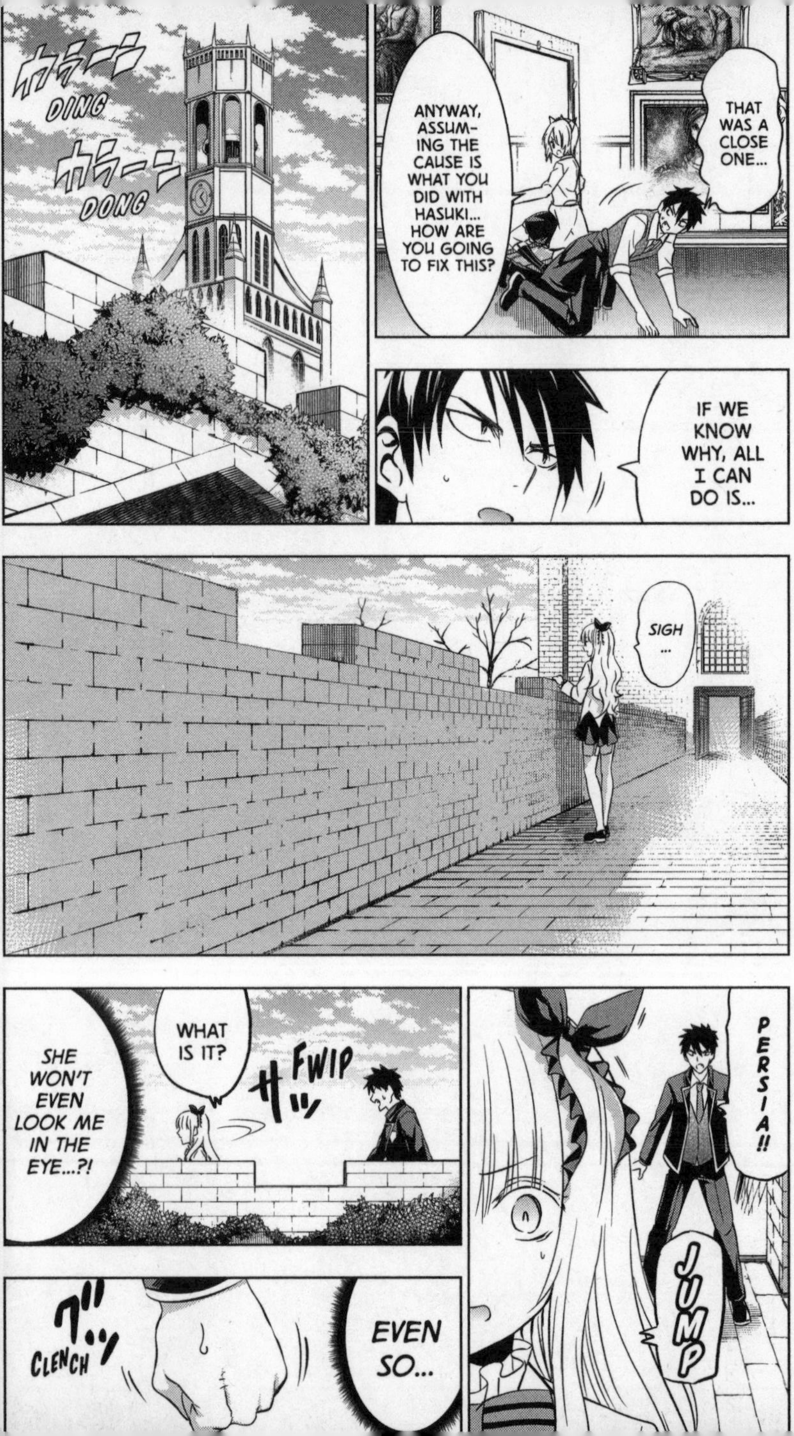
THAT WAS A CLOSE ONE...
ANYWAY, ASSUMING THE CAUSE IS WHAT YOU DID WITH HASUKI... HOW ARE YOU GOING TO FIX THIS?
IF WE KNOW WHY, ALL I CAN DO IS...
カラーン
DING
カラーン
DONG
SIGH...
PERSIA!!
JUMP
WHAT IS IT?
ハッ
FWIP
SHE WON'T EVEN LOOK ME IN THE EYE...?!
EVEN SO...
グッ
CLENCH

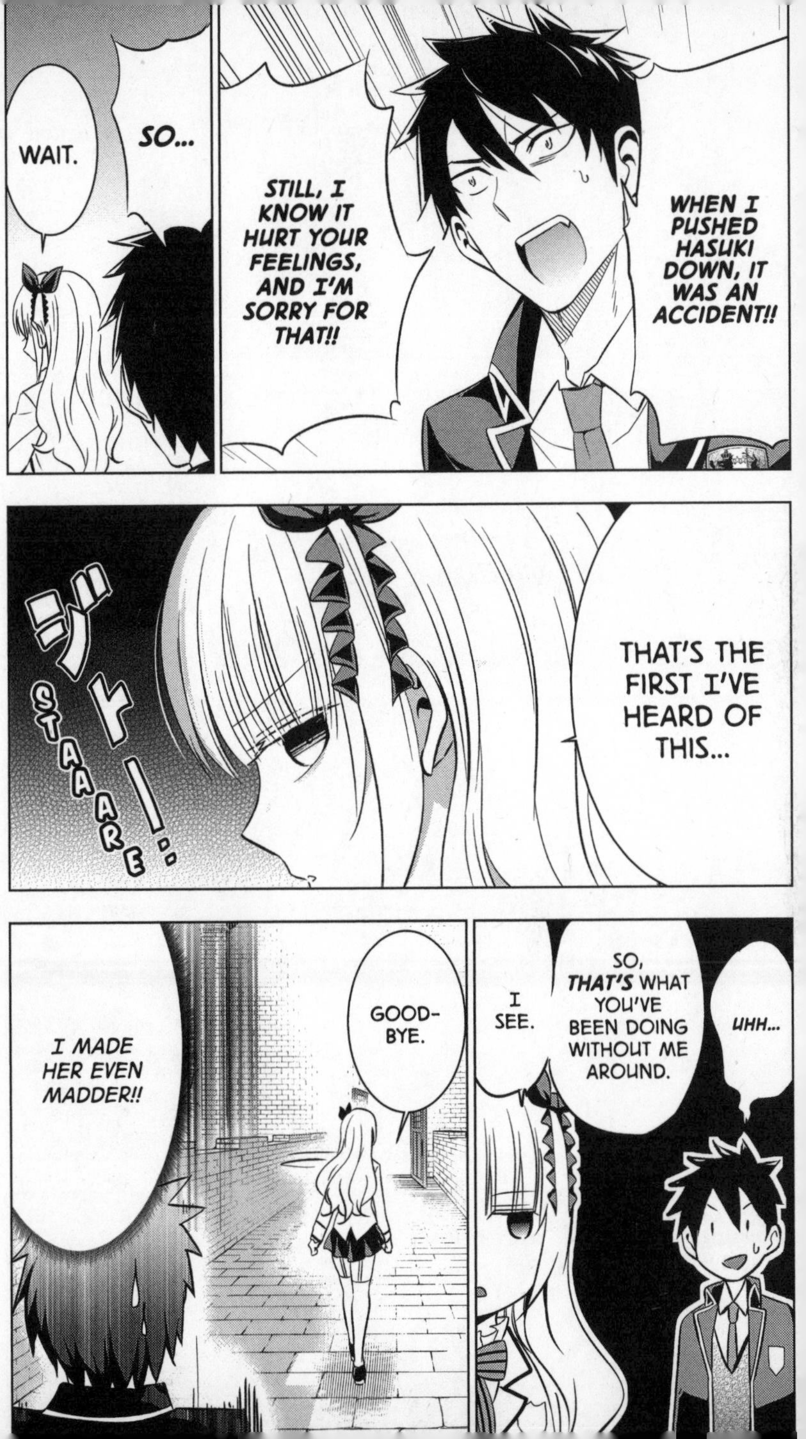
WHEN I PUSHED HASUKI DOWN, IT WAS AN ACCIDENT!!
STILL, I KNOW IT HURT YOUR FEELINGS, AND I'M SORRY FOR THAT!!
SO...
WAIT.
THAT'S THE FIRST I'VE HEARD OF THIS...
STAAAARE!!
UHH...
SO, *THAT'S* WHAT YOU'VE BEEN DOING WITHOUT ME AROUND.
I SEE.
GOOD-BYE.
I MADE HER EVEN MADDER!!

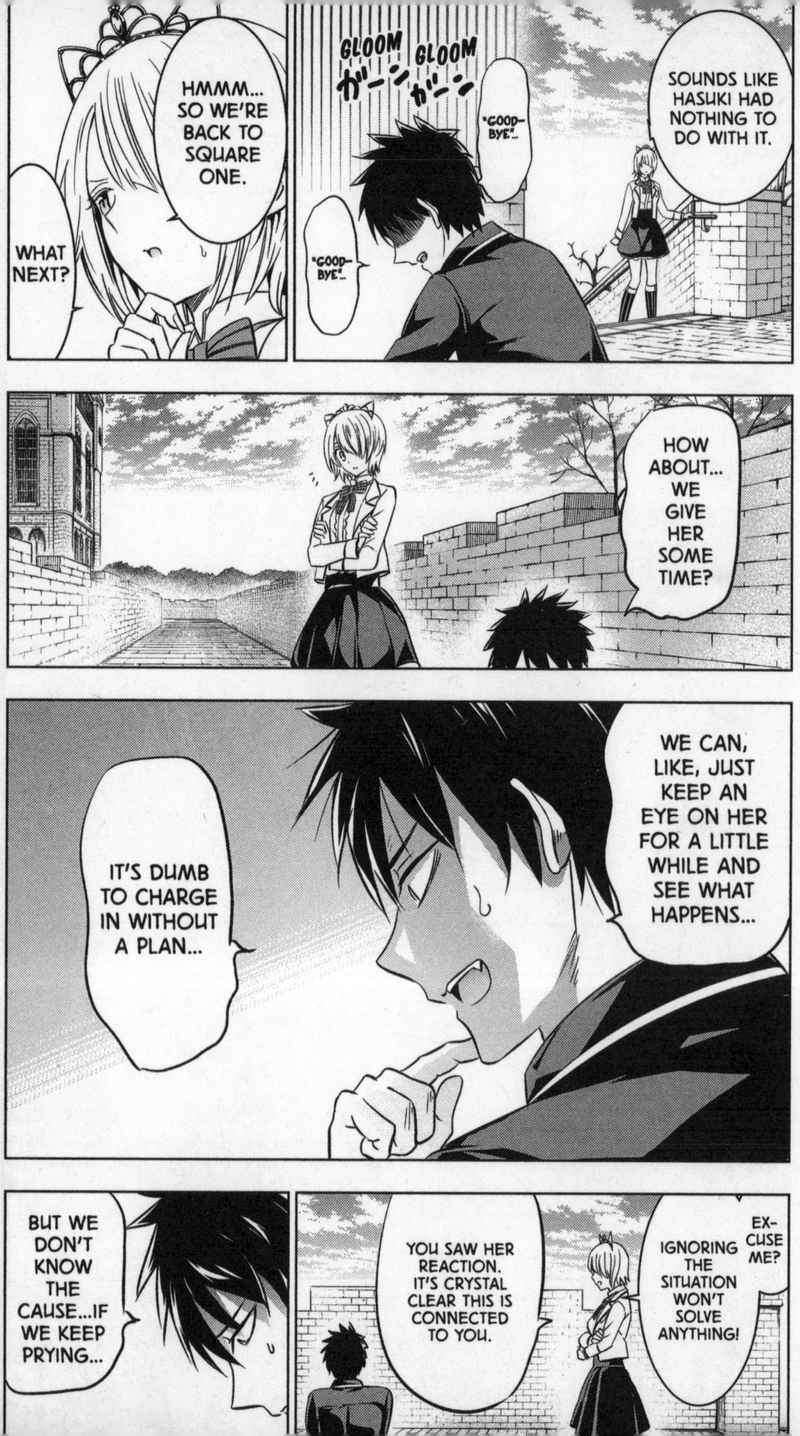
SOUNDS LIKE HASUKI HAD NOTHING TO DO WITH IT.
GLOOM
GLOOM
ガーン
ガーン
"GOOD-BYE"...
"GOOD-BYE"...
HMMM... SO WE'RE BACK TO SQUARE ONE.
WHAT NEXT?
HOW ABOUT... WE GIVE HER SOME TIME?
WE CAN, LIKE, JUST KEEP AN EYE ON HER FOR A LITTLE WHILE AND SEE WHAT HAPPENS...
IT'S DUMB TO CHARGE IN WITHOUT A PLAN...
EX-CUSE ME?
IGNORING THE SITUATION WON'T SOLVE ANYTHING!
YOU SAW HER REACTION. IT'S CRYSTAL CLEAR THIS IS CONNECTED TO YOU.
BUT WE DON'T KNOW THE CAUSE...IF WE KEEP PRYING...

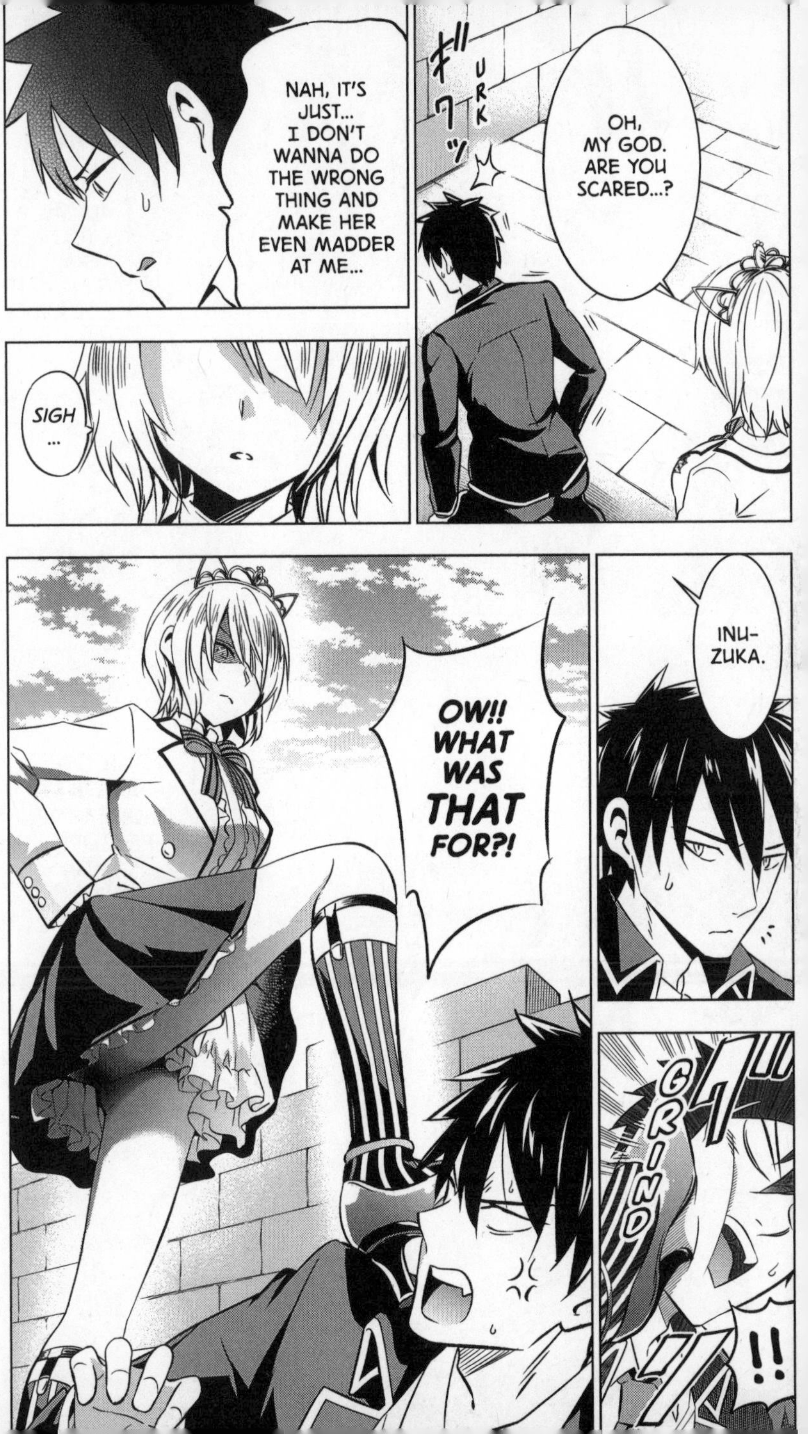
URK
OH, MY GOD. ARE YOU SCARED...?
NAH, IT'S JUST... I DON'T WANNA DO THE WRONG THING AND MAKE HER EVEN MADDER AT ME...
SIGH...
INU-ZUKA.
GRIND
!!
OW!! WHAT WAS THAT FOR?!

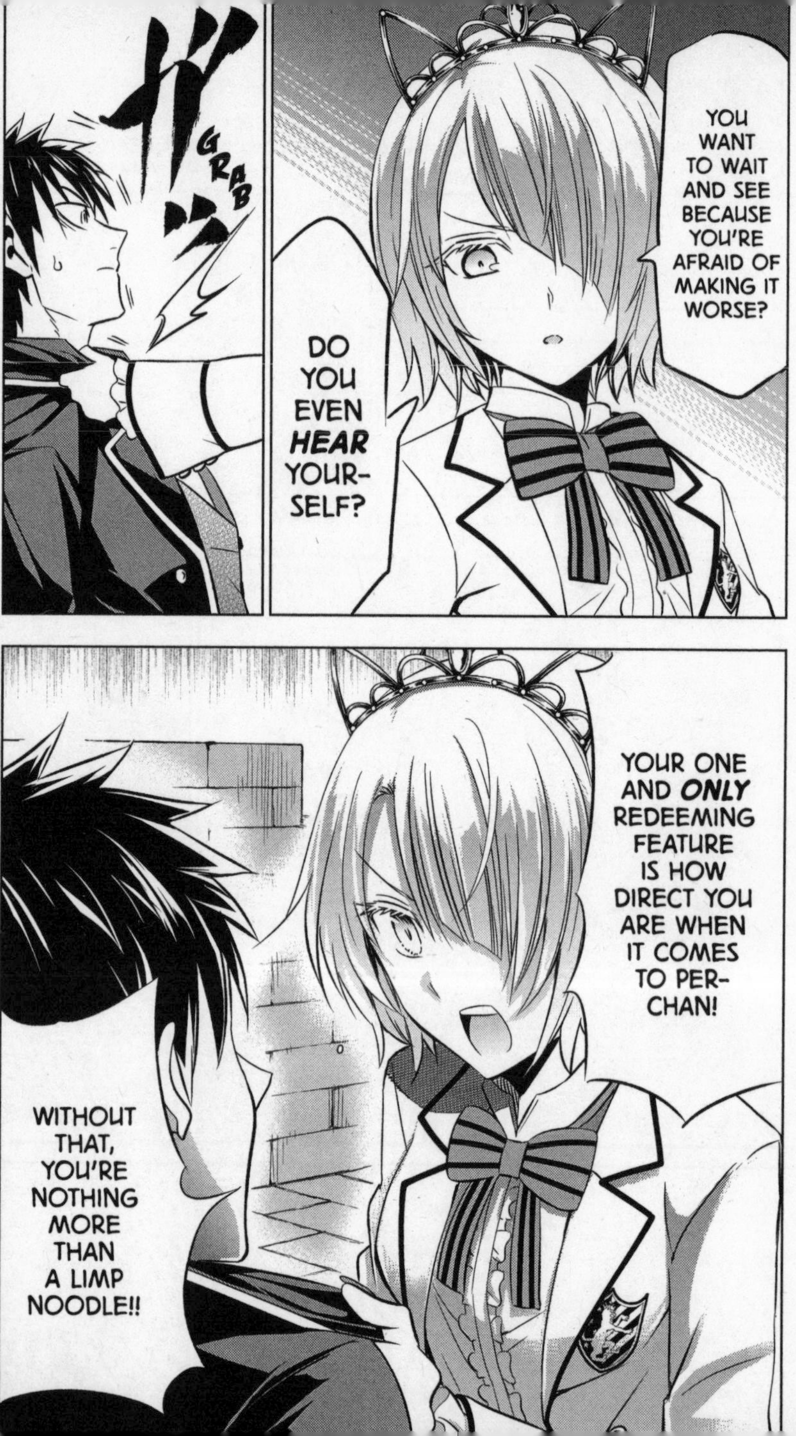
YOU WANT TO WAIT AND SEE BECAUSE YOU'RE AFRAID OF MAKING IT WORSE?
DO YOU EVEN *HEAR* YOURSELF?
GRAB
YOUR ONE AND *ONLY* REDEEMING FEATURE IS HOW DIRECT YOU ARE WHEN IT COMES TO PER-CHAN!
WITHOUT THAT, YOU'RE NOTHING MORE THAN A LIMP NOODLE!!

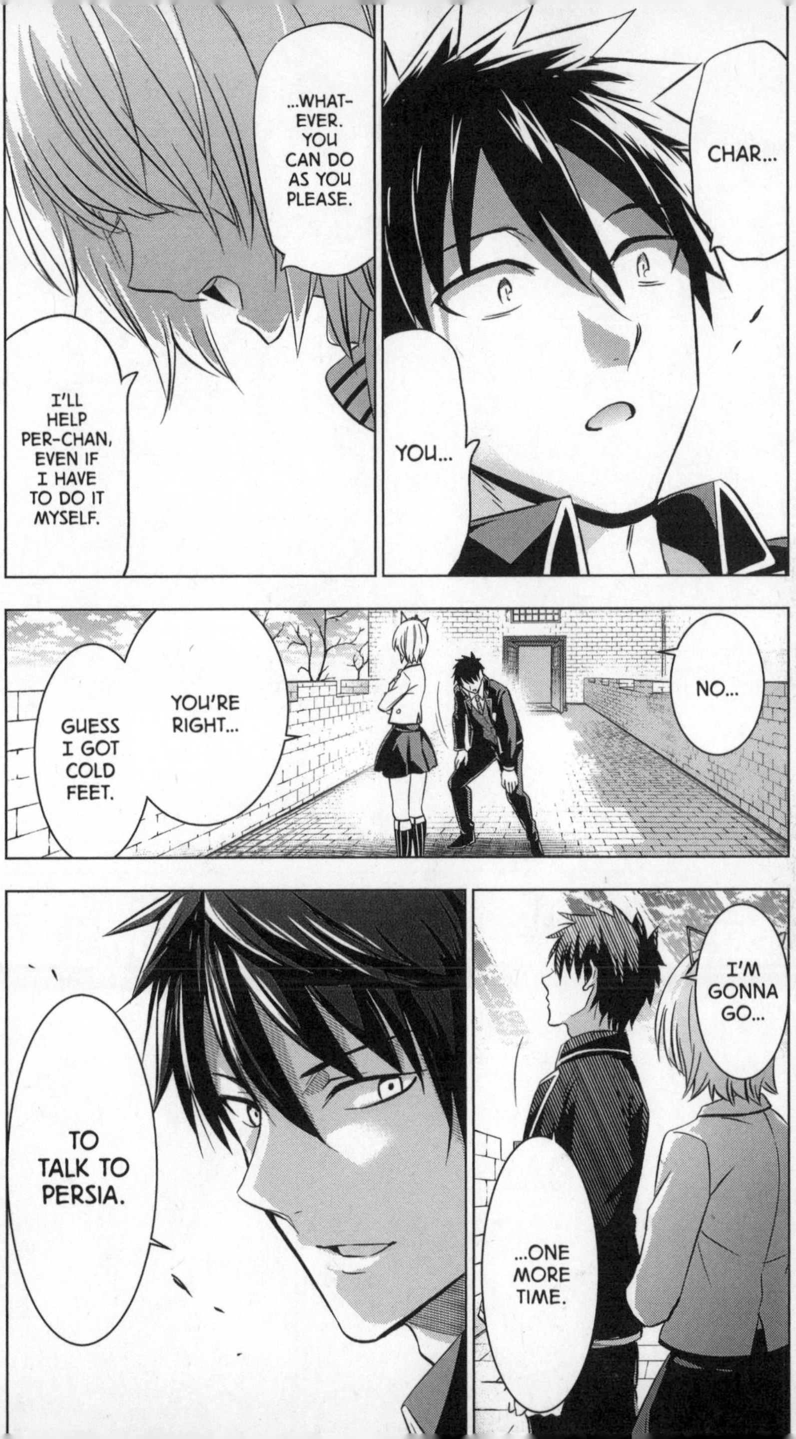
CHAR...
YOU...
...WHAT-EVER. YOU CAN DO AS YOU PLEASE.
I'LL HELP PER-CHAN, EVEN IF I HAVE TO DO IT MYSELF.
NO...
YOU'RE RIGHT...
GUESS I GOT COLD FEET.
I'M GONNA GO...
...ONE MORE TIME.
TO TALK TO PERSIA.

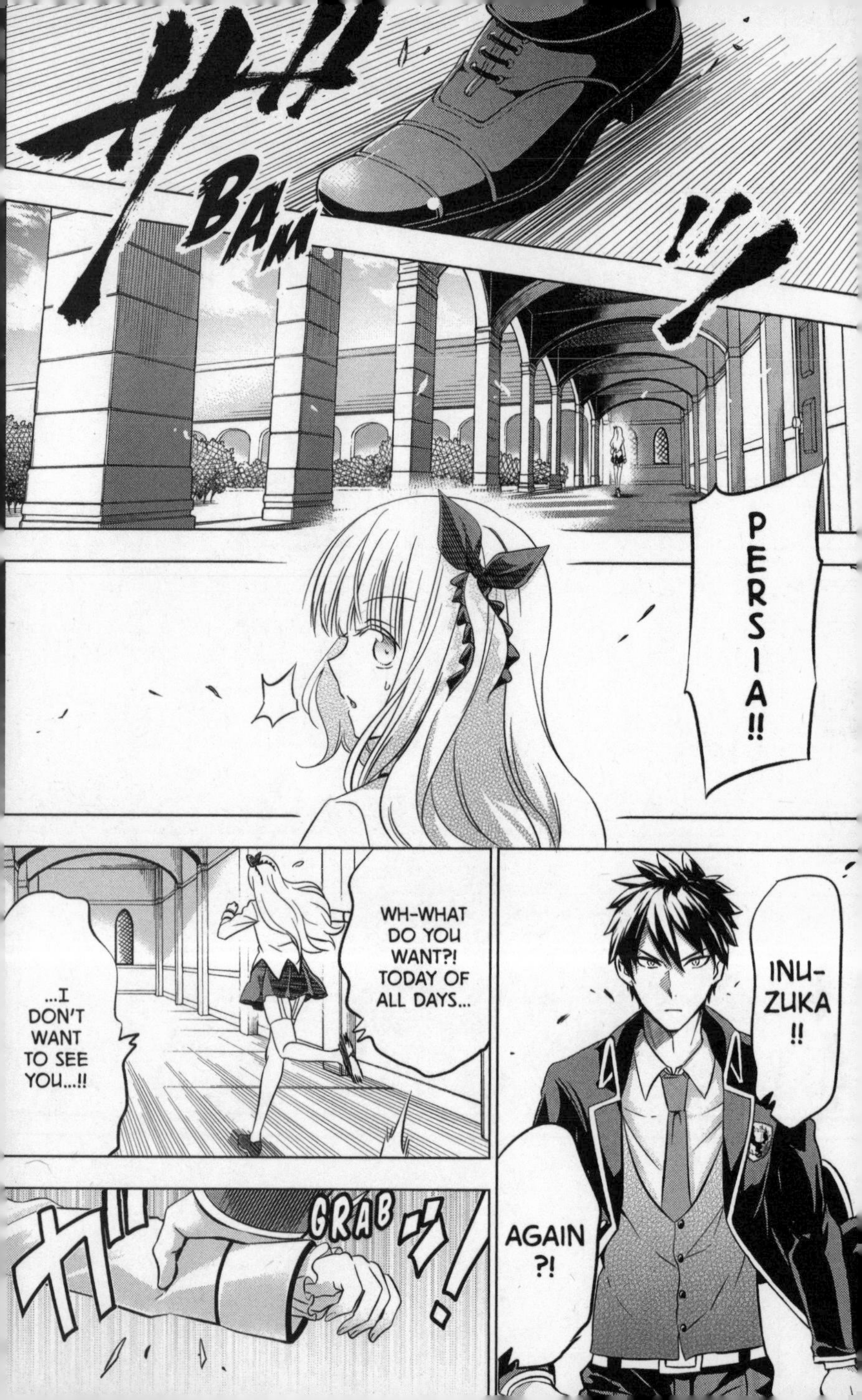
BAM!!
PERSIA!!
INU-ZUKA!!
AGAIN?!
WH-WHAT DO YOU WANT?! TODAY OF ALL DAYS...
...I DON'T WANT TO SEE YOU...!!
GRAB

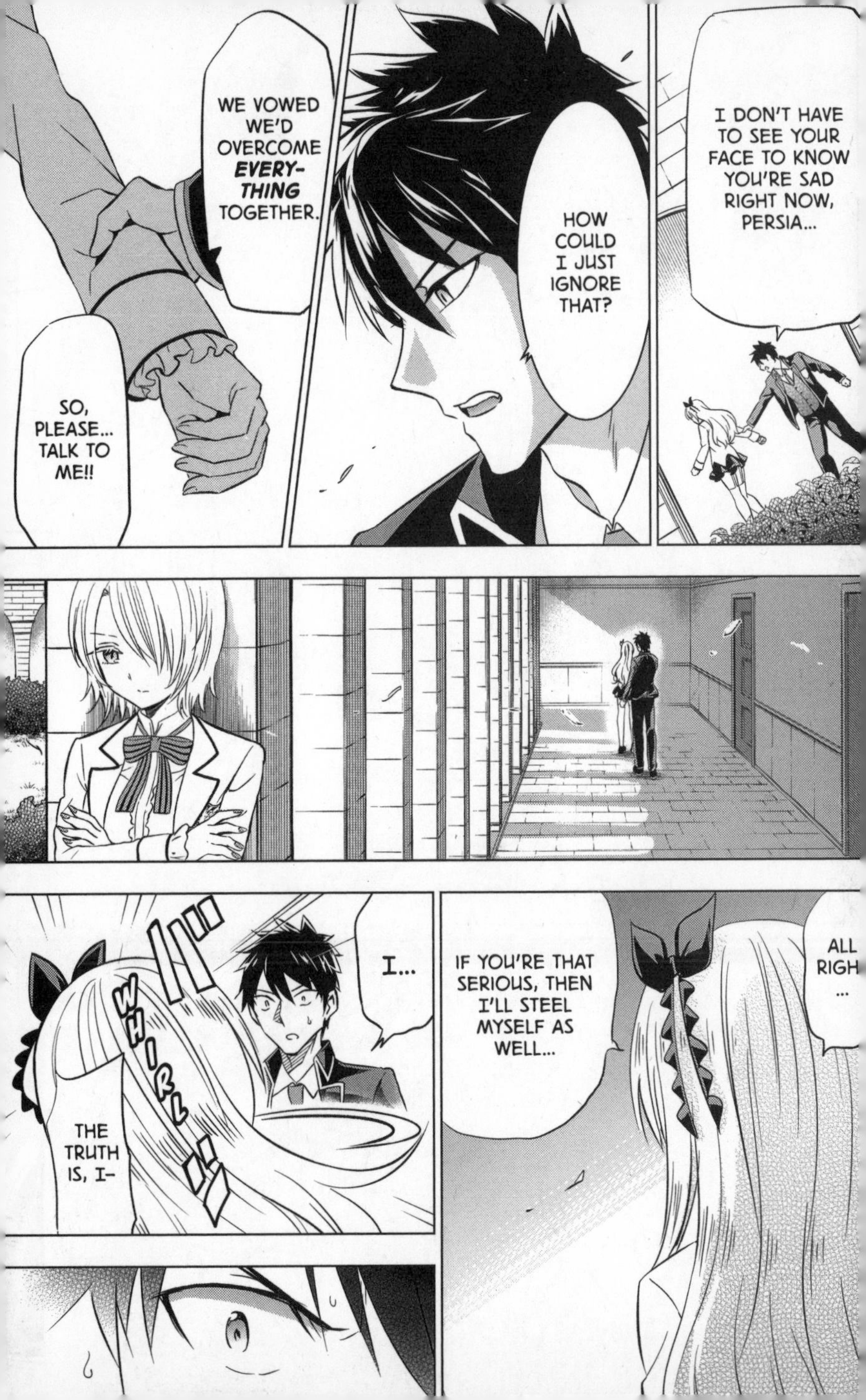
I DON'T HAVE TO SEE YOUR FACE TO KNOW YOU'RE SAD RIGHT NOW, PERSIA...
HOW COULD I JUST IGNORE THAT?
WE VOWED WE'D OVERCOME EVERYTHING TOGETHER.
SO, PLEASE... TALK TO ME!!
ALL RIGH ...
IF YOU'RE THAT SERIOUS, THEN I'LL STEEL MYSELF AS WELL...
I...
WHIRL
THE TRUTH IS, I–

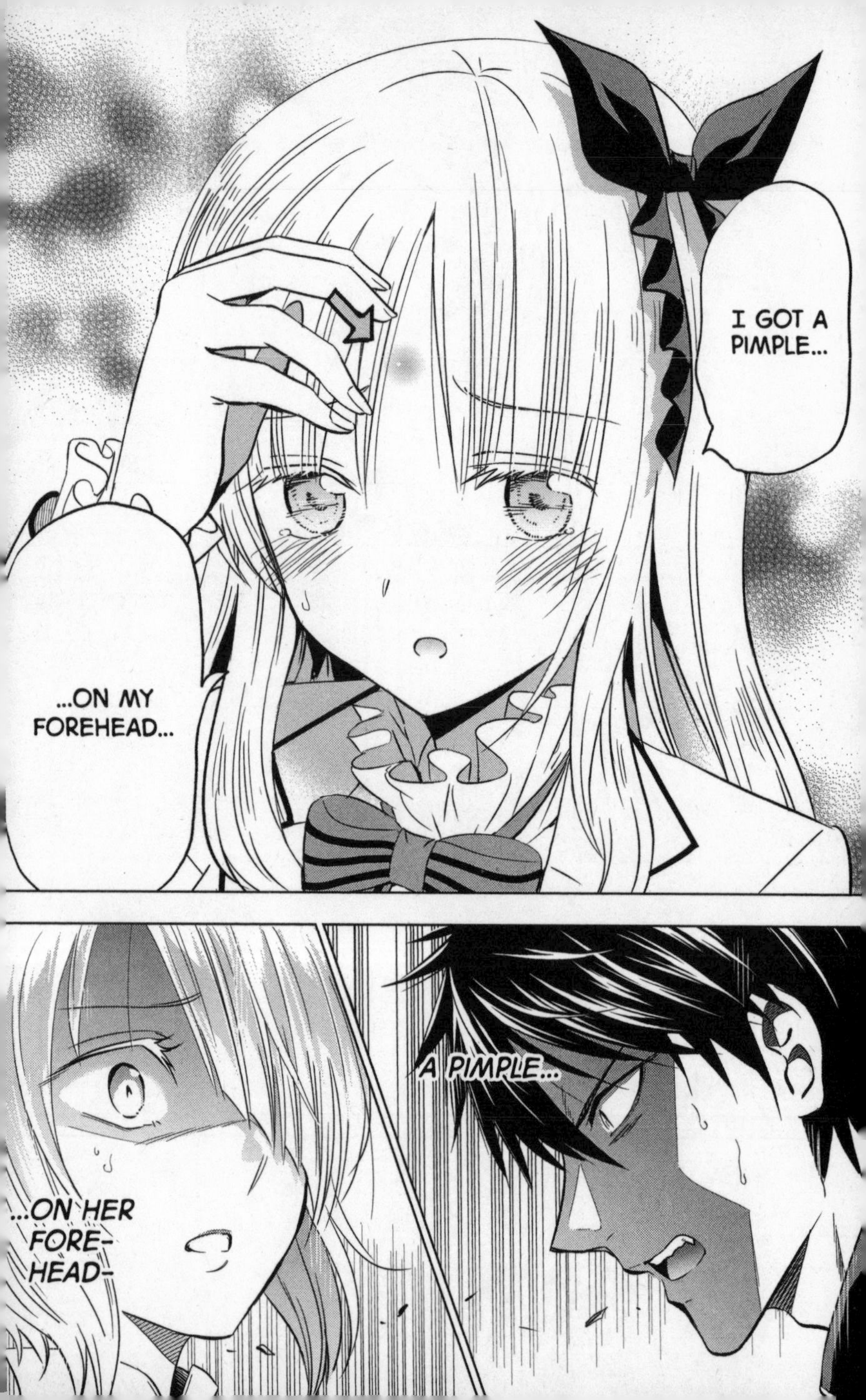
I GOT A PIMPLE...
...ON MY FOREHEAD...
A PIMPLE...
...ON HER FORE-HEAD-

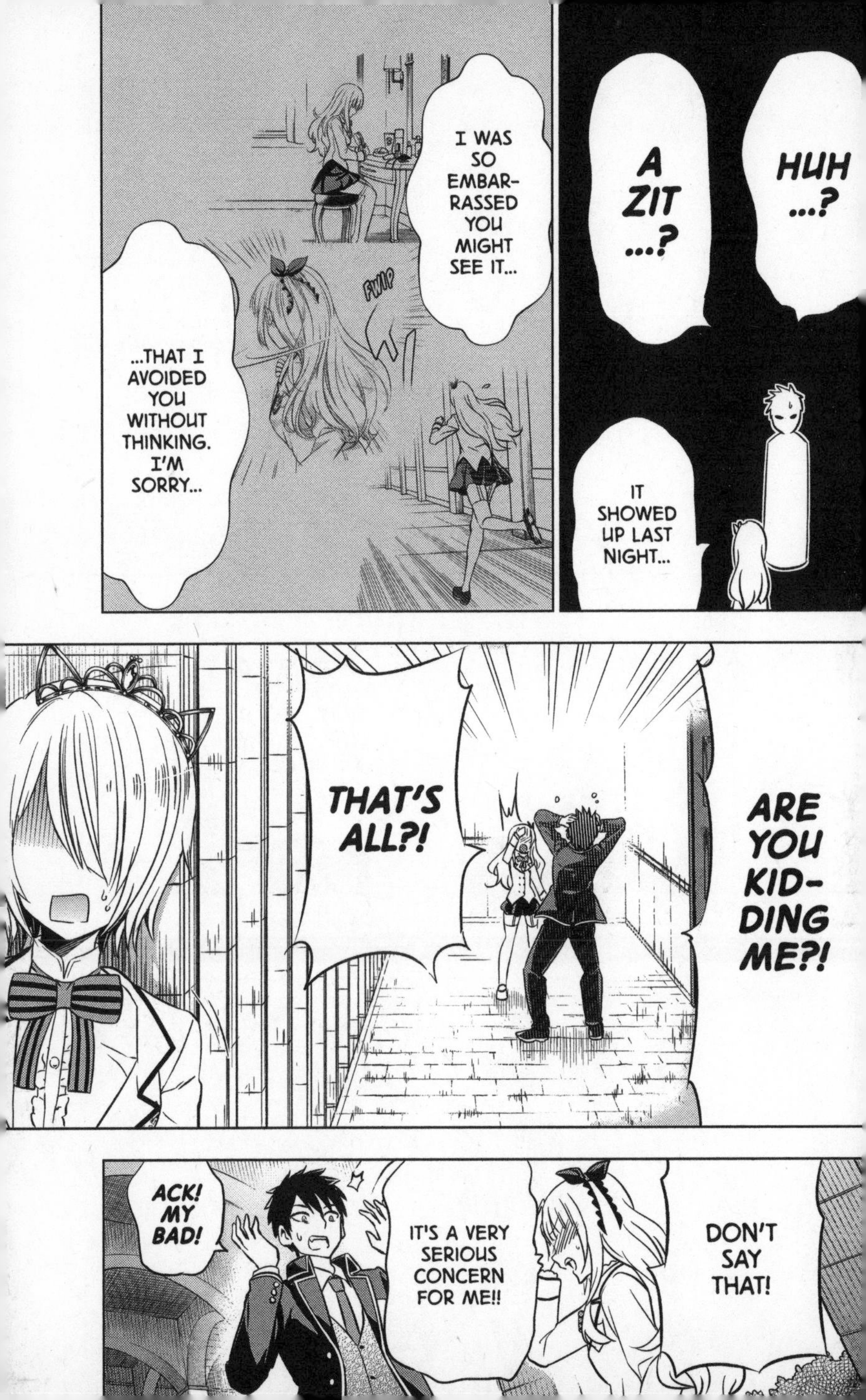
HUH ...?
A ZIT ...?
IT SHOWED UP LAST NIGHT...
I WAS SO EMBARRASSED YOU MIGHT SEE IT...
FWIP
...THAT I AVOIDED YOU WITHOUT THINKING. I'M SORRY...
ARE YOU KIDDING ME?!
THAT'S ALL?!
DON'T SAY THAT!
IT'S A VERY SERIOUS CONCERN FOR ME!!
ACK! MY BAD!

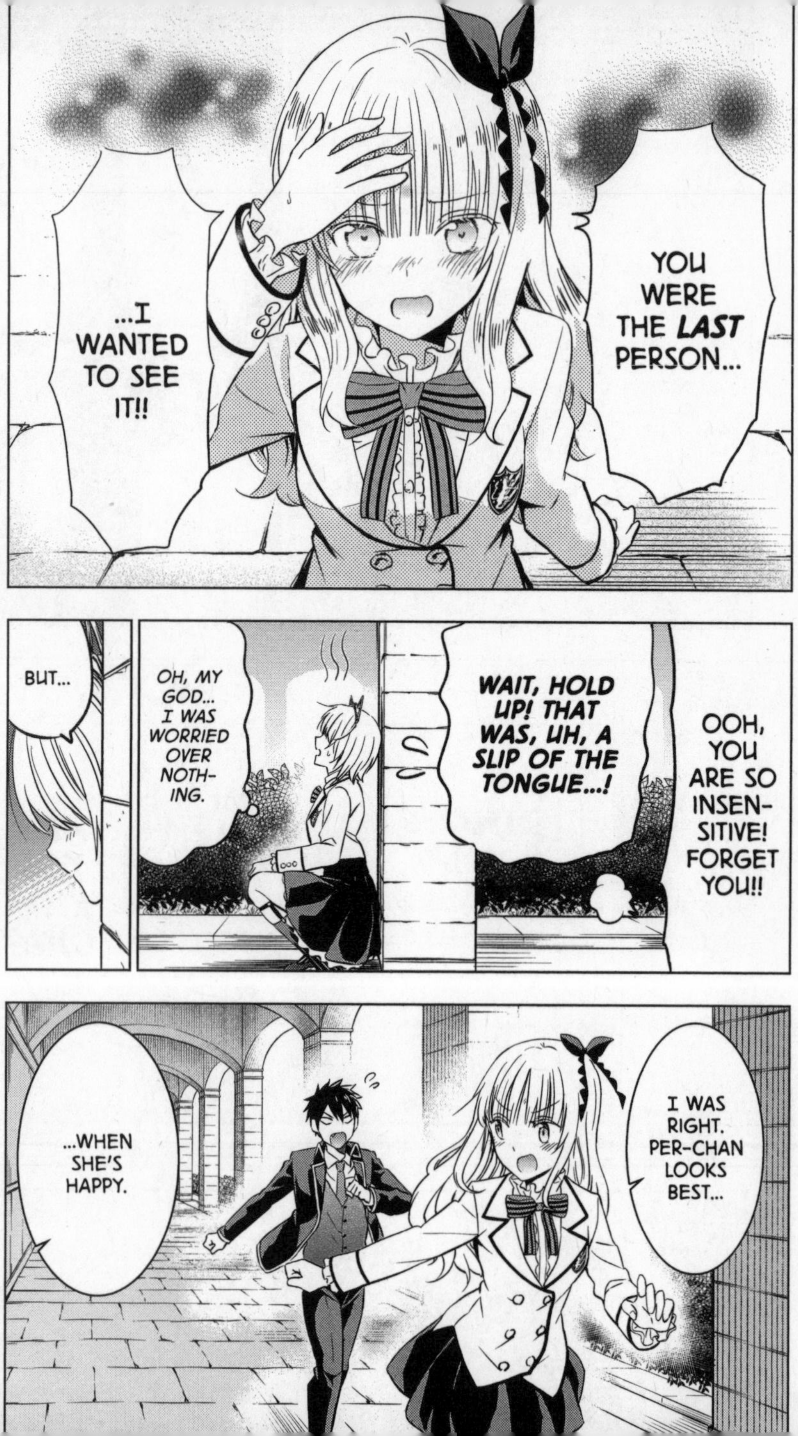
YOU WERE THE *LAST* PERSON...
...I WANTED TO SEE IT!!
OOH, YOU ARE SO INSEN-SITIVE! FORGET YOU!!
WAIT, HOLD UP! THAT WAS, UH, A SLIP OF THE TONGUE...!
OH, MY GOD... I WAS WORRIED OVER NOTH-ING.
BUT...
I WAS RIGHT. PER-CHAN LOOKS BEST...
...WHEN SHE'S HAPPY.

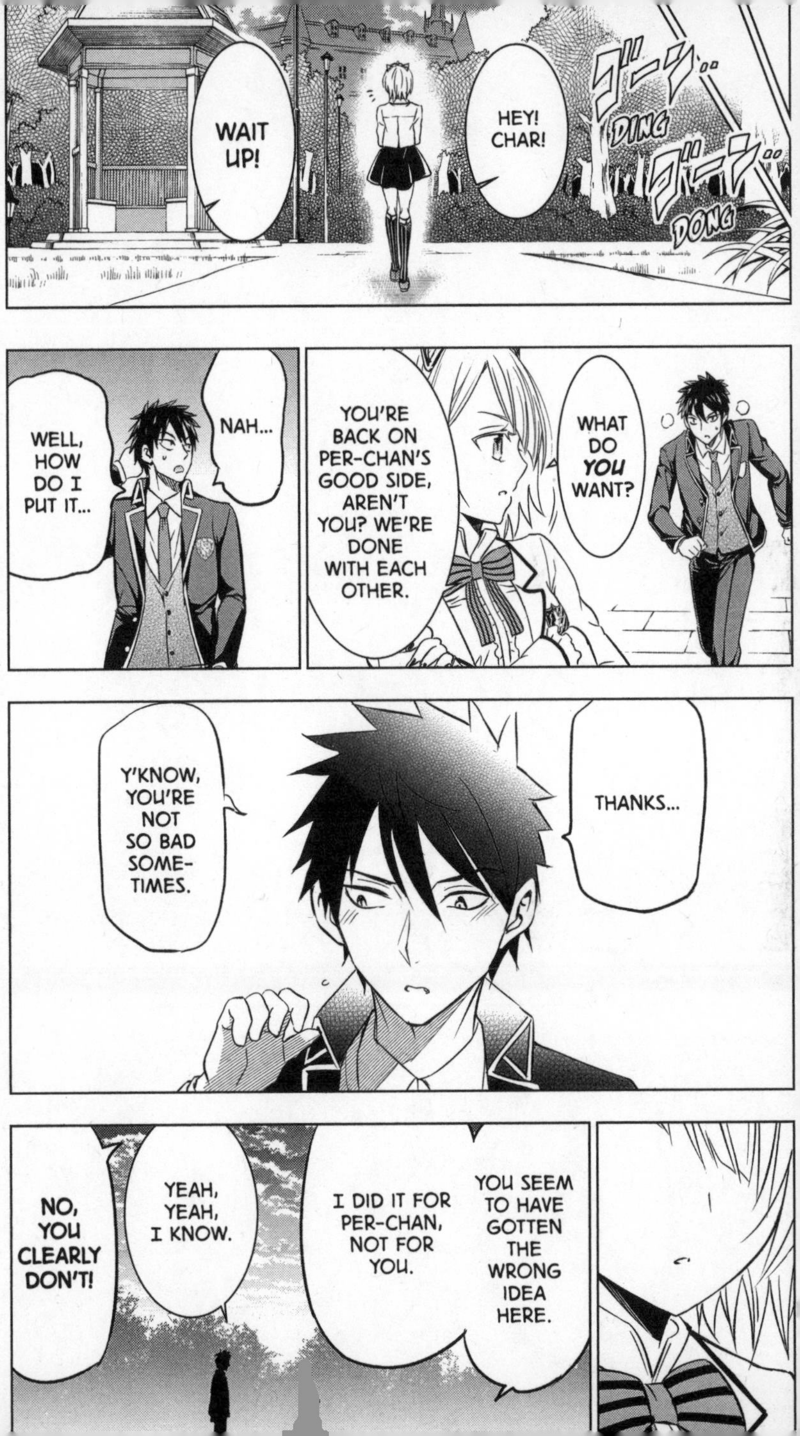
DING
DONG
HEY! CHAR!
WAIT UP!
WHAT DO *YOU* WANT?
YOU'RE BACK ON PER-CHAN'S GOOD SIDE, AREN'T YOU? WE'RE DONE WITH EACH OTHER.
NAH...
WELL, HOW DO I PUT IT...
THANKS...
Y'KNOW, YOU'RE NOT SO BAD SOME-TIMES.
YOU SEEM TO HAVE GOTTEN THE WRONG IDEA HERE.
I DID IT FOR PER-CHAN, NOT FOR YOU.
YEAH, YEAH, I KNOW.
NO, YOU CLEARLY DON'T!

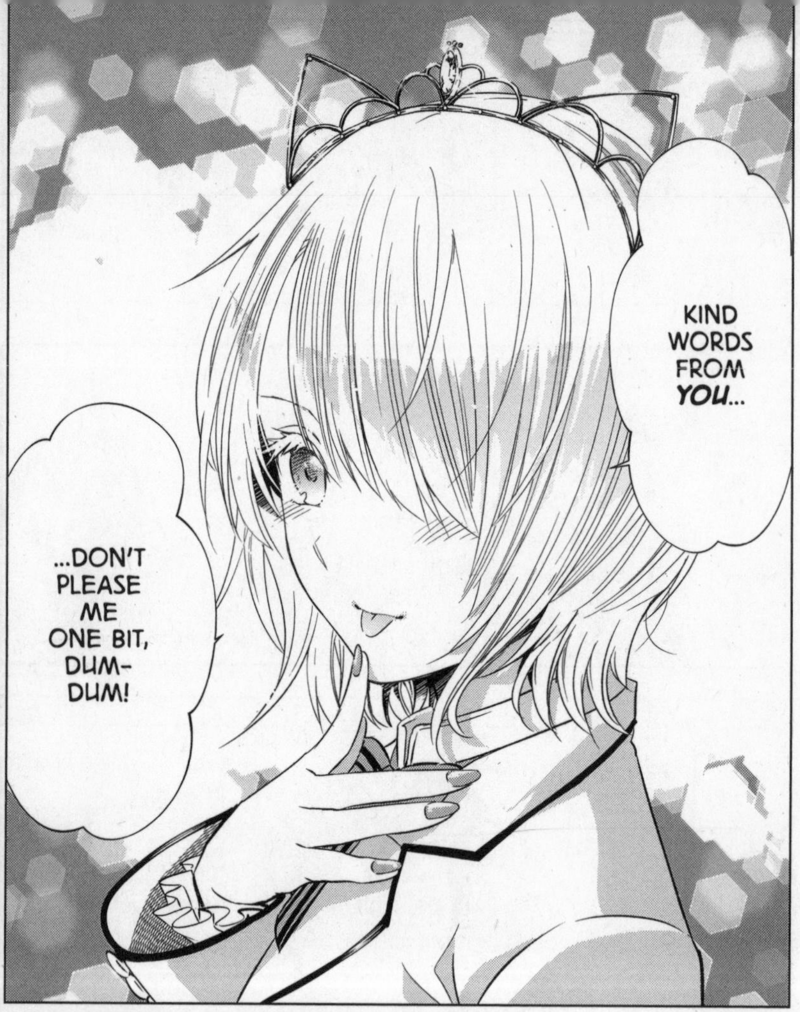
KIND WORDS FROM ***YOU***...
...DON'T PLEASE ME ONE BIT, DUM-DUM!

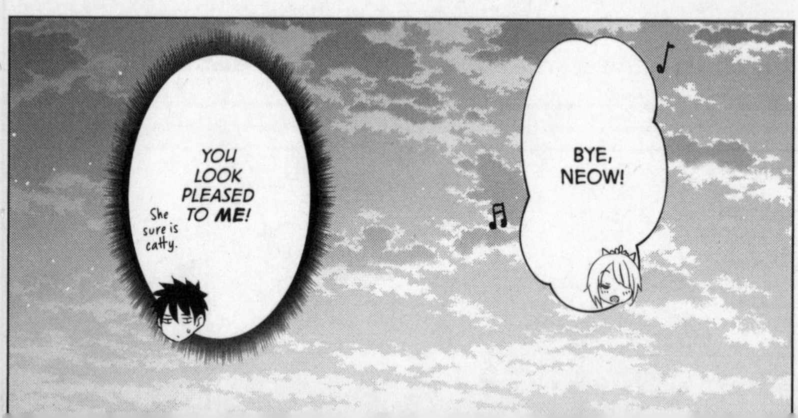
BYE, NEOW!
*YOU LOOK PLEASED TO **ME**!*
She sure is catty.

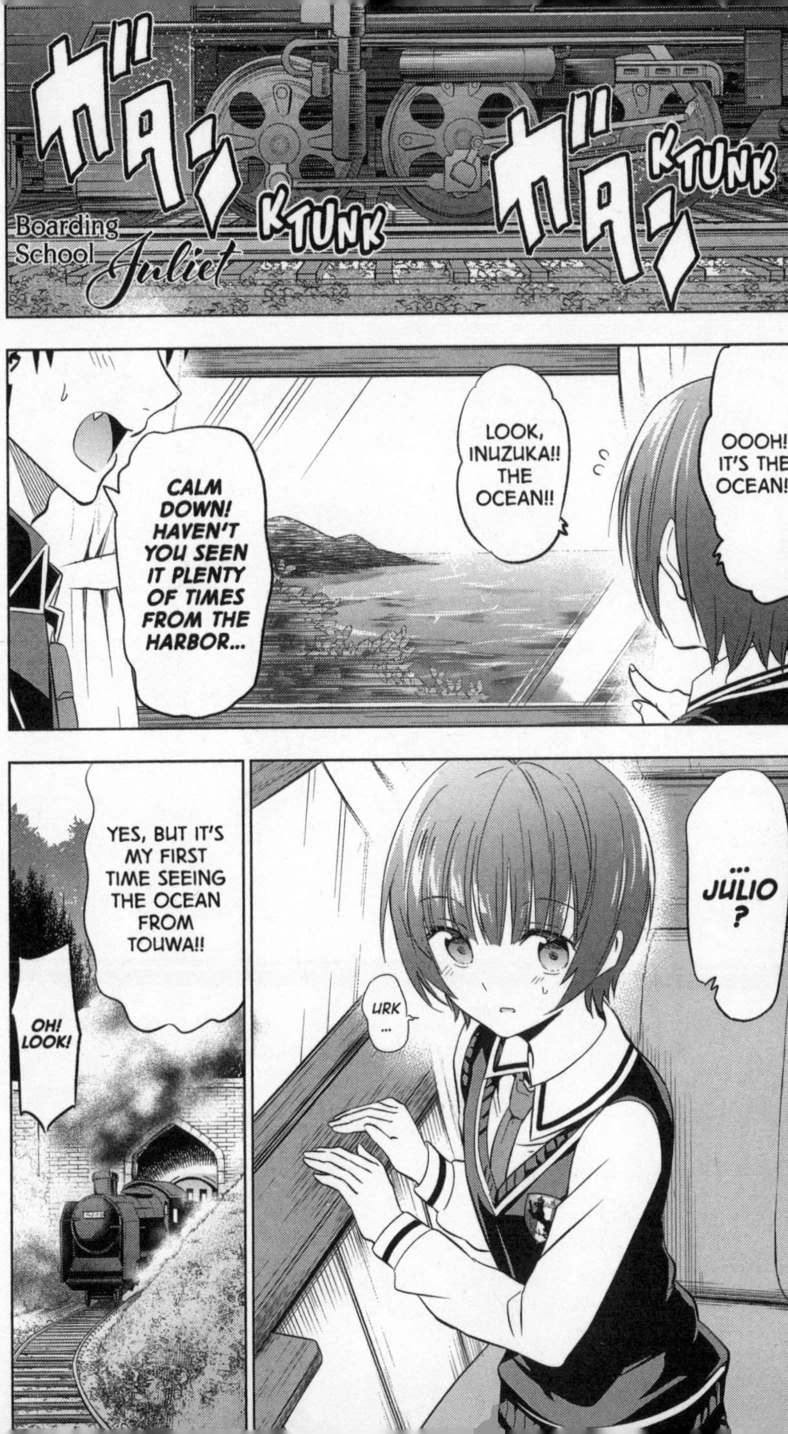
ガタン
KTUNK
ガタン
KTUNK
Boarding School Juliet
OOOH! IT'S THE OCEAN!!
LOOK, INUZUKA!! THE OCEAN!!
CALM DOWN! HAVEN'T YOU SEEN IT PLENTY OF TIMES FROM THE HARBOR...
...JULIO?
URK...
YES, BUT IT'S MY FIRST TIME SEEING THE OCEAN FROM TOUWA!!
OH! LOOK!

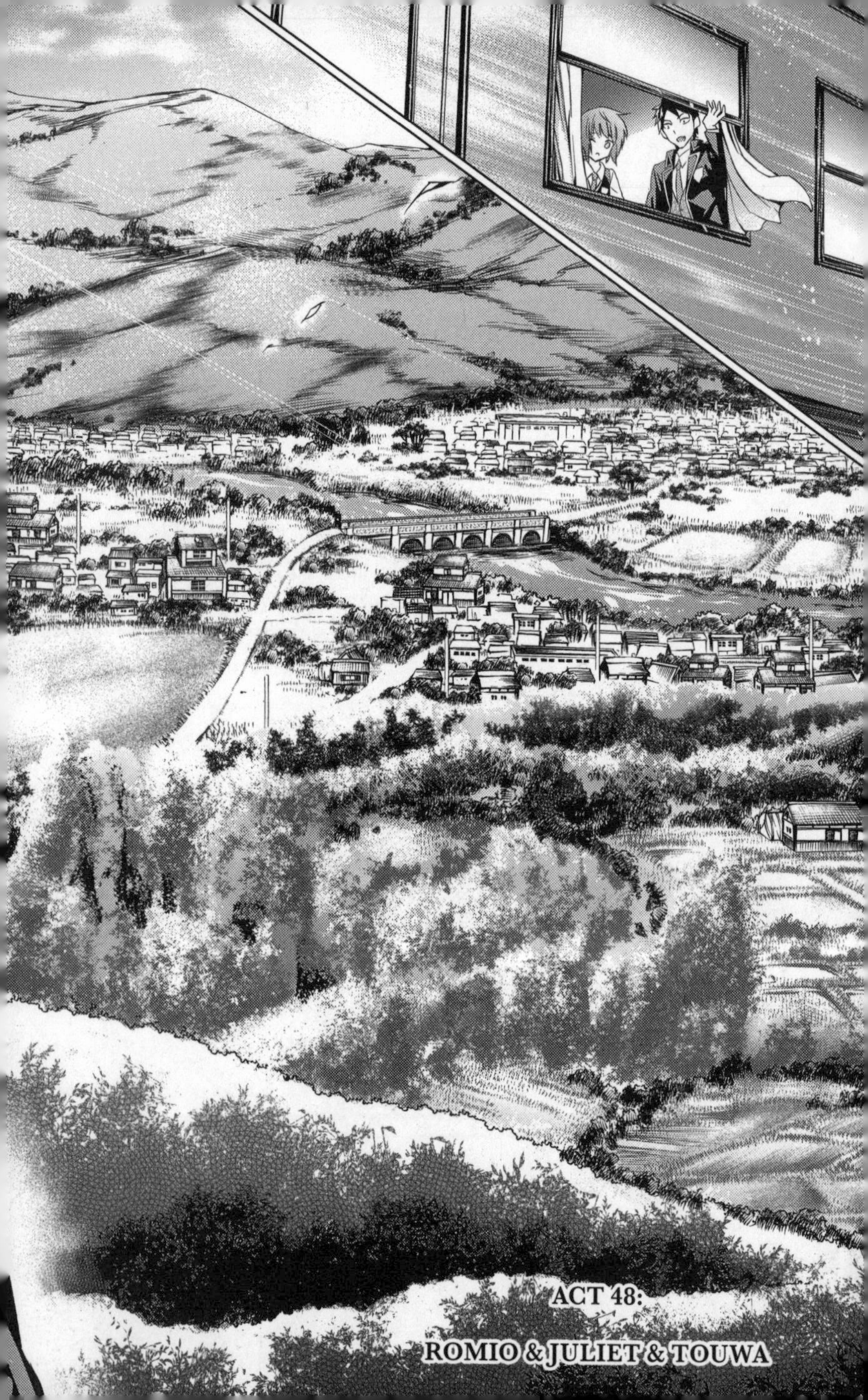
ACT 48:
ROMIO & JULIET & TOUWA

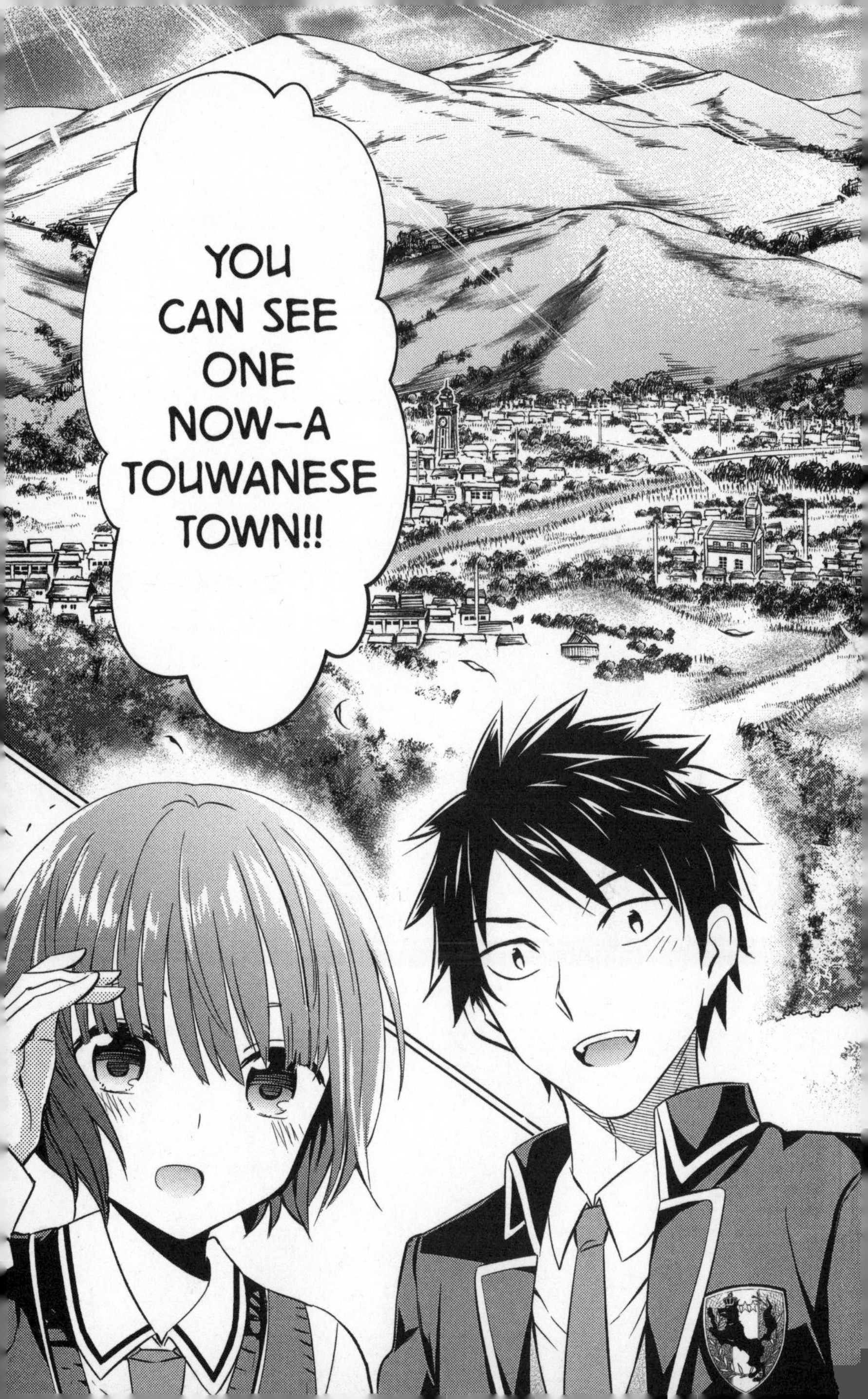
YOU CAN SEE ONE NOW—A TOUWANESE TOWN!!

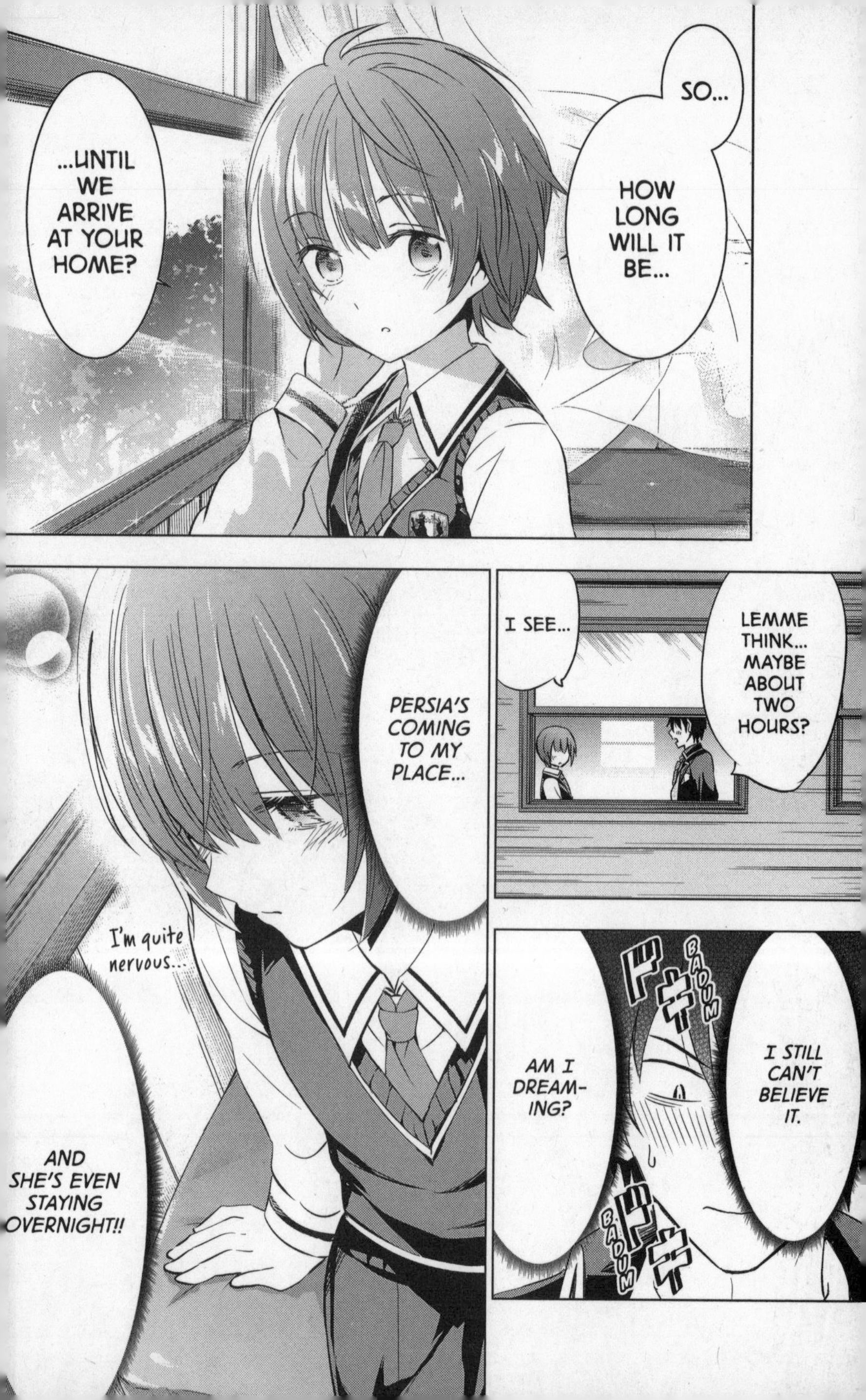
SO... HOW LONG WILL IT BE...
...UNTIL WE ARRIVE AT YOUR HOME?
LEMME THINK... MAYBE ABOUT TWO HOURS?
I SEE...
I STILL CAN'T BELIEVE IT.
ドキ BADUM
AM I DREAMING?
ドキ BADUM
PERSIA'S COMING TO MY PLACE...
AND SHE'S EVEN STAYING OVERNIGHT!!
I'm quite nervous...

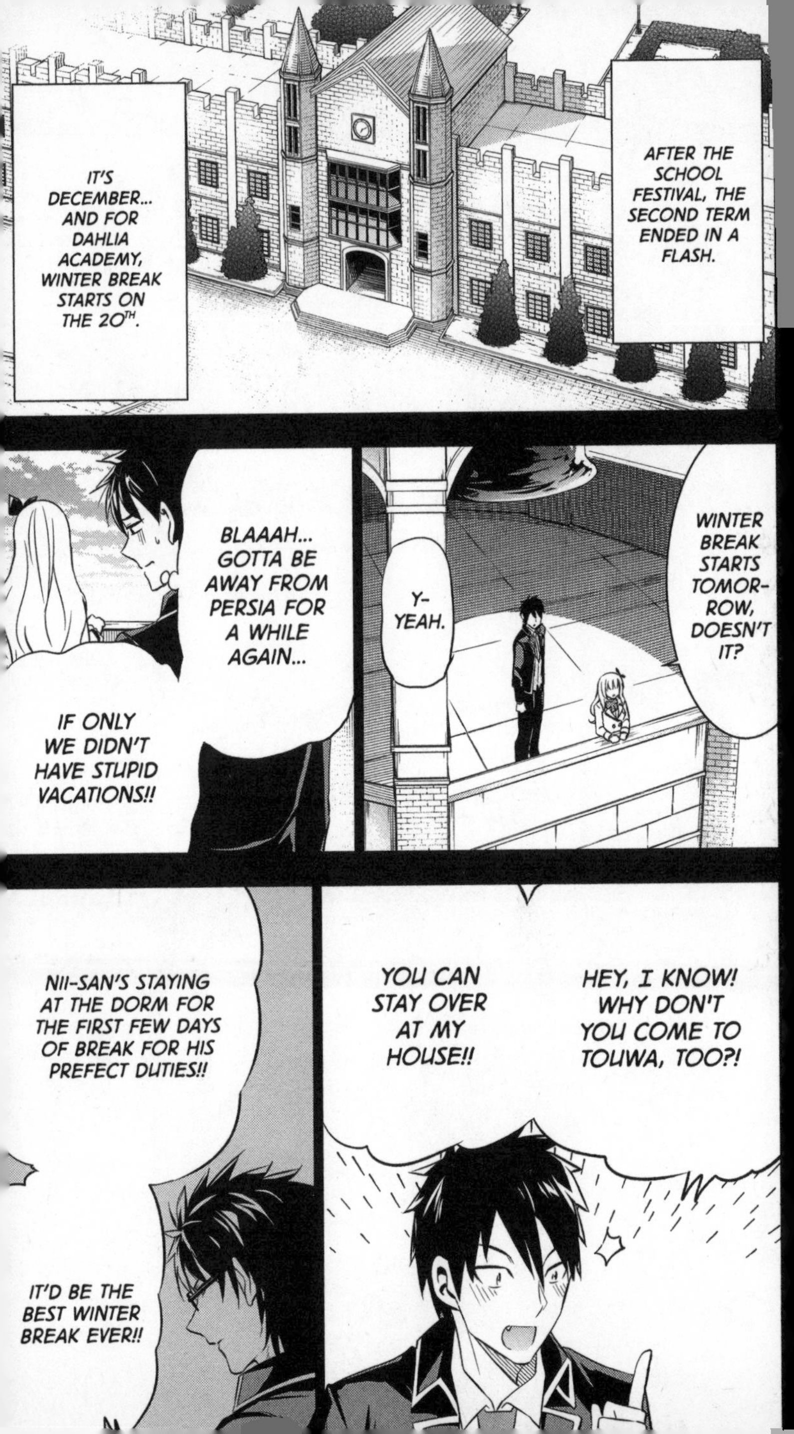
AFTER THE SCHOOL FESTIVAL, THE SECOND TERM ENDED IN A FLASH.
IT'S DECEMBER... AND FOR DAHLIA ACADEMY, WINTER BREAK STARTS ON THE 20TH.
WINTER BREAK STARTS TOMOR-ROW, DOESN'T IT?
Y-YEAH.
BLAAAH... GOTTA BE AWAY FROM PERSIA FOR A WHILE AGAIN...
IF ONLY WE DIDN'T HAVE STUPID VACATIONS!!
HEY, I KNOW! WHY DON'T YOU COME TO TOUWA, TOO?!
YOU CAN STAY OVER AT MY HOUSE!!
NII-SAN'S STAYING AT THE DORM FOR THE FIRST FEW DAYS OF BREAK FOR HIS PREFECT DUTIES!!
IT'D BE THE BEST WINTER BREAK EVER!!

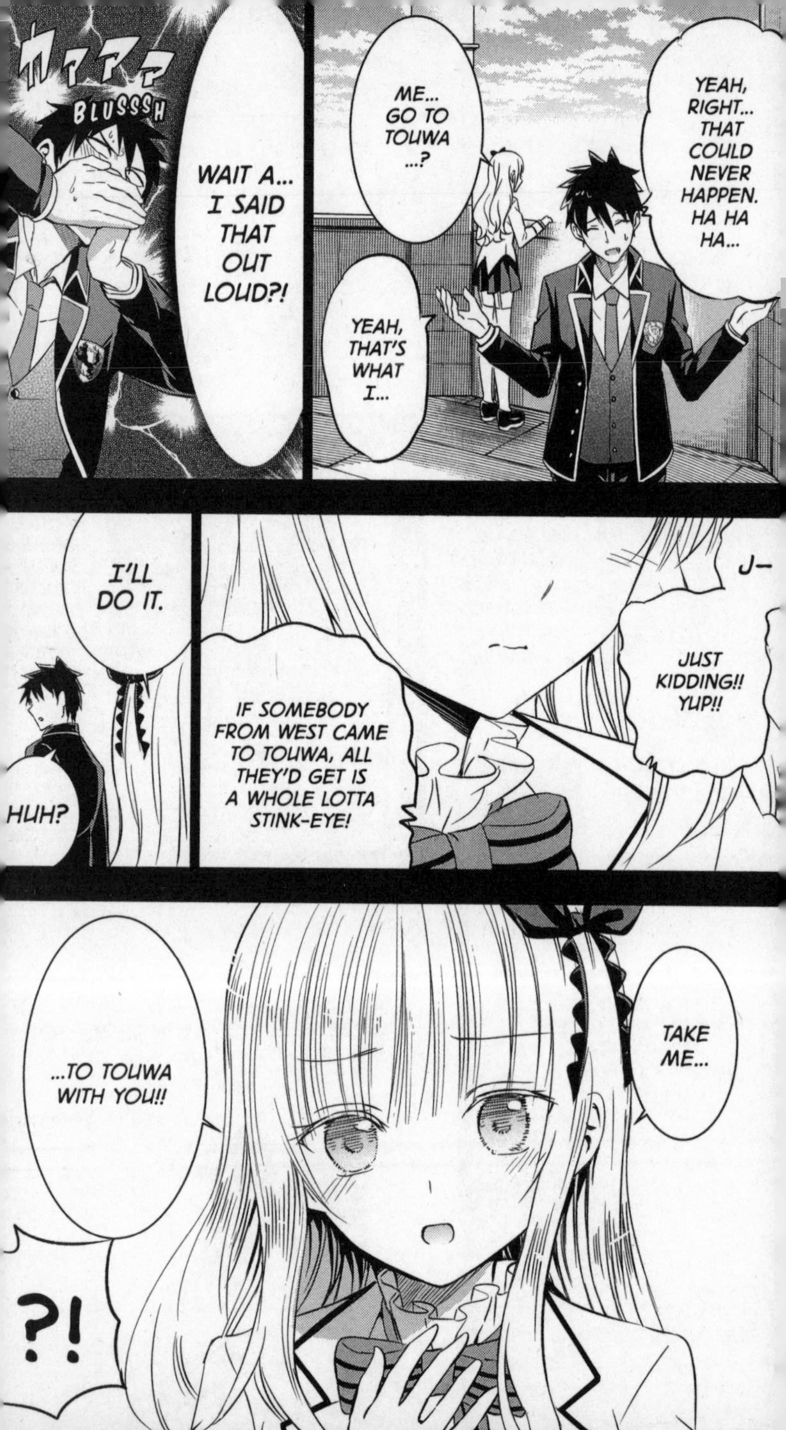
YEAH, RIGHT... THAT COULD NEVER HAPPEN. HA HA HA...
ME... GO TO TOUWA ...?
YEAH, THAT'S WHAT I...
BLUSSSH
WAIT A... I SAID THAT OUT LOUD?!
J—
JUST KIDDING!! YUP!!
IF SOMEBODY FROM WEST CAME TO TOUWA, ALL THEY'D GET IS A WHOLE LOTTA STINK-EYE!
I'LL DO IT.
HUH?
TAKE ME...
...TO TOUWA WITH YOU!!
?!

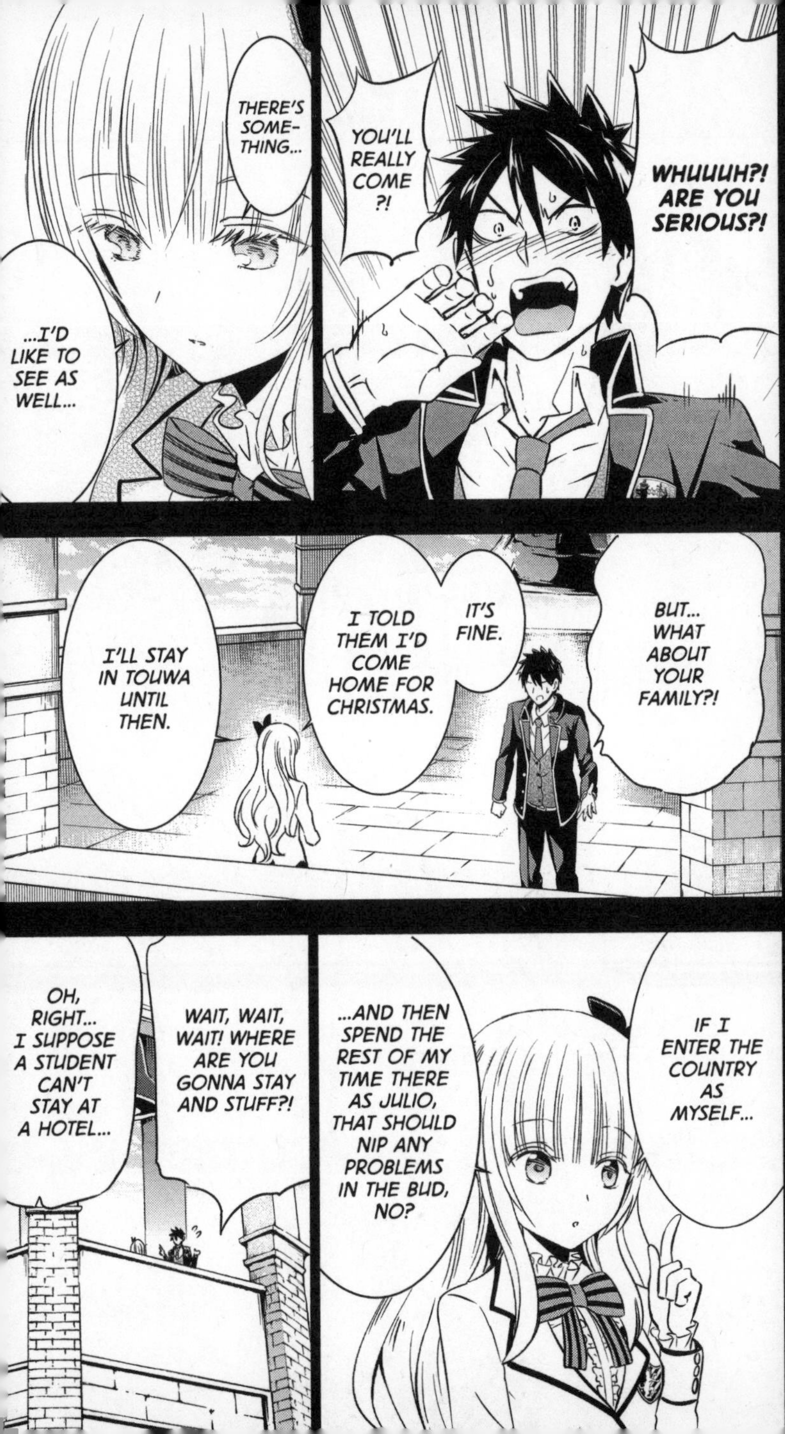
WHUUUH?! ARE YOU SERIOUS?!
YOU'LL REALLY COME ?!
THERE'S SOME-THING...
...I'D LIKE TO SEE AS WELL...
BUT... WHAT ABOUT YOUR FAMILY?!
IT'S FINE.
I TOLD THEM I'D COME HOME FOR CHRISTMAS.
I'LL STAY IN TOUWA UNTIL THEN.
IF I ENTER THE COUNTRY AS MYSELF...
...AND THEN SPEND THE REST OF MY TIME THERE AS JULIO, THAT SHOULD NIP ANY PROBLEMS IN THE BUD, NO?
WAIT, WAIT, WAIT! WHERE ARE YOU GONNA STAY AND STUFF?!
OH, RIGHT... I SUPPOSE A STUDENT CAN'T STAY AT A HOTEL...

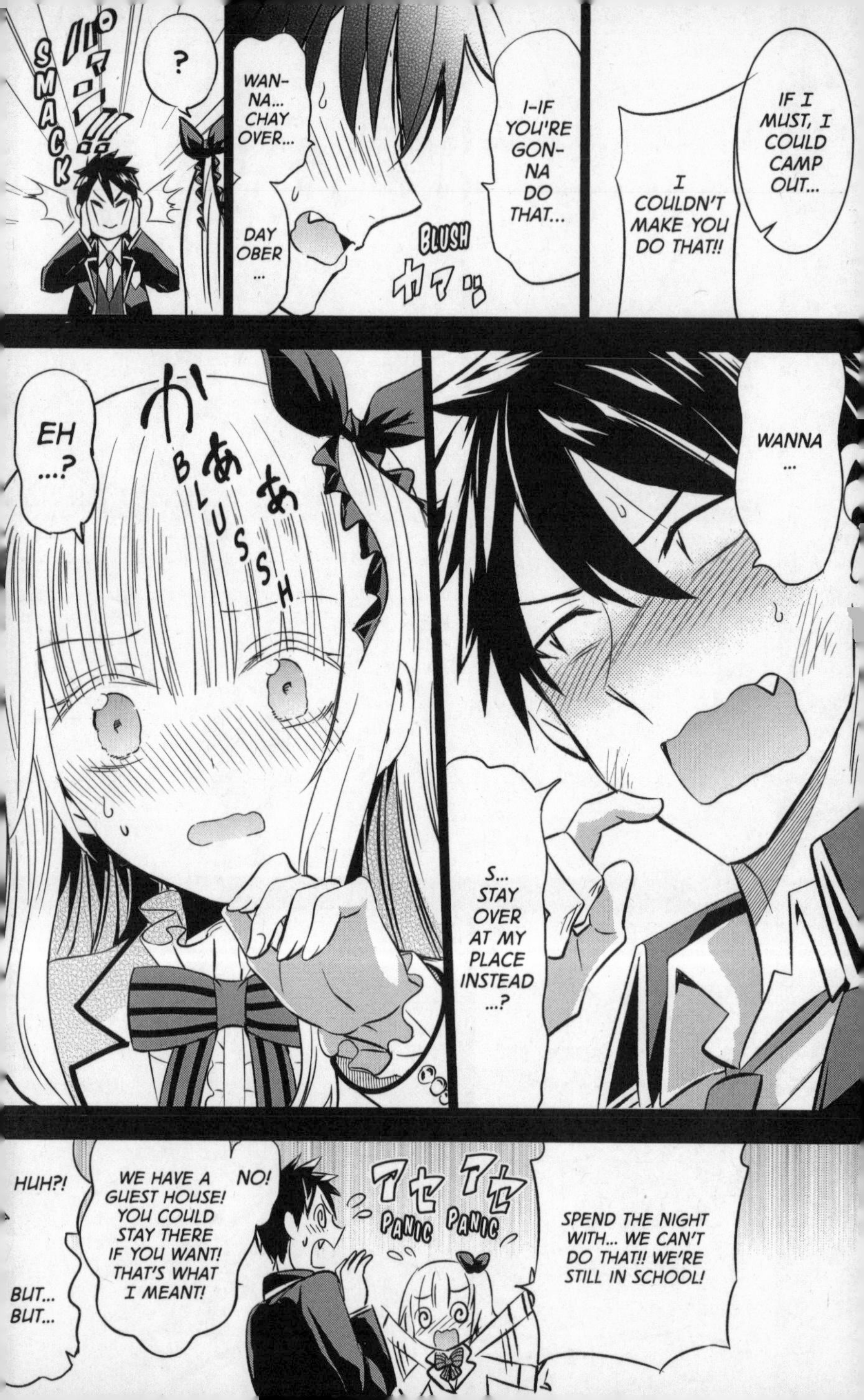
IF I MUST, I COULD CAMP OUT...
I COULDN'T MAKE YOU DO THAT!!
I-IF YOU'RE GON-NA DO THAT...
BLUSH
カァッ
WAN-NA... CHAY OVER...
DAY OBER...
?
SMACK
パァンッ
WANNA...
S... STAY OVER AT MY PLACE INSTEAD...?
EH...?
BLUSSH
かぁぁ
SPEND THE NIGHT WITH... WE CAN'T DO THAT!! WE'RE STILL IN SCHOOL!
アセアセ
PANIC PANIC
NO!
WE HAVE A GUEST HOUSE! YOU COULD STAY THERE IF YOU WANT! THAT'S WHAT I MEANT!
HUH?!
BUT... BUT...

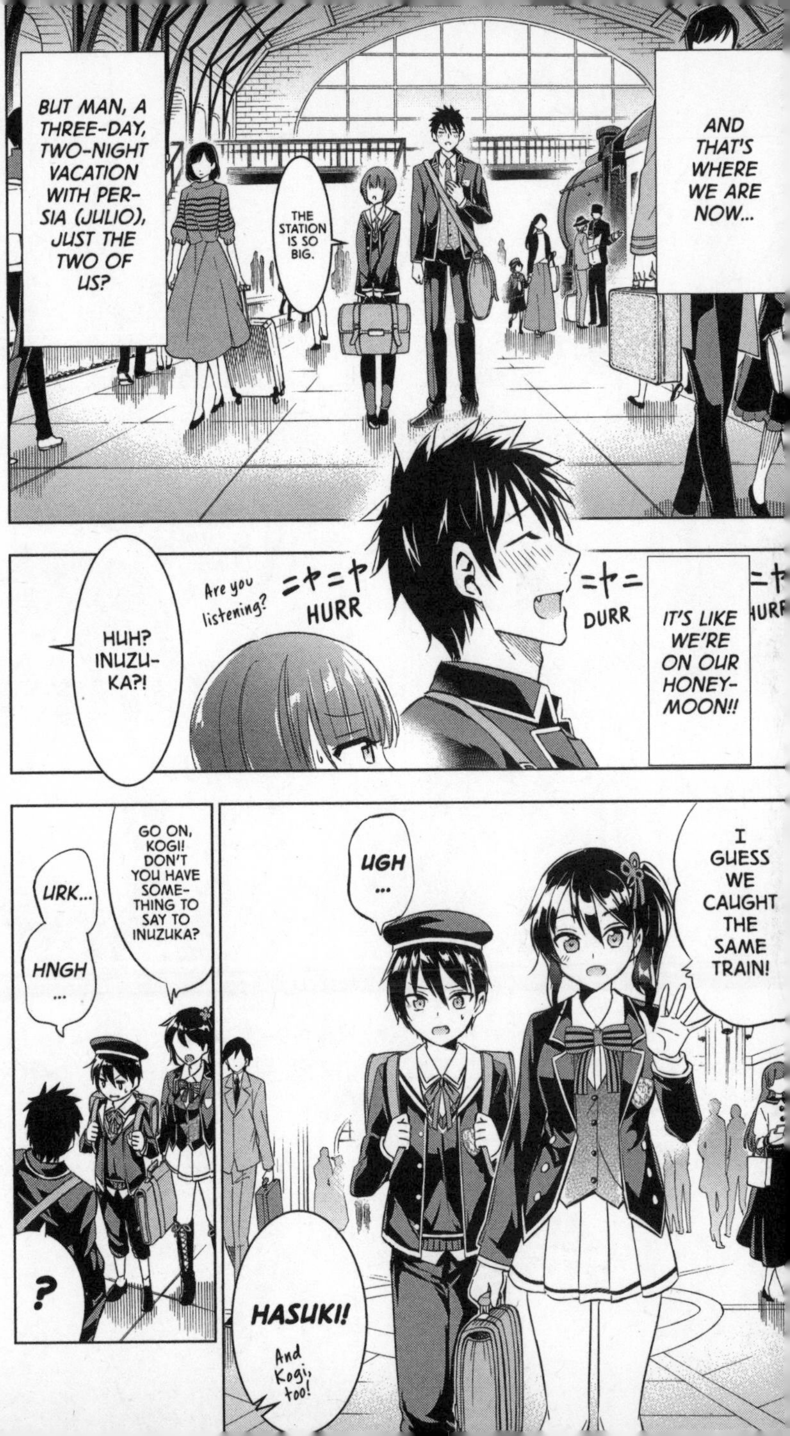
AND THAT'S WHERE WE ARE NOW...
THE STATION IS SO BIG.
BUT MAN, A THREE-DAY, TWO-NIGHT VACATION WITH PERSIA (JULIO), JUST THE TWO OF US?
IT'S LIKE WE'RE ON OUR HONEYMOON!!
HURR
DURR
HURR
Are you listening?
HUH? INUZUKA?!
I GUESS WE CAUGHT THE SAME TRAIN!
UGH...
HASUKI!
And Kogi, too!
GO ON, KOGI! DON'T YOU HAVE SOMETHING TO SAY TO INUZUKA?
URK...
HNGH...
?

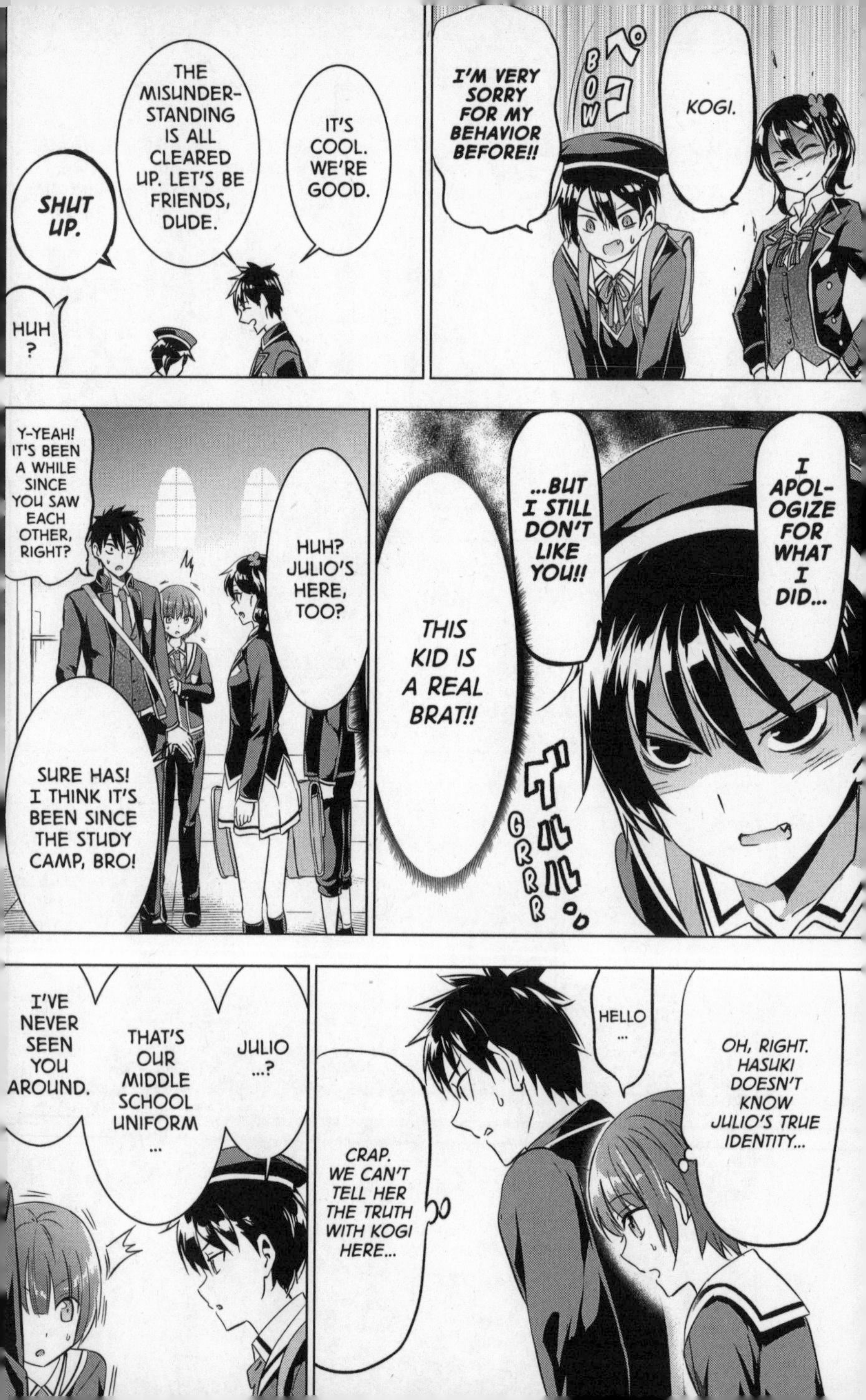
KOGI.
BOW
I'M VERY SORRY FOR MY BEHAVIOR BEFORE!!
IT'S COOL. WE'RE GOOD.
THE MISUNDER-STANDING IS ALL CLEARED UP. LET'S BE FRIENDS, DUDE.
SHUT UP.
HUH?
I APOLOGIZE FOR WHAT I DID...
...BUT I STILL DON'T LIKE YOU!!
THIS KID IS A REAL BRAT!!
GRRR
HUH? JULIO'S HERE, TOO?
Y-YEAH! IT'S BEEN A WHILE SINCE YOU SAW EACH OTHER, RIGHT?
SURE HAS! I THINK IT'S BEEN SINCE THE STUDY CAMP, BRO!
OH, RIGHT. HASUKI DOESN'T KNOW JULIO'S TRUE IDENTITY...
HELLO...
CRAP. WE CAN'T TELL HER THE TRUTH WITH KOGI HERE...
JULIO...?
THAT'S OUR MIDDLE SCHOOL UNIFORM...
I'VE NEVER SEEN YOU AROUND.

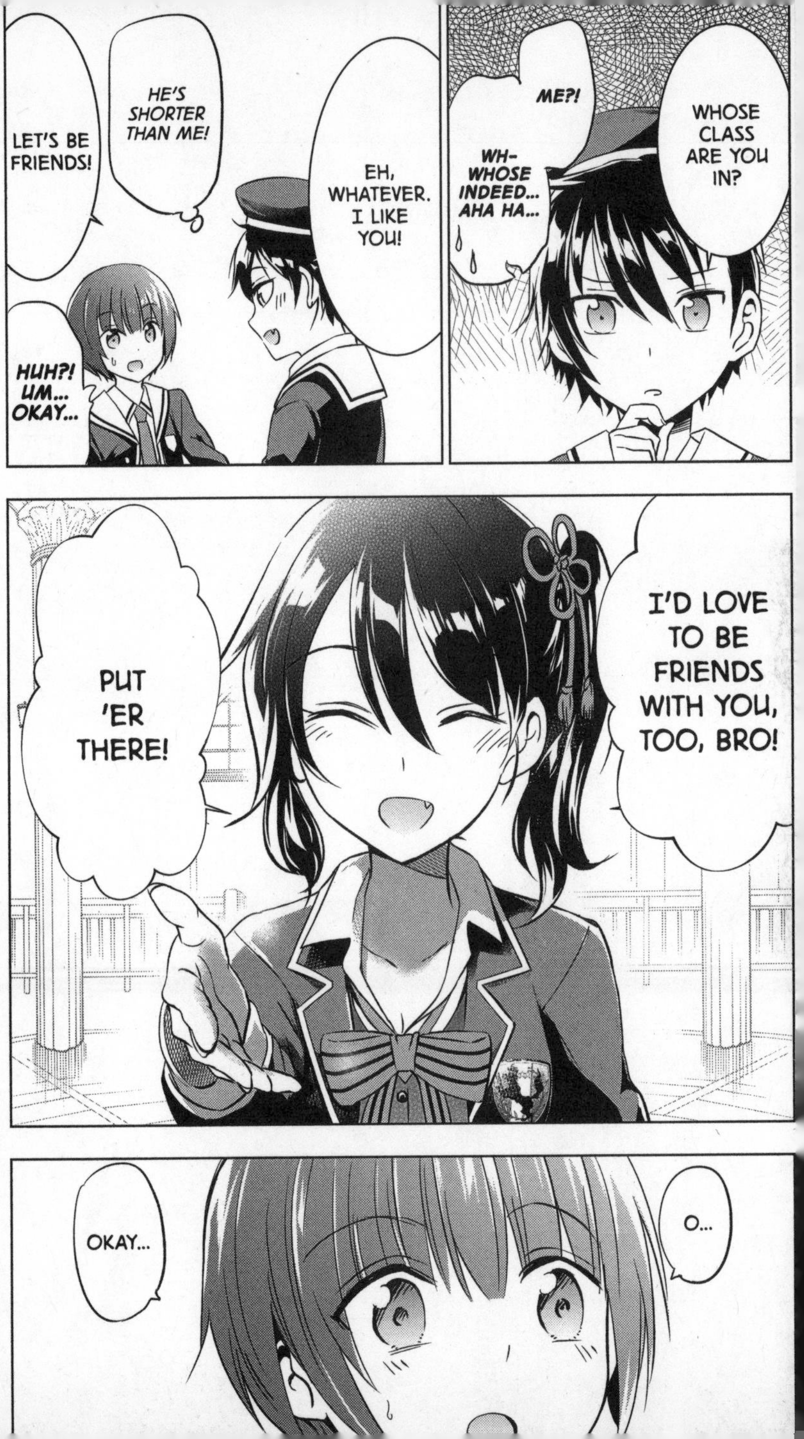
WHOSE CLASS ARE YOU IN?
ME?!
WH- WHOSE INDEED... AHA HA...
EH, WHATEVER. I LIKE YOU!
HE'S SHORTER THAN ME!
LET'S BE FRIENDS!
HUH?! UM... OKAY...
I'D LOVE TO BE FRIENDS WITH YOU, TOO, BRO!
PUT 'ER THERE!
O...
OKAY...

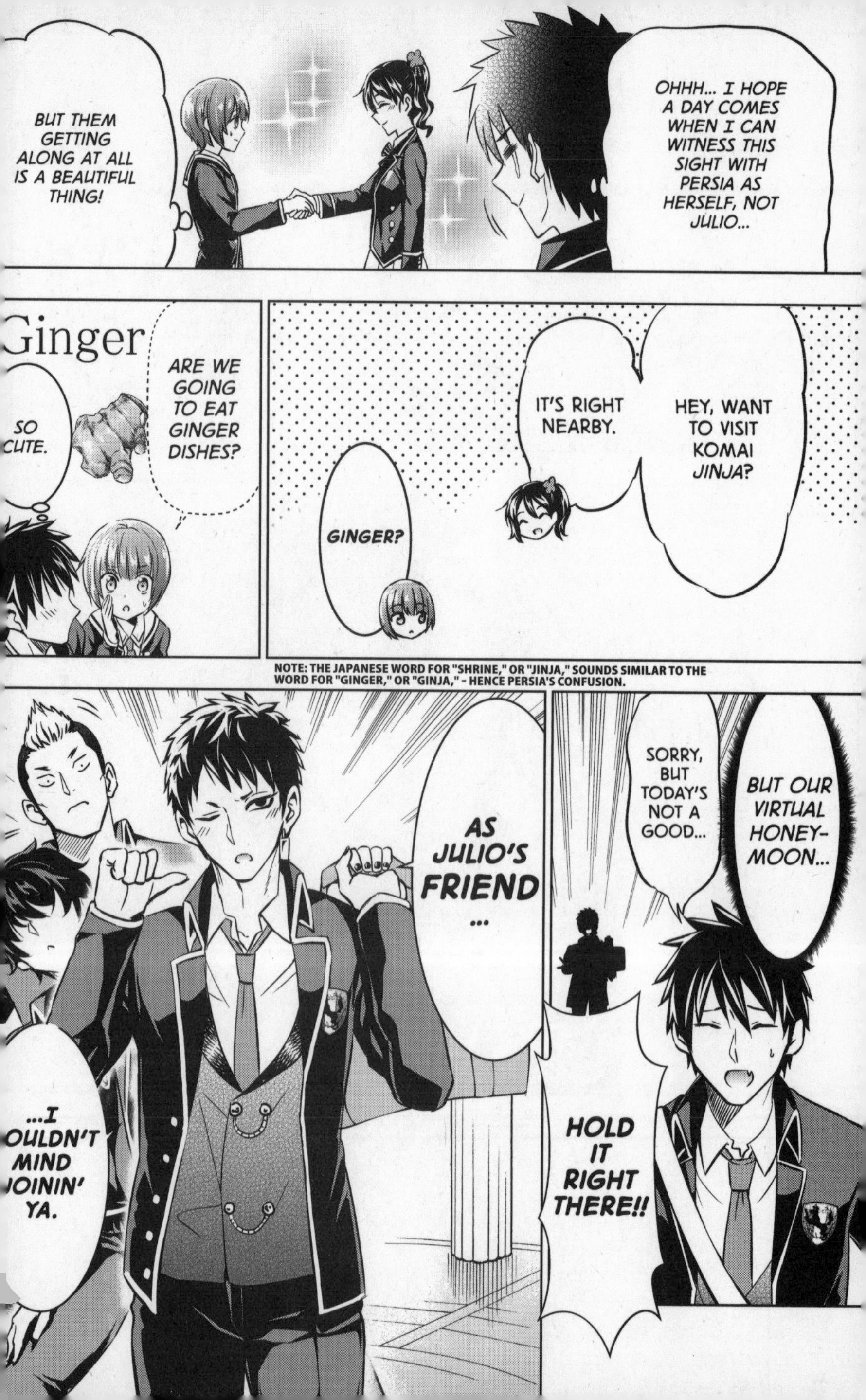

OHHH... I HOPE A DAY COMES WHEN I CAN WITNESS THIS SIGHT WITH PERSIA AS HERSELF, NOT JULIO...
BUT THEM GETTING ALONG AT ALL IS A BEAUTIFUL THING!
HEY, WANT TO VISIT KOMAI JINJA?
IT'S RIGHT NEARBY.
GINGER?
ARE WE GOING TO EAT GINGER DISHES?
SO CUTE.
Ginger
NOTE: THE JAPANESE WORD FOR "SHRINE," OR "JINJA," SOUNDS SIMILAR TO THE WORD FOR "GINGER," OR "GINJA," - HENCE PERSIA'S CONFUSION.
BUT OUR VIRTUAL HONEY-MOON...
SORRY, BUT TODAY'S NOT A GOOD...
HOLD IT RIGHT THERE!!
AS JULIO'S FRIEND ...
...I OULDN'T MIND OININ' YA.

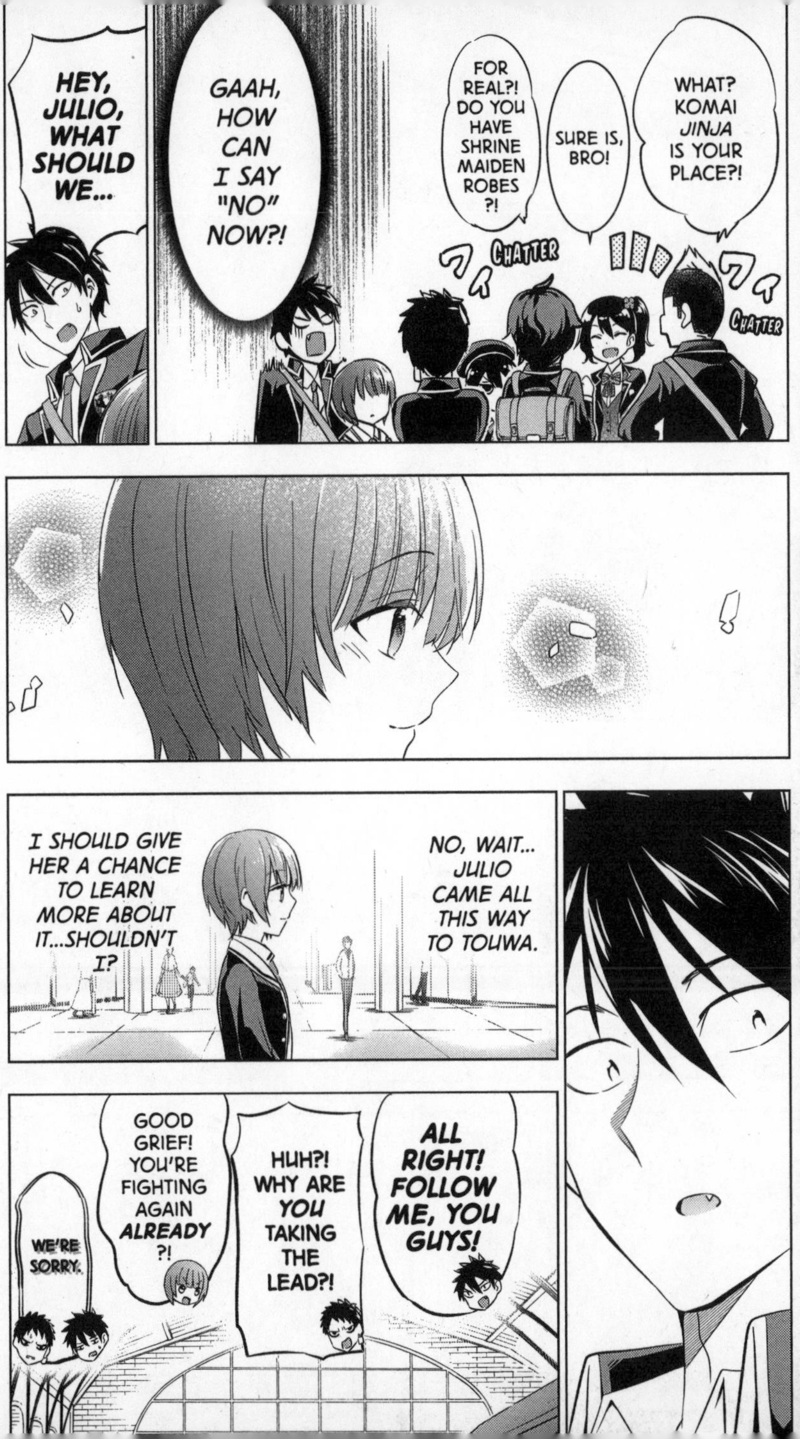
WHAT? KOMAI JINJA IS YOUR PLACE?!
SURE IS, BRO!
FOR REAL?! DO YOU HAVE SHRINE MAIDEN ROBES?!
CHATTER
CHATTER
GAAH, HOW CAN I SAY "NO" NOW?!
HEY, JULIO, WHAT SHOULD WE...
NO, WAIT... JULIO CAME ALL THIS WAY TO TOUWA.
I SHOULD GIVE HER A CHANCE TO LEARN MORE ABOUT IT...SHOULDN'T I?
ALL RIGHT! FOLLOW ME, YOU GUYS!
HUH?! WHY ARE YOU TAKING THE LEAD?!
GOOD GRIEF! YOU'RE FIGHTING AGAIN ALREADY?!
WE'RE SORRY.

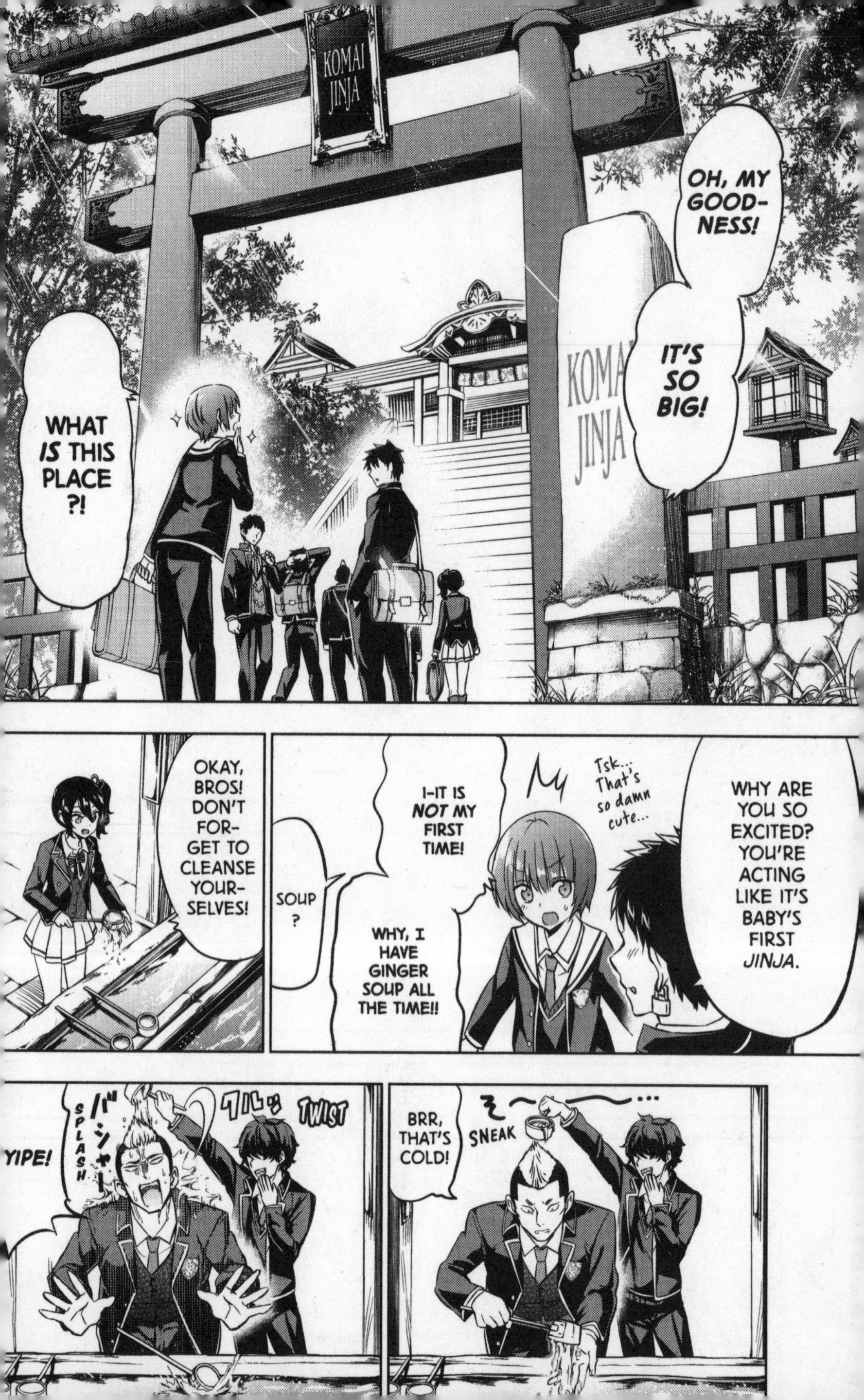

KOMAI JINJA
OH, MY GOOD-NESS!
IT'S SO BIG!
KOMAI JINJA
WHAT IS THIS PLACE ?!
WHY ARE YOU SO EXCITED? YOU'RE ACTING LIKE IT'S BABY'S FIRST JINJA.
Tsk... That's so damn cute...
I-IT IS NOT MY FIRST TIME!
WHY, I HAVE GINGER SOUP ALL THE TIME!!
SOUP ?
OKAY, BROS! DON'T FOR-GET TO CLEANSE YOUR-SELVES!
SNEAK
BRR, THAT'S COLD!
TWIST
SPLASH
YIPE!

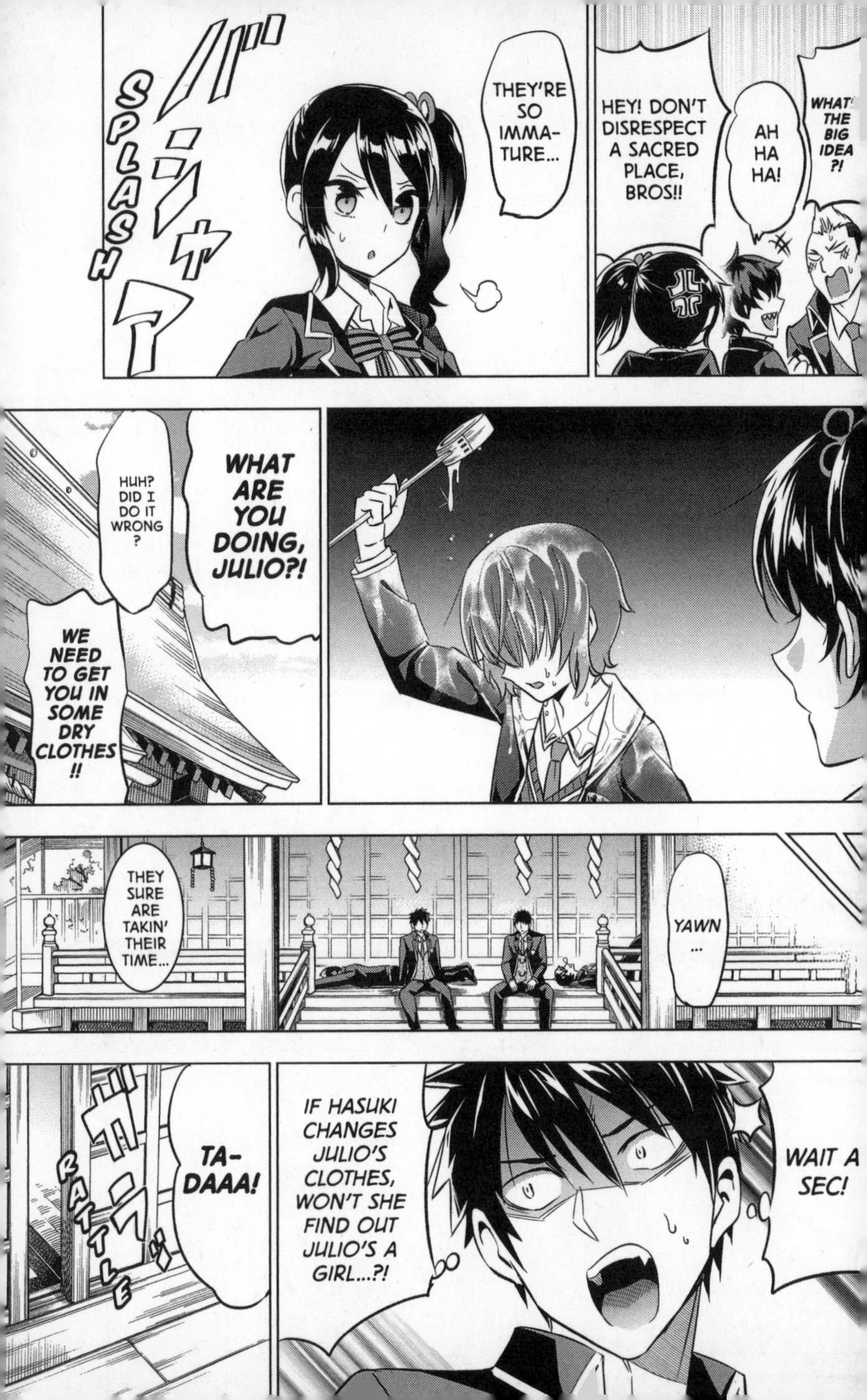
WHAT' THE BIG IDEA ?!
AH HA HA!
HEY! DON'T DISRESPECT A SACRED PLACE, BROS!!
THEY'RE SO IMMA-TURE...
SPLASH
WHAT ARE YOU DOING, JULIO?!
HUH? DID I DO IT WRONG ?
WE NEED TO GET YOU IN SOME DRY CLOTHES !!
YAWN ...
THEY SURE ARE TAKIN' THEIR TIME...
WAIT A SEC!
IF HASUKI CHANGES JULIO'S CLOTHES, WON'T SHE FIND OUT JULIO'S A GIRL...?!
TA-DAAA!
RATTLE

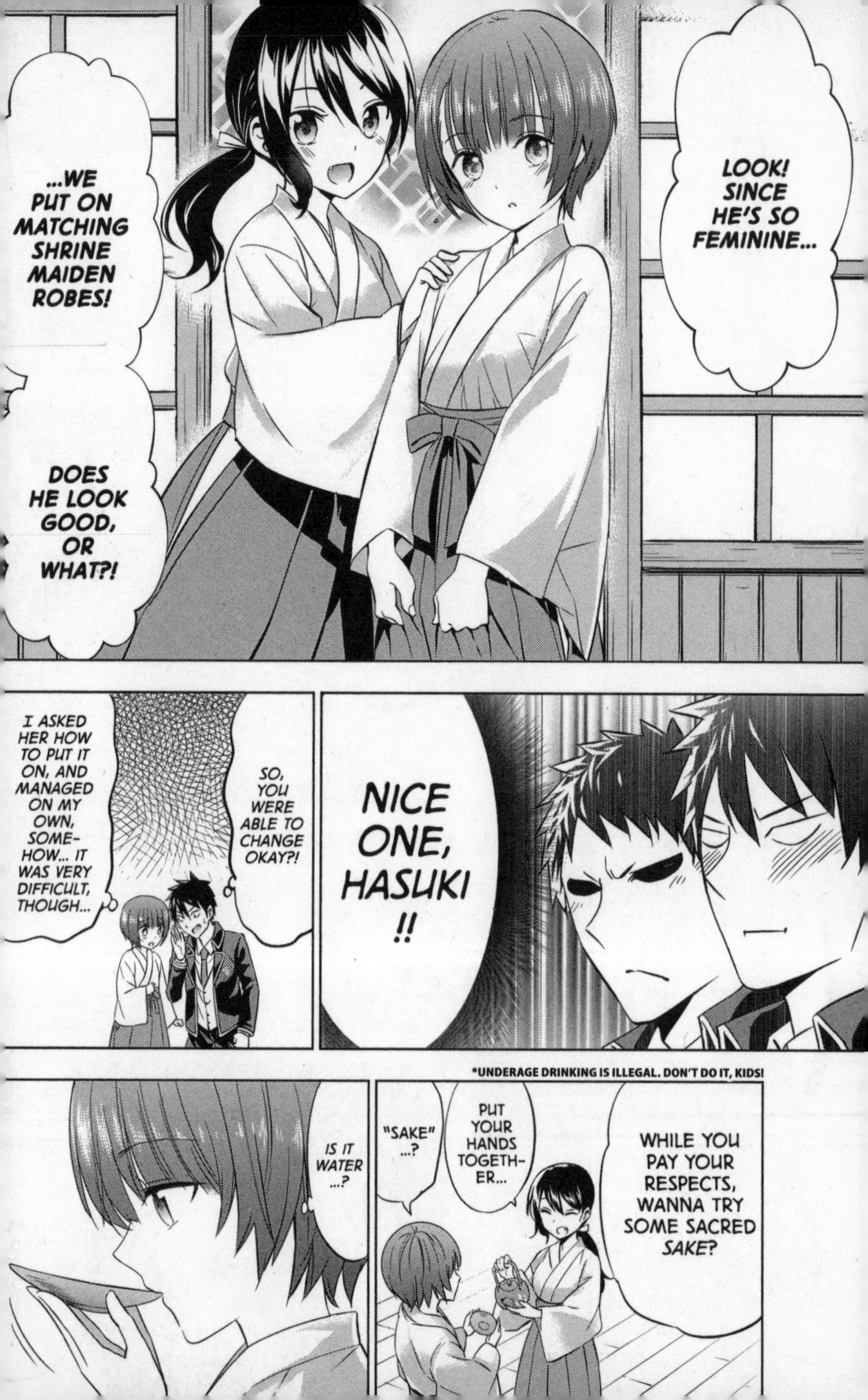
LOOK! SINCE HE'S SO FEMININE...
...WE PUT ON MATCHING SHRINE MAIDEN ROBES!
DOES HE LOOK GOOD, OR WHAT?!
NICE ONE, HASUKI!!
SO, YOU WERE ABLE TO CHANGE OKAY?!
I ASKED HER HOW TO PUT IT ON, AND MANAGED ON MY OWN, SOMEHOW... IT WAS VERY DIFFICULT, THOUGH...
*UNDERAGE DRINKING IS ILLEGAL. DON'T DO IT, KIDS!
WHILE YOU PAY YOUR RESPECTS, WANNA TRY SOME SACRED SAKE?
PUT YOUR HANDS TOGETHER...
"SAKE" ...?
IS IT WATER ...?

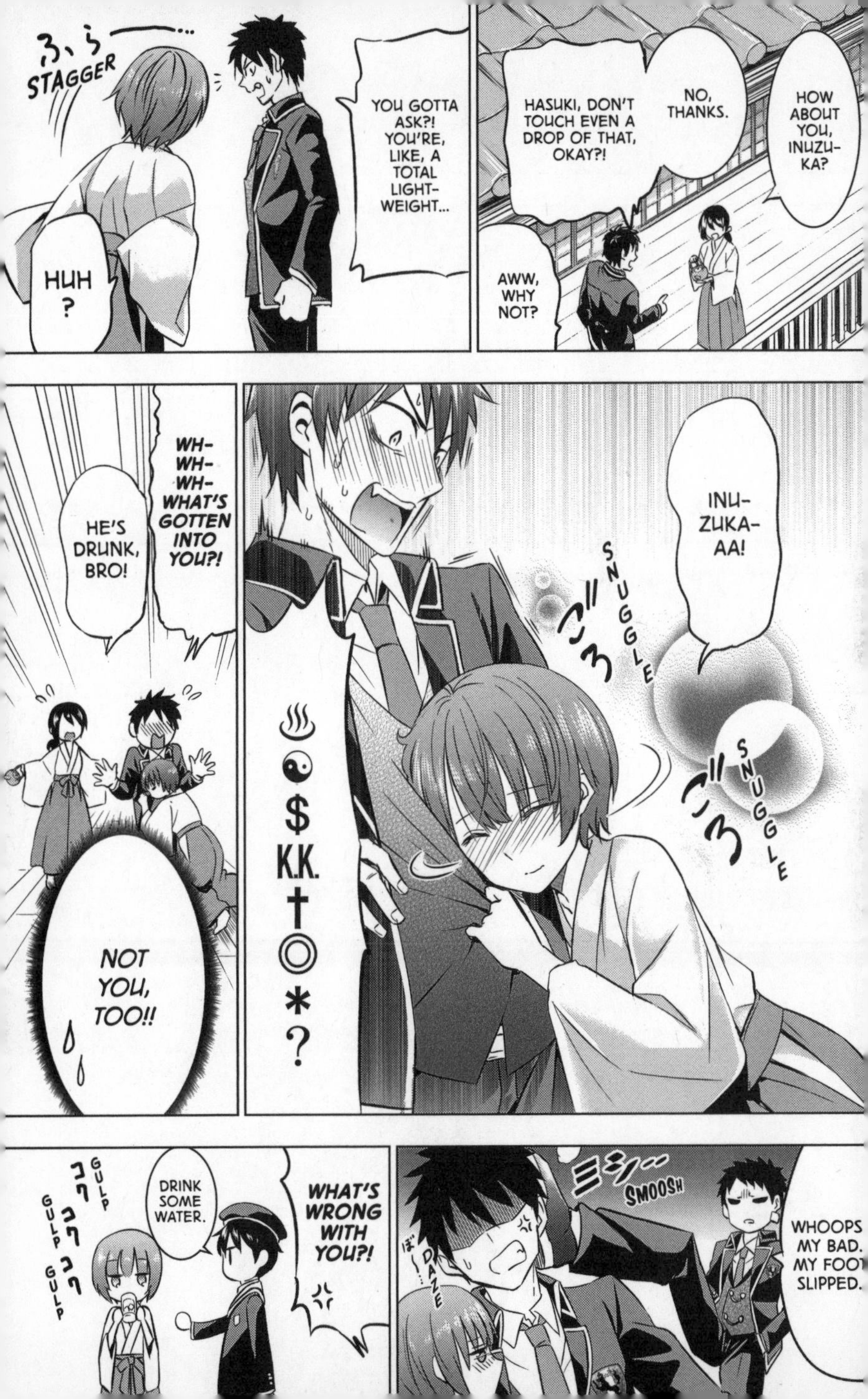
HOW ABOUT YOU, INUZUKA?
NO, THANKS.
HASUKI, DON'T TOUCH EVEN A DROP OF THAT, OKAY?!
AWW, WHY NOT?
YOU GOTTA ASK?! YOU'RE, LIKE, A TOTAL LIGHT-WEIGHT...
ふら—…
STAGGER
HUH?
INU-ZUKA-AA!
SNUGGLE
SNUGGLE
♨ ☯ $ K.K. † ◎ * ?
WH-WH-WH-WHAT'S GOTTEN INTO YOU?!
HE'S DRUNK, BRO!
NOT YOU, TOO!!
WHOOPS MY BAD. MY FOOT SLIPPED.
SMOOSH
DAZE
WHAT'S WRONG WITH YOU?!
DRINK SOME WATER.
GULP
GULP
GULP

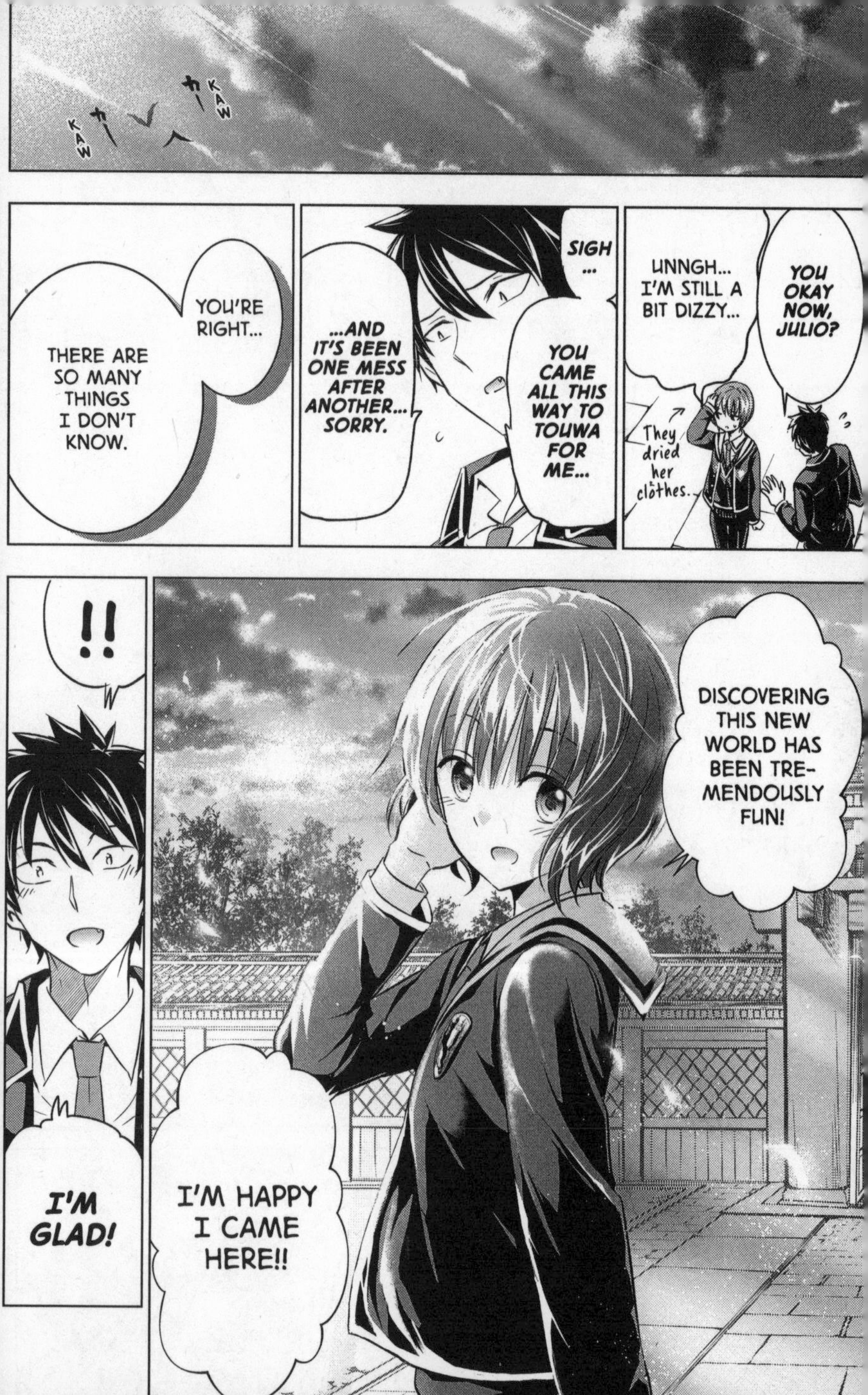
KAW
KAW
YOU OKAY NOW, JULIO?
UNNGH... I'M STILL A BIT DIZZY...
They dried her clothes.
SIGH...
YOU CAME ALL THIS WAY TO TOUWA FOR ME...
...AND IT'S BEEN ONE MESS AFTER ANOTHER... SORRY.
YOU'RE RIGHT...
THERE ARE SO MANY THINGS I DON'T KNOW.
DISCOVERING THIS NEW WORLD HAS BEEN TRE-MENDOUSLY FUN!
I'M HAPPY I CAME HERE!!
!!
I'M GLAD!

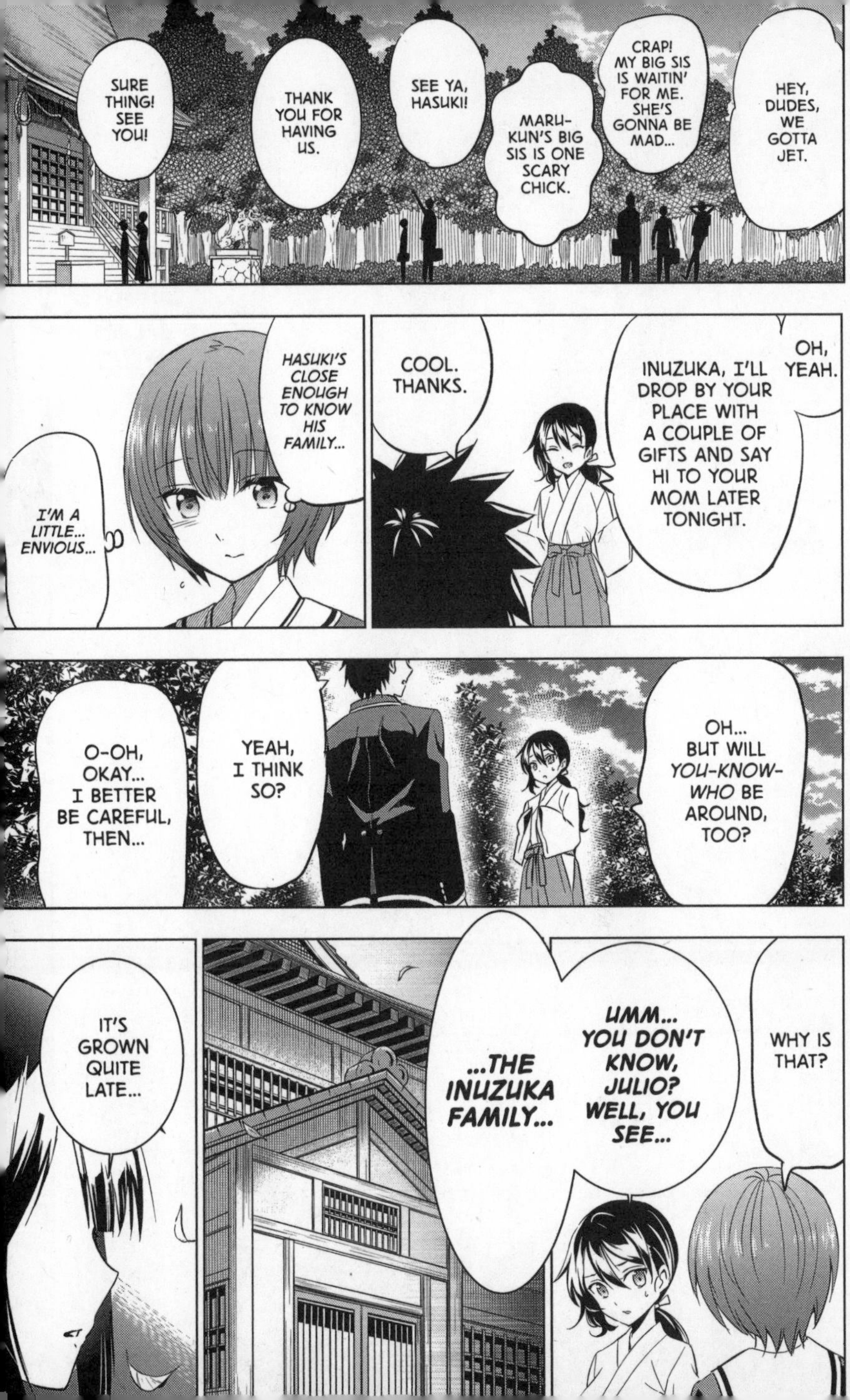
HEY, DUDES, WE GOTTA JET.
CRAP! MY BIG SIS IS WAITIN' FOR ME. SHE'S GONNA BE MAD...
MARU-KUN'S BIG SIS IS ONE SCARY CHICK.
SEE YA, HASUKI!
THANK YOU FOR HAVING US.
SURE THING! SEE YOU!
OH, YEAH.
INUZUKA, I'LL DROP BY YOUR PLACE WITH A COUPLE OF GIFTS AND SAY HI TO YOUR MOM LATER TONIGHT.
COOL. THANKS.
HASUKI'S CLOSE ENOUGH TO KNOW HIS FAMILY...
I'M A LITTLE... ENVIOUS...
OH... BUT WILL *YOU-KNOW-WHO* BE AROUND, TOO?
YEAH, I THINK SO?
O-OH, OKAY... I BETTER BE CAREFUL, THEN...
WHY IS THAT?
UMM... YOU DON'T KNOW, JULIO? WELL, YOU SEE...
...THE INUZUKA FAMILY...
IT'S GROWN QUITE LATE...

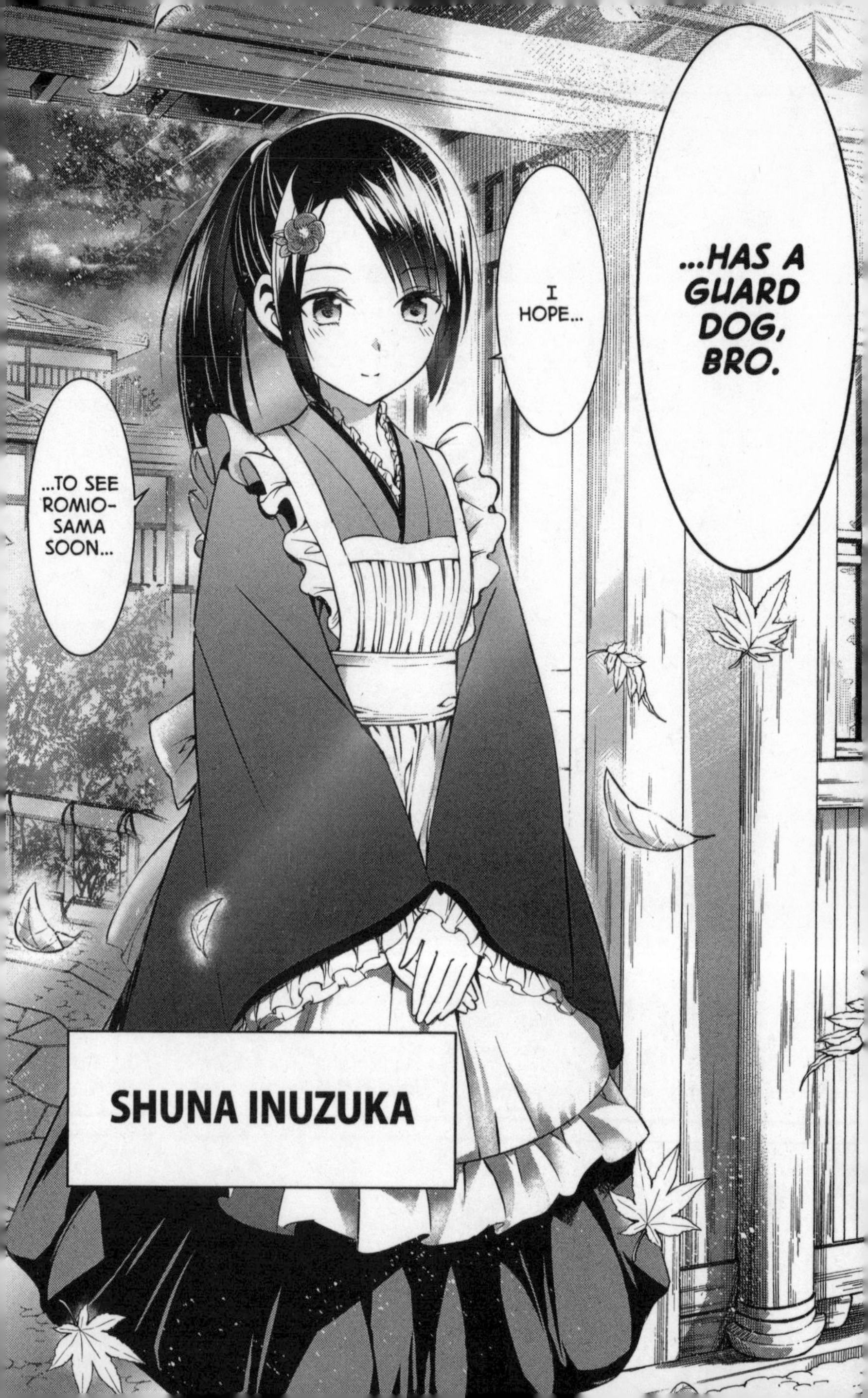
...HAS A GUARD DOG, BRO.
I HOPE...
...TO SEE ROMIO-SAMA SOON...
SHUNA INUZUKA

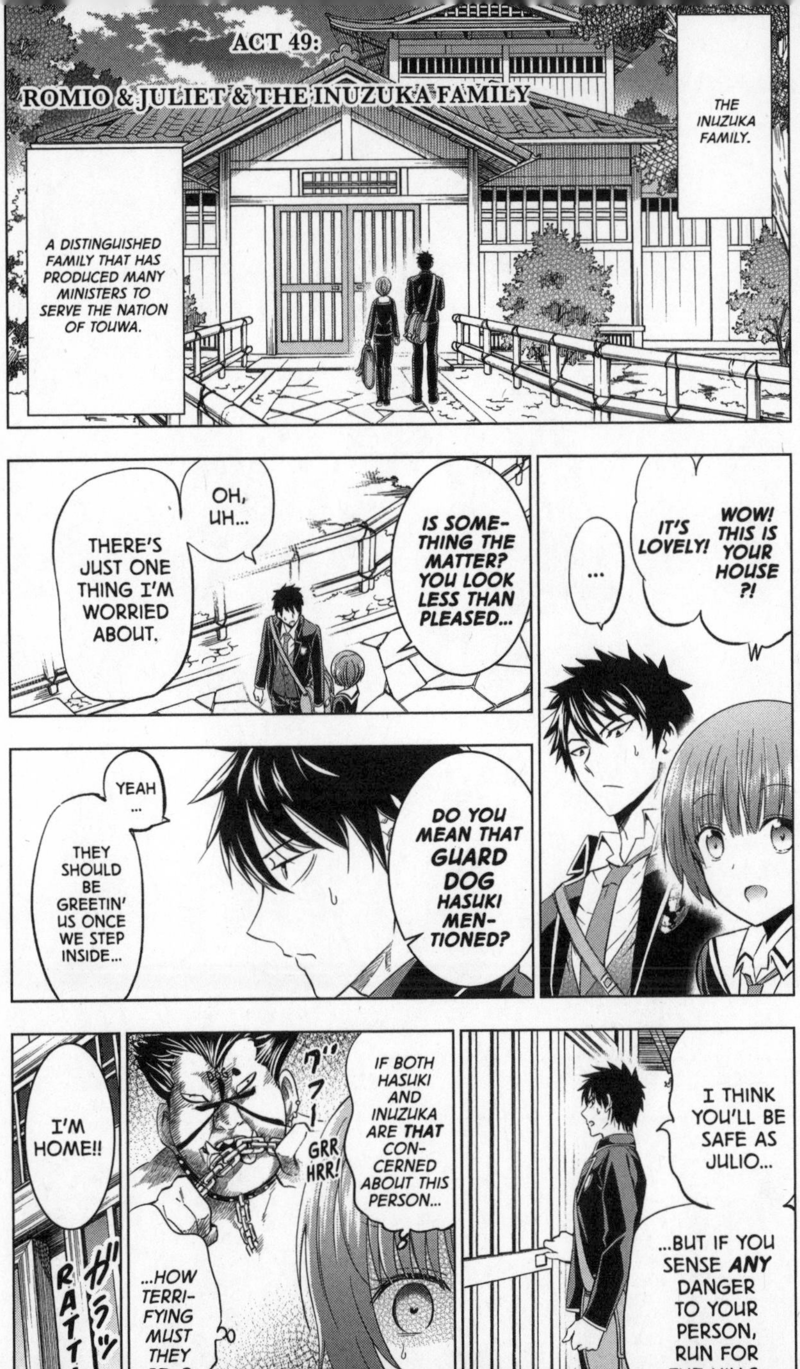
ACT 49:
ROMIO & JULIET & THE INUZUKA FAMILY
THE INUZUKA FAMILY.
A DISTINGUISHED FAMILY THAT HAS PRODUCED MANY MINISTERS TO SERVE THE NATION OF TOUWA.
WOW! THIS IS YOUR HOUSE?!
IT'S LOVELY!
...
IS SOME-THING THE MATTER? YOU LOOK LESS THAN PLEASED...
OH, UH...
THERE'S JUST ONE THING I'M WORRIED ABOUT.
DO YOU MEAN THAT GUARD DOG HASUKI MEN-TIONED?
YEAH...
THEY SHOULD BE GREETIN' US ONCE WE STEP INSIDE...
I THINK YOU'LL BE SAFE AS JULIO...
...BUT IF YOU SENSE ANY DANGER TO YOUR PERSON, RUN FOR THE HILLS. PLEASE.
IF BOTH HASUKI AND INUZUKA ARE THAT CON-CERNED ABOUT THIS PERSON...
GRR HRR!
...HOW TERRI-FYING MUST THEY BE...?
I'M HOME!!
RATTLE

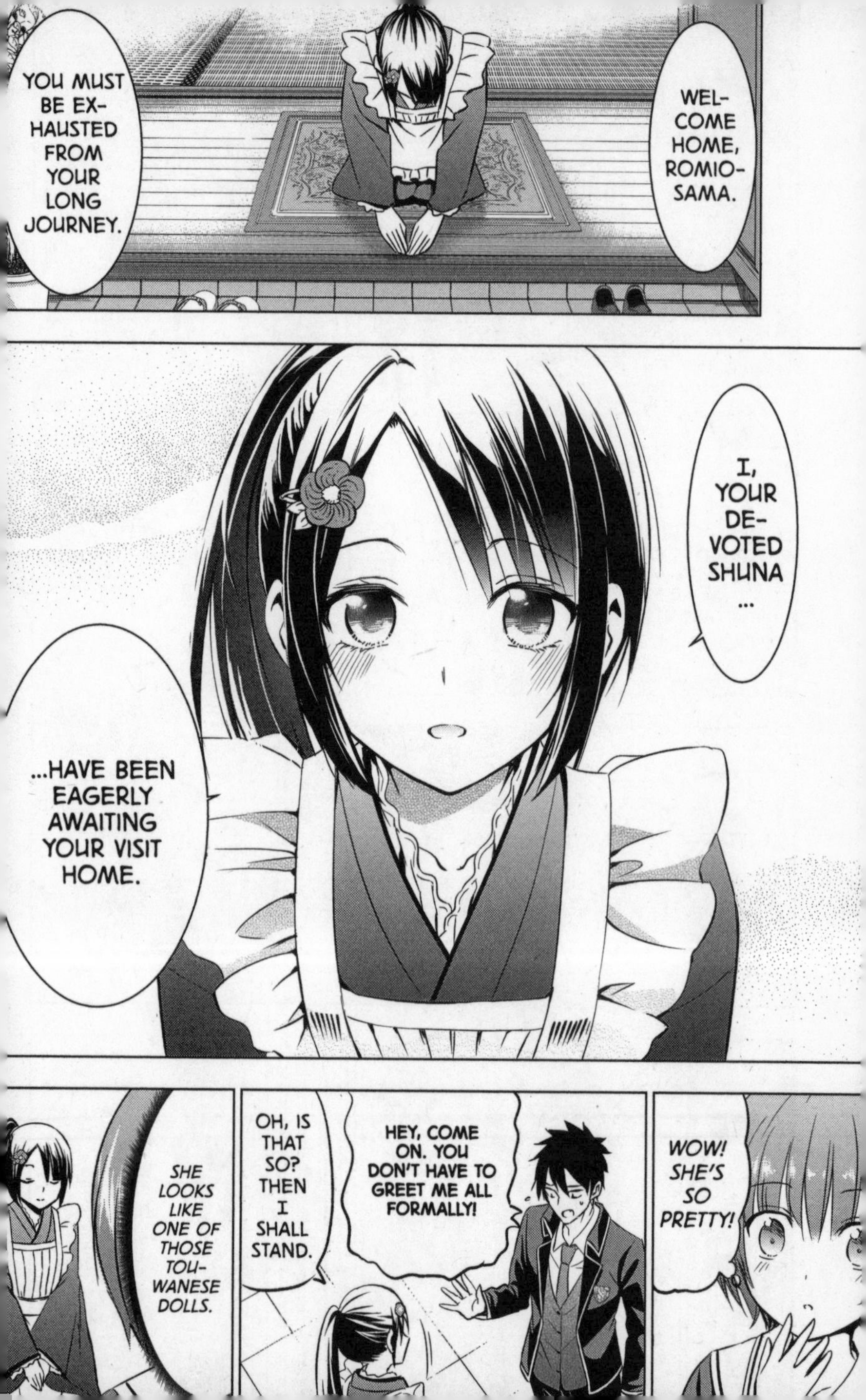
WELCOME HOME, ROMIO-SAMA.
YOU MUST BE EXHAUSTED FROM YOUR LONG JOURNEY.
I, YOUR DEVOTED SHUNA...
...HAVE BEEN EAGERLY AWAITING YOUR VISIT HOME.
WOW! SHE'S SO PRETTY!
HEY, COME ON. YOU DON'T HAVE TO GREET ME ALL FORMALLY!
OH, IS THAT SO? THEN I SHALL STAND.
SHE LOOKS LIKE ONE OF THOSE TOUWANESE DOLLS.

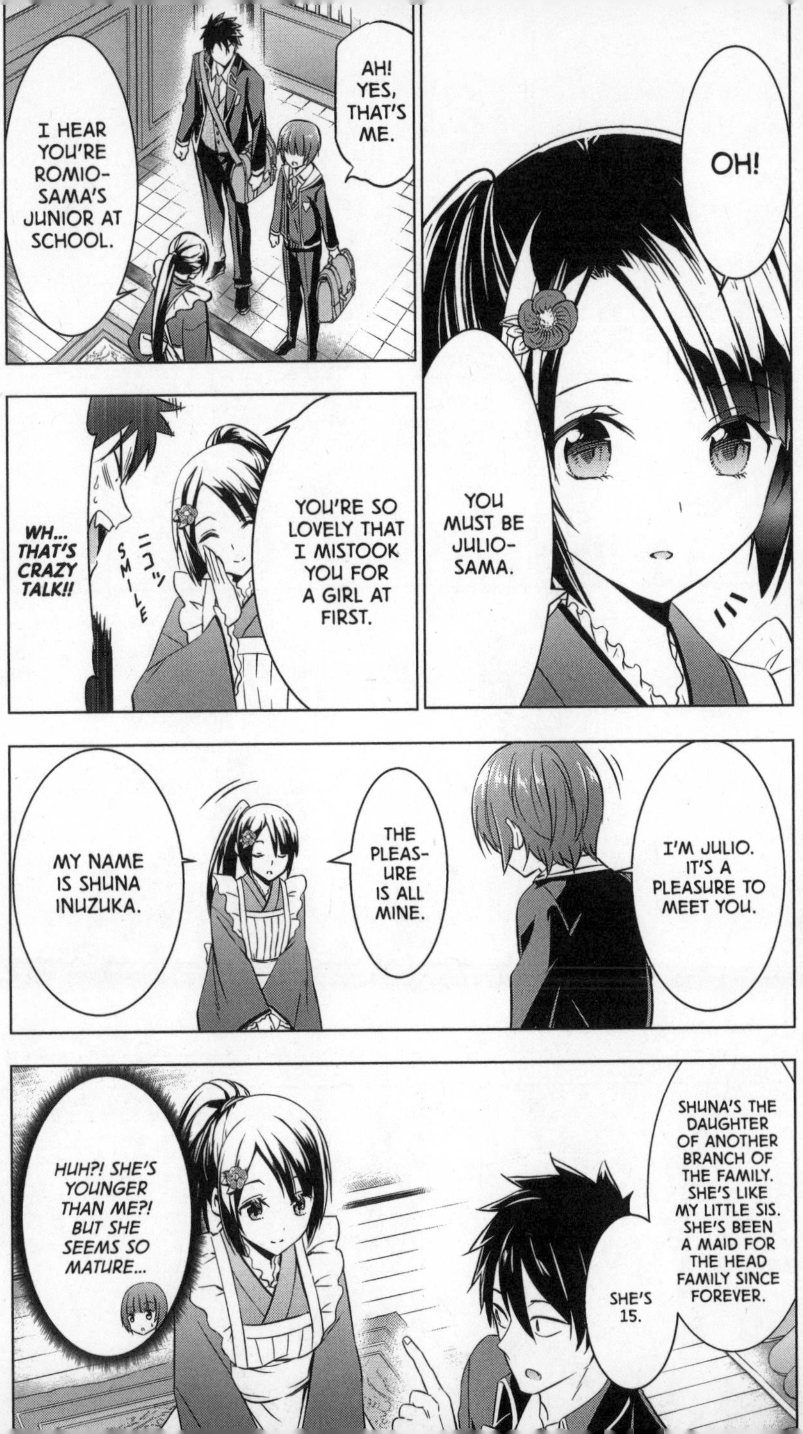

OH!
YOU MUST BE JULIO-SAMA.
I HEAR YOU'RE ROMIO-SAMA'S JUNIOR AT SCHOOL.
AH! YES, THAT'S ME.
YOU'RE SO LOVELY THAT I MISTOOK YOU FOR A GIRL AT FIRST.
SMILE
ニコッ
WH... THAT'S CRAZY TALK!!
I'M JULIO. IT'S A PLEASURE TO MEET YOU.
THE PLEASURE IS ALL MINE.
MY NAME IS SHUNA INUZUKA.
SHUNA'S THE DAUGHTER OF ANOTHER BRANCH OF THE FAMILY. SHE'S LIKE MY LITTLE SIS. SHE'S BEEN A MAID FOR THE HEAD FAMILY SINCE FOREVER.
SHE'S 15.
HUH?! SHE'S YOUNGER THAN ME?! BUT SHE SEEMS SO MATURE...

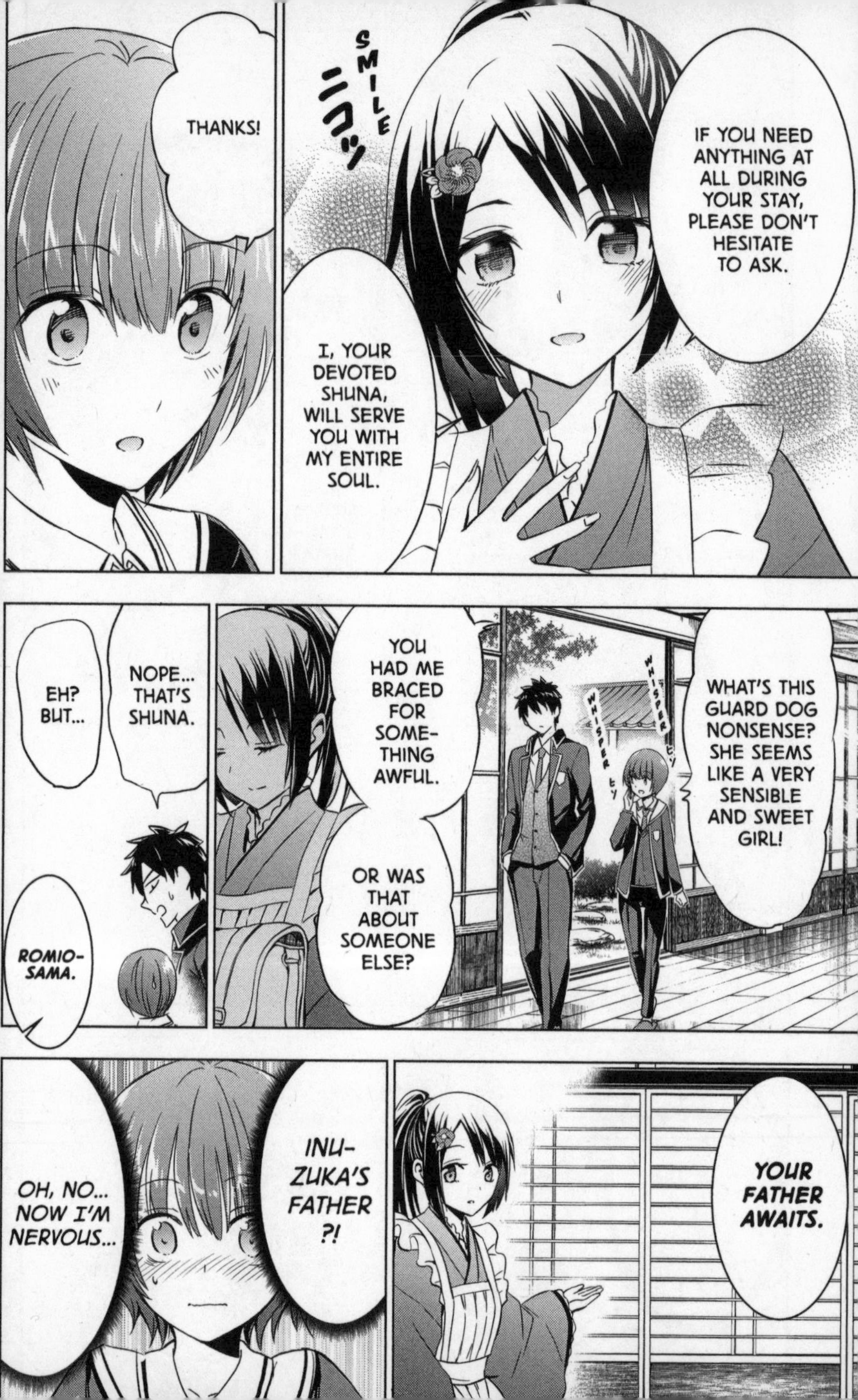
IF YOU NEED ANYTHING AT ALL DURING YOUR STAY, PLEASE DON'T HESITATE TO ASK.
SMILE
ニコッ
I, YOUR DEVOTED SHUNA, WILL SERVE YOU WITH MY ENTIRE SOUL.
THANKS!
WHAT'S THIS GUARD DOG NONSENSE? SHE SEEMS LIKE A VERY SENSIBLE AND SWEET GIRL!
WHISPER
WHISPER
YOU HAD ME BRACED FOR SOME-THING AWFUL.
OR WAS THAT ABOUT SOMEONE ELSE?
NOPE... THAT'S SHUNA.
EH? BUT...
ROMIO-SAMA.
YOUR FATHER AWAITS.
INU-ZUKA'S FATHER ?!
OH, NO... NOW I'M NERVOUS...

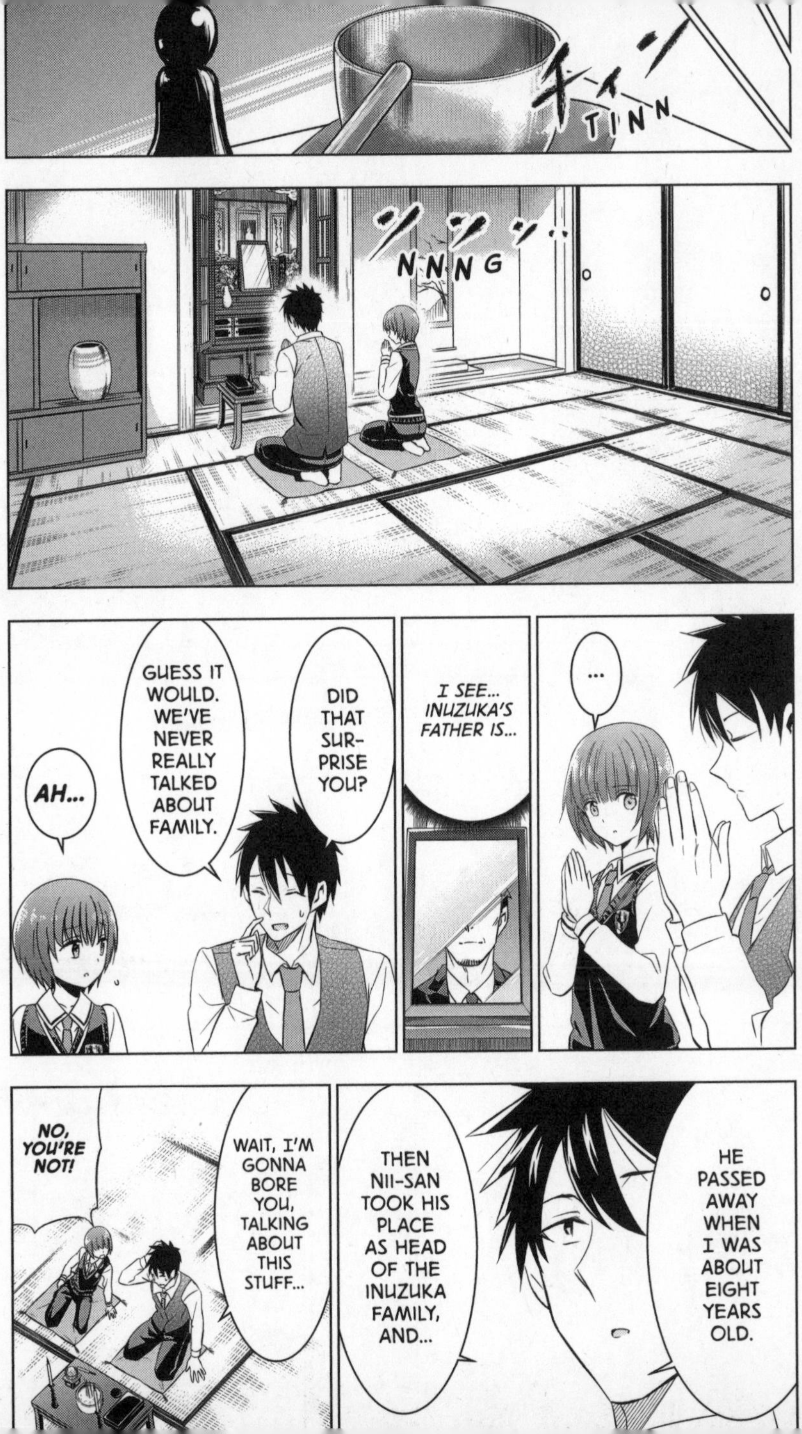
TINN
NNNG
...
I SEE... INUZUKA'S FATHER IS...
DID THAT SUR-PRISE YOU?
GUESS IT WOULD. WE'VE NEVER REALLY TALKED ABOUT FAMILY.
AH...
HE PASSED AWAY WHEN I WAS ABOUT EIGHT YEARS OLD.
THEN NII-SAN TOOK HIS PLACE AS HEAD OF THE INUZUKA FAMILY, AND...
WAIT, I'M GONNA BORE YOU, TALKING ABOUT THIS STUFF...
NO, YOU'RE NOT!

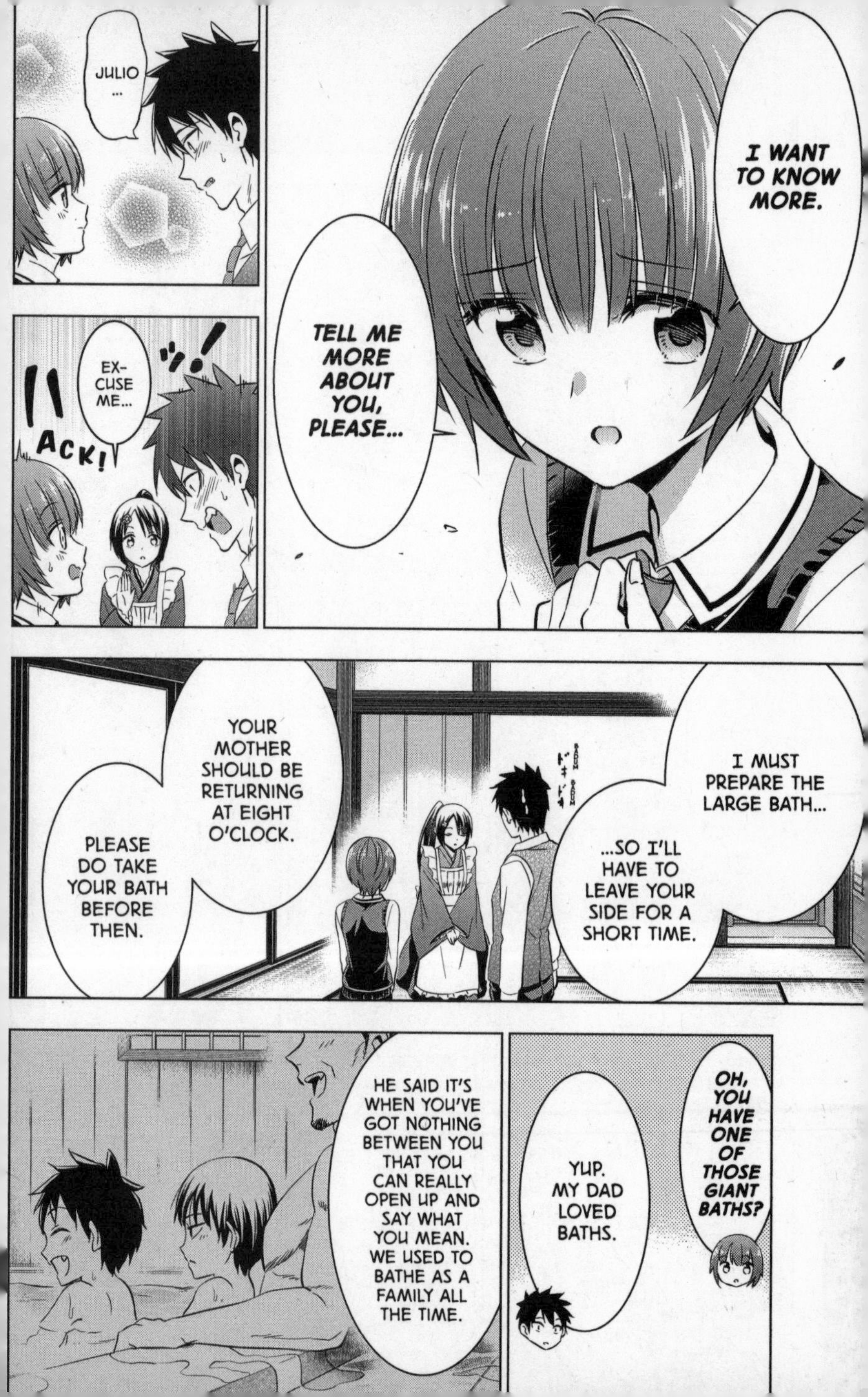
I WANT TO KNOW MORE.
TELL ME MORE ABOUT YOU, PLEASE...
JULIO ...
EX-CUSE ME...
ACK!
I MUST PREPARE THE LARGE BATH...
...SO I'LL HAVE TO LEAVE YOUR SIDE FOR A SHORT TIME.
BADUM BADUM
YOUR MOTHER SHOULD BE RETURNING AT EIGHT O'CLOCK.
PLEASE DO TAKE YOUR BATH BEFORE THEN.
OH, YOU HAVE ONE OF THOSE GIANT BATHS?
YUP. MY DAD LOVED BATHS.
HE SAID IT'S WHEN YOU'VE GOT NOTHING BETWEEN YOU THAT YOU CAN REALLY OPEN UP AND SAY WHAT YOU MEAN. WE USED TO BATHE AS A FAMILY ALL THE TIME.

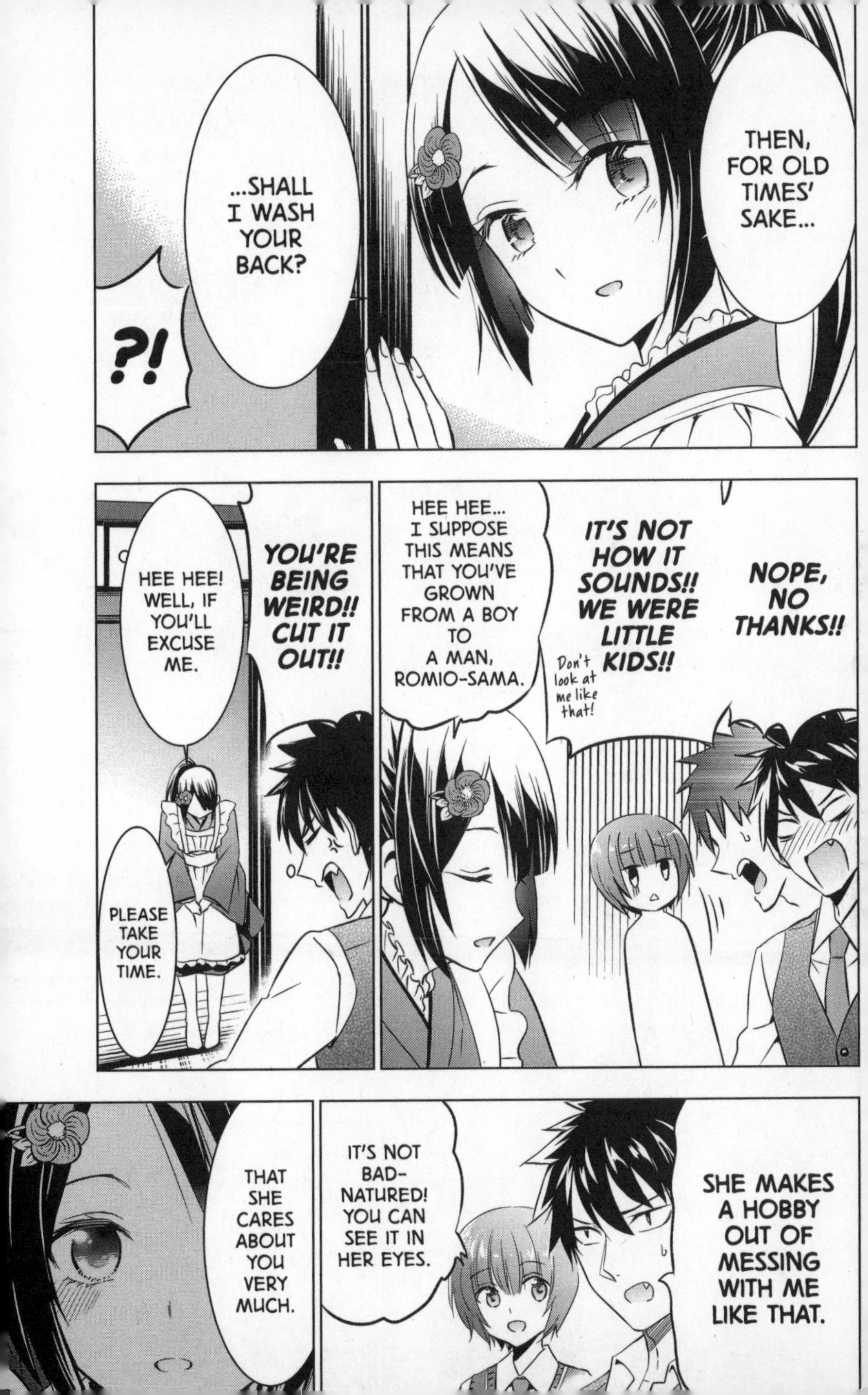
THEN, FOR OLD TIMES' SAKE...
...SHALL I WASH YOUR BACK?
?!
NOPE, NO THANKS!!
IT'S NOT HOW IT SOUNDS!! WE WERE LITTLE KIDS!!
Don't look at me like that!
HEE HEE... I SUPPOSE THIS MEANS THAT YOU'VE GROWN FROM A BOY TO A MAN, ROMIO-SAMA.
YOU'RE BEING WEIRD!! CUT IT OUT!!
HEE HEE! WELL, IF YOU'LL EXCUSE ME.
PLEASE TAKE YOUR TIME.
SHE MAKES A HOBBY OUT OF MESSING WITH ME LIKE THAT.
IT'S NOT BAD-NATURED! YOU CAN SEE IT IN HER EYES.
THAT SHE CARES ABOUT YOU VERY MUCH.

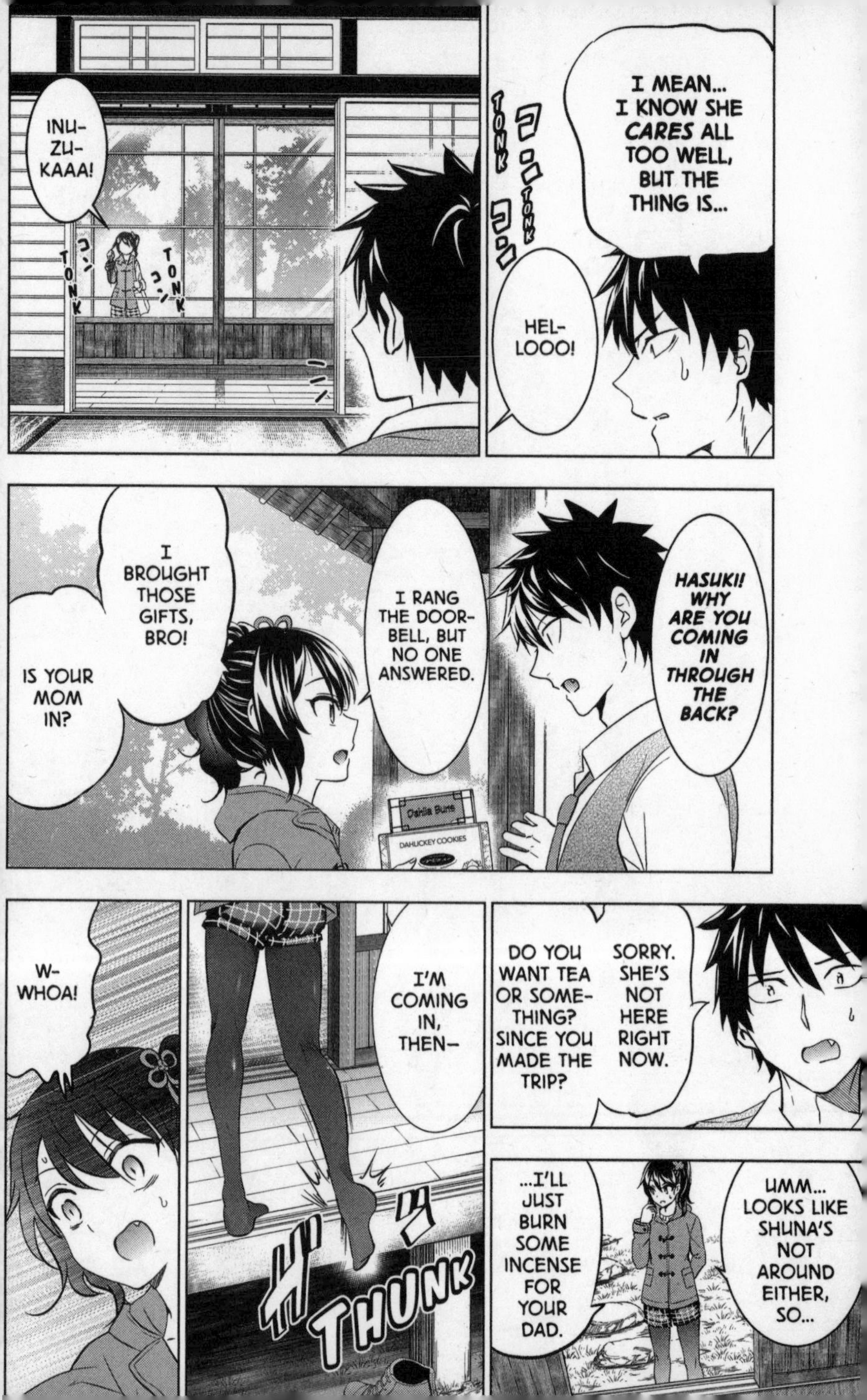
I MEAN... I KNOW SHE CARES ALL TOO WELL, BUT THE THING IS...
TONK TONK
HEL-LOOO!
INU-ZU-KAAA!
TONK TONK
HASUKI! WHY ARE YOU COMING IN THROUGH THE BACK?
I RANG THE DOOR-BELL, BUT NO ONE ANSWERED.
I BROUGHT THOSE GIFTS, BRO!
IS YOUR MOM IN?
DAHLICKEY COOKIES
SORRY. SHE'S NOT HERE RIGHT NOW.
DO YOU WANT TEA OR SOME-THING? SINCE YOU MADE THE TRIP?
UMM... LOOKS LIKE SHUNA'S NOT AROUND EITHER, SO...
...I'LL JUST BURN SOME INCENSE FOR YOUR DAD.
I'M COMING IN, THEN—
THUNK
W-WHOA!

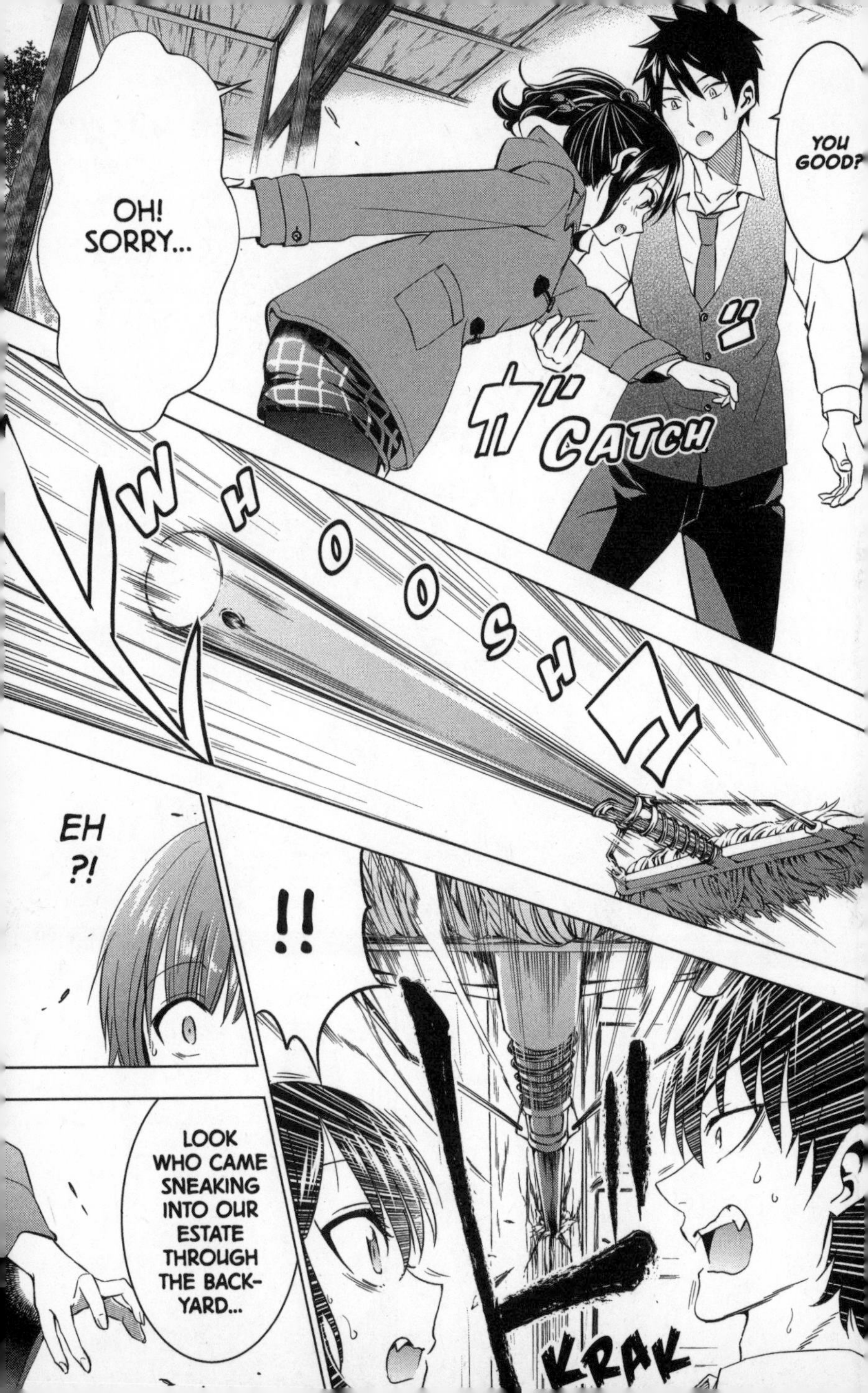
YOU GOOD?
OH! SORRY...
CATCH
WHOOSH
!!
EH ?!
KRAK
LOOK WHO CAME SNEAKING INTO OUR ESTATE THROUGH THE BACK-YARD...

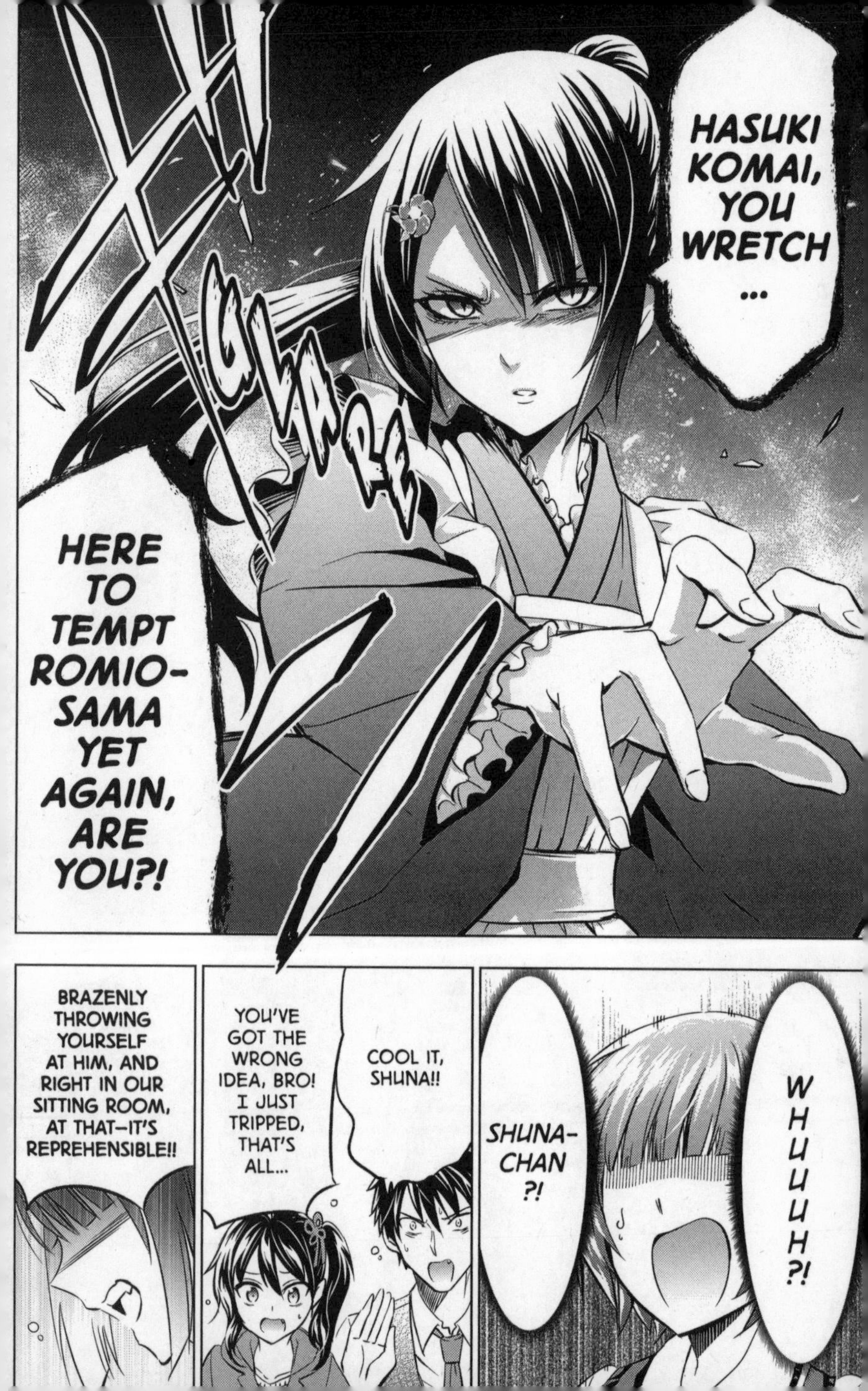
HASUKI KOMAI, YOU WRETCH ...
GLARE
HERE TO TEMPT ROMIO-SAMA YET AGAIN, ARE YOU?!
WHUUUUH?!
SHUNA-CHAN ?!
COOL IT, SHUNA!!
YOU'VE GOT THE WRONG IDEA, BRO! I JUST TRIPPED, THAT'S ALL...
BRAZENLY THROWING YOURSELF AT HIM, AND RIGHT IN OUR SITTING ROOM, AT THAT—IT'S REPREHENSIBLE!!

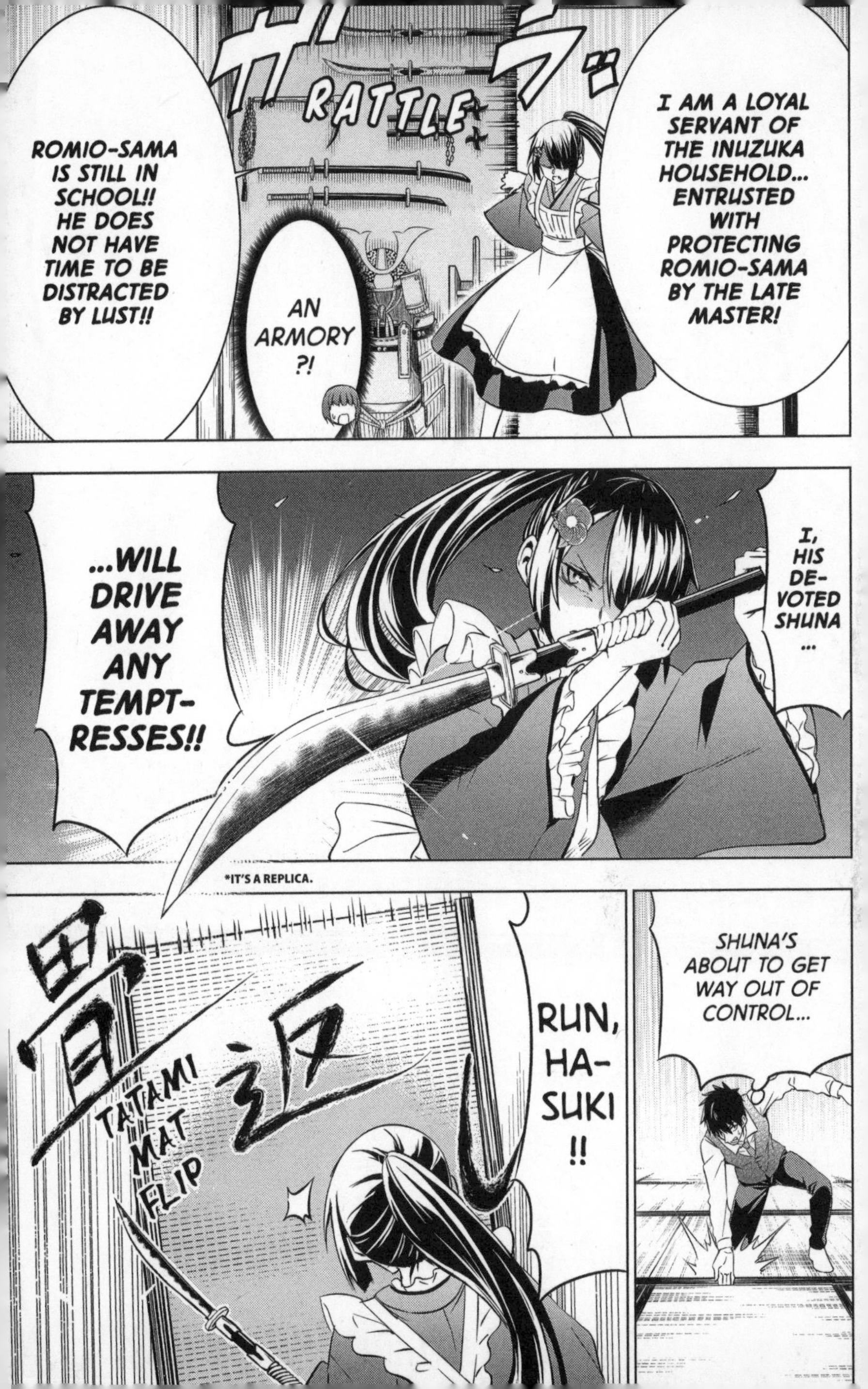
I AM A LOYAL SERVANT OF THE INUZUKA HOUSEHOLD... ENTRUSTED WITH PROTECTING ROMIO-SAMA BY THE LATE MASTER!
RATTLE
ROMIO-SAMA IS STILL IN SCHOOL!! HE DOES NOT HAVE TIME TO BE DISTRACTED BY LUST!!
AN ARMORY?!
I, HIS DE-VOTED SHUNA...
...WILL DRIVE AWAY ANY TEMPT-RESSES!!
*IT'S A REPLICA.
SHUNA'S ABOUT TO GET WAY OUT OF CONTROL...
RUN, HA-SUKI!!
TATAMI MAT FLIP

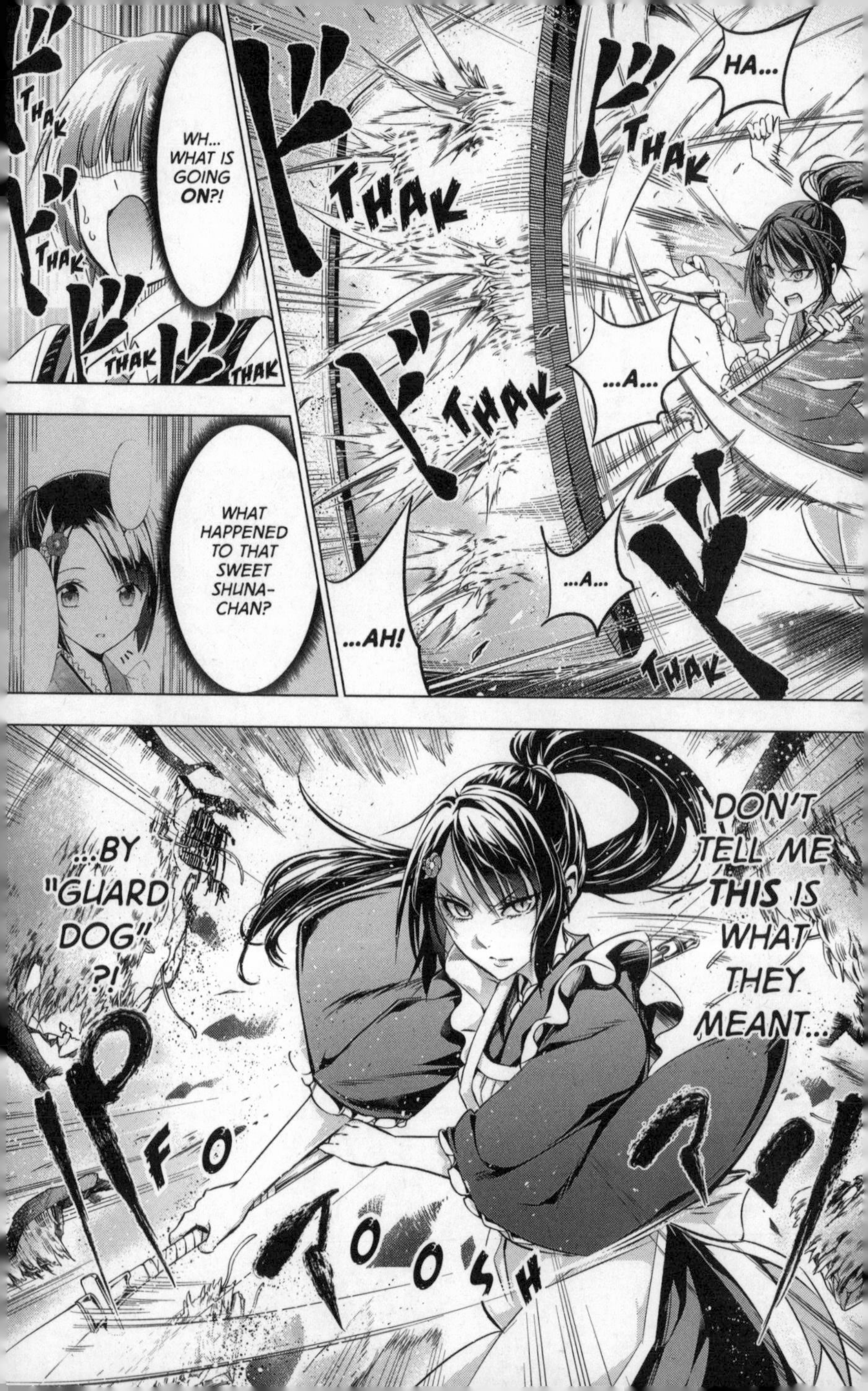
HA...
THAK
THAK
...A...
THAK
...A...
THAK
...AH!
THAK
THAK
THAK
THAK
WH... WHAT IS GOING ON?!
WHAT HAPPENED TO THAT SWEET SHUNA-CHAN?
DON'T TELL ME THIS IS WHAT THEY MEANT...
...BY "GUARD DOG"?!
FOOOOSH

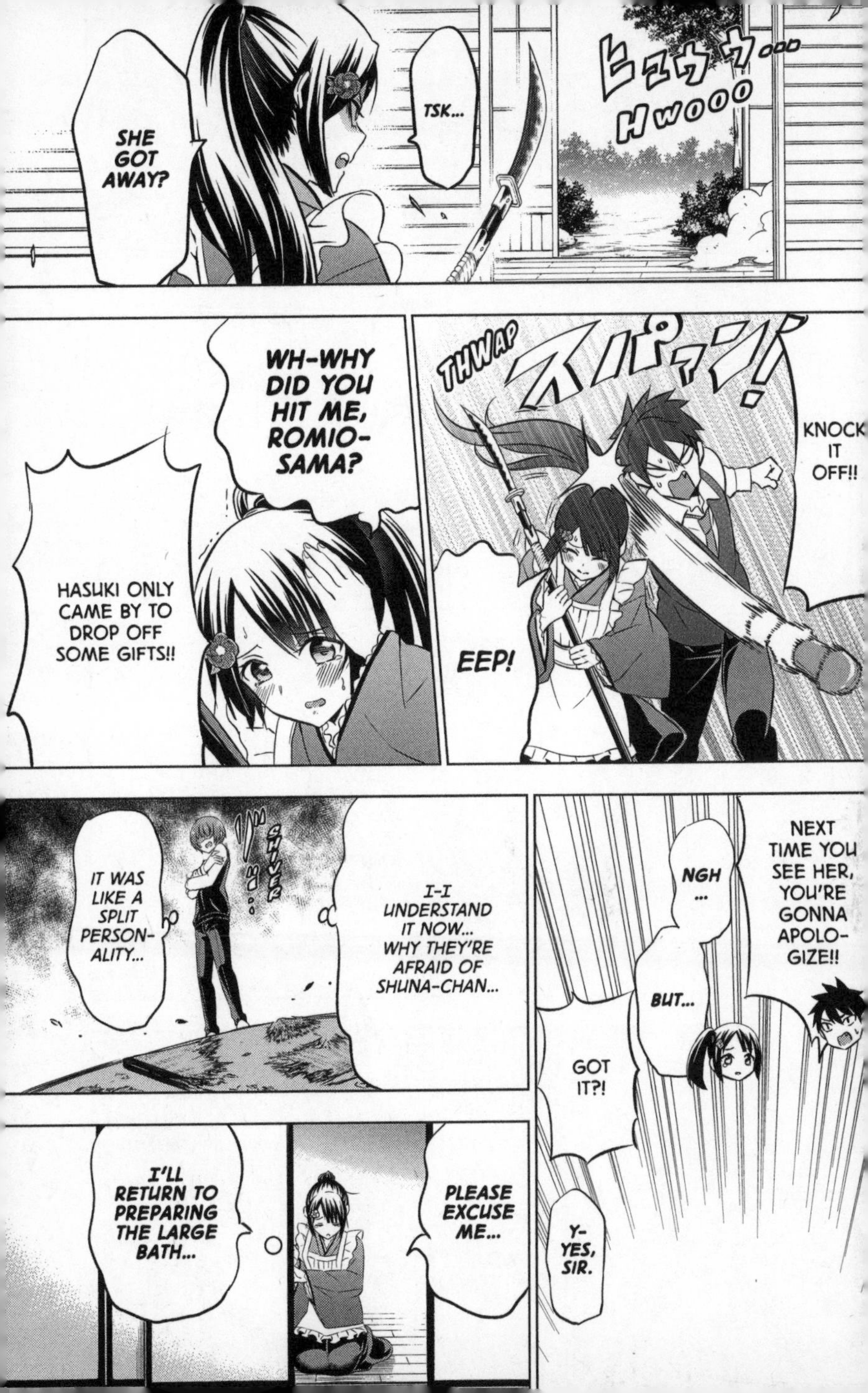
ヒュウウ…
HWOOO
TSK...
SHE GOT AWAY?
THWAP
スパァン!
KNOCK IT OFF!!
EEP!
WH-WHY DID YOU HIT ME, ROMIO-SAMA?
HASUKI ONLY CAME BY TO DROP OFF SOME GIFTS!!
NEXT TIME YOU SEE HER, YOU'RE GONNA APOLOGIZE!!
NGH...
BUT...
GOT IT?!
Y-YES, SIR.
I-I UNDERSTAND IT NOW... WHY THEY'RE AFRAID OF SHUNA-CHAN...
SHIVER
IT WAS LIKE A SPLIT PERSONALITY...
PLEASE EXCUSE ME...
I'LL RETURN TO PREPARING THE LARGE BATH...

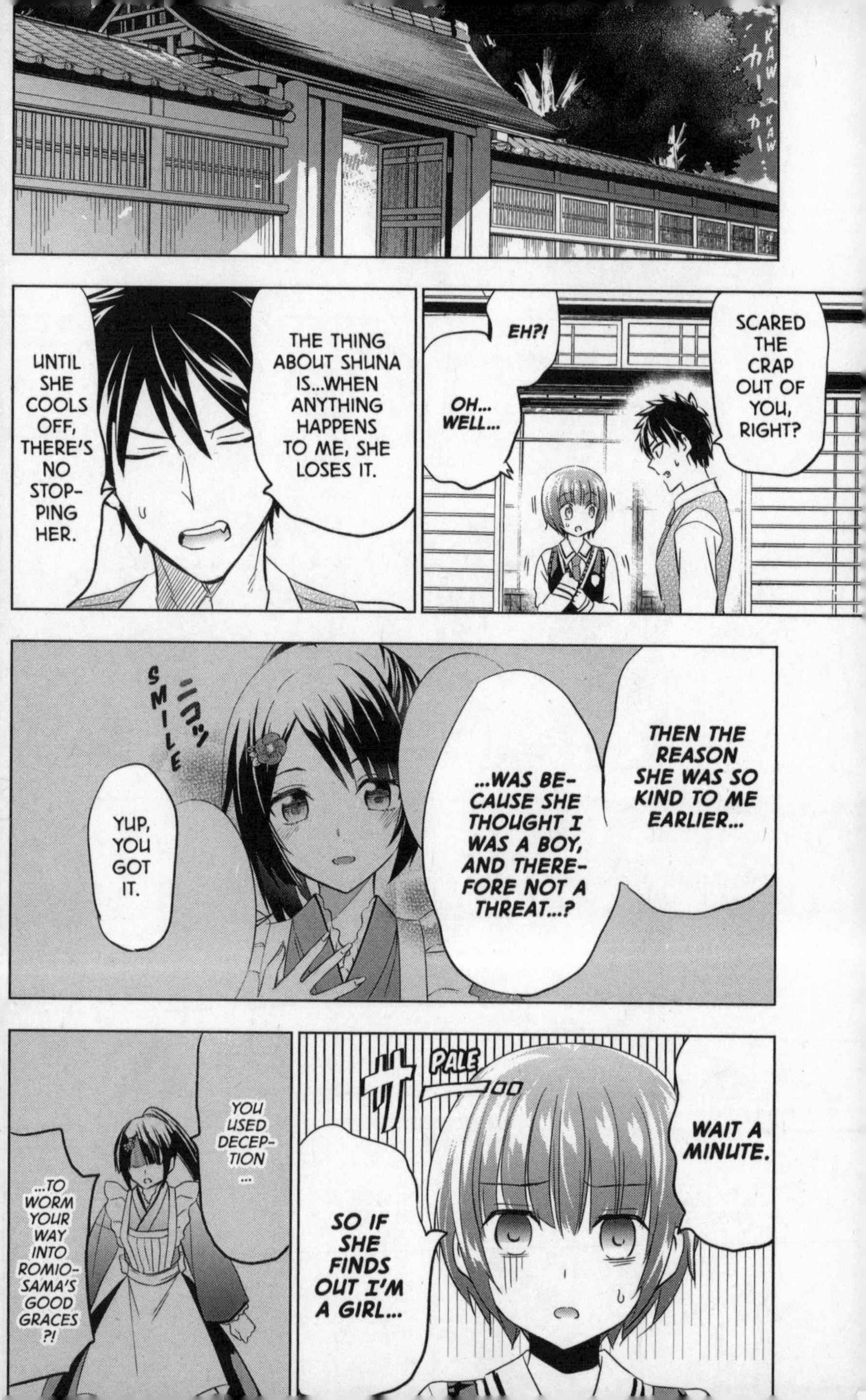
KAW
KAW
SCARED THE CRAP OUT OF YOU, RIGHT?
EH?!
OH... WELL...
THE THING ABOUT SHUNA IS...WHEN ANYTHING HAPPENS TO ME, SHE LOSES IT.
UNTIL SHE COOLS OFF, THERE'S NO STOPPING HER.
THEN THE REASON SHE WAS SO KIND TO ME EARLIER...
...WAS BECAUSE SHE THOUGHT I WAS A BOY, AND THEREFORE NOT A THREAT...?
SMILE
YUP, YOU GOT IT.
PALE
WAIT A MINUTE.
SO IF SHE FINDS OUT I'M A GIRL...
YOU USED DECEPTION...
...TO WORM YOUR WAY INTO ROMIO-SAMA'S GOOD GRACES?!

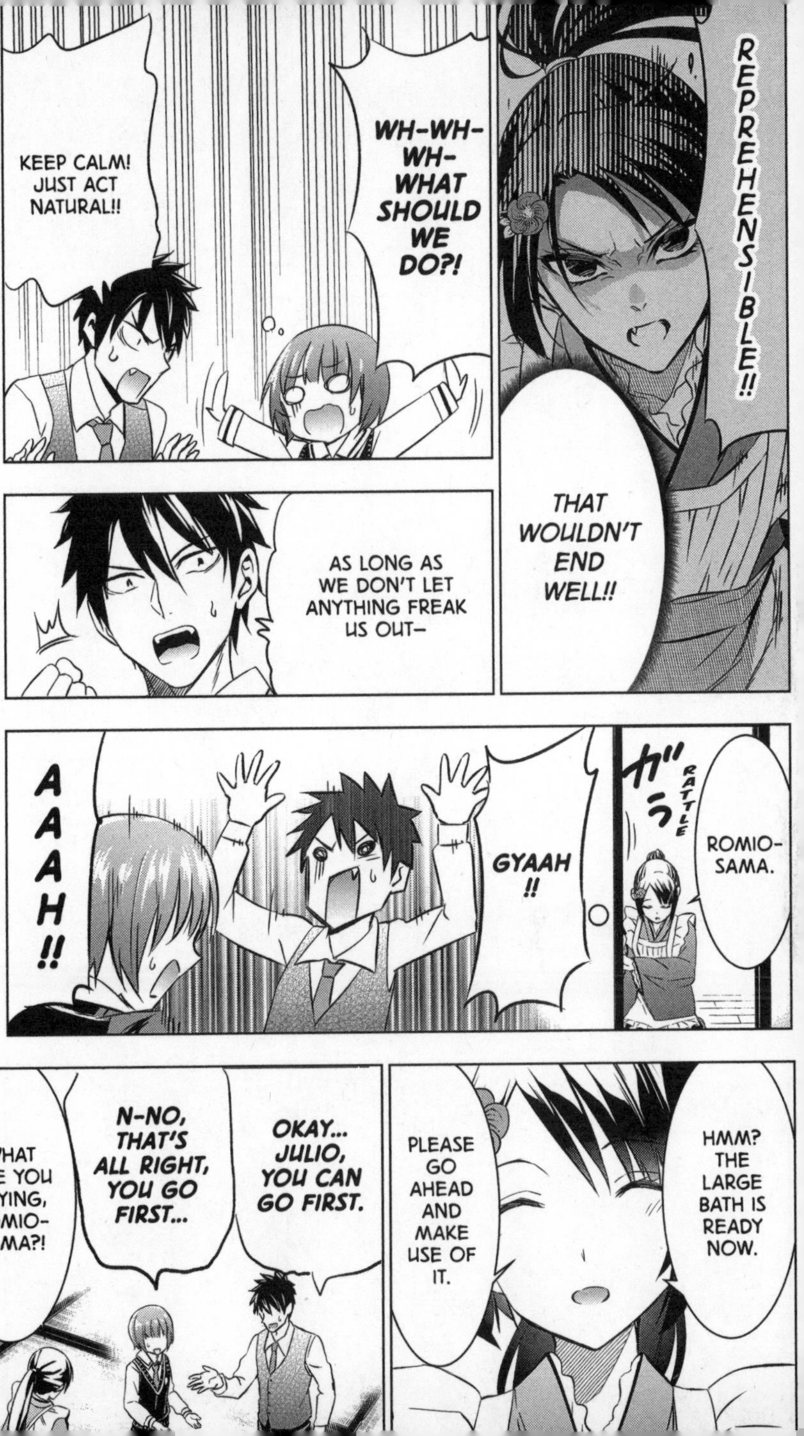
REPREHENSIBLE!!
THAT WOULDN'T END WELL!!
WH-WH-WH-WHAT SHOULD WE DO?!
KEEP CALM! JUST ACT NATURAL!!
AS LONG AS WE DON'T LET ANYTHING FREAK US OUT–
ROMIO-SAMA.
ガラ
RATTLE
GYAAH!!
AAAAH!!
HMM? THE LARGE BATH IS READY NOW.
PLEASE GO AHEAD AND MAKE USE OF IT.
OKAY... JULIO, YOU CAN GO FIRST.
N-NO, THAT'S ALL RIGHT, YOU GO FIRST...
WHAT ARE YOU SAYING, ROMIO-SAMA?!

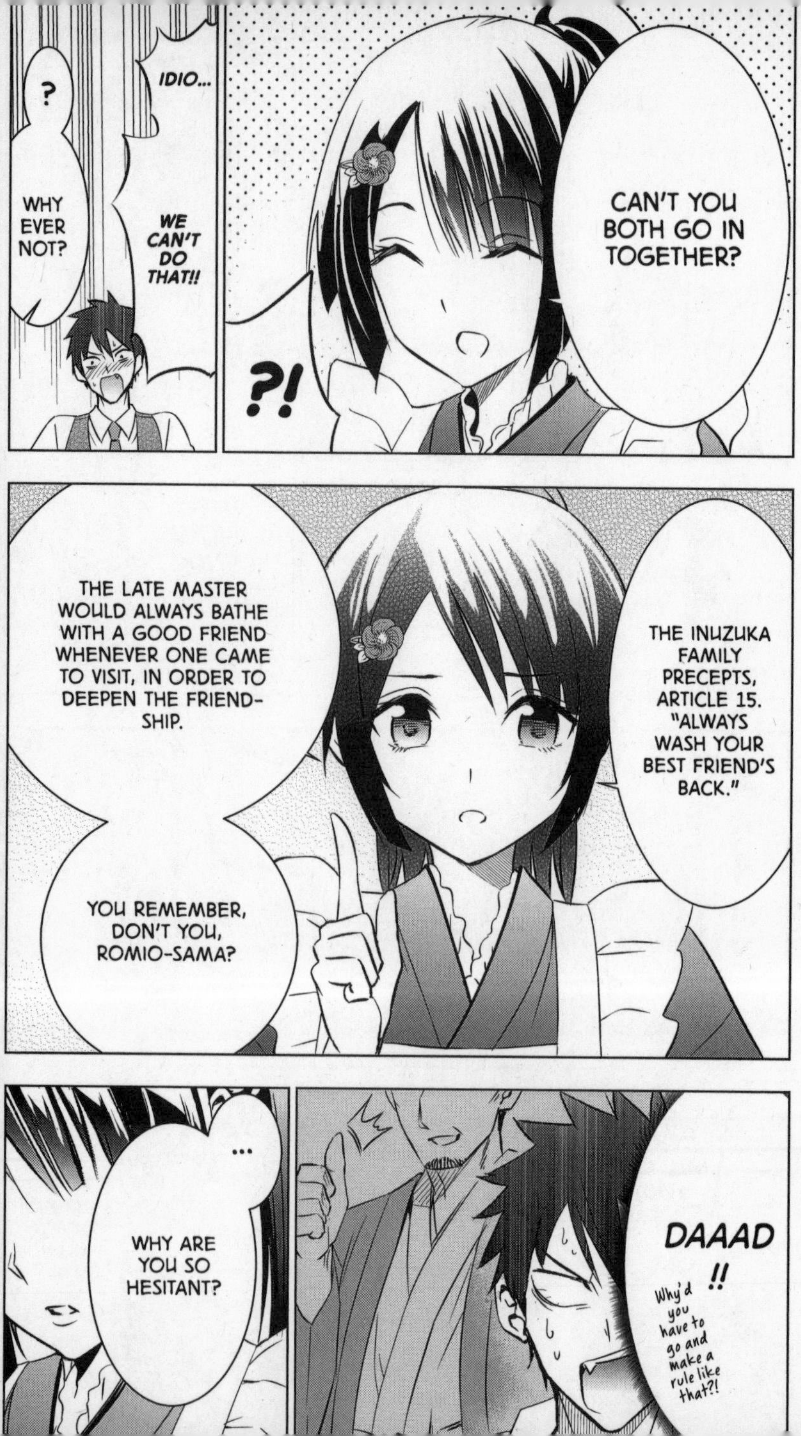
CAN'T YOU BOTH GO IN TOGETHER?
?!
IDIO...
WE CAN'T DO THAT!!
?
WHY EVER NOT?
THE INUZUKA FAMILY PRECEPTS, ARTICLE 15. "ALWAYS WASH YOUR BEST FRIEND'S BACK."
THE LATE MASTER WOULD ALWAYS BATHE WITH A GOOD FRIEND WHENEVER ONE CAME TO VISIT, IN ORDER TO DEEPEN THE FRIEND-SHIP.
YOU REMEMBER, DON'T YOU, ROMIO-SAMA?
DAAAD !!
Why'd you have to go and make a rule like that?!
...
WHY ARE YOU SO HESITANT?

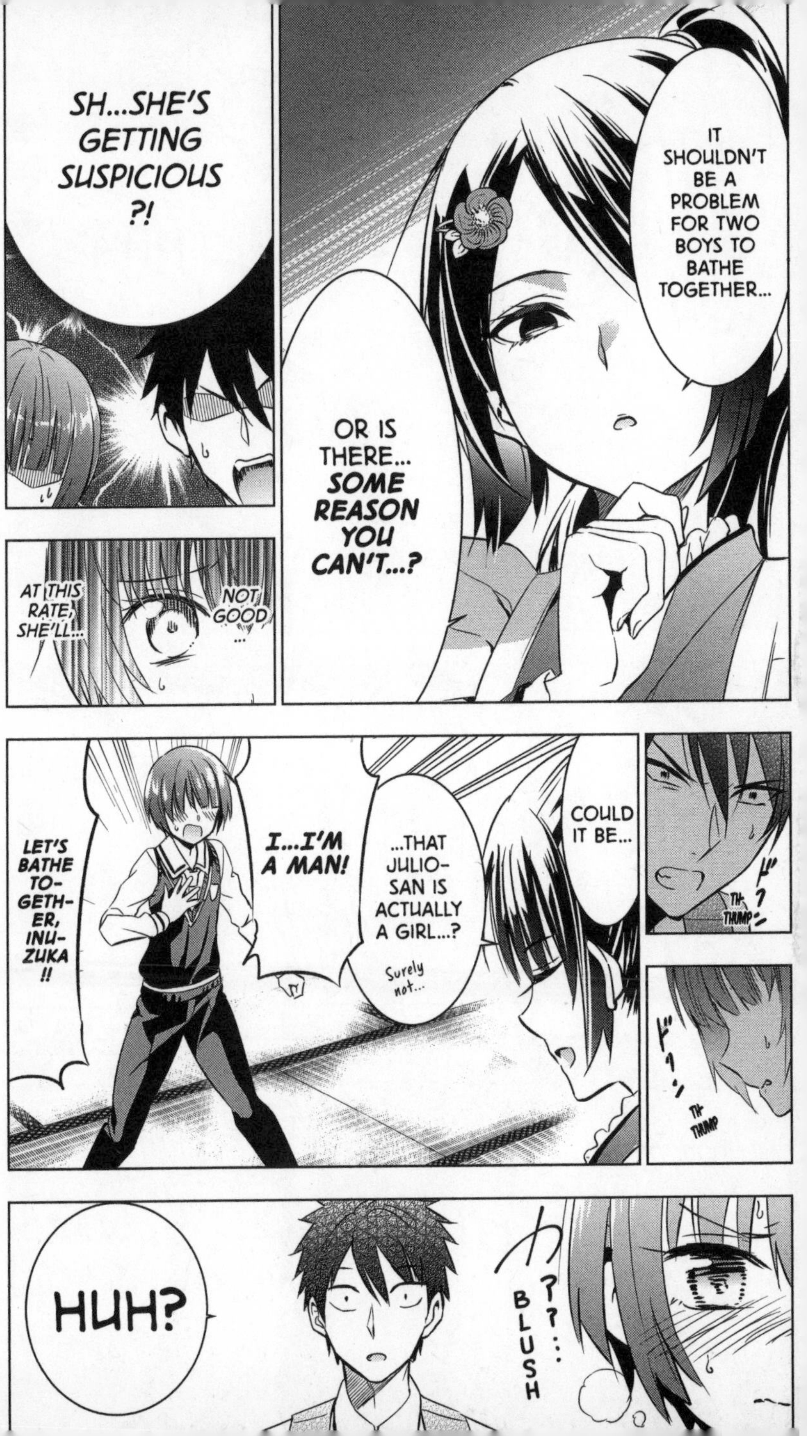
IT SHOULDN'T BE A PROBLEM FOR TWO BOYS TO BATHE TOGETHER...
OR IS THERE... SOME REASON YOU CAN'T...?
SH...SHE'S GETTING SUSPICIOUS ?!
NOT GOOD...
AT THIS RATE, SHE'LL...
TH-THUMP
TH-THUMP
COULD IT BE...
...THAT JULIO-SAN IS ACTUALLY A GIRL...?
Surely not...
I...I'M A MAN!
LET'S BATHE TO-GETH-ER, INU-ZUKA!!
BLUSH
HUH?

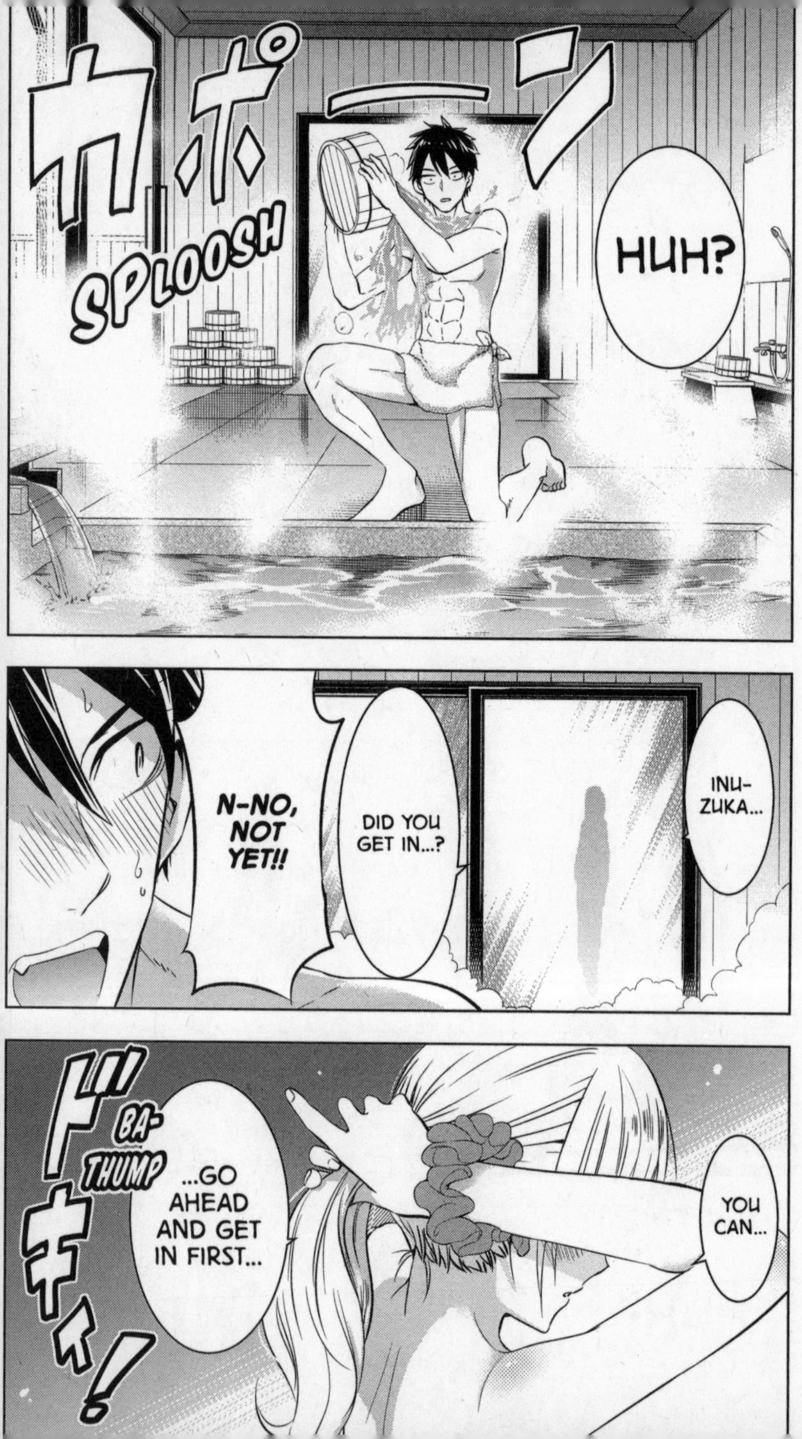
SPLOOSH
HUH?
INU-ZUKA...
DID YOU GET IN...?
N-NO, NOT YET!!
YOU CAN...
...GO AHEAD AND GET IN FIRST...
BA-THUMP

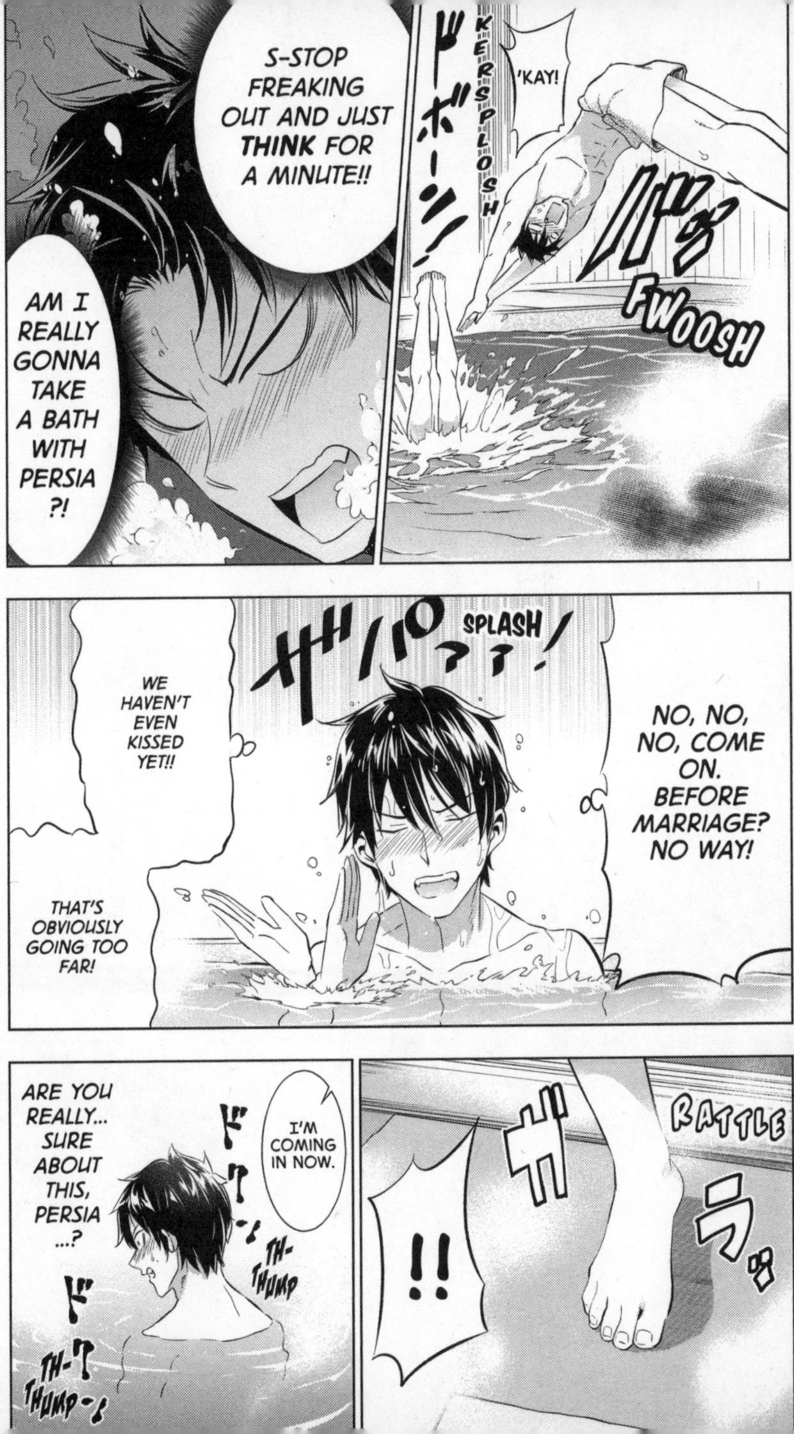
'KAY!
KERSPLOSH
FWOOSH
S-STOP FREAKING OUT AND JUST **THINK** FOR A MINUTE!!
AM I REALLY GONNA TAKE A BATH WITH PERSIA ?!
SPLASH
NO, NO, NO, COME ON. BEFORE MARRIAGE? NO WAY!
WE HAVEN'T EVEN KISSED YET!!
THAT'S OBVIOUSLY GOING TOO FAR!
RATTLE
!!
I'M COMING IN NOW.
ARE YOU REALLY... SURE ABOUT THIS, PERSIA ...?
TH-THUMP
TH-THUMP

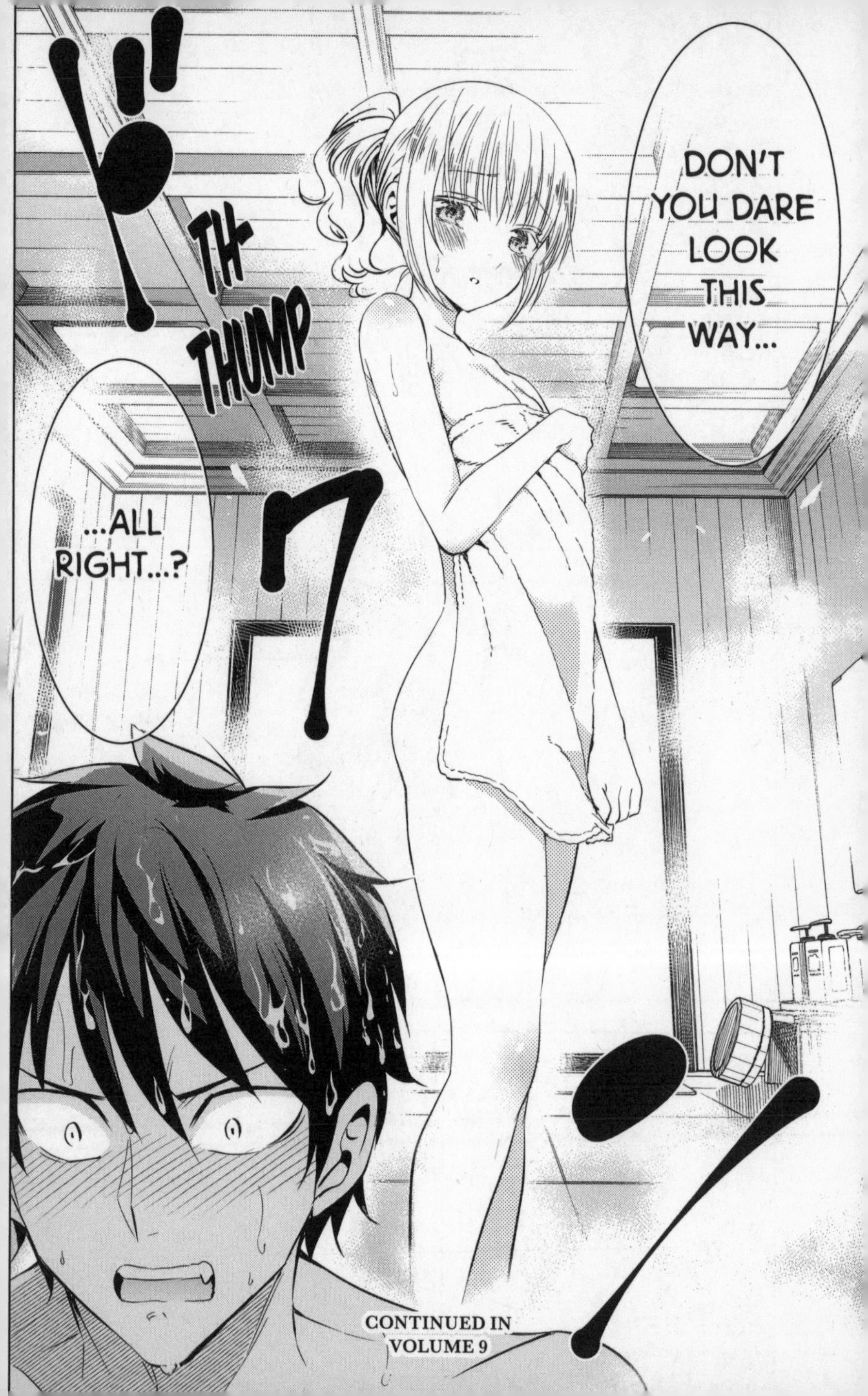
DON'T YOU DARE LOOK THIS WAY...
TH
THUMP
...ALL RIGHT...?
CONTINUED IN VOLUME 9

BONUS MANGA: RAGDOLL'S PAST

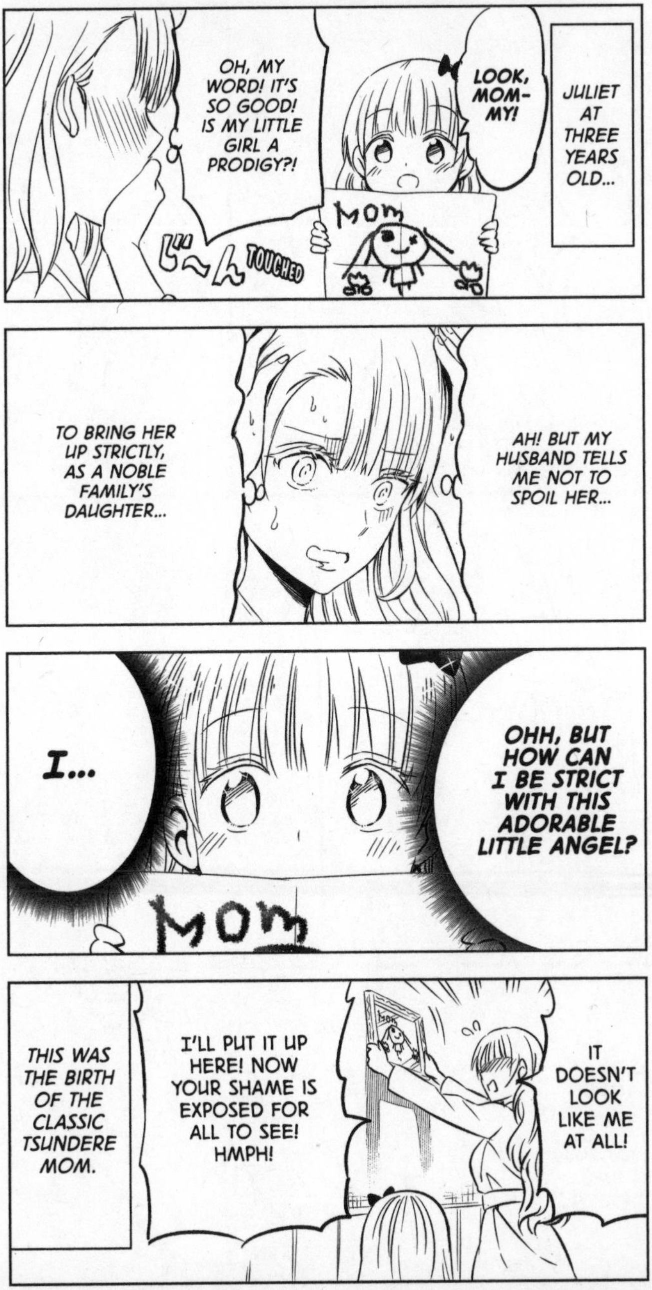
JULIET AT THREE YEARS OLD...
LOOK, MOM-MY!
OH, MY WORD! IT'S SO GOOD! IS MY LITTLE GIRL A PRODIGY?!
MOM
じ~ん TOUCHED
AH! BUT MY HUSBAND TELLS ME NOT TO SPOIL HER...
TO BRING HER UP STRICTLY, AS A NOBLE FAMILY'S DAUGHTER...
OHH, BUT HOW CAN I BE STRICT WITH THIS ADORABLE LITTLE ANGEL?
I...
MOM
IT DOESN'T LOOK LIKE ME AT ALL!
I'LL PUT IT UP HERE! NOW YOUR SHAME IS EXPOSED FOR ALL TO SEE! HMPH!
THIS WAS THE BIRTH OF THE CLASSIC TSUNDERE MOM.

AFTERWORD

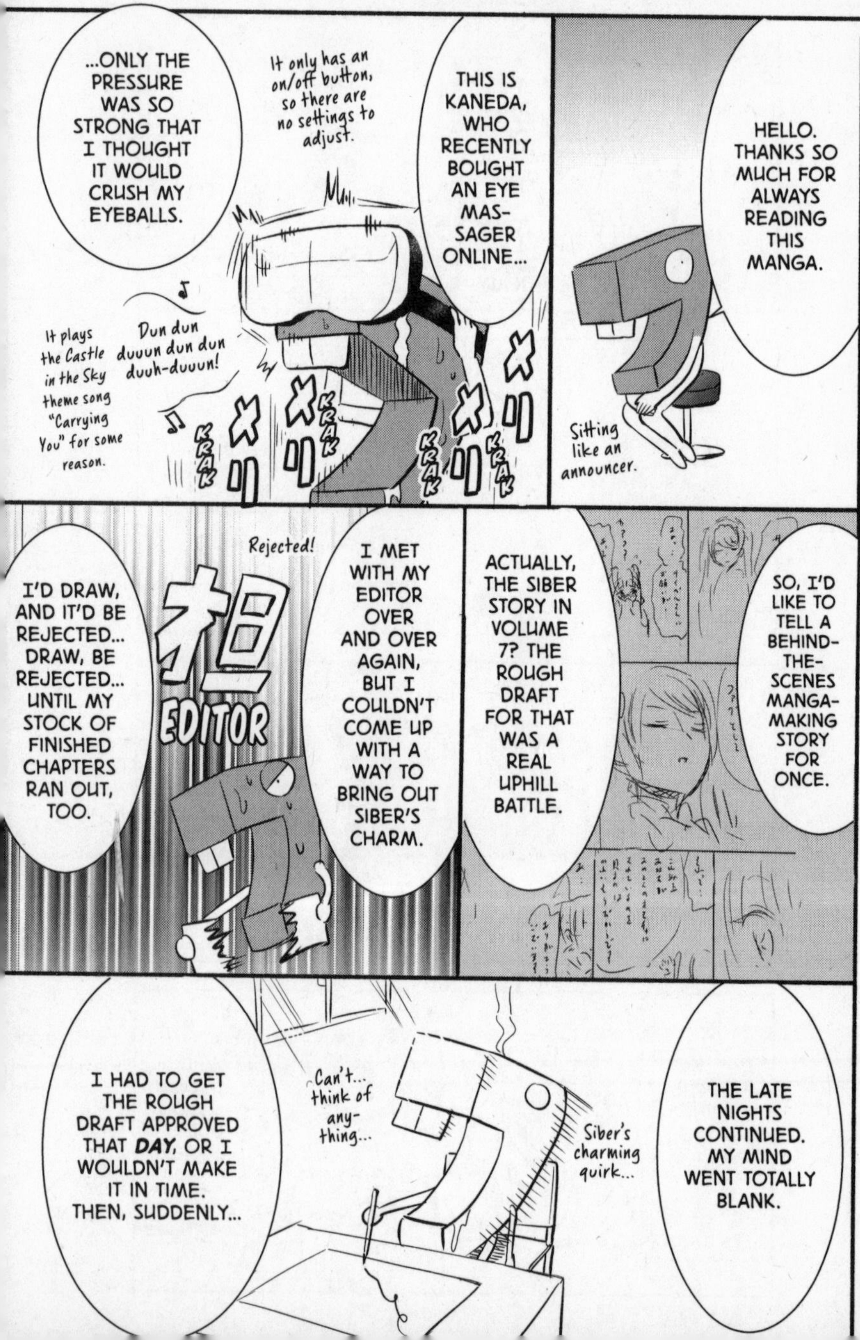
HELLO. THANKS SO MUCH FOR ALWAYS READING THIS MANGA.
Sitting like an announcer.
THIS IS KANEDA, WHO RECENTLY BOUGHT AN EYE MAS-SAGER ONLINE...
It only has an on/off button, so there are no settings to adjust.
...ONLY THE PRESSURE WAS SO STRONG THAT I THOUGHT IT WOULD CRUSH MY EYEBALLS.
Dun dun duuun dun dun duuh-duuun!
It plays the Castle in the Sky theme song "Carrying You" for some reason.
KRAK
KRAK
KRAK
KRAK
SO, I'D LIKE TO TELL A BEHIND-THE-SCENES MANGA-MAKING STORY FOR ONCE.
ACTUALLY, THE SIBER STORY IN VOLUME 7? THE ROUGH DRAFT FOR THAT WAS A REAL UPHILL BATTLE.
I MET WITH MY EDITOR OVER AND OVER AGAIN, BUT I COULDN'T COME UP WITH A WAY TO BRING OUT SIBER'S CHARM.
Rejected!
EDITOR
I'D DRAW, AND IT'D BE REJECTED... DRAW, BE REJECTED... UNTIL MY STOCK OF FINISHED CHAPTERS RAN OUT, TOO.
THE LATE NIGHTS CONTINUED. MY MIND WENT TOTALLY BLANK.
Siber's charming quirk...
Can't... think of any-thing...
I HAD TO GET THE ROUGH DRAFT APPROVED THAT ***DAY***, OR I WOULDN'T MAKE IT IN TIME. THEN, SUDDENLY...

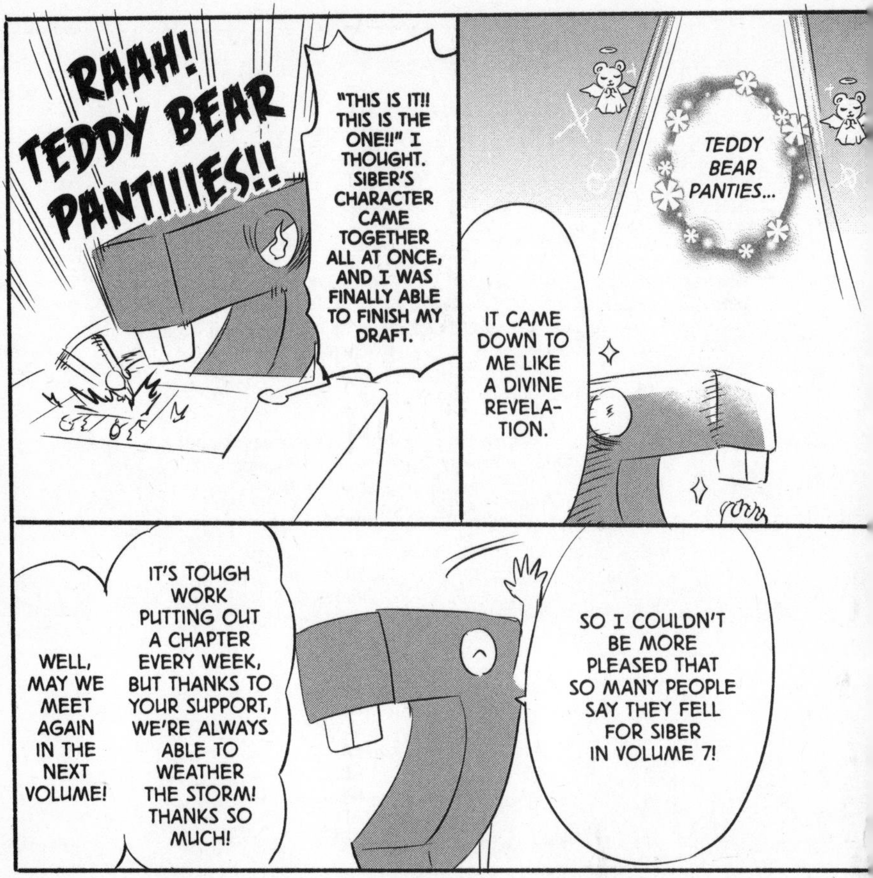
TEDDY BEAR PANTIES...
IT CAME DOWN TO ME LIKE A DIVINE REVELA-TION.
"THIS IS IT!! THIS IS THE ONE!!" I THOUGHT. SIBER'S CHARACTER CAME TOGETHER ALL AT ONCE, AND I WAS FINALLY ABLE TO FINISH MY DRAFT.
RAAH! TEDDY BEAR PANTIIIIES!!
SO I COULDN'T BE MORE PLEASED THAT SO MANY PEOPLE SAY THEY FELL FOR SIBER IN VOLUME 7!
IT'S TOUGH WORK PUTTING OUT A CHAPTER EVERY WEEK, BUT THANKS TO YOUR SUPPORT, WE'RE ALWAYS ABLE TO WEATHER THE STORM! THANKS SO MUCH!
WELL, MAY WE MEET AGAIN IN THE NEXT VOLUME!

I'M ON TWITTER: **@YOUSUKEKANEDA**

Boarding School *Juliet*

THERE'S SOMETHING BIG COMING IN VOLUME 9!

Boarding School Juliet volume 8 is a work of fiction. Names, characters, places, and incidents are the products of the author's imagination or are used fictitiously. Any resemblance to actual events, locales, or persons, living or dead, is entirely coincidental.

A Kodansha Comics Trade Paperback Original.

Published in the United States by Kodansha Comics,
an imprint of Kodansha USA Publishing, LLC, New York.

Publication rights for this English edition arranged through
Kodansha Ltd., Tokyo.

First published in Japan in 2018 by Kodansha Ltd., Tokyo, as
Kishuku Gakkou no Jurietto volume 8.

ISBN 978-1-63236-830-0

Printed in the United States of America.

www.kodanshacomics.com

9 8 7 6 5 4 3 2 1

Translation: Amanda Haley
Lettering: James Dashiell
Editing: Erin Subramanian and Tiff Ferentini
Kodansha Comics edition cover design: Phil Balsman